MDCCCXCVIII.

# Modern Astrology

With which is incorporated
## "The Astrologers' Magazine"
(Volume VIII.)

ESTABLISHED AUGUST, 1890.

⊹ A ✳ Work ⊹

DEALING SOLELY WITH

## Astrological Matters.

✳ ✳ ✳ ✳ ✳

" The Wise Man rules his Stars, the Fool obeys them."

Published at the Editorial Offices :

**Vol. 3.**

Old Series:
Vol. 8.

# 1 & 2, BOUVERIE ST., FLEET ST.,
LONDON, E.C.

Price
**7/-**

# Kessinger Publishing's Rare Reprints
## Thousands of Scarce and Hard-to-Find Books!

# INDEX.—VOL. III.

15°♉ 52'

♉24°

♏11°33'

♋29°

♃18°21'℞

♌

27°31'

♏17°

♈12°

15°♏ 52'

♌24°

♑29°

♂20°10'℞

27°34'

♒

♓1 7

♄29°10'

♎15°19'

♐12°

♃8°25'
☉14°51'47"
☿20°11'℞

♄27°36'
Regulus

*Alan Leo*

The Editor of Modern Astrology.

Born 5.49 a.m., August 7th, 1860, London.

# Modern Astrology

Edited by
ALAN LEO, P.A.S.

The Official Organ of the Astrological Society.

Vol. 3, No. 1.  ✳  AUGUST, 1897.  ✳  Price 1s.

THE one great fact that must impress itself upon the minds of all who investigate the science of Astrology, is the wonderful intelligence behind all manifested existence. Not only does the horoscope help us to see ourselves as in a looking-glass, but it may also enable us in time to understand what is the Will of God.

✳     ✳     ✳     ✳     ✳     ✳     ✳

For ages the destiny of the world has been mapped out in the sky, but there have been few men pure enough to interpret the mysterious handwriting of the Supreme Ruler. We can only realize through pain and sorrow that we alone are the builders of our own future, and the rulers of our own destiny.

✳     ✳     ✳     ✳     ✳     ✳     ✳

"Be not deceived," say the scriptures, "God is not mocked; whatsoever a man soweth, that shall he also reap." Each man reaps what he himself hath sown, and he comes back for the harvest.

✳     ✳     ✳     ✳     ✳     ✳     ✳

The secret of Planetary influence lies behind Spirit-Matter. When we can perceive the unity in this duality we shall understand the law that governs all action and re-action. We may logically compare the observed facts in nature with the subtle unseen forces which are in reality the causes of all phenomena. We feel through matter, cold and heat physically; we can also cognize love and hatred through the senses, yet these are polar opposites of the same spirit-substance,

▲

just as Mars and Saturn are the same in essence though manifesting so differently.

       *      *      *      *      *      *      *

The wise man does not rule his stars until he understands them, which he is ever seeking to do, but the fool does not trouble himself about them; he is content to obey that which he has not the will or desire to understand. The stars rule all who are not complete masters of themselves.

       *      *      *      *      *      *      *

Self-consciousness is a word often used by occultists and Astrologers, the meaning of which conveys so much to the intelligent mind. All life is conscious, but not self-conscious. There are many states of consciousness operating through various planes or conditions. There is the waking consciousness which we possess in our physical body while active in our daily life. To be self-conscious on that plane we must concentrate our thoughts, and know ourselves. While scattered in mind, and attracted by any passing object we are not *self*-conscious, for then the SELF within is not acting with deliberation and free choice. To be self-conscious is to be fully alive, and possessed of self-control. Then there is the dreaming state, half awake and half asleep. Our consciousness is then in a critical state, neither passive nor active, but hovering between the two, influenced by circumstances and surroundings. Finally there is what is called the state of deep sleep. In this condition we have entirely withdrawn the consciousness from the body and the physical plane, and live in a new world where all is bliss. We are not all self-consciously acting in this plane, the majority being only conscious of the purely physical or concrete. When we fully realize that we are not the body but the Spirit within it, then we become self-conscious on the physical plane and begin to rule our stars.

       *      *      *      *      *      *      *

> If ye lay bound upon the wheel of Change,
> And no way were of breaking from the Chain,
> The Heart of boundless Being is a curse,
> The Soul of Things fell pain.
>
> Ye are not bound! the Soul of Things is sweet,
> The Heart of Being is celestial rest;
> Stronger than woe is Will: that which was good
> Doth pass to Better—Best.
>
>                                        LIGHT OF ASIA.

# A Simple Method of Instruction in the Science of Practical Astrology.

## ENVIRONMENT, HEALTH AND FINANCE.
### *INTRODUCTION.*

Ho ! Ye who suffer ! know
Ye suffer from yourselves.   None else compels,
None other holds you that you live and die,
And whirl upon the wheel, and hug and kiss
It's spokes of agony,
It's tire of tears, it's nave of nothingness.

THE above lines from the beautiful verses in " The Light of Asia," contain the secret of our environment, as we find it upon awakening into the concrete matter of our physical existence.  We are simply immortal sparks from the great flame, becoming *self*-consciously individualized by our experiences in the physical world, and thereby slowly building our character and environment.

When we consider that our character as we find it to-day, is the result of our past thoughts and actions, we can easily see how important it becomes that we should study the future moulding of our character.  It is the centre of the circle which is ever expanding, with each expansion becoming more powerful, more loving and more wise.

It is out of our character, and the use of the mental qualities, that the whole of our future is made ; our mental attitude toward objects decide the steps we shall take, and if objects are presented to us out of which we have not had sufficient experience, then we are attracted by what appears pleasurable, to painfully extract knowledge from the contact therewith.

All moral character is built up from painful experiences, for how can we decide to abandon evil until we know its undesirable nature ; and until we deliberately choose the good in preference to the evil, we are not free from the contact of all that is without us.  If we can clearly follow this line of thinking we shall see that the centre of us is the will, colored, as it were, by experience, into character. The will when joined to love moves to good, but when linked to the desires of the personal self, the tendency is to evil.

The first object of our lives should be to purify our desires, for assuredly we are drawn to whatever we desire, be it good or evil. The lust of the senses, no matter what may be its nature, binds us to the wheel of fate as sure as we live. The lust for gold will bind our energies to the acquirement of gold, as much as the sensual desires bind the sensualist for the time to the object of his attraction. In this way the whole of the character may be chained to its environment by the desires, either of the flesh or of the mind. We ARE our CHARACTER, and not our SENSES or our MIND, both of which we only use as instruments, as we use the physical casket called the body. We came to this world to inhabit the physical form prepared for us, attracted to the environment by an affinity which it alone could offer, for us to work out those desires, which were contained in that part of our conciousness desiring the experience. We are the sower and the reaper, our will being limited within the circle of our desires and mental vision. Realizing these facts we begin to understand the nature of our environment, the quality of our mind and the strength of our will.

## CHAPTER I.

### ENVIRONMENT.

To environ is to encompass, surround, and encircle. When used in an Astrological sense the environment embraces the whole of the physical condition into which the Soul is drawn at birth, being attracted to the environment most suitable to give expression to the mind and character. Not once, but many times, does the Soul environ itself in matter as a vehicle or instrument through which it can function. Just as a ray of the Sun focuses itself upon, and permeates the flowers as they grow, so does our soul permeate the form to which it is attached for physical manifestation, and as we have remarked, it ensouls the form more than once, otherwise the study of Astrology is nonsense. This is why there is so much difference in the environment of each individual. The soul with the qualities of a prize fighter would never be drawn to a form in which the most refined tastes, and gentle manners were the characteristics of its make-up.

We do not propose to argue the point with regard to the re-embodiment of the soul, but we intend to prove it, and we maintain that, short of illumination, Astrology is the only science that will once and for all time definitely decide this important question. No one can believe in Astrology without accepting this truth, for upon this and its accompanying idea of action and re-action are the laws of Astrology based. How otherwise can we be fated to good or evil if there is not in us the qualities necessary to work out this way.

Through many races and many nations we have come, and change after change of environment has made us readily adapt ourselves to our circumstances, and accept the position as we find it.

For several months previous to the natal day the form that the ego, or soul, is to inhabit is being slowly builded. An insight into this may be gained by reading Revelations, Chap. VII, in which the sealing of the twelve tribes of Israel is described, each coming under a sign of the Zodiac.

The real man is attracted to the form by that peculiar sound to which he must ever respond having in himself the same vibratory chord. The desire to enter physical life comes from within, and all through the period of physical manifestation this desire prompts the speech and action. Behind the whole of the manifesting life is this desire; it stands behind the Will, and is the cause of motion, life and energy.

The environment best fitted for the soul's manifestation is chosen by those Great Ones in whose hands the government of the world's evolution is placed, and only as the qualities in us are developed, can we respond to the highest vibrations of sound which emanate from harmonious surroundings, and thus attract us to peaceful and beneficial circles. The coarse and gross in whose soul only the unrefined qualities abound, are drawn toward those discordant sounds which offer them the best means of expression for their soul-qualities. Upon this plan is justice carried out, and each soul is fitted with the best vehicle for its use. There is no disorder in the Divine plan; all is harmony. There is no injustice in God's work ; no confusion or chance.   We suffer from ourselves.

As like attracts like, so are we drawn to the evironment to which we can the most readily respond.   The sensualist finds a sensual body, and the pure are drawn into the home-life of the pure.   The lover of gold is attracted to other souls who worship gold. The drunkard and the glutton, the philosopher and the saint, are all drawn to their own levels.   This is the secret of heredity that is ever going on, and the cause is in ourselves.   We must reap what we have sown.

But in the present work we will not enter the domain of the Esoteric, leaving the consideration of ante-natal causes to that branch. We shall now concern ourselves with the physical environment, as indicated by the horoscope, merely remarking that it is a representation of only a part of the real man, and *not the whole*.   When the whole of the man is able to express himself, then the real natal star alone must be judged, and to do this the adeptship that goes beyond ordinary Astrology is reached, and instead of only one of the seven keys being used to enter the temple of truth, the whole are known, and those planes of being are explored which are beyond all that the ordinary man can conceive.

There are twelve signs of the zodiac through which the planets pass in their periods.   These signs run in the following numerical order and ever remain the same.

| | | | | | |
|---|---|---|---|---|---|
| 1.—♈ ... | Aries | house of | ♂ | Mars | ... Day Positive. |
| 2.—♉ ... | Taurus | ,,  ,, | ♀ | Venus | ... Night Negative. |
| 3.—♊ ... | Gemini | ,,  ,, | ☿ | Mercury | ... Day Positive. |
| 4.—♋ ... | Cancer | ,,  ,, | ☽ | Moon | ... Night Negative. |
| 5.—♌ ... | Leo | ,,  ,, | ☉ | Sun | ... Day Positive. |
| 6.—♍ ... | Virgo | ,,  ,, | ☿ | Mercury | ... Night Negative. |
| 7.—♎ ... | Libra | ,,  ,, | ♀ | Venus | ... Day Positive. |
| 8.—♏ ... | Scorpio | ,,  ,, | ♂ | Mars | ... Night Negative. |
| 9.—♐ ... | Sagittarius | ,,  ,, | ♃ | Jupiter | ... Day Positive. |
| 10.—♑ ... | Capricorn | ,,  ,, | ♄ | Saturn | ... Night Negative. |
| 11.—♒ ... | Aquarius | ,,  ,, | ♄ | Saturn | ... Day Positive. |
| 12.—♓ ... | Pisces | ,,  ,, | ♃ | Jupiter | ... Night Negative. |

When divided into twelve divisions each sign becomes a house, and plays an important part in the environment.

The first division governs the life and form, temperamant and energies, the natural disposition and personal feeling. It is positive and expressive. In its original condition, it is similar to iron, the object being to temper it into steel, or exalt it into fine gold.

The second division governs the financial condition in the external world, and marks the strength of the Will. The alchemists used the sign ruling this house as the symbol to represent copper. It is one of the four vital houses and extremely important in all interior considerations.

The third division is allotted to the mind, in which the mental condition is mirrored. Like quicksilver, the mind may be divided into many parts and scattered. This is the house of duality; in it unity is needed to reflect properly.

The fourth division represents the centre of the environment, the home-life and all general affairs at the close of the life. It is *silvered* by the mercurial influence of the mind, collecting as it does, each separated drop of quicksilver that falls from the houses of Mercury.

The fifth division is the house of construction, generation, and the creative power. It is used for pleasure and speculation, whereas it should be used in true feeling and deliberate action. It governs all the golden emotions of the heart producing unions out of which marriage may spring.

The sixth division is generally the house of pain, sickness and death to the physical body. In reality it is the house of service, but there are few who truly serve except for personal gain or limited motives, therefore, physically, it is considered one of the evil houses, indicating the nature of disease and ill-health which we shall fully explain.

These six houses are the first half of the circle, the first three the intellectual triad, finding their duplicates in the maternal trinity, the positive portion synthesizing all the active pursuing qualities; the negative, the latent and preserving nature.

| POSITIVE. | NEGATIVE. | POSITIVE. |
|---|---|---|
| 1st ♈ | 2nd ♉ | 3rd ♊ |
| Fate or Environment. | Will or Character. | Mind or Reflection. |
| 4th ♋ | 5th ♌ | 6th ♍ |
| NEGATIVE. | POSITIVE. | NEGATIVE. |

We may now take up our study from the fourth angle.   The centre of the environment is governed by the fourth house, and the sign Cancer, synthesizing itself in the moon.   The fourth house forms the focussing point for the whole of the other signs and houses, this being the magnetic spot to which all the manifesting life is drawn,   as it represents the downward half of the triangle as follows :

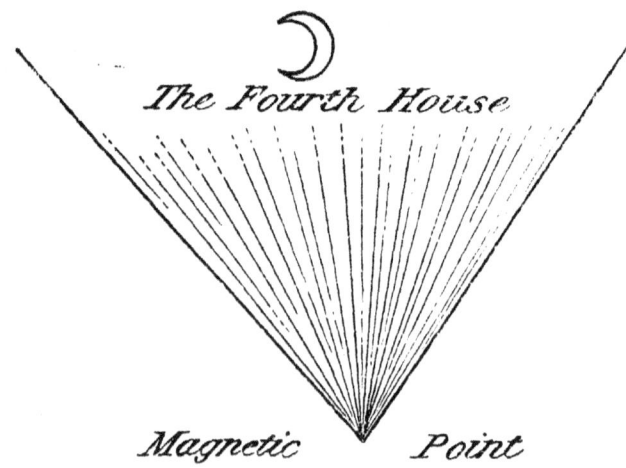

The sum total of our past is registered in the Sun, and this is reflected upon the Moon, coloring our manifested life ;   therefore,  to it we must look for the fate or environment.

The rulers of the first six signs and houses of the zodiac are Mars, Venus, Mercury, Moon and Sun.   Mars and Venus are duplicates, dualistic in their manifestation when considered  separately,  but acting as one or the other when indrawn.   When Mars is positive and active, Venus is latent and inactive ; both cannot be expressed at the same time. Thought must precede careful action ; the idea must come before the form.   We cannot love and hate at the same moment ; neither can we have war and peace acting simultaneously.   All anger and strife is apart from love, even up to the highest form of righteous indignation.   We are two and not one when we can be drawn from our centre by emotion, no matter how refined the quality.   In gradual steps we rise from Mars to Venus moulding the iron at each step, until from Aries, the exaltation of Venus is reached in the last sign, Pisces, when the circle has entirely surmounted the cross, from whence we pass on into the Sun or Nirvana, the realm of the blest.   In the pairs of opposites we may study all the rulers.   The Moon is but a reflection of the Sun;

without the latter's light the Moon is dead and void; and Mercury is the winged messenger of the Sun, the interpreter which moulds itself to the slightest vibration.

We have always known that the Sun represents gold, the Moon silver, and Mercury quicksilver, called Mercury. It is common knowledge that Mercury is used in silvering mirrors, but it is not generally known that in Mercury we see ourselves as others see us. Mercury is the mind and the reflector of mental images, which the Sun creates. The Moon acts as a collector of the impressions made upon her by the reflections of the principles signified by the planets. There we are living in an illusion of false appearances mistaking the unreal and changeable for the real. We make our own environment by creating our own images, and we follow the shadow, mistaking it for the substance. Before dipping into the practical demonstration of all this, we must grasp the idea that our character makes the whole of our future, as it made the past, and that the future also makes our character, paradoxical as it may seem. Realizing that *we* are our character because it is our individuality, we can see that all else must be illusive and whatever environment in which we may be placed, it must be colored either by our individuality or— color us. No matter how we look at Astrology or any other science we must have a centre from which to start, and that centre for us is the Sun, from out of which is pouring spirit-substance, in essence one, in manifestation dual. Viewing all manifestation from the central point of spirit, we have unity, we alone making the division in ourselves, therefore, we must realize that we are always one behind the two. We must hold fast to the fundamental idea of unity, the Sun, individuality or character, call this unity what we will. Now let us introduce the thought of the Personality— what is it? and what part does it play in our life and environment?

Every student will admit that the highest point of ideality for humanity in its manifested condition is Love,—Love, pure, unselfish and sacrificial. In touching this we touch God, for God is Love. From this highest state of consciousness we come down to feeling; when we begin to analyze our feelings we start thinking and create or produce mind, this mind ascending from the lowest perceptions of the animal and animal man, up to the most lofty conception of wisdom. Now let us think of these two great principles which are either active or latent in us, in their very lowest forms of manifestation acting as sense or instinct. We can trace the various manifestations of the one sense through all the five senses, realizing that to cognize them or discover their values we shall need a mind by which to know them. It is in this experience by analysis that we produce the first germs of mind, and as our experience grows, our mind expands, and we become more and more conscious, until we can readily perceive the nature of any article by touching it; by sight we get a further insight into the object, and then by taste or scent a still wider judgment of its nature, all the while storing up our impressions as memory, until we come to the condition of having obtained so much abstract knowledge that we are enabled to use what we call our intuition, to perceive readily the whole nature of all that comes before us, and thus convert the five senses into one sense.

Now it is while limited or held to anyone of these five senses that we become personal, and only when we have full realization, or what is called self-consciousness, that we become individualized. We consider the Moon as the significator of the personality for this reason: as the collector of all impressions she goes out from the Sun month after month. From her own sign, Cancer, to the opposite point, Capricorn, she encompasses the half-circle of the zodiac, and in that sign metaphorically crystallizes the whole of her collections, and from this point Saturn embodies the experience. In the order of the signs, Capricorn is the tenth, mid-heaven, or culminating point of the zodiac. The personality is limited to the concrete and objective side of life. It is concerned only with the practical and can only judge from the sense perceptions, admitting only the material or substance side of the duality, which had sprung from the unity of the one spirit-substance. Its concern is with the dark side of nature until illuminated by the Sun's rays. It governs the whole of the personal, limited, concrete, one-life-self, and those who worship Diana believe in but one life, for they know of no other; having always followed the shadow, nothing can be permanent or fixed, all is changed.

When we can steady this changeableness and fleeting attraction to objects and objective life, we begin to reflect, and turn round upon ourselves, as it were; we feel and see by reflecting upon the past, the errors and mistakes we have made and the accompanying pain it brought us. Thus it is that Mercury acts, for in it is stored the Memory of our past which now becomes a guide for the future. No longer acting upon impulse or desire for sensation, we think and reason, and choose our own course of action with regard to the circumstances of our environment.

It is imperative that we know that we suffer from ourselves, otherwise, we are not seeking causes, which we must be doing if we study this science with the true spirit of the truth-seeker, but are simply playing with a mighty science either for curiosity, or to cheat our fate— an impossible thing for us ever to do.

Every student of Astrology should examine his motives for becoming such. If through his brain-mind he has not yet realized that his soul is seeking an explanation of the mysteries, he should quietly watch the trend of his thought when engaged in this stupendous study.

To illustrate the subject of environment we shall be compelled to dip into the lives of some personalities, but in no single study of a life can the whole of the truth be extracted, as it contains merely a minute part. Therefore we shall study this subject first in the abstract, through ideas which each student can, if he is willing, make practical for himself.

When dealing with health we shall go back to the days of herbs and the old alchemists, but even here we shall bring into the subject the proof that we suffer from ourselves, therefore, in ourselves will lie the cure. Every effort will be made, however, to make the whole subject as practical as possible, and give the science the best illustration it has had in modern times. We shall now proceed to deal with poverty and wealth as essentials to environment.

*To be continued.*

---

Mercury with an unfortunate planet in the eleventh, denotes the establishment of some severe or unjust laws in the world.

  &#42;  &#42;  &#42;  &#42;  &#42;  &#42;

A conjunction of Mars and Saturn in the sixth or eighth houses, especially in a human sign, signifies a great pestilence.

  &#42;  &#42;  &#42;  &#42;  &#42;  &#42;

If wars be signified note the angle of the figure wherein Mars is posited, for from that part the enemies shall come.

# The Esoteric Side of Astrology.

OR every human soul there is a natal star, a star so brilliant and luminous that naught on earth can equal its splendour and radiance ; no physical language can describe its beauty or its nature ; no mind can paint its loveliness for mortal eyes to see and live. This star is immortal and essentially divine. Its chart lays in the never-ending circle, and its boundary is within the consciousness of divinity. Beyond the understanding of the ordinary mind, and only faintly cognized by the human soul, this star shines on for ever ; each ray as it goes forth ensouls anew and afresh the re-incarnating individual self : beyond all that becomes manifest, this star *is*, being the one permanent reality of each successive re-incarnation. It is not born, neither can it die. Its change is in color, and its echo, sound ; voiceless, it speaks through our soul's intuition, silently it gleans fragrance of each life : slowly but surely it guides, and controls. To it, vice and virtue are one ; the principle alone containing the essence of what is to become. Each earth-life is its playground and its school, the cream of which alone is skimmed, some lives must yield but little, others much ; in no single one can its purpose be obtained. They who sought the Holy Grail, did pursue this star, which only the pure could find. The faith to search must needs be first, and then the will to dare, but only the pure in heart shall find it. Its wonderous diamond-splendour can not be fully realized until its mission through substance is over, but its rays may be felt as the color deepens in quality, and the breath of aspiration carries the soul within the sphere of its influence. Great teachers in all climes and ages have proclaimed its being, and the testimony of those who tread the path are obtainable by all who enquire of its mystery. Sooner or later we shall one and all set out in search for our Natal Star. Its being dates from the beginning of its immortality ; its birth in essence it had none ; from whence it came none may know until it knows itself as a drop in the ocean ; it is one with the Absolute, its differentiation is the development of its consciousness, but to the all it is but the spark from a mighty flame. To intellectually

understand it is one thing, to know it is everything ; it is the only real portion of ourselves ; in seeking to know the one we shall know the many.

One in essentials, but manifesting differently, we are all spiritually the same. The mass of clay which moulds the potter's bowl, yields its form to the will of the workman. Each vessel used by the soul must bend to the will of the higher self, the outward form is but the vehicle by which our experience is to be gained through us for that Natal Star. As the Sun is to the solar system so is this Natal Star to the sum of our being and existence. As the photospheres envelope the Sun's centre, so is the Natal Star enveloped in its own Auras. As the planets are to the Sun the Media of its attributes, so are the principles to our star. The correspondences as correspondences only find their expression as follows, the full explanation of which may be given so far as our intellect is able to perceive through the likeness in the words, "As above so below."

| SOLAR SYSTEM. | NATAL STAR. | | HUMANITY. |
|---|---|---|---|
| | *Higher Principles. Immortal.* | | |
| ☉ Sun. | Vital Essence (Principle) | Over-Soul | ○ Individual. |
| ☿ Mercury. | Reflector (Vehicle) | The Messenger | ✡ Memory. |
| ♀ Venus. | Love and Wisdom (Principle) | Manas | ♀ Human Soul. |
| ♃ Jupiter. | Compassion (Vehicle) | The Egg | ○ Individuality. |
| | *Lower Expression. Mortal.* | | |
| ♂ Mars. | Fohat—Energy (Secondary Principle) | Expansion | ▽ Life Forces. (Animal qualities) |
| ♄ Saturn | Time and Space (Vehicle) | Limit (Astral Body) | ⊹ Brain Intellect. (Personality) |
| ☽ Moon. | Etheric Condition (Collector—Ephemeral) | — | ☐ Personal Mould |
| ⊕ The Earth. | Substance—Matter (Changeable) | — | ⊕ Physical Body |

We are distinctly seven in one from the physical standpoint, but in reality only three in one, being the Spirit, or Vital essence, the Soul or consciousness, and the body or vehicle through which these may manifest.    If we consider ourselves from the seven-in-one-standpoint we are but ONE using six sheaths, or vehicles, to express ourselves, the one being formless and abstract.    The Physical body at what we call death disintegrates and passes back into the earthy elements, the remaining six withdrawing into the  mould upon which the physical was built : but this also disappears, leaving the saturnine astral  vehicle to hold the others until the life-forces have exhausted themselves in  the purgatory of the Roman Catholics and the Hell of the Christians.  When this has been  accomplished and the grosser desires expended, the triad rises with its Jupiterian vehicle  into the Deva Land, the heaven of the Christian, to again, after a long period of rest, re-clothe itself with the concrete elements whereby it may gain fresh experiences, give effect to previous causes and obtain unacquired Virtues.    For, the triad must know and realize itself, and only by contact with its opposite in Nature, can it test its Power, Love and Wisdom.    The test of real growth is Compassion, the Jupiterian quality.    When the colored Individuality has known and felt all the earth's joys and sorrows, and realized the impermanent and illusive nature of form and substance, then it can feel for others,  struggling along the path to freedom ; it is then that the egg which has been brooded over by the higher principles is ready to burst its shell and realize its immortality.

There are many  to-day who although at times  identifying themselves with the physical body, know that *they* are not the  body, which is only a vehicle to hold  the real self.    There are a few who to-day, although often identifying themselves with their mind, know that *they* are not  the  mind it being  merely an instrument through which experience is obtained.

No one who has given careful thought and  study  to  this great subject can  help realizing that they take up many new physical bodies through which they can express themselves and obtain fresh experiences. The Soul can never die ; in fact there is no  death,  the  very earth will some day return to its  original condition.    We are all sparks from  the great  flame,  coloring  and  adding  to  our  consciousness continually ; primarily one in  essence, we are colored by  our  experiences differently. To realize the one throughout the diversity of manifested existence is to become wise.    To see the good in all and overcome evil by good is to be filled with Love.    To be complete masters of ourselves is to have Power.

*To be Continued.*

# Astrological Stories.

## No. I.

T WAS a beautiful summer evening. The Sun was slowly sinking, and all the world was peaceful, still and calm; that is, so far as Nature was concerned within the sphere of what was Willie Arter's world. He knew of no other world than the little village in Hertfordshire in which he drew his first breath of life. He had often heard of the market town a few miles away from the village, and knew quite well the carrier's cart and the carrier, Sam; but that was the full extent of his knowledge of any outside surroundings to the village. It was a pretty spot to live in. The inhabitants were scattered and poor, and the only sensation to be obtained by the villagers was the "goings on at the Squire's house," and it was on the occasion of one of these events that Willie first began to think of a bigger world than that in which he lived. It was Willie's birthday, and he had spent it as usual in the fields with his father, a labourer on the Squire's farm.

Willie had been sent on an errand to the Squire's house by one of the servants, and he was returning through the grounds when a sweet little girl, dressed all in white, ran after him crying out with a musical voice:

"Oh! Willie Arter, I am so glad to see you. It is my birthday to-day, and I am going to give you a present," and, dropping a bright yellow coin into Willie's cap, which he held in his hand, she ran away, leaving him quite startled. In a moment he recovered himself and suddenly started off in pursuit of the little maiden and, overtaking her, exclaimed:

"But it is my birthday, too. I'm ten to-day!"

"And so am I," she said. How funny; oh, do come and tell papa," and taking Willie's hand, she ran with him through the great hall of the Squire's house, and did not stop until she stood before her father in one of the large rooms at one end of the hall.

"Why, little Bessie, who have you brought," he exclaimed.

"It's Willie Arter; he's got a birthday, too, and he's ten to-day, like me," said Bessie, all in a breath.

" Well, well," said the Squire, " we must see Willie's father and he must let him come to the party and keep his birthday, too." With these words he told the boy to go in search of his father and ask him to come to the court-yard, and, bidding Bessie stay in the room for a few moments, the Squire walked out to meet him.

" It is singular," he muttered; " both born on the same day. I wonder if the stars speak truly. We shall see," and pacing up and down the court-yard, he waited the coming of his servant.

" William," he said, on the approach of the farm labourer, " what hour was your son born ten years ago to-day, which I learn is the lad's birthday ? "

" At ten o'clock in the night, sir, with more than the last quarter of the Moon rising."

" And this, you believe, will cause the boy to rise in life ? "

" Well, sir, Doctor King said he thought it was strange that the rich and the poor should come on the same day. No offence, I hope, sir ?"

" No, no, William; the boy shall be a guest at Bessie's party, and be well cared for. We must see about his future. I shall take an interest in him, and this is why I wished to see you. Have you any more children ? "

" No, sir ; the next were twins, but they died."

" Well, well, call for the boy in two hours' time. Until then he shall have a birthday to remember," and, dismissing his servant, he re-entered the house and went in search of his wife, who was busily engaged in preparations for the celebration of Bessie's birthday.

" Miriam, dear," he exclaimed on finding her, " Sapal's words have come true. Surely there can be no truth in such humbug as planet ruling, and yet I remember so well your brother's words—" In her tenth year the line of fate will begin. Do you remember, dear, how emphatic Sapal was with regard to Bessie's future ? When the party is over we will both read her nativity again, and decide our course of action for her future welfare."

*(To be continued).*

# On the Divisions of a Horoscope.

## By Zariel.

———

HE diagrams given in "The Horoscope Revised" have been thought by some of my critics to be wrong indications of the meaning I wished to convey by them, and since the whole subject seems yet in a state of doubt, I would like to make a clear illustration of the equal division of the horoscope in contradistinction to the orthodox method by oblique Ascension, as in the Tables of Houses, with a few additional, and perhaps more suitable, designs than those formerly used in "The Horoscope Revised." These, I think, will convey the real distinction between the two methods, and, at the same time, prove the correctness of my first diagrams when considered from the same point of view. This matter has not yet received anything like the attention it requires, but perhaps my readers have not fully understood the importance of the position I wished to convey.

If the equal method is identical with the Ptolemaic system, which seems highly probable, how can we expect the old and valued rules of Ptolemy to apply when we have, through the march of time, adopted a different arrangement of the horoscopic frame? If we follow the rules of Ptolemy, must we not, if we desire the best results, apply them to the method for which they were adopted? The modern system of obtaining the cusps by considering the visible horizon with the oblique Ascensions, which causes a frequent change, and often much unevenness in the cusps and divisions, requires a revised code of rules to suit the alteration, which is of a more complex nature. Both methods are almost equally definite so far as the relation of the heavens to the earth is concerned, but based upon different laws. The equal division is more simple in accurate construction, and has *more connection with*

B

*the earth's centres of daily axial motion* instead of the mere visible
heavens.

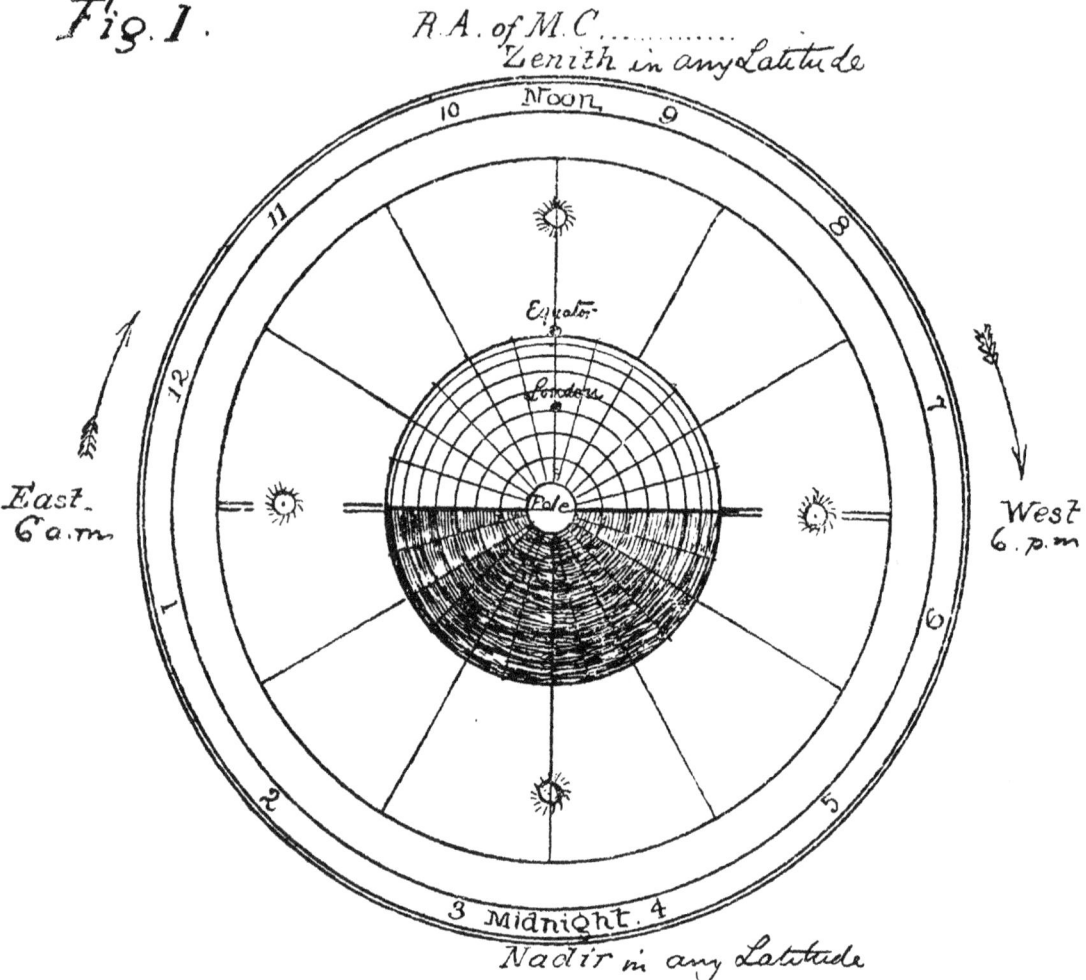

Fig. 1.

R.A. of M.C.............
Zenith in any Latitude

Fig. 1 shows the earth in the centre of the horoscope, with the polar
axis at right angles to the zenith.   The circumference of the globe in
this case represents the Equator; the dot on the top shows a place on
the Equator for which the horoscope is drawn, and here, the twelve
houses would have an equal, or nearly equal division of ecliptic longitude by either method; the Eastern line or Ascendant giving the place
of the Sun at 6 a.m.; the upper meridian at noon; the Descendant at 6
p.m., and the under Meridian at midnight.

It is the elevation of the Pole for various latitudes which causes the
unequal division of ecliptic longitude, in the different houses, when
arranged by right and oblique Ascension from the *visible* horizon.   This
often produces that distorted appearance in the horoscope to which I

referred in "The Horoscope Revised," but the following illustration may give a clearer indication of my meaning :

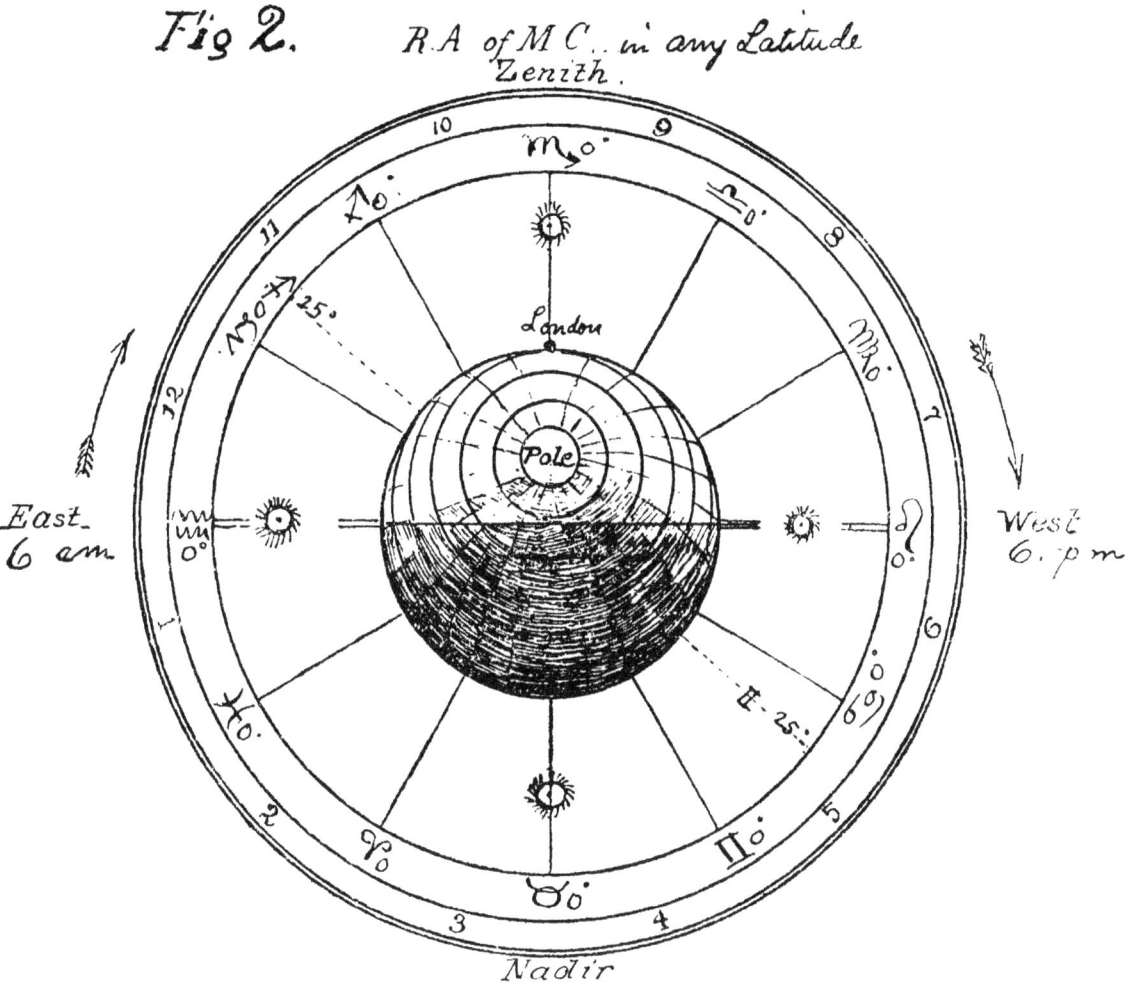

*Fig 2.*  *R.A of MC. in any Latitude*
*Zenith.*

Here the globe is shown with the pole elevated above the plane of the *Celestial horizon*, but, as may be plainly seen, this in no way disturbs the position of the celestial horizon, though, of course, it alters the circle of vision from the position of the spectator in a proportionate ratio to the polar elevation. It is evident the natural division of the twelve houses into equal parts of ecliptic longitude, will remain unaltered, so far as the whole circle is concerned, from the observer's position; the only alteration being in the visible portion of that circle. The sun would occupy the same cardinal points as before, at the stated times. The dot on the top of the globe in Fig. 2 is given to represent the position of London. Now, in the latitude of London, when the beginning of the sign ♏ (Scorpio) occupies the cusp of the tenth, there is a very unequal division of ecliptic longitude in the twelve houses when measured by the visible horizon, giving a very short space from the rising degree to the Meridian, and a very long space from the Meridian to the setting degree, as shown by the dotted line in Fig. 2. The visible Ascendant in this case falls in ♐ (Sagittarius) 25° (see dotted line), while the Descendant falls in ♊ (Gemini) 25°. This indication corresponds exactly with the illustration in "The Horoscope Revised" and proves the correctness of what was there advanced.

But why should the pole be elevated in one case and not in the other? When a man travels from the Equator to London, the North pole does not move upwards to meet him; he simply moves towards the pole which remains fixed in the same position as before. His line of visible horizon alters, of course, in proportion to the distance he travels towards the pole, but this does not affect his relation to the circle of the ecliptic so long as he remains on the same line of longitude. This is shown by referring again to Fig. 1, where the positions of a place on the Equator and the relative situation of London are indicated by spots on the same longitudinal line. There is certainly a change in the Astronomical positions, but "*an Astronomical appearance may not always be an Astrological necessity.*"

I will now view the two methods by an illustration from another standpoint which shows how the differences arise when certain signs culminate.

In Fig. 3, the circle represents the earth; N, the north pole; A, the position of an observer at the Equator; B, the position of an observer in London, when the sixth degree of ♏ (Scorpio) culminates. As ♏ (Scorpio) is a Southern sign, he has to look a little beyond the line of the Equator to that point as shown by the dotted line of sight from B to M C. D D would, in this case, represent the line of visible horizon to the position at B, and at this time the beginning of ♑ (Capricorn, the extreme Southern declination) would rise on this line at G, which is *considerably above the line of Polar axis S, N, at this point;* while on the Western setting point at H, the beginning of ♋ (Cancer), (extreme Northern declination), will be found. This gives the short ecliptic space in the Oriental upper quadrant, and the long space in the upper occidental quadrant, as shown by the dotted line in Fig. 2.

But if the ecliptic is measured from the Meridian to the *Celestial Ascendant*, which is always *parallel to the Polar axis without reference to visibility, and coincides with the focus of the earth's daily motion*, the longitudinal space will be equal in the four quadrants without any possibility of intercepted signs.

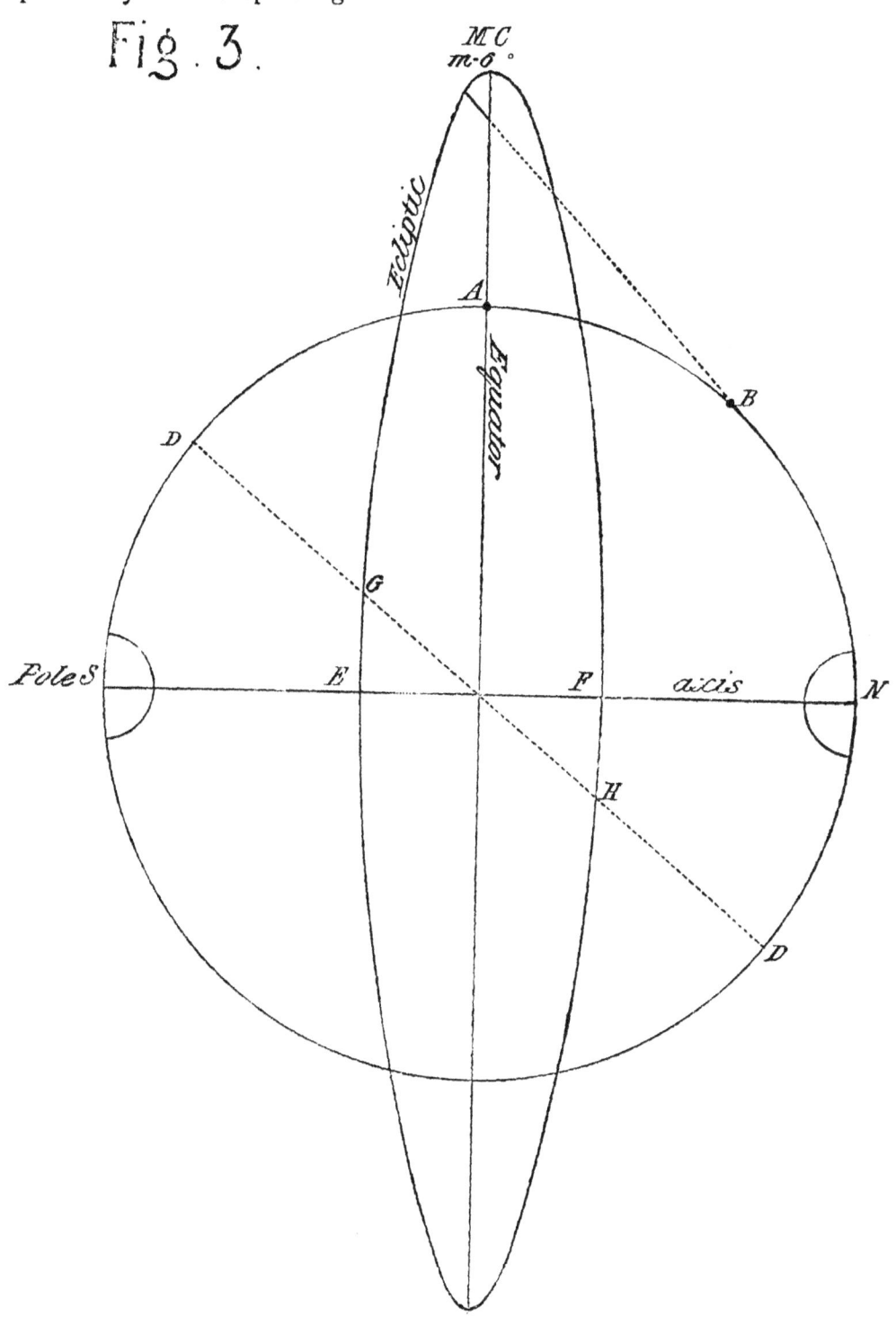

Fig. 3.

The foregoing illustrations and remarks clearly show that both systems are founded upon well defined lines of observation, and both require to be judged by the results of practical experience in their use, applied to well-timed cases. If the equal division was the method used by the ancient Astrologers up to the time of Claudius Ptolemy, it is surely of sufficient importance to warrant a close investigation. The results I have so far obtained by the equal method are more accurate in general indications than I have observed from the unequal modern system, but students must judge for themselves, which they can only do by a thorough trial in a number of carefully-timed horoscopes.

Mundane latitude, as it nears or recedes from the ecliptic, causes a distinct local influence on persons, places and things, owing to the increase or decrease of the Solar and planetary rays; but this does not necessarily require that Mundane latitude must be taken as a factor in the general significations of the Zodiacal twenty-four hour circle when measured from a given Meridian, because we have to consider the *whole of it, irrespective* of local vision, and the six houses below the Ascending line are as potent in their indications as those above it.

------------

If Cancer ascends, and the Moon be in a movable or common sign, especially remote from an angle, the native is credulous, light and inconstant.

\*        \*        \*        \*        \*

He that has Mercury well posited but the Moon afflicted shall understand well, but deliberate ill, and therefore such, though they may advise others excellently, yet shall manage their own affairs foolishly.

\*        \*        \*        \*        \*

When the Moon and Mercury, and lord of the Ascendant shall be all in double bodied signs, the native will be naturally addicted to old opinions and curious religious notions.

\*        \*        \*        \*        \*

When Venus is with Saturn and Mars, and in opposition to the place of the Moon, the native will be egotistic.

\*        \*        \*        \*        \*

In sickness, the Ascendant or its Lord signifies the patient, the seventh house the disease, the luminaries the patient's strength, the infortunes the strength of the disease, but the eighth house always has a share in the signification. The seventh and its lord signify the physician.

# Interesting Items.

The Arctic ship " Windward " cleared the dockhead of St. Katherine's, at 8.30 a.m., June 10, 1897, outward bound for the third time to the North Pole region of Franz Joseph Land, from which we anticipate her safe return from what will practically be a fruitless journey, as signified by the malefics in the fourth house. Students will find the map interesting. The horoscope of the well-known skipper, Captain James Brown, also that of her owner, Mr. Harmsworth, would be useful.

Sir James Franklin, with Captains Crozier and Fitz James in H.M.S. " Erebus " and "Terror," carrying in all 138 souls, sailed on his third Arctic expedition of discovery and survey from Greenhithe, on May 19th, 1845. The planetary positions and aspects for that day were as follows: ⊙ 28° ♉ ; ☽ 28° ♎ ; ☿ 13° ♉ ℞ ; ♀ 29° ♉ ; ♂ 11° ♒ ; ♃ 27° ♈ ; ♄ 18° ♒ ; ♅ 9° ♈ ; ♆ 26° ♒ (about). The Moon was in opposition to Jupiter, applying to the Square of Saturn and Mars, and the opposition of Mercury, and before the Sun had set the Moon had entered the sign of death, Scorpio. There were no good aspects on that day, save the Moon's separation from the trine of Neptune. A more unfortunate day for such an undertaking could not have been chosen. The year was under the cycle of Jupiter and the influence of Mars.

✳    ✳    ✳    ✳    ✳

## THE VALUE OF NAMES.

There is much fascination in the value of names and numbers. The value of the title, MODERN ASTROLOGY, is as follows :—

| | | | | | | KEY. |
|---|---|---|---|---|---|---|
| M | 4 × 6 | = | 24 | A 1 × 9 = 9 | | 0 |
| O | 7 × 5 | = | 35 | S 3 × 8 = 24 | | 9 |
| D | 4 × 4 | = | 16 | T 4 × 7 = 28 | | 9 |
| E | 5 × 3 | = | 15 | R 2 × 6 = 12 | | 1 |
| R | 2 × 2 | = | 4 | O 7 × 5 = 35 | | 4 |
| N | 5 × 1 | = | 5 | L 3 × 4 = 12 | | 8 |
| | | | | O 7 × 3 = 21 | | — |
| | | | 99 | G 3 × 2 = 6 | | 31 |
| | | | | Y 1 × 1 = 1 | | |
| | | | | 148 | | |

Added together thus : 99148, equals 31, which, according to Kabalistic Astrology, gives the Key number to the names. There being no higher number than 22 in our table, we add together 3 and 1 giving the key number 4. The explanation from the Tarot is :—

Point IV.—The Stone Cube.

*Divine World :* The perpetual and successional realization of the virtues contained in the Absolute Being.

*Intellectual World :* The realization of the ideas of dependent being by the fourfold working of the Spirit : Affirmation, Negation, Discussion, and Solution.

*Physical World :* The realization of acts directed by true knowledge, right will and good work.

*Horoscopical :* Nothing can resist the stedfast will, based upon the consciousness of Truth and Justice. To wish for that which is right and true, and to fight for its realization is more than a right : it is a duty. The man who triumphs in this struggle has only accomplished his mission. He who falls has acquired immortality. The realization of a man's hopes depends upon one more powerful than he ; let him, therefore, strive to know that One, and to gain help therefrom.

The subject of numbers is full of interest and may be used by any person without prejudice. Pythagoras says " The world is formed by numbers, and all the affairs of life are governed by numbers."

The number-value of each letter of the English alphabet is as follows :—

| | | | | |
|---|---|---|---|---|
| A = 1 | F = 8 | K = 2 | P = 8 | U = 6 |
| B = 2 | G = 3 | L = 3 | Q = 1 | V = 6 |
| C = 2 | H = 8 | M = 4 | R = 2 | W = 6 |
| D = 4 | I = 1 | N = 5 | S = 3 | X = 6 |
| E = 5 | J = 1 | O = 7 | T = 4 | Y = 1 |
| | | | | Z = 7 |

The points of the Tarot are as follows :—

| POINT. | SYMBOL. | POINT. | SYMBOL. |
|---|---|---|---|
| 1 = | The Magician. | 11 = | The Muzzled Lion. |
| 2 = | The door of the Hidden Sanctuary. | 12 = | The Sacrifice. |
| 3 = | Isis-Urania. | 13 = | The Reaping Skeleton. |
| 4 = | The Stone Cube. | 14 = | The two Urns. |
| 5 = | The Master of the Secrets. | 15 = | Typhon. |
| 6 = | The Two Ways. | 16 = | The Blasted Tower. |
| 7 = | The Chariot of Osiris. | 17 = | The Star of the Magician. |
| 8 = | The Balance and the Sword. | 18 = | The Twilight. |
| 9 = | The Veiled Lamp. | 19 = | The Resplendent Light. |
| 10 = | The Sphinx. | 20 = | The Awakening of the Dead. |
| | | 21 = | The Crown of the Magician. |

22 = The Blind Fool.

Mercury in Pisces lays an impediment on the tongue, making a person absurd in speech and uttering unawares what is not conceived in mind; this obtains if that sign ascends.

\*    \*    \*    \*    \*

Jupiter, very potent in a geniture, always promises some extraordinary happiness, and if he be in the mid-heaven, near the cusp in Capricorn, he gives a great deal of good fortune by means of violence and power under pretence of justice, but the same will have an unfortunate issue.

\*    \*    \*    \*    \*

When the lord of the figure, in a nativity, shall be retrograde and both ways cadent, the native will be a weak, poor spirited, dejected fellow, bringing nothing to perfection.

\*    \*    \*    \*    \*

Sol in Leo alone raises a man, and if the same sign ascends, it buoys up his spirit with hope, and makes him master of more than ordinary reason.

# Horoscope of Mr. Barney Isaacs Barnato.

## By THAUT.

Lat. 51° 31″ N.   Long. 0° 6′ W.     R.A.M.C., 34° 30′

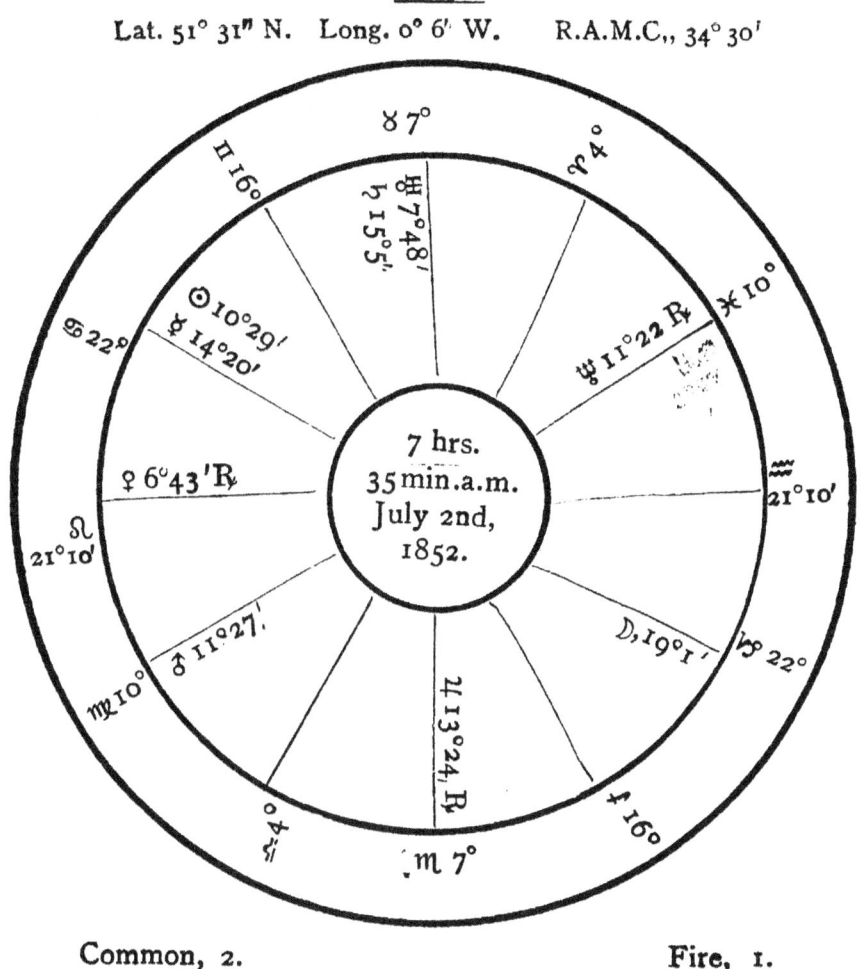

7 hrs. 35 min. a.m. July 2nd, 1852.

| | | |
|---|---|---|
| Common, 2. | | Fire, 1. |
| Cardinal, 3. | | Earth, 4. |
| Fixed, 4. | | Air, 0. |
| Exalted, 0. | | Water, 4. |

Positive, 1.     Negative, 8.

| Planet. | Sign. | House. | Declins. | Lat. | General Aspects. |
|---|---|---|---|---|---|
| ☉ | ♋ | 11 | 23° N 3′ | — | ☌ ☿, △ ♃, ♆, ✶ ♂, ♄ ♅ P ☽, ☿ |
| ☽ | ♑ | 5 | 23 S 0 | 1° S 3′ | 8 ☿, △ ♄, ✶ ♃, P. ☉ ☿ |
| ☿ | ♋ | 11 | 24 N 12 | 1 N 35 | ☌ ☉, △ ♃, ♆, ✶ ♂, ♄, 8 ☽, P. ☉ ☽ |
| ♀ | ♌ | 12 | 16 N 58 | 1 S 40 | □ ♅ |
| ♂ | ♍ | 2 | 8 N 4 | 0 S 54 | ✶ ♃, ☉, ☿, △ ♅, ♄, 8 ♆ |
| ♃ | ♏ | 4 | 14 S 51 | 1 N 5 | ✶ ♂, ☽, △ ♆, ☉, ☿ 8 ♄, ♅ |
| ♄ | ♉ | 10 | 14 N 13 | 2 S 15 | 8 ♃, ✶ ♆, ☉, ☿, △ ♂, ☽, P. ♃ ♄ |
| ♅ | ♉ | 10 | 13 N 41 | 0 S 28 | 8 ♃, ✶, ☉, ♆ □ ♀, P♃ ♅ |
| ♆ | ♓ | 8 | 8 S 7 | 0 S 54 | ✶ ♄, ♅, △ ♃, ☉, ☿, 8 ♂ |
| M.C. | ♉ | — | — | — | |
| Ascen. | ♌ | — | — | — | |

# MR. BARNEY ISAACS BARNATO.

## By Thaut.

"—Alterius vitæ quoddam initium ordimur."
—Cicero "*Epistles*."

VERY man serves his end, good, bad or indifferent, even if it be only as an object-lesson to his fellow creatures— to compel for a moment or two an eager attention and thenceforth fade from the mundane mind into an oblivion generally merited. And in the nature of things, Barney Barnato will be more surely forgotten than last year's snow for he has fulfilled his mission, and in the end it has fallen upon him. Nothing vital will remain. He has become *usé*.

Whether he ever realized the zenith of his ambition was known only to himself. It concerns us not. His life forces have reached their Nadir and have poured themselves out through the negative fourth house, but can anyone examine the horoscope of his birth and doubt that his Tanha, at the present moment maybe, still strongly appeals to his earth-instincts and draws him madly again into its feverish sphere? I believe not.

Barney Barnato was immersed in a purely physical sense-life, as is well exhibited by the position of the planets at his birth; but in every respect bearing upon that life it is almost a magnificent chart. One finds it sufficient to glance down the list of aspects to be convinced that the man was born with what the outside world terms *luck*, and a sight of the map itself adds full confirmation thereto. Yet while it is an unequivocal exhibition of a sanguine, happy-go-lucky temperament, joined with an enterprising and mercenary calculating spirit; while it shows the hard, perishable brain-mind, existing in and for itself, how is it with that fifth principle of the human constitution belonging to the upper triad, the Sanscrit *manas*! Of course such a consideration as this is too trivial for our journalist friends, but I am hoping one day they will get their eyes opened and cry *peccavi*. Meanwhile I would refer them to an article in *Lucifer* for May of this year on " The Ignorance of Learned Men."

Barney Barnato's story is too well-known for us to occupy valuable space in recounting for the thousand and first time. The name alone has been for years one to arouse envy in the hearts of less fortunate human beings than the one to which it belonged, and to the feverish cosmopolitan speculative world dabbling in stocks and shares it was at one time a magnet, and a golden dew itself.

This man whose name was so powerful a talisman or excitant throughout all classes, was the son of an " old clo'" merchant, and even stood himself in the " Lane " and shouted his wares. But he was always different from his confréres, and in a short while he rose from chaffering over old vests in dingy Whitechapel to floating Barnato Banks and Consols in the South African Commonwealth, and signing cheques for £5,000,000 sterling. Barney Barnato was a Solar man, born as the twenty-second degree ot Leo appeared on the eastern horizon, consequently his ruling planet is the Sun which is found located in the eleventh, in the positive-martial portion of the second decanate of Cancer, and this combination will sufficiently well describe him.

*Profession, Wealth, Speculation.*—For the profession consider the Sun and the tenth house, how they are aspected and with what planets configurated. The Sun *mainly* dominates the profession, according to aspecting planet. We shall notice in the first place, that the solar orb conjoins with Mercury, while both have the trine of Jupiter from mundane fourth house (that of mines, minerals, concealed treasure, etc.) ; at the same time they both occupy Cancer, this being the *Zodiacal* fourth and having the same signification as the fourth house does in the world. Cancer rules Africa. Now the conjunction of Sun and Mercury renders the mind apt for business and bargaining, which the aspect of Jupiter increases. The latter also indicates the nature of such transactions. These however are not the only aspects the Sun receives, for there are besides a trine of Neptune, and sextiles of Mars, Saturn and Uranus. Saturn is a big dealer in mines. He calculates acutely and hazards warily, and *his* influence is exerted to the degrees held by the glorious Sun at birth. From Mars on the cusp of the second house, a diametrically opposed influx comes. These cross aspects are just those that puzzle students in their initial stages of study in astral dynamics. But in a case like this, when both aspects are constitutionally of the same nature, there should be little difficulty in apprehending the perfect feasibility of influxes of Saturnine and Martial beams to a common point at one and the same time.

The Saturnine ray alone will steady and crystallise the character, almost to hardness or miserliness. It will calculate minutely and never risk without due and even excessive thought. It plans, but lacks what the Americans call " snap ; " it advises but does not act. But lo, you ! when the Martial ray impinges. The hand becomes more open, the active will is enforced, the bargain is clinched at just the precise moment, for directly the Saturnine portions of the brain (viz. those occupying the front and hinder parts of the head and comprising the powers of reflection and the selfish sentiments in general)—directly these cease to act, having gravely done theirwork, the Martial side turns up and establishes concretely the abstractions of the calculating son of Cœlus and Titheia—in fact to use a Londonism "*cuts it fat.*"

The horoscope at present engaging our attention shows a remarkable abundance of resource in this particular, and a wonderful sympathy for fourth and second house matters. Eventually the ego was to gain experience in the physical Taurean department of human life, and that indeed appears the main end of this incarnation. But the lesson is not yet learned, and must be repeated time after time until he becomes Solon enough to break the bonds he has himself forged aforetime, and realise that to reap of the spirit one must sow to the spirit ; and that the material and sense-life is unerringly cultivated at the expense of what sits higher enthroned, and so *vice versa.*

Referring to the horoscope it is noted that Mars is in the second house, well aspected, and in an earthy sign, thus showing again the source of his wealth, and that much would be gained, but that at the same time, he would possess a lavish hand and never be mean or stingy. There is no text for a moral homily, however, on that account, for it would be an impetuous open-handedness—in fact he was *un bon diable* in this matter, as the French say—the result of Mars' position and nothing more.    If read by the zodiac it is the same, and here we actually find Taurus, the second sign, equivalent to the second mundane house, on the cusp of the tenth, with Saturn therein well configurated, except for the opposition of Jupiter retrograding in Scorpio, in the fourth.    Again, Mercury rules the second (that of personal wealth) and read with its configurations leads to the same results.    In whatever way the point is regarded, the conclusions drawn are splendid for the native's temporal welfare.

The Sun, the centre of his life, character, and interest, occupies Cancer and this sign rules Africa as is well known to Astrologers, and thither of course it was natural for Barney to fly, in the hope of making a fortune when the proper directions arrived, which happened in 1873.    They were ☉ ☌ ♀ P. (Sun conjunction Venus Progressive) in Cancer, twelfth house, and ☽ △ ♂ (Moon trine Mars), Mars being lord of the ninth, the house of long voyages, etc.    He went over as an entertainer, ☉ ☌ ♀ (Sun conjunction Venus) for he had always possessed strong leanings this way, and what man, my dear penetrating critic of the English and Foreign Press, who discovers after his birth that he has Uranus conjunction M.C., and square Venus does not desire to take up such a calling as entertainer, actor or some other equally Bohemian and public vocation?    It must also be noted that the Sun with Mercury is located in the watery, emotional Cancer and that they are aspected by the self-deceptive and imitative Neptune, a ray from which is so wonderfully pregnant an auxiliary to wearers of the buskin, sock or cothurnus.

At an early age this tendency showed itself in the young Barnato, and helped to foster his talent for bartering and speculation, for both he and his brother Harry were accustomed to display the whole art of legerdemain to the *jeunesse dorée* of Whitechapel at a rate which appeared to satisfy all concerned.

The Moon located in fifth gave a great impetus to the speculative faculties, and being in a cardinal, movable sign in the fifth (theatres, amusements, speculation) and lord of the twelfth (that of foreign parts, Cancer on cusp) it bears directly upon the purpose of his going out. Had not the indications of money-making by quite different methods over-ridden those of the histrionic he would have found his true vocation in the stage.   As it was, this particularly imitative art offered him merely an *avocation*, but his ambitions lay strongly in that direction and with very great reason, as students can perceive for themselves, especially when it is also noted that his temperament was the Physical-emotional.   (Four planets in earthy and a like number in watery signs).

Much of his success is due to the configuration between Mars, Jupiter and Mercury, which gave him a hopeful, sanguine nature, and a capacity for clinching a bargain, and forging ahead at exactly the right moment.   He never threw his chance away.   "There is a tide in the affairs of men," but the majority do not even know when it has arrived.   Astrology shows plainly such tides in men's lives, when they are at flood, when at ebb, and teaches how to make the greatest use of the opportunities offered.   The so-called "lucky" individual apprehends these times intuitively because of the happy constitution of his radix,   in contradistinction to the more unfortunate ones, the small promise of whose horoscopes needs careful watching and waiting for, indeed, with all the arts the astrologer has at his disposal, and the harvest reaping close to the stubble.   Barney Barnato knew the identical moment his tide had arisen and he not only knew when it occurred but also how to take advantage of it to the furtherance of his own material interests.

But we find Saturn elevated in the tenth and this certainly but surely would have brought him down from his pedestal in South African financial affairs sooner or later.   It has done so, although forming a gloomy sequel to what I suppose for conventionalism's sake we must term a successful career.   Until 1895 when the boom showed unmistakeable signs of collapse he had nearly the whole of the speculative world at his heels, and if students will take an ephemeris for the year 1852, they will note that during those years in which he derived most, or we may say all, of his pecuniary success he had the progressive Jupiter forming a trine with his radical Mercury, and when this passed his success wavered, and there was a collapse ; and practically all 'booms' were over.   The critical point was ahead, viz.—☉ Par. ♅ ℞, and ♄ ℞ (Sun Parallel Uranus radix and Saturn radix) ; and ☉ ∠♂ P. (Sun semi-square, Mars) ; and when the former directions came up, the end came—a watery one as is decisively shown in his chart. It was his fate to be drowned like a dog.

*Au premier coup d' œil* the mental organs do not appear to be much afflicted, the representative Mercury only bearing the opposition of the Moon, but she is in her fall and opposed also by the Sun, which is decidedly not good for the mental balance. He was born at the full Moon and on the day of his death the Moon fulled.

That there is a lack of balance is gathered from the oppositions from cardinal, common and fixed signs—Mars as representative of the external will and Neptune of the subjective consciousness are in twain as are the animal consciousness and the active conditioned mind.

The kind of death is well attested by the opposition of Mars and Neptune, the latter planet always conveying in some shape or form, affairs peculiar, unannounced, chaotic and embarrassed. It is here in *the watery sign Pisces on the cusp of the house of death.* It points out plainly that control over the subjective consciousness would be lost and then reason would inevitably totter, and that the watery element would be finally involved in his death. Discriminating by the zodiac we find Scorpio, the eight sign on the cusp of the fourth mundane house, both ruling death, and the end of life, occupied by Jupiter, opposed by Saturn. These positions scarcely need remark. In conclusion we may be allowed to quote some of Barnato's ruling maxims. They are what are known as *smart*, and illustrate the man's character :—

" Never let a man put his hand on you without giving him what for ; and always have the first hit."

" You have no right to spoil another man's game so long as he plays it cleverly ; he will expose himself soon enough when he ceases to be clever at it."

" Never play the game above the people's heads, but as they think they understand it ; you have a bit in hand every time then."

" Always wind up with a good curtain, and ring it down before the public gets tired or has had time to find you out."

Well may we regard him as an object lesson and cry, *O dii boni !* *vanitas vanitatum !*

[NOTE.—This horoscope was cast from time furnished to the delineator by Mr. Barnato himself. ED.]

# Calendar  for August.

 ELATIVE time is measured by the earth's motion, and is divided into years, months, weeks, days, hours, minutes and seconds. It has its origin in movement; its existence creates change, and by it we compute the planetary aspects and positions at any given period. The time of Astronomical phenomena, when carefully noted by the objective perception, is the key to the real meaning of planetary influence, and reveals the effect from which we deduce our Astrological judgment, having already by observation, and the enlightenment of our consciousness, learned the nature of these aspects and positions.

The wisdom of the ancients, added to our own individual experience, has taught us that Jupiter and Venus are benefics, while Saturn and Mars are malefics, simply because the former are more refined, less gross, and of higher vibrations than the latter. Saturn and Mars offer nothing beyond the physical vibrations to mortal man, while Jupiter and Venus influence humanity through the feelings and the most refined thought. The very fine electric currents of the whole of the planets may be abused by the misuse of their principles, but this depends solely upon planetary aspects and positions, the square producing conflict and discord, the trine harmony and peace, as we shall proceed to judge.

## THE PHENOMENA DATA.

### Moon's Aspects with the Sun and Planets.

| ⊙ Sun. ⊙ | ☿ Mercury. ☿ |
|---|---|
| ✶ 3rd, 11.30 a.m., ✶ ☽. | ✶ 1st, ☿ ✶ ♀. |
| ✕ 5th, 6.25 p.m., □ ☽. ♄ Par. | ✶ 4th, 10.30 p.m., ✶ ☽. |
| ✶ 8th, 0 25 a.m., △ ☽. | ✕ 7th, 7.40 a.m., □ ☽. |
| ✕ 12th, 2.23 p.m., ☍ ☽. | ✶ 9th, 4.15 p.m., △ ☽. |
| 14th, ⊙ ✶ ♅. | 11th, ☿ ☌ ♄, Par. ♃. |
| ✶ 17th, 3.10 p.m., △ ☽. | ✶ 12th, 8.52 p.m., ☿ ☌ ♃. |
| ✕ 17th, ⊙ □ ♄, ♅. | ✕ 14th, 1.50 p.m., ☍ ☽. |
| ✕ 20th, 8.20 a.m., □ ☽. | 18th, ☿ □ ♆, Par ♂. |
| ✶ 23rd, 2.0 a.m., ✶ ☽. | ✶ 20th, 0.20 a.m., △ ☽, ✶ ♄. |
| 28th, 3.29 a.m., New ☽. | ✶ 21st, ☿ ✶ ♅. |
| | ✕ 22nd, 7.15 p.m., □ ☽. |
| | ✕ 24th, ☿, Par. ♂. |
| | ✶ 25th, 11 a.m., ✶ ☽. |
| | ✕ 26th, ☿ ☌ ♂. |
| | 30th. 5.22 a.m., ☌ ☽. |

**♀ Venus. ♀**

| | | | |
|---|---|---|---|
| ✱ | 1st, | ♀ ✱ ☿ | |
| × | 2nd, | 9.35 a.m., | □ ☽. |
| ✱ | 4th, | 5.40 p.m., | △ ☽. |
| × | 9th, | 7.15 a.m., | ☍ ☽. |
| ✱ | 14th, | 0.45 a.m., | △ ☽. |
| × | 16th, | 2.10 p.m., | □ ☽. |
| ✱ | 19th, | 7.40 a.m., | ✱ ☽. ✱ ♃. |
| ✱ | 24th, | 8.0 p.m., | ☌ ☽. |
| ✱ | 27th, | ♀ △ ♄. | |
| ✱ | 29th, | 5.30 p.m., | ✱ ☽ △ ♅. |

**♂ Mars. ♂**

| | | | |
|---|---|---|---|
| × | 1st, | 1.0 p.m., | ☌ ☽. |
| ✱ | 6th, | 1.15 a.m., | ✱ ☽ |
| × | 8th, | 6.0 a.m., | □ ☽. |
| ✱ | 10th, | 10.55 a.m., | △ ☽. |
| | 13th, | ♂ □ ♆. | |
| × | 15th, | 2.30 a.m., | ☍ ☽. |
| ✱ | 16th, | ♂ ✱ ♄. | |
| | 18th, | ♂ Par. ☿ | ✱ ♅. |
| ✱ | 20th, | 8.30 a.m., | △ ☽. |
| × | 22nd, | 10.5 p.m., | □ ☽. |
| × | 24th, | ♂ Par. ☿. | |
| ✱ | 25th, | 11.30 a.m., | ✱ ☽. |
| × | 26th, | 2.45 a.m., | ♂ ☌ ☿. |
| × | 30th, | 3.32 a.m., | ☌ ☽. |

**♃ Jupiter. ♃**

| | | | |
|---|---|---|---|
| ✱ | 1st, | 7.40 a.m., | ☌ ☽. |
| ✱ | 5th, | 4.45 p.m., | ✱ ☽. |
| × | 7th, | 8.0 p.m., | □ ☽. |
| ✱ | 9th, | 11.15 p.m., | △ ☽. |
| × | 14th, | 10.0 a.m., | ☍ ☽. |
| ✱ | 19th, | 8.0 a.m., | △ ☽. |
| × | 21st, | 9.30 p.m., | □ ♃. |
| ✱ | 24th, | 9.55 a.m., | ✱ ☽. |
| ✱ | 29th, | 1.3 a.m., | ☌ ☽. |

**♄ Saturn. ♄**

| | | | |
|---|---|---|---|
| ✱ | 2nd, | 5.35 a.m., | ✱ ☽. |
| × | 6th, | 0.22 p.m., | ☌ ☽. |
| ✱ | 10th, | 5.45 p.m., | ✱ ☽. |
| × | 12th, | 10.0 p.m., | □ ☽. |
| ✱ | 15th, | 4.45 a.m., | △ ☽. |
| × | 17th, | ♄ □ ☉. | |
| × | 20th, | 4.30 a.m., | ☍ ☽. |
| ✱ | 25th, | 1.40 a.m., | △ ☽. |
| × | 27th, | 9.0 a.m., | □ ☽. |
| ✱ | 29th, | 2.0 p.m., | ✱ ☽. |

**♅ Uranus. ♅**

| | | | |
|---|---|---|---|
| ✱ | 2nd, | 7.0 a.m., | ✱ ☽. |
| × | 6th, | 1.45 p.m., | ☌ ☽. |
| ✱ | 10th, | 7.0 p.m., | ✱ ☽. |
| × | 12th, | 11.15 p.m., | □ ☽. |
| ✱ | 15th, | 5.50 a.m., | △ ☽. |
| × | 17th, | ♅ □ ☉. | |
| × | 20th, | 5.40 a.m., | ☍ ☽. |
| ✱ | 25th, | 2.35 a.m., | △ ☽. |
| × | 27th, | 9.45 a.m., | □ ☽. |
| ✱ | 29th, | 2.40 p.m., | ✱ ☽. |

## The Value of the Aspects.

The symbols of the planets and aspects are not generally known, therefore, we shall use common symbols for good and so-called evil days, so that the full advantage of the calendar may be obtained by all interested. It is not possible to enter into all the details of each individual life, therefore, the general tendencies which may be applied in single cases are noted as follows :—

The corresponding marks found below may be traced to each date above, and the tendencies for that day learned by very little study of both, the Star (✱) indicating good ; the Cross (+) evil.

*Sun* ☉, ✱.—On these days, seek all persons from whom you require favours, such as employment or help ; it is good for pleasure, children's affairs, courtships, marriage, partners, and all things connected with authority, position, honour, credit, health, and speculative finance.

*Sun* ☉, +.—On these days the reverse of the foregoing may be expected, and persons in authority should be avoided.

*Mercury* ☿, ✳.—These days are good for travel ; all literary affairs and correspondence, and dealing with printers, publishers and editors, sending MSS. and writing generally. It is a good time to study, acquire languages, etc. The days marked with the + are not good ; on these, beware of thieves, falsehood and treachery.

*Venus* ♀, ✳.—All these days will be good for love affairs, social gatherings, visiting, and pleasure generally ; it will favour courtships, marriage, the engagement of servants and all domestic affairs ; these will also be good financial days. When marked by the +, affairs connected with females will not go well, and pleasures will end sorrowfully ; the tendencies will be toward disappointment and grief.

*Mars* ♂, ✳.—These are good days to exert the energies for profitable results ; all business affairs and travelling will go well ; surgeons and dentists may be favourably consulted ; also mechanics and military men. But when marked + females should avoid males, and temperance should be exercised in every way. The latter days are likely to produce quarrels and accidents, and very unfortunate disputes: arguments should then be avoided, and the senses held in check. Financial losses occur on these days.

*Jupiter* ♃, ✳.—These are good days for all matters, and especially important undertakings, such as opening new business, extension of business, etc. ; for consulting lawyers, clergymen, philosophers, etc. In a broad and general sense it is good for everything that is essentially good in motive and purpose. The days marked + are not evil but delay and hinder, and bring one in contact with hypocrites and deception.

*Saturn* ♄, ✳.—These are good days for agriculture, gardening, and building ; a good time to commence building, buying land, dealing in mines and all things of a heavy and concrete nature ; dealing with aged and elderly persons ; for constancy, contemplation, and matters requiring patience. The days marked + are evil, causing delays, disappointments, slow and prolonged troubles, and all matters that in the end, cause deep sorrow.

*Uranus* ♅, ✳.—Good for travel, Bohemian habits, and adventure ;

metaphysical studies and all romantic undertakings, and affairs having much speculation in them, such as inventions, and extraordinary and peculiar events. The + days are evil for all those things.

| D M | D W | Moon at Noon. | | THE LUNAR POSITIONS. |
|---|---|---|---|---|
| | | ° ′ | | |
| I | S | 14♍ 9 | M | Virgo, ♍, governs the bowels ; diarrhœa and dysentry |
| 2 | M | 27 ,, 47 | ,, | will be prevalent with the ☽ in ♍. |
| 3 | Tu | 11♎37 | C | Libra, ♎. This is the sign of justice and Equilibrium. |
| 4 | W | 25 ,, 36 | ,, | It favours love and peace. |
| 5 | Th | 9♏ 44 | F | Scorpio, ♏, governs the secret parts. It is a critical sign |
| 6 | F | 23 ,, 58 | ,, | ruling the deep emotions. |
| 7 | S | 8♐16 | M | Sagittarius, ♐, the sign of activity, sports and all |
| 8 | S | 22 ,, 34 | ,, | expressed feelings. |
| 9 | M | 6♑49 | C | Capricorn, ♑, is the sign of power, fame and the aris- |
| 10 | Tu | 20 ,, 58 | ,, | tocracy. It governs politics. |
| 11 | W | 4♒58 | F | Aquarius, ♒, the human nature sign. It is the sign of |
| 12 | Th | 18 ,, 44 | ,, | perception. It governs the eyes and the blood. |
| 13 | F | 2♓14 | M | Pisces, ♓, the sign of duality or double dealings. It governs |
| 14 | S | 15 ,, 27 | ,, | the ocean and all spiritualistic phenomena. |
| 15 | S | 28 ,, 21 | ,, | Mediumistic in tendency ; it purifies the emotions. |
| 16 | M | 10♈57 | C | Aries, ♈, governs the head ; it is the sign of leadership, |
| 17 | Tu | 23 ,, 18 | ,, | independence and liberty. |
| 18 | W | 5♉25 | F | Taurus, ♉, governs the throat, the taste and voice. Its |
| 19 | Th | 17 ,, 23 | ,, | tendencies are toward feastings and pleasure and |
| 20 | F | 29 ,, 17 | ,, | physical development. |
| 21 | S | 11♊ 9 | M | Gemini, ♊, governs the lungs. It is an intellectual sign, |
| 22 | S | 23 ,, 7 | ,, | dual in nature and refined. |
| 23 | M | 5♋13 | C | Cancer, ♋, rules the home life and all domestic affairs ; |
| 24 | T | 17 ,, 33 | ,, | also the emotions ; a sensitive sign. |
| 25 | W | 0♌ 9 | F | Leo, ♌, governs the heart, the creative powers, and gives |
| 26 | Th | 13 ,, 5 | ,, | wisdom born of deep feelings and love emotions ; it |
| 27 | F | 26 ,, 20 | ,, | is the sign of strength. |
| 28 | S | 9♍55 | | The New Moon of to-day is beneficial to commercial |
| 29 | S | 23 ,, 47 | | interests, and favours employés and all persons |
| 30 | M | 7♎52 | | whose business depends upon small profits and quick |
| 31 | Tu | 22 ,, 7 | | returns. It is favourable to all matters of speed, and the minor affairs of life. |

There are certain days in which the moon passes through either a Fixed, Cardinal, or Common sign marked in the above calendar of the lunar positions, as follows : F, Fixed ; C, Cardinal ; M, Mutable. Under the influence of the Fixed signs matters are likely to be lasting and binding ; under the Cardinal, changeable and uncertain ; and under the Common, undefined and indefinite ; these signs have a double influence and undercurrent of uncertainty. The Fixed signs give stability and lasting good or evil, the influence of the other signs may be altered and changed.

# 𝔅𝔦𝔯𝔱𝔥𝔡𝔞𝔶 𝔍𝔫𝔣𝔬𝔯𝔪𝔞𝔱𝔦𝔬𝔫.

## OR GENERAL CHARACTERISTICS OF ALL PERSONS BORN IN THE MONTH OF AUGUST.

### *The Twelve Signs of the Zodiac.*

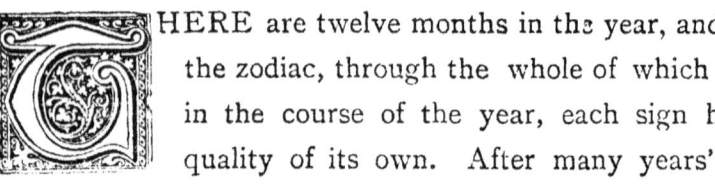

| Aries. | Taurus. | Gemini. | Cancer. | Leo. | Virgo. | Libra. |
|--------|---------|---------|---------|------|--------|--------|
| ♈ | ♉ | ♊ | ♋ | ♌ | ♍ | ♎ |

| Scorpio. | Sagittarius. | Capricorn. | Aquarius. | Pisces. |
|----------|--------------|------------|-----------|---------|
| ♏ | ♐ | ♑ | ♒ | ♓ |

### *Planets.*

| Sun. | Moon. | Mercury. | Venus. | Mars. | Saturn. | Jupiter. | Uranus. | Neptune. |
|------|-------|----------|--------|-------|---------|----------|---------|----------|
| ☉ | ☽ | ☿ | ♀ | ♂ | ♄ | ♃ | ♅ | ♆ |

THERE are twelve months in the year, and twelve signs of the zodiac, through the whole of which the Sun passes in the course of the year, each sign having a special quality of its own. After many years' careful study it has been found that all persons come more or less under the influence of one of these signs.

The sign ruling this month is Leo (The Lion), the fifth sign of the zodiac, fiery, and fixed in Nature.

The principle from which all persons coming under this sign Act is Feeling.

They are kind-hearted, generous, sympathetic and magnetic, emotional and very intuitive. They like to plan better than execute, and are not fond of details. They are lovers of pleasure, the opposite sex and children. They have strong passions, are self-confident, very determined, inclined to be hasty in temper, and very violent, and ungovernable, when not under self-control, and provoked. They may obtain great honours and celebrity; they have a royal spirit, and possess universal sympathies. They find more pleasure in giving than receiving; are always constant, noble, and ambitious. They are capable of great undertakings from an adventurous spirit, and always rise in life. Their highest powers are SELF-CONTROL, FAITH, and INTUITION.

Mentally they are best fitted to become speakers, writers, novelists, actors, overseers or managers. They are liable to heart troubles, back and kidney derangements and fevers. They should think well before they marry, and choose a partner with more head force than themselves, being liable to great mistakes in marriage. They are governed by the Sun; their gems are the ruby and diamond; colours red and green.

*N.B.—Owing to the Sun's change of sign taking place about the 21st of each month all persons born after the 20th of this month will partake of the nature of the sign Virgo (♍), which rules over September.*

## THE PROGRESSIVE BIRTHDAY.

There are few amongst us who are not curious to know what the year following our birthday is going to bring forth. If we know of trouble ahead we think it would help us to overcome much of our fate. The desire to know the future is very strong in the majority of minds. Some think it unwise to probe into the future; others consider it foolish, while there are those who even go so far as to say it is nothing short of wickedness to seek to unravel nature's secrets, but the real facts are rarely dreamed of by those who question. There is no future, past or present. All is Now. We make time by our limitations; the Sun is ever shining in a perpetual day. Night is merely the result of accident, dependant upon the earth's revolution on its axis. We have stored in us the whole of our own past, and that past has made the present and shapes our future. While bound to earth and the flesh we use the terms past, present and future, and we read the future by the past. When we can deliberately choose our future we shall have profitably gained by our past. It is undoubtedly possible to predict the future of those who continue to identify themselves with the body, mind and senses; but it is not possible to foretell ordinary events for those who are no longer ruled by their stars.

All persons born in the month of August have the root of their nature in the maternal trinity; out of the deepest emotions and powerful feeling their life is affected, so that all matters connected with feeling, pride, and ambition will have the power to move them from their centre. This is the test of all prediction for any one of the twelve signs. The Sun indicates the centre, and for the Leos that centre is the heart; therefore, all affections, passions, and moral qualities will be the centre from which life in its broadest aspects will be viewed, more from principles than particulars.

The will of the Leos, is strong though silent. They make no fuss about doing a thing, but do it; once their mind is made up, they are determined and carry out whatever they plan. Heart-sorrow is often caused through this. The ideals of persons born in Leo are high, and their moral standard of the best. From the lowest plane of desire for sensation and pleasure, they work through the emotions to the highest devotion of a pure and unselfish love, in which the sentiment is expressed, nothing is *mine* but all *yours*.

In judging the future of those born under this sign we must judge how the transits and lunar positions will affect them during·the coming year. From the 1st to the 31st the Sun receives the following aspects :—4th, ⚹ ♃ ; 5th, Par. ♄ ; 14th, ⚹ ♅ ; 17th, □ ♅, □ ♄. The 5th and 17th are therefore evil birthday anniversaries to those who have not very strong horoscopes; for should the Sun at birth be well aspected, then these afflictions will have no power to affect them, and this brings up this very important consideration: we can only be affected by evil of a similar nature to that which is in ourselves.

We will dismiss from our minds all thought of the Nativity, and give the general tendencies of the aspects on each day during August, presuming that the mutual and lunar aspects have the power to affect those whose birthdays occur on the days mentioned.

### EPHEMERAL INFLUENCES ON BIRTHDAY ANNIVERSARIES.

The world's horoscope is our own, in a general way. Taking the world *en masse* we are all linked and inter-linked. Each nation comes under a particular sign of the zodiac, and acts in accordance with the characteristics of that sign. India comes under Capricorn, and the rule of the slow and ponderous Saturn, while Britain is under the rule of Aries, the fiery and martial planet Mars being its ruler. All Britishers come more or less under the National influence of Mars, having in them the go-ahead, enterprising and energetic spirit of Mars. In judging the destinies of Great Britain the planet Mars will require chief attention, just as the ruling planet in the Natal Chart requires the primary consideration with regard to the particular fate of individuals.

The daily motions of the planets affect the nation in proportion to the nation's progress, and the process of changing iron into highly tempered steel applies as much to the individual as it does to the whole. It is in this important feature of Astrology that the judgment of the Astrologer is required; this fact must always be remembered, or the following attempt to predict for all will be a failure. We come under planetary influence only while we have in our own composition the qualities to respond to either good or evil.

## TRANSITS.

Those persons whose progressive Moon is passing through 25° of Scorpio will have grief and sorrow this month, those with the Moon passing through 10° to 15° Virgo will be beneficially affected, and those whose Moon is from 20° to 30° of the same sign must avoid acting through impulse. The transits are not good for those born about the 16th to the 19th of this month.

All persons in whose horoscopes the Sun is afflicted by Saturn and Uranus, will suffer this month from persons signified by this planet.

## LUNAR INFLUENCES DURING AUGUST.

1st.—This is a good birthday. Financial success, attended with much energy and business enterprise, will be the lot of those who avail themselves of the good influences that set in this day. Extravagance should be avoided; all excess in diet will affect health; temperance should be studied to avoid feverish complaints.

2nd.—Those born before noon will make beneficial changes in their surroundings, but will experience some sorrow through friends; they should not lend money, but give it instead; care will be needed in signing papers connected with finance. Those born in the afternoon will have love troubles, unpleasantness in social gatherings and in their relationship with acquaintances.

3rd.—Trouble through relatives, and many short journeys may be expected; marriages in the family circle, and some benefits, in a general way, will come during the year.

4th.—Those born in the morning have a good birthday; a happy year is promised; finances will be good and gain through correspondence, friends and acquaintances; it will be a pleasant year. Those born in the afternoon will have changes in the home life, and may hear of the death of some one in the family circle.

5th.—This will not be a good birthday ; great changes in the home-life, and some heavy disappointments, with the probability of gain through the decease of a relative.   The honour should be guarded.

6th.—Expect sudden changes and unexpected events ; probability of a long journey which will bring success eventually ; it will be a year of adventure.

7th.—There will be trouble through friends and acquaintances, financial worries and troublesome correspondence ; deaths may occur in the circle, and the health of children should be guarded ; pleasures will end painfully, yet through it all there will be bright glimpses of sunshine.

8th.—Avoid large assemblies ; be careful in speech and think very carefully before acting ; some painful news from abroad may be expected.  It is not a good year for any but those who possess a religious spirit.

9th.—The health will suffer this year, yet there will be some very pleasant and happy days ; gains and losses financially, but help from friends.

10th.—You will have desires to improve your position, and will succeed if you persevere and use your energies in that direction. Avoid an attitude of selfish exactitude, and look well after health. Keep the circulation active.

11th.—This may prove an unfortunate year unless you avoid society, and do not fall in too readily with strangers and acquaintances. The health will not be good ; take care of the lungs.

12th.—You will desire to travel, and be liable to many misfortunes during the year.   Protect the eyes and be very careful with whom you associate ; think well before you marry, and avoid romances.

13th.—You will have some dual experiences ; keep your own council ; avoid the water, steamships and pleasure boats especially.

14th.—You will either hear of or see a death occur in your family circle, probably the death of a friend, in which finance will be involved. Keep away from the water and seaside resorts.

15th.—Be temperate this year, doing nothing rash and impulsive. Some home trouble with regard to domestic affairs probable.

16th.—This is an unlucky birthday.  If married the partner's relatives will cause serious trouble.   Do not take long journeys ; avoid all pleasure parties, and persons who hold authority.

17th.—You will travel and come in contact with some peculiar persons. With care you may obtain much useful information this year. Avoid extremes.

18th.—Financial loss, changes in employment or profession, and many unpleasant occurrences.

19th.—This is a good birthday; the year will bring financial success, much honour and prosperity, advancement and some permanent good.

20th.—If before noon your birth occurred, expect scandal, many trials, worry and annoyance. If after noon, gain through friends; help, but difficulty with employers and persons having authority.

21st.—The loss of friends, social troubles, loss of finance and some double experiences, also annoyances through children may be expected.

22nd.—This is not a good birthday. Avoid everything of a speculative nature; keep your own counsel; be careful in correspondence, and be surety for none.

23rd.—A changeable year with mental troubles; some of the desires will be fulfilled; the emotions will be active.

24th.—This will be a good year; new friends, and many pleasant changes; you may undertake new ventures with success.

25th.—This will be a very prosperous year: all things will go well. Whatever sorrow comes it can be traced directly to your own actions. You may make the year a very happy one.

26th.—The year will be uneventful. You will only suffer through your own inaccuracy; therefore, be truthful and careful in your desires.

27th.—Mental troubles, bothers through brethren and relatives, and some anxiety may be anticipated.

28th.—You will have an entirely new set of experiences, which, although of a minor order, will give you some new realizations.

29th.—This will be a very good year, and success will attend all your efforts in business matters; all will go well and finance improve.

30th.—Females will be inclined to marry this year, and for them it will be an eventful year, bringing suitors and offers of marriage. For males it is an active year, and one of progress.

31st.—The year on the whole will be tame and uneventful; finance will fluctuate, and though, on the whole, changeable, the inclination will be toward marriage.

## To the Members of the Astrological Society, and to all Liberal-Minded Men.

THE Council of the Astrological Society are of opinion that, with a view of protecting the interests of duly qualified Astrologers, the time has now arrived for founding a fund for providing legal aid to assist those who may be prosecuted for practising Astrology.

At present the Council consider that it would be wise to confine their assistance solely to Members of the Society, and the Council will render such aid, only when in their absolute discretion, the Council are of opinion that a fit and proper case has arisen. But in time, as the proposed fund increases, the Council would be disposed to offer legal aid in all deserving cases.

The Council propose that the Fund shall be known as—

### "THE LEGAL AID FUND."

The Council earnestly urges upon the Members of the Astrological Society that such a fund is absolutely necessary for the following reasons :—

1st. That it is preposterous and intolerable, in this age of so-called freedom, toleration, and liberality, that men should be prosecuted for holding and expressing opinions of any sort, upon questions of Natural Science; or even as to the probable results of the positions and aspects of certain planets in the Zodiac.

2nd. That the Statute of 5 Geo. IV. c. 83, when applied to the prosecution of duly qualified Astrologers, is a disgrace to the age in which we live, as it savours of persecution and dogmatism, and is in restraint of the exercise of reason, the faculty with which men are endowed "for " arriving, by abstraction and generalization at the laws and principles " of things."

3rd. That the enforcement of this Act of 5. Geo. IV. c. 83, against duly qualified Astrologers, who are educated and honourable men, and householders, is a misapplication of the Act, and is in unlawful restraint of the liberty of the subject.

4th. That the Council are advised that, if properly organized resistance is offered to these prosecutions, it is *now* (having regard to recent decisions, and especially to the recent judgment of the Lord Justice Clerk, Lord Young in Scotland, in March 1896, in the case of Jane Smith) highly probable that these prosecutions or persecutions, will cease.

(Zadkiel's Almanac for 1897, contains an article upon this case, which should be read by all Astrologers).

5th. That this Act having been rightly described as " a very questionable " Act of Parliament, a criminal statute highly penal, investing Justices

" with a somewhat unconstitutional power, and as therefore if the slightest
" doubt exists as to its construction, the Justices should refrain from
" exercising their jurisdiction " (*see* " Principles of Punishment," by Mr.
Serjt. Cox) and the Council having been advised that very great doubt
exists as to whether the Act should be enforced at all against
Astrologers, as it was clearly never the original intention to include
Astrologers in its operation, and as the Council have been further
advised that, in the event of a test case being properly argued, no
conviction could take place, the Council think it desirable that the
question should be submitted to the Courts of Law as soon as the
opportunity offers.

6th, That " the Act, being a penal Act, must be construed strictly *against*
" the Statute and in favour of the defendant. Every word must be read
" in its most restricted meaning, and no meaning is to be strained for any
" purpose whatever "——Yet, nevertheless, the word " pretending " (in
sec. 4 of the Act) is constantly improperly strained in the cases of con-
victions of Astrologers, and the Council are therefore of opinion that the
time has come to demonstrate that Astrological predictions, made in
accord with the laws of Astrology, are not a pretence, and that the
strongest evidence can be given to rebut such an unwarrantable inference.

7th. That the Statute was originally intended to apply to " that class of
" persons who wander about the country with no fixed abode, no desire to
" enter upon honest labour, and no legitimate means of protracting their
" idle, and apparently useless, existence "——but it was not intended to
apply to householders, or to respectable and educated persons, acting and
thinking in accordance with an honest conviction, founded upon
experience.

8th. That it is desirable an opportunity should be afforded of arousing a
healthy public opinion upon the question as to whether or not persons
are to be prosecuted in this Nineteenth Century for holding and expressing
opinions and beliefs which such men as Kepler and Bacon affirmed to be
true, and as to which Kepler himself said that " a most unfailing experi-
" ence of the excitement of sublunary natures by the conjunctions and
" aspects of the planets, has instructed and compelled my unwilling
" belief."

For these reasons, the Council of the Astrological Society have
determined to take action with a view to check these prosecutions, as
soon as " The Legal Aid Fund," for which they now solicit subscriptions from every true Astrologer, and every lover of fair-play, shall be
in a sufficiently satisfactory condition to enable them to do so.

Donations and Annual Subscriptions to " The Legal Aid Fund "
should be sent in as soon as possible to the Hon. Secretary of the
Astrological Society, 1 & 2 Bouverie Street, Fleet Street.

(Signed) A. V. BIRCH, Hon. Sec.
By Order of the Council.

# Editorial Comment.

IT has been usual to say a few words in the first issue of each new volume as to the progress of our work and our future plans. After seven years' experience of public work in connection with Astrology we are convinced that a great change is taking place in public opinion with regard to this science. The people as a whole are beginning to think for themselves, and are no longer bound by the opinions of bigots ; they have begun to investigate the subject for themselves, the result being a satisfactory conclusion in favour of our contention, in spite of foolish opposition for the past seven years. The rising generation have more of the occult and mystical in their mind aura than those who must soon give way to them, and the display of childish ridicule as regards a great science must, therefore, soon yield to a more enlightened and progressive condition of thought. It is extremely painful to hear otherwise intelligent men criticise a subject they have never taken the slightest trouble to investigate. We are acquainted with a most earnest and sincere co-worker in other lines of useful and progressive work, who is still content to class all students of this profound science as mentally aberrated, and this in the face of the fact that dozens of his own fellow-students have proved by investigation the truth of Astrology. Yet this gentleman is contented to follow, in this particular, the track of ordinary minds, who even fail to understand his own splendid investigation into the history of the Christian religion of the earlier centuries. Why he does not devote a few hours to look into the claims of Astrology we fail to understand. Either he should do this or remember that the remarks he applies to Astrology are equally applicable to himself when considered from the lower mind standpoint, when his own work is critiscised. This, however, is not strange when we consider that the idiosyncrasies of human nature are fully borne out, showing that we are wise only to the extent of our actual experience. There are those who think that the mind of the truth-seeker should be focussed above such considerations as Astrology, but we would remind them of a sensible lecture by Mr. A. P. Sinnett on " Super Physical Research," delivered at St. James's Hall, on July

11th, in which this broad-minded writer and speaker drew the attention of his audience to the fact that all super-physical investigations should be considered as a means to an end. It is undoubtedly true that altruism is the goal that all souls should seek, but, to get in direct touch with the highest, is not such an easy matter as one might suppose. There are many short bye-paths leading to the high road of truth, and we claim for Astrology that it shows the working of the law of cause and effect. A direct perception of truth is not general to all human souls at the present stage of our evolution, and the great Teacher once said "give not strong meat to babes." We can only regret the *silent* hindrance to a pure motive, the chief desire being to place before the world one of the keys to wisdom. It must be admitted that man on the downward arc is compelled by the forces without, and only when he is master of himself can he rule his stars. If those who consider it foolish to dabble in the stars can convince us that *they* have overcome their stars, then we shall understand why they object to an investigation of the law, but until then we think it would be wise to have enough patience and, at the same time, desire for the manifestation of truth, no matter in what guise she may come.

It will not be out of place here to quote from that great occultist and teacher H. P. B. In the posthumous work, the third volume of the "Secret Doctrine," just published, she says: "The Occultists and Theosophists are the first to confess that there is white and black Astrology. Nevertheless, Astrology has to be studied in both aspects by those who wish to become proficient in it; and the good or bad results obtained do not depend upon the principles, which are the same in both kinds, but in the Astrologer himself. Thus Pythagoras, who established the whole Copernican system by the book of Hermes 2,000 years before Galileo's predecessor was born, found and studied in them the whole science of Divine Theogony, of the communication with, and the evocation of the World's Rectors—the Princes of the "Principalities" of St. Paul—the Nativity of each planet of the Universe itself, the formulæ of incantations, and the consecration of each portion of the human body to the respective Zodiacal sign corresponding to it. All this cannot be regarded as childish and absurd—still less "devilish"—*save by those who are, and wish to remain tyros in the Philosophy of the Occult Sciences.* The italics are ours.

# Important.

## PRIZES FOR ALL READERS.

THE following is the list of prizes to be given during the issue of the present volume :—

**Ten Pounds.** To the Astrologer who sends the best article, or series of articles on directions. The articles may contain explanations of all the systems advocated by Ancient and Modern Astrologers, or be entirely new. All well-known and professional Astrologers are invited to compete. The conditions are these :—The whole of the article or series of articles must be sent and marked outside " Competition," and the name of the writer given in full, either by letter, or on the back of the copy. MSS. will be returned when not accepted, if stamps are enclosed. All articles published will be paid for if required, and this be stated at the time of sending, the prize going as a reward of merit to the successful writer, as judged by the readers themselves, the Editor in all cases to have the casting vote. *Noms de plume* may be used if desired.

**Five Pounds** is the next prize which we shall give, to the Collector of the greatest number of verified dates and times of birth of notable persons, or those whose names have been drawn before the public attention.

**Five Pounds** will also be given to the Critic who turns the tables on us by proving that our science is not a true one, but instead is founded on delusions, etc. *We shall be glad if any reader hearing unjustified ridicule of Astrology by its opponents will call their attention to this paragraph.*

**One Guinea** will be given to the reader sending the greatest number of verified data concerning persons who are afflicted in any way of the five senses, such as deaf mutes, the dumb or blind, cripples, etc.

**One Guinea** is offered to the prophet making the best definite prediction during the next twelve months. The Astrological reasons must be given in every case, and the prediction must be clear and concise, and in no way vague.

**One Guinea** will be given to the reader sending satisfactory answers to the questions that may be unanswered in these pages during the next twelve months.

**Free Horoscopes.** Free Horoscopes will be given to all who are already subscribers introducing a new subscriber, whose name has not before appeared on our books.

**Guinea Subscribers.** Those who send One Guinea as a subscription to MODERN ASTROLOGY may have a complete horoscope, or one year's directions, to which special attention will be given, the work having the Editor's personal attention.

**Jubilee Prizes.** All subscribers having children born within the next twelve months, on sending the certificate of birth, may have a free horoscope. Any subscriber who marries during the year may, on sending the marriage certificate have a free horoscope or directions.

**Photo Prize.** We also offer three prizes of one, two, and three guineas each, to the sender of the greatest number of Photographs of persons whose EXACT time of birth is known, the same to be stated on the back of each card. Every reader can compete for these Prizes, and to encourage Students we shall offer Consolation Prizes, the object being to obtain reliable data and photos for the purpose of discovering the correct descriptions from the Ascending degree.

We hope that our efforts to induce interest will be fully appreciated by our numerous subscribers scattered all over the world. Those readers who have deeply studied Astrology should compete for the directions prize. Persons residing in the United States may subscribe through the Occult Publishing Company, Boston, Mass.; others should send direct to ALAN LEO, 9, Lyncroft Gardens, West Hampstead, London, N.W.

---

When the Moon applies to planets of a nature contrary to that of the distemper, the disease will be changed for the better especially if they be fortunes.

An election signifies nothing, or very little, unless it corresponds with the nativity, and time wherein you elect.

# Letters to the Editor.

Letters of general interest alone are inserted.    Correspondents desiring reply tmus
    please enclose a stamped addressed envelope.
All correspondents should give full name and address, not necessarily for publica-
    tion, but as a token of good faith.
N.B.—Writers of signed articles are alone responsible for the opinions therein
    contained.

DEAR SIR,—H. S. Green, in your April number, which I have just
received, rather unjustly raps me over the knuckles for my letter (p. 253, vol. ii).
I never argued that the Zadkiel-Raphael-Lilly system, relative to ascendant,
    erroneous.   On the contrary, when I said, " There can be no denial of the
fact that wherever we are, there is *our* centre," I thought that I very emphat-
ically declared in favour of their system.   Mr. Green, doubtless, knows that
no other Geocentric ascendant of the native can be had than from his own
centre, where the umbilical cord was tied.   I therefore think the "burden of
proof," is with Mr. Green, to prove wherein I denounced the Geocentric
system.   I have practised it for more than a quarter of a century.

Now, in a friendly way, and in the interest of the Divine (mark that word)
Science of Astrology, I wish to curb Mr. Green in his loose assertions concerning the " Tarot," which he admits, apparently, he is not clearly familiar
with.   Ely Star's and Sepharial's Kabalistic systems we may call one, for
Sepharial evidently translated Star's, or else both authors gathered from the
same source, as their presentations are almost identical ; almost *verbatim et
literatim*, Sepharial's in English, Star's in French.   Sepharial, however,
applied to the Geocentric Ascendant what Star gave to the zodical position of
the Sun.   Now do not the laws of Zadkiel, Raphael and Lilly, lead us to consider that there is some reason in this.   Should any one attempt by these
ancient teachings to judge a native by the Geocentric Ascendant without
considering and blending the position of the Sun.   These teachers also include
the Moon and lord of the Ascendant.   Now, the Ascendant marks the
beginning point of earth-life, because the earth progresses from that point.
Are not the places of the Sun, Moon and the other bodies the starting points
from whence they progress ? Might not these be termed " Ascendants" *for the
spheres of life* over which they rule, just the same as the cusp of each house in
the horoscope is the Ascendant for that relationship to the life which they are
supposed to govern ? Why then does Mr. Green declare that they are not
astronomical ascendants. If they furnish us with any knowledge of their relative
positions they are astronomical, and if their places ascend (i.e., move on) while
they progress, are not their places Ascendants without in any way destroying
our knowledge of, or faith in, the geocentric ascendant ? My experience proves
that he who ignores the natal places of the Sun and Moon, as ascendants, to
be treated in like manner (according to their spheres) as the geocentric
ascendant, is as inconsiderate as he who works by heliocentric system,
ignoring the geocentric.   Are we not told that Ptolemy worked by circles of

spheres, and when we are taught to look to the " Disposers," are not these disposers equivalent to the " lord of the ascendant ;" that is to say, is not the disposer of the Sun, the "lord" of the Sun's Ascendant ? I claim that the system taught by Zadkiel, Raphael and Lilly, is a system which *combines all* of the other systems, and if we wish a perfect reading of a native we must do as they tell us to do, *judiciously mix* the various rulers of the various ascendants, and not depend solely upon the geocentric ascendant, that, at its best, is only the *Horary* ascendant,—the Ascendant of the *hour of birth*,— for no calculations are made from it but such as are governed by that hour. A horoscope (scope of the hour) is an horary figure, drawn for the hour of birth, and in many respects is independant of the Soloscope, or the Lunascope, or any other scope, and to be confined to any one particular scope, is a wise thing for new beginners in Astrology, but as the mind advances in the Science, the student will discover that, if he lives as old as Methusalah, there will yet be unlimited scope to his far-reaching, God-given mind, in a science which includes *all things*.

Mr. Green wishes me to remember that certatn systems are but " Kabalistic," or " divinatory," like unto cards, symbolical. What of it ? Does it make any difference what it is, if only there be Truth in it ? Is not our whole science Kabalistic to those who do not understand it ? Wise men of old would not unite themselves secretly and mysteriously without sense or reason. Our object should be to get at the sense and reason which actuated them, and not imagine that we know it all because we have arrived at some truths. Astrology is all symbolical : figures, logarithms, letters and astrologic signs are but symbols. Everything representing the forces of nature—even our own bodies-- are only symbols, and largely used for divining, divinatory or Divine purposes He is wise who uses these symbols to divine or divining ends. Ely Star gives an excellent system of cartomancy in his major and minor Arcanes, alike applicable to Nativities, and here you will find the " World Divine, Intellectual Physical and Horoscopical," or in other words the spheres to which the various ascendants belong.

If Mr. Green wishes further elucidation let him get " The Tarot of the Bohemians," by Papus. The ancients employed cards, by which to arrange their horoscopes, just as we now use pen and paper to arrange ours, and the " tables" spoken of by Isaiah, as " spewed upon by the drunken," divines, diviners, or "priests," were the tables upon which they made their " spreads," each card having distinguishing marks by which they could hold their findings in place.

Excuse me for so long a letter, but I do not think I have said anything that is without interest to your readers, and I thank Mr. Green for his excellent articles on the Theoretical Basis of Astrology. He is unravelling Kaballa.

Yours, &c.,

PROF. HENRY.

D 1

# Reviews.

Cheiro's "Language of the Hand," 12/6, Messrs. Nichols & Co., Oxford Street, W.C.

This is one of the best books we have seen on what is called the science of Cheirognomy and Cheiromancy. Its artistic cover, and beautiful style of printing and binding make it quite a work of art, apart from its literary merit. Each chapter is in logical sequence, leading the student from step to step in a practical manner, and they are written in a style that is at once clear, lucid and concise. Cheiro simplifies the subject and treats it with an originality that could only be obtained from facts gathered from first hand observation.

The chief point of difference between his teachings and others' seems to lie in his classing the various lines under different heads, treating of each particular point clearly. The line of life is taken and classified as regards life, its length, etc., etc. The line of head describing the mental abilities and qualities with all that relates to the mind, and so on with the other details. The line of marriage is very interesting, being clearly defined and illustrated, and many items are noticed which are not mentioned in other popular works on the subject.

The numerous plates are beautiful illustrations, and there are quite a number of plates of the hands of celebrities all of which cannot fail to be of the deepest interest to students of this interesting subject. It is a work that we can confidently recommend; it does Cheiro great credit for the pains he has taken to make the study of Cheiromancy instructive and useful. The book is well worth the price charged for it.

L.B.

---

"Practical Astrology," A Simple Method of Instruction in the Science of Astrology, by ALAN LEO, President of the Astrological Society, and Editor of Modern Astrology. Price 3s. 6d. Modern Astrology, 1 & 2, Bouverie Street, E.C., London.

This is a manual of over 200 pages, having for its sole aim and object the placing of the ancient Chaldean and Assyrian methods of reading the stars in all clearness and perspicuity before the minds of devout students of the True Astrology. There is no straining after effect within its pages, unless it be the lasting effect of simple Truth. The Author has a devout appreciation of the "Wisdom Religion," and expresses himself throughout under the quiet and reverential assurance that the stars in their courses are intentionally given as the handwriting of the "unseen hand," and as such may be read and acted upon with confidence by all who have pleasure therein. All modern discoveries up to date which carry upon them the impress of Truth are set forth in it with clearness; but where uncertainty lingers, the author contentedly works on the principle that "all things come to him who waits." Its style is marked with considerable originality, and with abounding fearlessness; and shows throughout a large degree of intuition which will cause the work to meet with much appreciation by all who are understanding the value of, and becoming intent upon, soul culture. On the understanding that the science and art of Astrology puts its possessors in the perfect way of reading the end from the beginning, it is very certain that its devout student should do all in full and reverential view of the great unseen force which finds its clearest and most significant expression in the orbs of the firmament. This Alan Leo has aimed at and successfully done in the pages of this manual. It is well calculated to meet a want that has arisen, of something like scientific accuracy and precision that can be regarded as unerring and reliable, so as to make one's progress along the perplexing paths of life as certain as may be. The true Astrology has always from time immemorial been able to do that; so to strip it of every accretion which can only mar its usefulness and value, and put the eternal—or shall we not rather say the time-serving—verity itself before the world, is exactly all that is in it attempted. The Author is evidently no fatalist. He unmistakeably believes with all his heart that man in every case makes or mars his own destiny by his own exertions; and that if he is prepared to make intelligent sacrifices of everything superfluous and empty, thereby to win the priceless verity of greatness and capacity of soul, that every such worker is bound to realise proportionately to the energy and the wisdom displayed. No one can rise from its perusal and help realising that the little work is the best effort of one who has a clear and intelligent grasp of the great subject he handles, and of one also who is desirous before all things that the student of Astrology should have nothing to encumber him which has not already borne, and will also continue still to bear, all the severe tests of keen criticism and time. Under these circumstances it is possible to predict with much quiet assurance that the little manual will be received by the devout and the thoughtful everywhere with a marked and a growing appreciation, for it supplies what may be regarded as a much felt want.        THEODORE WRIGHT.

---

"INTELLIGENCE," issued by The Metaphysical Publishing Company, 503, Fifth Avenue, New York, made its appearance in June as the continuation of "The Metaphysical Magazine," which has been before the public for the last two years and a half. In its new form the magazine is more attractive than ever, having been enlarged in size, changed in style, broadened in character and scope, and improved generally, while the subscription price has been reduced to the popular rate of one dollar a year, and ten cents a number. Mr. Leander Edmund Whipple will edit "Intelligence," and that he has a keen sense of the needs of thoughtful readers is shown by the table of contents of the June number, a part of which follows :—

"Man and Nature," by C. Staniland Wake ; "Modern Astrology," by Alan Leo ; "Philosophy of the Divine Man," by Hudor Genone ; "Mazdaism and 'Being'—The Iranian Dualism and Fire Worship," by C. H. A. Bjerregaard ; "Bhagavad Gita—Songs of the Master"—by Charles Johnston.

M.R.A.S. ; " Esoteric Puritanism," by Henrietta Christian Wright ; " Leaves from a Metaphysician's Diary (A Summer Idyll)," by Helen Marshall North ; " Strange Experience in the Rockies," by William H. Hamby ; Odors of Flowers in the Orient," by M. Eugene Mesnard.

The attractiveness of " Intelligence " is greatly increased each month by a fine half-tone portrait of some one of the prominent workers in occult and metaphysical directions.   The June number contains an excellent portrait of Mr. Leander Edmund Whipple, founder of " The Metaphysical Magazine."

### THE HEAVENS DECLARE.

With stately tread yon mighty orbs
   Of heaven round us swing,
And, vibrant with celestial waves,
   Of God's great glory sing.

From day to day, in circuit vast,
   Majestic truths are told,
While night to night, in mystic sign,
   Deep wonders they unfold.

Each mortal child a planet is,
   By God's omniscient plan,
His orbit, too, he fully rounds ;
   Its measure—who can scan ?

Yet in this human planet reigns
   A prince of royal line ;
His mission, like the stars of heav'n,
   To speak his source divine.

O ye, thus heav'n endowed, shine forth !
   Thy parentage proclaim !
Attuned to constellations vast,
   Sing pæans to His name !

Be this thine aim, to manifest
   Thro' thy Deific powers
His love, who, thro' deep realms of space,
   Safe guides this world of ours.

The foregoing is reproduced from a little volume entitled, " Truth in Song, for the Lovers of Truth Everywhere," by Mrs. Clara H. Scott, Chicago, Ill.   As stated in the preface, the issuing of the small collection is an attempt, to meet the needs of a rapidly growing number of Christian people who are not fettered by chains of dogma, but who recognize in " Christ's " teaching a design broad enough to cover all conditions and races of men, together with their ultimate redemption.—Price, in boards only, 1/2, or 25 cents, post paid.   To be had from the author, 1351, Lexington Avenue, Chicago.

———

" Ye Booke of ye Cards," by Zuresta, The Roxburghe Press, 15, Victoria Street, Westminster, London.   Paper 1/- ; cloth 1/6.

Notwithstanding its quaint-sounding title, it is an up-to-date little volume of 113 pp., containing a dozen or more methods of card divination, with a brief interpretation of the Tarot.   For those who have not the time in this age of bustling activity to delve into books exhaustively treating on the subject, this volume will be of great service, its terseness and clear-cut style recommending it to all who are appalled by the vast deal of verbiage usually accompanying works of this kind.

# Weather for August.

The following weather forecasts have been prepared by Mr. Charles Bowen, who has studied astro-meteorology for some time. If his predictions for August are as correct as those for a portion of July have been, his system of astro-meteorology will be worth while looking into. The weather for each day during the month will be as follows :—

1st.— An ideal summer day.
2nd.—Overcast in early morning; fine day.
3rd.—Breezy, fine day.
4th.—Dull; bright intervals. Fine on the whole.
5th.—Pleasant day; cooler.
6th.—Fine day.
7th.—Fine, unsettled in p.m.; local thunder storms, but not London.
8th.—Fine, cool; breezy in the p.m.
9th.—Fine on the whole; overcast in the p.m.
10th.—Dull at times, but fine on the whole.
11th.—Fine breezy day.
12th.—Fine, warm.
13th.—Fine all day; thunder on coasts.
14th.—Bright, fine day.
15th.—Overcast early morning; fine on the whole.
16th.—Breezy, bright, fine.
17th.—Fine in the a.m.; fresh afternoon.
18th.—Dull at times; fine on the whole.
19th.—Fine, bright, pleasant day.
20th.—Doubtful in the a.m.; fine on the whole.
21st.—Fresh, pleasant, breezy day.
22nd.—Fine, breezy day.
23rd —Fine, summer day.
24th.—Doubtful in the a.m., but fine on the whole.
25th. –Cloudy, bright intervals.
26th.—Overcast, but fine.
27th.—Gusty, windy, but fine.
28th.—Fine on the whole; evening overcast, doubtful.
29th.—Cumuli, but fair weather.
30th.—Fair in the a.m.; evening doubtful, overcast.
31st.—Fair weather on the whole.

We may say of August: A fine, dry month; no rain, except a thunder shower or two. The reason for this is that all the rain producers are neutralized by their longitudes being about the same as that of the Sun, Moon and Lunation for, when the Moon by transit makes an angle to Mars, Venus, Uranus, or Saturn, she, at the same time makes an angle the Sun, Moon, Jupiter or Lunation, or Neptune, the result being that they are neutralized, and a few clouds is the only outcome of aspects which would otherwise bring rain. The above forecast is more especially applicable to London.

# Questions answered by the "Astrologer."

N.B.—*If you are in doubt as to the future, seeking advice upon the problems of life or desirous of testing the truth of Astrology, then consult the Astrologer into whose hands the management of this part of the Magazine has been entrusted. All communications should be addressed to the offices of MODERN ASTROLOGY, 1 and 2, Bouverie Street, E.C., and the envelopes marked QUESTION. The correspondence must be written upon one side of the paper only, and no more than one question asked at the time of sending. We shall require the following particulars with the question :—Time, date, and place of birth, full name and address, or instead, a suitable nom de plume, which alone will be used when sent. All questions are answered free of charge. Answers will be sent by post to subscribers if desired, or on receipt of twelve stamps to non-subscribers. Questions are answered in rotation as received. The numbers to each question have reference to the map which has been erected for future requirements. The particulars of question run through in the following order :—No——, nom de plume, birth data, place, question. Notes follow the question for the information of students. Then the answer. The letter M indicates male and F female. A for a.m., and P for p.m.*

---

No. 1.—*Bookseller, m, 8 a., February* 21, 1853, *Ireland. Q. Terminus vitæ? Father died May* 14, 1871. *A.*—In your 82nd year.

No. 2.—*Lillian, f,* 9.30a, *September* 24, 1879, *Ohio. Q.—Marriage prospects? A.*—A successful marriage in your 30th year to a man extremely devoted to you. He will have a martial appearance, and a strong love nature, and live mostly in his senses. You will have to avoid disputes, and soften his hasty temper. He will be very fond of pleasure.

No. 3.—*M.L.B., f,* 2a., *July* 5, 1878, *Ohio. Q.—When shall I marry? A.*—Your marriage will be delayed through the intervention of your intended's relatives. I judge you will not marry before your 33rd year.

No. 4.—*Lola, f,* 9.35a, *March,* 23, 1881, *Cincinnatti. Q.—Terminus vitæ? Afflicted with spinal curvature, which began in second year; health fairly good, but has not grown since fourth year. A.*—In her 22nd year a very critical stage is reached, I do not think she will survive it.

No. 5.—*Minneapolis, m, midnight. April,* 11, 1851, *Minnesota. Q.—Voyages? A.*—A voyage, West, next year.

No. 6.—*M.K.B., f,* 6.45p, *March* 27, 1870, *Ipswich. Q.—In what way will my next marriage prove disastrous, and can I avoid it? A.*—The significator or ruling planet of the husband is placed in the sixth which is the twelfth of the partner, hence, self-undoing, sorrow, and confinement as judged by the separation of Mars from Saturn. If your Will and Love is strong enough to protect him—yes. But it would be a most unselfish devotion to another to bear their burdens for them. Your first marriage was unfortunate; to prevent recurrence, choose the best day you can get for marriage.

*No. 7.—Anglo-American, m, 6a, March 5, 1843, Warwick. Q.—Date of death?* A.—You mean the time you will withdraw from physical existence. 85 is the limit, hold on until then.

*No. 8.—Uranus Rising, f, 2a, June 2, 1850, Yorkshire.* A.—Travel. New thought, some benefits, pleasure and family increase.

*No. 9.—Faithful, f, 0.45a, March 5, 1834, Shropshire. Q.—When may I expect a change?* A.—Before this year is out there will be a change for the better.

*No. 10.—♄ in Asc., m, 3p, July 25, 1869, Lat. 39° 57″ N., Long. 75° W. Q.—Vocation?* A.—The musical profession is decidedly the best for you. You may display talent in this direction, all you want is tact.

*No. 11.—Mercury in Leo, m, 9.45a, July 21, 1871, Manchester. Q.—Employment.* A.—You will have many different employments, and in the end will be connected with a society, association, or in some club, or where many people congregate.

*No. 12.—Dhanons, f, 11a, September 10, 1858, India. Father died October 1866. Mother now fatally ill.* A.—Household changes. A new friend who will become much attached, some irritability.

*No. 13.—Isis, f, 10p, September 6, 1835, Kent. Father died July, 1840, Mother, February 2, 1881. Married a widower, September 15, 1867, 23 years older. He died January 1, 1872. Disappointed in love in 1860.* A.—Beneficial changes and some good fortune. Renewed health and a fresh lease of life.

*No. 14.—Vulcan, m, midnight, October, 11, 1874, Portsmouth.* A.—You will have an opportunity to enter Government employ this year.

*No. 15.—Uranus, m, midnight, June 20, 1848, Lat 30° Q, 6 hours W.* A.—Yes, you have sufficient ability to enable you to become a good astrologer.

*No. 16.—A better change, m, 5.30a, May 27, 1865.* A.—If you must change let it be in September next.

*No. 17.—Vega, m, 10a, May 4, 1837, Iowa. Mother died April 29, 1888, Father, July 22, 1896.* A.—It is true that the current of our lives change, every 30 years, this being the cycle of Saturn. Your third promises to be similar to the first. The end will be good.

*No. 18.—True Friction, 7 to 8 a.m., December 22, 1846, Stockport. Q.—A what time am I likely to marry, if at all? Father died October 23, 1860; mother April 5, 1895.* A.—You will never marry.

*No. 19.—Lassie, 3.40 p.m., May 6, 1872, Kingston. Q.—Description of persons best avoided. Father died December 1874.* A.—While you are seeking to avoid those who you think work against your interests which, after all, is self, you will have to avoid every one with whom, in the past, your interests have clashed—persons older than yourself. To secure perfect freedom of action, therefore, avoid aged persons.

*No. 20.—November, 4.30 a.m., November 5, 1870, Albany, N.Y., U.S.A. Q.—Description of person likely to marry?* A.—Well-proportioned form, dark brown hair, with streaks of auburn, youthful face.

*No. 21.—Pearl, 6.30a, February 13, 1869, London. Q.—Date of death? Married June 20, 1892. Father died when quite young.* A.—During your forty-seventh year.

*No. 22.—L. H., 4.50 p, December 5, 1872. Portsmouth. Q.—What is the effect of the Moon in this map.* A.—The Moon is in Aquarius in the ninth. This will give deep understanding upon all religious and philosophical questions; an active mind and a tendency to hold peculiar views, and some magical ability. The Moon is well placed here and keeps you from much evil.

*No. 23.—X.Y.Z., 2.45 p., June 30, 1839. Lat. 50° 48' N. Q.—Will I benefit financially to any great extent from death or otherwise of an aged friend?* A.—The square of the Sun to Saturn does not promise you much financial benefits from the death, although something is promised when the Moon enters Taurus, though this is only *probable.*

*No. 24.—Jelf, 3 a, May 9, 1865, Dunmore, Pa. Q.—Will she recover from her present illness?* A.—She will recover.

*No. 25.—Spoart, 4 p, March 26, 1843, Ayrshire, Scotland. Q.—Is the Superintendent of my mining interests in Honduras, C.A., strictly honest.* A.—No, he is not *strictly* honest.

Isaac Harris.—We require more data.

*No. 26.—B.T.—Terminus vitæ?* A.—If you survive a serious accident likely to prove fatal in your 52nd year. The limit of life is reached at 72.

*Cheira.*—Yes, you will marry a widower, and certainly one of French origin would be the most likely. We feel very much for you, and hope your troubles will soon pass away.

*Hypatia.*—Hour of birth required.

N.B.—Please quote these numbers in all future questions.

───────────

The disease is desperate, when the significator of the sick, either in his nativity or the decumbiture has dominion in the fourth house.

When Saturn passes out of one sign into another, strange meteors and splendid meteoric displays may be expected for several days together.

LONDON :

Printed by the Law & General Printing Co., 1 & 2, Bouverie St., & Camberwell; and Published Monthly by the Proprietor, Alan Leo, at 9, Pleydell St., Fleet St., E.C.

# Modern Astrology

Edited by
ALAN LEO, P.A.S.

The Official Organ of the Astrological Society.

Vol. 3, No. 2.　　✳　　SEPTEMBER, 1897.　　✳　　Price 1s.

## Some Higher Thoughts.

N Him we move and have our being." In the bosom of the Absolute the whole of the Circle which forms our Solar system is moving. In this great circle millions of minor circles revolve. The nearer our little horoscopic circle corresponds to the greater horoscope, the more harmonious, and happy our lives become. What we continue to call evil is a misuse of our qualities. Humanity is free within the circle of its own limitations, and the more we expand this circle, the more we realize that our consciousness will expand until the possibilities of becoming more than human is cognized. We then perceive the value of the Great Teacher's words : " I and my father are one ; ye are my brethren."

✳　　✳　　✳　　✳　　✳　　✳　　✳

Around each one of us there is a great luminous mist, which corresponds to the atmosphere around the earth. In the atmosphere which surrounds us, called the Aura, our thoughts, good and bad strong or weak, are imprinted. Our body corresponds to the earth, our emotions to the dew and rain, governed by the watery signs, the mental conditions are like the wind, while the spiritual aspirations act like the sunshine, in vitalizing the reality of our self.

Every human being is surrounded by a zodiac of his, or her own, upon which the thought-currents act and react continuously, causing the Aura to become fine or coarse. The purer and stronger the life, the more delicate and beautiful will the radiation of the colours in our Aura become.

  *   *   *   *   *   *   *

Dr. Luys has described some experiments made by him, shewing the presence of luminous emanations which surround the human body, and he has demonstrated it, according to the *Electrical Review*, in the following extraordinary manner by means of photography. In the dark room, place your fingers for about twenty minutes on an ordinary photographic plate which is itself in a bath containing the usual solution of hydroquinone, and after this exposure fix the negative in the usual way. You will see not only your fingers and the lines on the skin reproduced, but also their pores, and, what is still more interesting, round the fingers a sort of zone or halo a third of an inch wide, which would lead one to believe that we live in a luminous fluid, which has enabled us to obtain a photographic print of itself and of the fingers, as if under the influence of light. Dr. Luys has tried the same experiment, but without any results, on patients whose hands were paralysed, benumbed, or insensible to touch. No image appeared on the plate.

  *   *   *   *   *   *   *

To keep the law we must first know the law. How can we love God until we know God: to work in harmony with the law and God we must obey His Will, but we must understand the commandments before we can keep them. In our prayer we say, " Our Father which art in Heaven, *Thy* Will be done on earth as it is in Heaven." The Harmony of the spheres are ever singing the glories of the Divine Ruler, but we cannot hear them until we have attuned our consciousness to its highest level.

  *   *   *   *   *   *   *

We must first love those whom we have seen, before we can love those whom we have not seen. The more we refine and purify our love, the more do we feel the meaning of the words " God is Love."

Pure love is a principle that can never be destroyed; it brings both power and wisdom. Wisdom is a blending of true knowledge and love. Power on any plane comes by wisdom. Love of the personality is limited, selfish and opposed to love of God. To love God is to love our real individuality: that which is undivided is a part of the whole. We are sparks from the great flame, and in essence a part of God.

Even if we doubted the existence of the all-loving, all-wise, and Almighty God, we know that there are those beyond us in love and intelligence whose life and precepts lead to a wider expansion of our own consciousness. There are living to-day on this earth great souls whose whole existence is devoted to the guidance and help of those struggling upward toward manhood. Animal man must be man *minus the animal* before he can become fit to understand the law of God.

As a spirit, you are a part of God or the Infinite Force or Spirit of Good. As such part, you are an ever growing power which can never lessen, and must always increase, even as it has in the past through many ages always increased, and built you up, as to intelligence, to your present mutual stature. The power of your mind has been growing to its present quality and clearness through many more physical lives than the one you are now living. Through each past life you have unconsciously added to its power. Every struggle to the mind—be it struggle against pain, struggle against appetite, struggle for more skill in the doing of anything, struggle for greater advance in the art or calling, struggle and dissatisfaction at your failings and defects—is an actual pushing of the spirit to greater power, and a greater relative completion of yourself,—and, with such completion happiness. For the aim of living is happiness.—From *The God in Yourself*, White Cross Library.

# How to Calculate Foreign Horoscopes, with Rules for South Latitudes.

THE *Nautical Almanac* and the annual ephemerides now in use among astrologers are calculated for the meridian of Greenwich ; and the following instructions are intended for the use of those who wish to erect foreign horoscopes while using these books.

It is pre-supposed that the reader is already acquainted with the method of erecting a horoscope for London, as described in the various works on the subject.

The rules for calculating foreign horoscopes are naturally classed under two heads. *Firstly*, the student must learn how to find the sidereal time for noon at the place for which he wishes to erect the figure. *Secondly*, he must know how to reckon the places of the planets correctly.

## PART I.

### To find the Sidereal Time for Noon at any place.

The Sidereal Time for noon, as given in the ephemeris, means noon at Greenwich. Therefore, to find the sidereal time for noon at any other place, a correction has to be made.

Ascertain the longitude of the place in question in degrees and minutes of space, and then turn it into hours and minutes of time by means of the following table.

> One degree of space equals four minutes of time.
> One minute of space equals four seconds of time.

Having found the longitude in time, the necessary correction has to be made for it. This is done by means of the " Table to reduce Mean to Sidereal Time." For each hour of longitude take 9·86 seconds ; and for each minute of longitude take 0·16 seconds, according to the table. This amount is to be *subtracted* from the sidereal time for

Greenwich noon in the ephemeris if the place is *east* longitude, and is to be *added* if *west*.

### TABLE TO REDUCE MEAN TO SIDEREAL TIME.

| FOR. Hours. | | TAKE. Min. | Sec. | FOR. Min, | | TAKE. Sec. |
|---|---|---|---|---|---|---|
| 1 | ... | 0 | 9·86 | 1 | ... | 0·16 |
| 2 | ... | 0 | 19·71 | 2 | ... | 0·33 |
| 3 | ... | 0 | 29·57 | 3 | ... | 0·49 |
| 4 | ·· | 0 | 39·43 | 4 | ... | 0·66 |
| 5 | ... | 0 | 49·28 | 5 | ... | 0·82 |
| 6 | ... | 0 | 59·14 | 6 | ... | 0·99 |
| 7 | ... | 1 | 9·00 | 7 | ... | 1·15 |
| 8 | ... | 1 | 18·85 | 8 | ... | 1·31 |
| 9 | ... | 1 | 28·71 | 9 | ... | 1·48 |
| 10 | ... | 1 | 38·57 | 10 | ... | 1·64 |
| 11 | ... | 1 | 48·42 | 20 | ... | 3·29 |
| 12 | ... | 1 | 58·28 | 30 | ... | 4·93 |
| | | | | 40 | ... | 6·57 |
| | | | | 50 | ... | 8·22 |
| | | | | 60 | ... | 9·86 |

Example I.—What is the Sidereal Time for noon on June 4th, 1897, at New York ?

Longitude of New York ... ... ... 74° 0′ w.
Equivalent in time ... ... ... ... 4H. 56M.
Correction for 4H. 56M. ... ... ... 48·64s.
Sidereal time noon, Greenwich, June 4th ... 4H. 52M. 45s.
Add correction for West ... ... ... 48·64s.
_____
Sidereal time noon New York ... ... 4H. 53M. 33·64s.

Example II.—What is the Sidereal Time for noon on June 4th, 1897, at Athens ?

Longitude of Athens ... ... ... ... 23° 41′ E.
Equivalent in time ... ... ... 1H. 35M.
Correction for 1H. 35M.... ... ... ... 15·61s.
Sidereal time noon, Greenwich, June 4th 4H. 52M. 45s.
Subtract correction for East ... ... 15·61s.
_____
Sidereal time, noon, Athens ... ... 4H. 52M. 29·39s.

Having thus found the sidereal time at noon for place in question, proceed to ascertain the sidereal time at the birth of the child (or right ascension of the mid-heaven in time), in the usual way. Add the time of birth if after noon, and subtract the difference between it and noon if before noon ; being careful not to forget the correction for the difference between mean and sidereal time, which is to be taken also from the " Table to Reduce Mean to Sidereal Time."

Example III.—Find the sidereal time of birth of a child born at New York, June 4th, 1897, at 10 p.m.

The sidereal time for noon at New York on the day in question has already been found by Example I., therefore we proceed thus :—

| | |
|---|---|
| Sidereal time, noon, New York ...     ... | 4H. 53M. 33·64s. |
| Add time elapsed       ...     ...     ...     ... | 10H. 0M. 0s. |
| Also add correction for 10H.      ...     ... | 1M. 38·57s. |
| Sidereal time of birth     ...     ...     .. | 14H. 55M. 12·21s. |

Example IV.—What is the sidereal time of birth of a child born at Athens on June 4th, 1897, at 10 a.m.?

The sidereal time for noon at Athens on the day in question has already been found by Example II.

| | |
|---|---|
| Sidereal time, noon, Athens...     ...     ... | 4H. 52M. 29·39s. |
| Subtract difference before noon     ...     ... | 2H. 0M. 0s. |
| | 2H. 52M. 29·39s. |
| Also subtract correction for 2H.     ...     ... | 0H. 0M. 19·71s. |
| Sidereal time of birth     ...     ...     ... | 2H. 52M. 9·68s. |

Taking the decimals as the nearest whole number, the sidereal time of birth in Example III. is 14h. 55m. 12s.; and in Example IV. 2h. 52m. 10s.

Having found the sidereal time of birth, the cusps of the mid-heaven and other houses are written in the figure by means of a table of houses for the latitude of the birth place ; or they may be worked out by trigonometry.

If the correction for longitude is wholly omitted, the error will never exceed two minutes—the less the longitude the less the error.

*(To be continued.)*

# Pu33le Ihoroscopes.

NE GUINEA is offered to the student who shall correctly state the event that happened to the native whose time of birth is given under the above heading each month We shall publish the data to which we require the solution of what we consider will be a puzzle to students. The subject for this month is :—

No. 1.—Male, born 3.45 a.m., January 2nd, 1872, in London. Puzzle: What was the nature of the remarkable event that happened to him on April 20th, 1887?

## REMARKABLE HOROSCOPES.

No. 1.—Male, born 4.45 a.m., February 8th, 1871, Lat. 52 N. Long. 2° W. He disagreed with his father, went to India, met with an accident, injured his foot, returned home, and in the summer of 1893 *shot himself.*

No. 2.—Female, born 1.40 a.m., March 4th, 1890, Lat. 52° N., Long. 2° W. This girl is tall, fair, blue eyes, round face, quick and active, and nothing is noticeably wrong with her until she begins to speak, when a defect is at once apparent. On asking the reason for the defect her parents showed me the roof of her mouth, which is cleft in two, and when a baby the liquid food would come back out of the nostrils. Her mouth is a series of roofs, none joining, but the cleft in each roof narrowing as far as can be seen. The passage is not closed now, as she can return food out of her nostrils. Outwardly, the mouth is perfect.

No.3.—Female, born January 2nd, 1841, at midnight ; Lat. 49 N., Long. 2° W ; married November 5th, 1863 ; husband died insane, February 24th, 1880. Married again, a widower, 6 children, June 11th, 1882. *No children* by either marriage, yet ♀ is in the 5th House, trine Mars, sextile ♄ ( ☿ ) ruler of 5th, Herschel is in 6th, but her constitution is a good one, and her chief illness has been quinsies. Had a tumour on the left cheek when a child. Is of a peaceful, mild disposition, fond of bodily comforts and approbation.

# A Simple Method of Instruction in the Science of Practical Astrology.

## CHAPTER II.

" By this, the slayer's knife did stab ; himself
The unjust judge, hath lost his own defender ;
The false tongue dooms its lie ; the creeping thief
And spoiler rob to render."

IF we could choose for ourselves, independently of any higher powers, the exact nature of our environment, we would, in the majority of cases, choose a different environment to that in which we find ourselves when we awake to a self-conscious realisation of our surroundings. But if, on awakening to self-consciousness, we were wise enough to understand the purpose of our physical existence, and the object in view, we should cease to rail against our fate, and immediately set to work to counteract the evil, or unfortunate conditions, by a corresponding amount of good or fortunate influences. This question of environment must always afford us a problem, the solution of which all systems of self-examination must first take into account, before the nature of human existence can be understood. The whole social problem rests upon this question of environment. To the Socialist the inequalities of the human race are matters of deep concern, and until the reasons for the same are understood, both by materialists and moulders of religious thought, no progress can be made to a satisfactory conclusion of the world's suffering and misery. In all the great cities of the world extremes meet, both as regards ignorance and knowledge, poverty and wealth, materialism and religion, cruelty and compassion, or evil and good, between each of which lies the middle path, known as the normal road of evolution. From birth to death thousands pass in ignorance of why they have followed in the tracks laid down for them in the plan of their nativities. Every-day experience alone brings its slowly dawning knowledge. Of those born into poverty, only a few are able to seize upon the opportunities to rise out of their often pitiful condition. The poor come into life heavily handicapped—born with fetters around them

that bind them to their surroundings—and yet no solution is offered by those who profess to teach the will of God. From 1881 to 1885 the writer was engaged in visiting the very lowest quarters of the East End of London, and has actually seen cases of families living in a stable, amidst filth and surroundings that were not fit for animals of the unclean type. In one four-roomed house in Whitechapel, sixteen adult persons resided, two families living and sleeping in the same room, the only division being a soiled, ragged sheet, suspended between the two walls of a small room. Some of the cases investigated were beyond description, and nothing short of first-hand knowledge of these cases could convince those whose environment is refined and secluded. And this is a Christian country, whose present day civilization is second to none. Happily, many of the worst slums in London are fast disappearing, and the sweater's victims are made cleaner and better housed by the advancing enquiry and philanthropic investigation into the condition of the poor. Within a stone's throw of these unfortunate conditions, it is not unusual to find the homes of the wealthy, on whose tables it is not thought extravagant to spend fifty pounds in floral decorations at an afternoon "at home" or dinner party. Why this great inequality is the question all students of human nature must ask. Is it an accident of birth under no wise control, or do we fall into that environment best suited for the soul's requirements ? The first duty of the Astrologer is to enquire for the causes behind this apparent inequality. To those who allow their common sense full play, neither poverty or wealth are desirable conditions of existence. In the one case the soul is heavily handicapped by its fate and in the other there is very little incentive to use the energies.

Experience has shown us that poverty comes under Mars, while great wealth may be found by the good influences of Saturn, the ethical interpretation of which lies in the fact that Mars governs the senses, while Saturn rules the mind. The troubles of the rich are more often of the mental kind, while those of the poor affect the physical and emotional side of life, yet this can be applied only in a general sense. But it may be taken as a safe rule that finance and character act and react upon each other. Persons of *strong* characters will take steps to improve their financial positions to suit their requirements, while the careless will drift on in an improvident manner, having little or no regard for themselves or those dependent upon them. A great deal is involved under the consideration of finance with regard to environment. The purely Martial types of humanity will be found in various degrees to act along the plane of the senses; and often it will be found that the Martial men and women who have not purified their prominent or chief planet, increase their social and domestic trials by a corresponding increase of family regardless of how they may be properly supported. The first consideration cannot be the children's future welfare, when we find young fathers and mothers producing children at the average rate of one per year. This is the primary evil at the root of the major portion of the extreme poverty cases, and the large family is more often taken as an excuse to impose upon the generosity of others, than it is an incentive to improve the financial condition. It is only when we have the courage to gaze upon the naked truth with regard to the unfortunate environment, that we find it true that, after all, we suffer from ourselves. We pay dearly in some cases for our experiences, but the debt for knowledge must be paid, for we ourselves forged the fetters which were ready at our birth to bind us, and no fatalist can ignore the fact, when reason is active, that we are the originators and makers of our own fate.

Planetary law explains every existing condition of environment. There never has been a horoscope describing wealth, in which the person was poor, or *vice versa*. Perhaps the greatest problem to many is why we often find some very clever persons who are always poor, and some dull and unintellectual persons who are rich. Some are inclined to think it is a case of luck, while others object to the idea of there being such things as lucky or unlucky conditions. It does not matter whether or not we use these terms, the fact remains that some succeed just where others fail.

A great deal depends upon our start in life, especially with regard to our social position. When we recognize the value of truths contained in the idea of re-incarnation, we can readily perceive the immense responsibility that is placed upon us, as we become both the parent and the child. We are each building up the world's future for our own inheritance, and in accordance with the seed we plant, so will the harvest be.

If measured by quality, the Moon and Mars, as the negative and positive, are capable only of the lowest vibrations, as compared with the Sun and Jupiter. The red and violet rays of the spectrum, corresponding to the former, are to be refined into the orange and blue of the latter. The first sign of the zodiac or house of the horoscope represented by Mars, governs the incoming life, which, from gross iron is to be finally transmuted into fine gold, hence the exaltation of the Sun in the sign Aries, or in the Eastern angle, called the Ascendant. This life, as expressed by the ruling planet, as the lord of the Ascendant is called, is always marked by the significator, the description of the person always answering to this ruling planet and the Ascendant, more or less, in a great or less degree as aspected and placed in the Nativity. In the same way the Moon may be considered. Her house is Cancer, the sign or natural ruler of the fourth house which represents the environment, the ultimate of which is Jupiter, the planet which is always exalted in Cancer, or the fourth house. In every case where the ruling planet, the Moon or fourth house, and its ruler, is heavily afflicted, the environment is not a good one, and should the ruler of the Nativity be much afflicted, then a hard struggle against adverse fate is the result.

A blending of the nativity is always necessary to judge the life and environment, but generally the fourth house conditions give the clue to the environment. The following contrast maps will help to show how judgment is obtained:

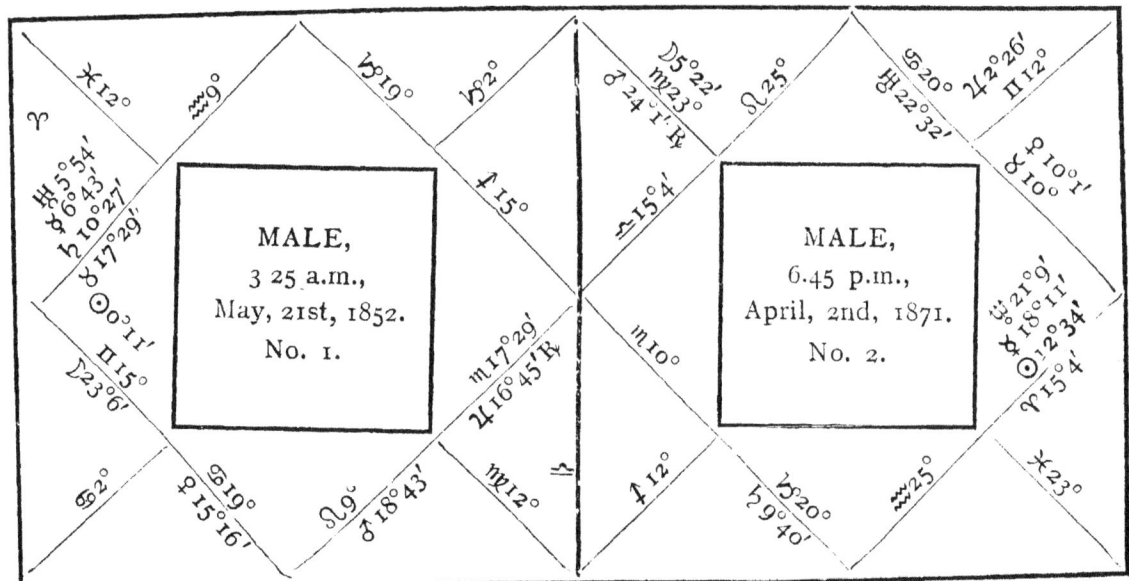

No. 1 lives a wretched life; he is a man of critical intellect ( ☿ ☌ ♄ ), a scholar, (ruler in third) and a mathematician, but always in poverty. He is a good Astrologer from the mathematical side, but his judgment is of the poorest. He has sudden and periodical drinking spells, and ruins his future prospects by his folly. Here the Moon rules the fourth, passing in affliction from Uranus and Mercury to Saturn. Now this is a case where the man has opportunities to rise in life but he lets them slip. With Venus, the ruling planet, so near the cusps of the fourth in trine aspect to Jupiter, he may close the account with interest, but as yet he has not passed Saturn and its affliction, to Jupiter. He is of the purely objective type, and never reasons and continually lapses into the influence of Mars square Jupiter. He has spent many days in the Union, to which he pays frequent visits. The critical position of the Sun between two signs gives him no real will, and his character is quite of the nature indicated by the second house, its ruler and the lunar position.

No. 2 was born into a very wealthy environment, but has run through many thousand of pounds foolishly. The ruler of the fourth is Saturn which is in trine aspect with Venus, to which planet the Moon is also in trine. The native's folly is indicated by Mars square Jupiter, and Sun square Saturn. Mars is ruler of the second and seventh. Through litigation he has lost what to some would be a fortune.

Both natives are born under the benefic Venus, but they are contrasts in every sense of the word. No. 2 has the ruler strong in its own sign, well aspected, while No. 1 has this planet beneath the earth at the lowest point. In this way the environment may be beneficially studied, the rules being simply as stated, the ruling planet with its position and aspects, and the fourth house, its ruler, etc.

It must not be supposed from the foregoing remarks that money is the only means to, or indication of, a good environment, for there are those born in the middle class who have not the extremes above mentioned. There is a condition of health to be considered; also peaceful and inharmonious surroundings. The Moon in a cardinal sign will give many changes of environment and surroundings, while the fixed signs will tend to give a steady sameness, and in common signs an ordinary and mutable condition in accordance with aspects and position.

When the life is taken up independently of the environment into which the ego is born, then all depends upon the ruling planet as to how the future will turn out to affect the environment, the fourth in reality showing the beginning and the end, the houses indicating the beginning, and the signs and rulers the end. In No. 1 map the beginning and the end will, in a manner, be similar, excepting that a dualistic or double-life tendency is indicated by the Moon in Gemini. It is in the power of every ego to make its own environment within the limits of the Sun and Jupiter; to reach either is to become the individual not limited to the personality or the physical and astral conditions.

*(To be continued.)*

THE DOG STAR.—As far as we know or are able to ascertain, Sirius, one of the giants among the "fixed stars," is one of the most magnificent specimens of God's handiwork. Sir John Herschel's astronomical labours during the early portion of the century and those of the brilliant French astronomer, Flammarion, during the past twenty-five years, have enabled us to know much about the distance to, the size of, and the intensity of the light of that distant orb. Sirius is situated about 52,000,000,000 leagues, or upwards of 225,000,000,000 miles, from our world, but the intensity of the light is such that it has been estimated by Flammarion to be at least two hundred and twenty-four times greater than that emitted by our sun! The distance to Sirius being so great, it follows that we do not see that orb as it is to-day, but as it was twenty-two years ago. The ray of light which comes to us from Sirius in this, the summer of 1897, was not emitted by that orb yesterday, or the day before, but early in the spring of 1875. Should Sirius be blotted out of existence to-day, we should know nothing of the calamity until about the middle of the year 1918.

\* \* \* \* \* \* \*

Man is the first dialogue that Nature held with God.—GOETHE.

\* \* \* \* \* \* \*

The house in which you dwell, the hall or church in which you assemble, first had form in the mind of the architect. Thus the ideas you entertain, the thoughts you think, are the architects of your future bodily conditions.

# Curious Horoscopes:

## HYPERTROPHIED HEART.

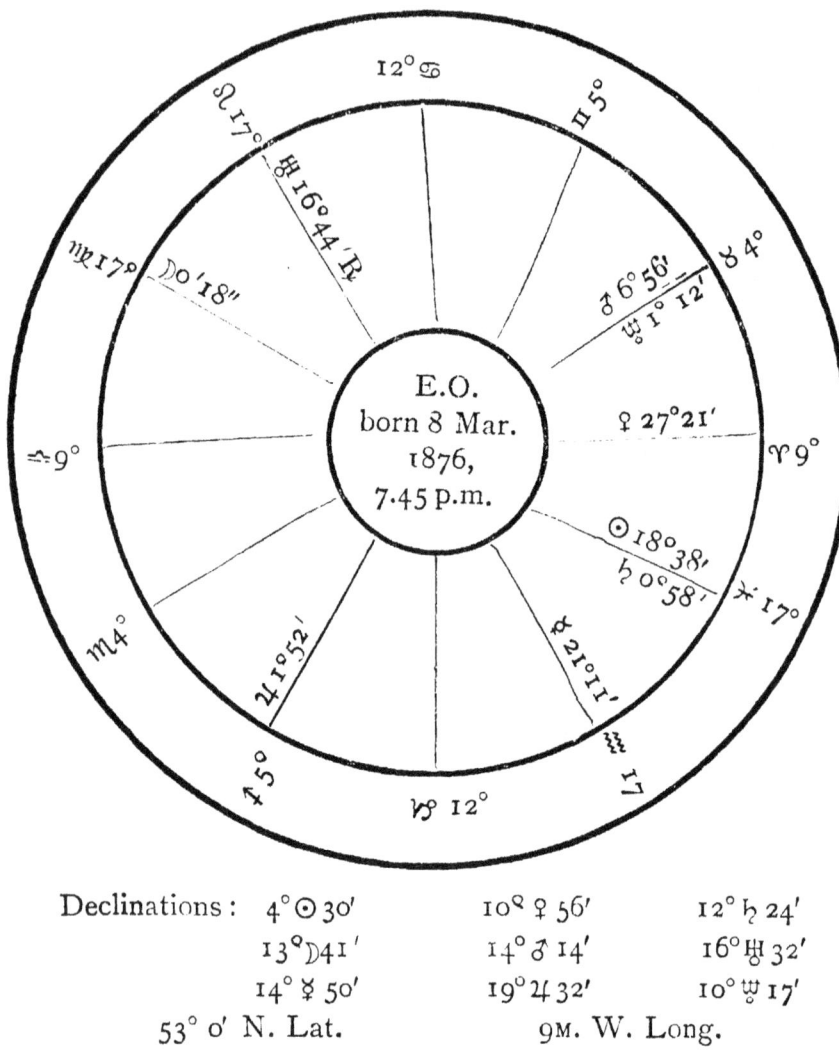

Declinations :  4° ☉ 30'       10° ♀ 56'       12° ♄ 24'

13° ☽ 41'       14° ♂ 14'       16° ♅ 32'

14° ☿ 50'       19° ♃ 32'       10° ♇ 17'

53° 0' N. Lat.                    9M. W. Long.

This young man was a " boy sorter" in the Post Office, and in June 1894, was preparing to pass the requisite examination for the post of "sorter." Before doing this it was necessary that he should be medically examined to see that he was in good physical health, as the regulations forbid anyone to hold this post who is otherwise than strong and sound. Greatly to his astonishment, and that of his parents, the doctor who examined him pronounced him to be suffering from hypertrophied or enlarged heart. This, if true, would disqualify him for the position he sought; but the doctor's report was overlooked by the authorities, as he failed to pass the examination referred to. In December, 1894, he passed the examination and was allowed to choose another doctor at a distance to report upon him again. The second report however fully confirmed the first as to the state of his heart; the doctor attributing it to his having overtaxed his strength by too rapid growth. At the age of eighteen he was over six feet in height. As a consequence of this the Commissioners refused to grant him a certificate of qualification as sorter, and he was thrown out of work. He finally left work at the Post Office on the 20th April, 1895. Neither he nor his parents had ever suspected the existence of any form of abnormality of the heart; and his health and strength had been quite as good as with most young men of his age. It is unncecessary to dwell upon the complete overthrow of all his prospects, and the trouble and anxiety this caused him and his parents.

On looking into his horoscope, we shall see very clear indications of all this. The heart is signified by Leo and the fifth house, and is influenced by the two rulers of these and by any planets contained therein. Here Leo contains Uranus, afflicted by the opposition of Mercury from the fifth house, and devoid of good aspects. This position of Uranus falls in very well with the very unexpected nature of the trouble. The fifth house contains Mercury and Saturn. Of these Mercury is well placed in Aquarius but receives and gives affliction in the manner just referred to; it is also a natural significator of letters and the Post Office (through Gemini) and when afflicted may be a source of disease or weakness (through Virgo). Saturn in the fifth would tend to weaken the heart slightly in any case, but here it is in square to Jupiter, its dispositor, lord of the sixth house (disease), and in opposition to the Moon. The Sun, a natural significator of the heart, is weakened in several ways in this figure.

(1) It is in the sixth house afflicted.

(2) It is in Pisces afflicted.

(3) It has the semi-square of Neptune and Mars from the sixth to the eighth.

(4) It has the sinister 150° aspect (= nature of sixth house) to Uranus in its own sign Leo.

(5) It is devoid of good aspects.

Here is more than sufficient to account for the state of the heart. Now let us turn to the significators of his occupation, the Post Office.

This is indicated by Gemini, the third house, and their rulers. Of Gemini, there is little to say, as it is not occupied by any planet; its ruler Mercury, however, is badly afflicted in the house of the heart and from the sign of the heart, as previously noticed. The third house has Jupiter in Sagittarius on its cusp. This position is decidedly fortunate, and, in the absence of the other afflictions, would have given him considerable success in his chosen occupation. But Jupiter is also lord of the sixth house, and is afflicted by the square of Saturn from the fifth and of the Moon from the eleventh, and is devoid of good aspects.

This horoscope, therefore, illustrates admirably these incidents in the native's life. It also exemplifies what I have previously pointed out : namely, that serious events are not always indicated by one malefic position only, but often by several pointing in a similar direction.

The reader will doubtless observe other points in the figure worthy of notice ; such as the parallel of Mars from the eighth to the Moon and Mercury ; and the bearing of the Moon opposition Saturn upon the mid-heaven and occupation.

It will be noticed that, according to Ptolemy's theory, the Moon is hyleg in this horoscope.

H. S. G.

To accomplish anything we must believe in our ability to accomplish, and this faith must at once be translated into action. Faith has no tentative efforts ; it begins in certainty of finishing, and works calmly as though it had omnipotence at its disposal and eternity before it.—MYSTERIES OF MAGIC.

*    *    *    *    *    *    *

That sign in which the significator of the disease is posited, and that to which he casts any aspects, show the members or parts of the body principally afflicted.

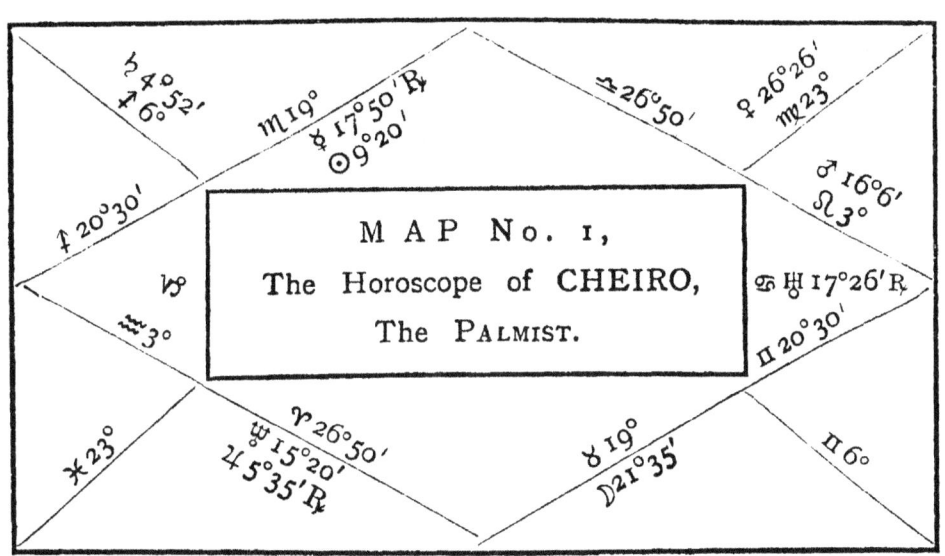

Common, 2         Positive, 4         Fire, 4
Cardinal, 3       Negative, 5         Earth, 2
Fixed, 4          Angular, 3          Air, o.
Elevated, ☉ ☿     Above ⊕, 6          Water, 3

| | | | | | |
|---|---|---|---|---|---|
| ☉ | ... 14° S. 37′ | ... | — | ... | ∠ ♀. |
| ☽ | ... 13° N. 20′ | ... | 5° S. | ... | ☍ ☿, ⚹ ♅, △ ♀. |
| ☿ | ... 18° S. 34′ | ... | 1° S. 28′ | ... | △ ♅, □ ♂. |
| ♀ | ... 2° N. 35′ | ... | 1° N. 17′ | ... | ∠ ☉, △ ☽. |
| ♂ | ... 17° N. 35′ | ... | 1° N. 38′ | ... | □ ☿. |
| ♃ | ... 0° N. 46′ | ... | 1° S. 35′ | ... | △ ♄. |
| ♄ | ... 19° S. 32′ | ... | 1° N. 37′ | ... | △ ♃. |
| ♅ | ... 22° N. 44′ | ... | 0° N. 25′ | ... | △ ☿. |
| ♆ | ... 4° N. 27′ | ... | 1° S. 40′ | ... | △ ♂. |

Many opinions have been given by various writers upon the merits and demerits of Cheirognomy and Cheiromancy, but few of these can be considered of much value unless the writers have taken the trouble to understand the science, or system of character delineation which is criticised. From time to time fresh stars arise in this profession as in

F

all others, each having a method or system of their own, meeting with success or otherwise as the abilities of the professor warrants. We have had the pleasure of testing the truth of palmistry by submitting our hands to the examination of many well-known professors. But out of the many to whom we have given the opportunity to distinguish themselves in our case, we have only obtained anything like satisfaction from Mrs. Katherine St. Hill, Miss Oxenford, Miss Amy C. G. Clapshaw, and the subject of this month's sketch, Cheiro.

Cheiro may be called the King of Palmists being the only male Palmist we know. The system he personally uses may be said to be dual, *i.e.*, scientific and intuitional. Therein he has the advantage of some of his brethren, who make use of but one. In his latest and best work, which we reviewed last month, so clearly is the whole system laid before the student that it cannot fail to win for Cheiro the admiration of all lovers of this ancient science. We are often asked to recommend a good work on this subject, and without the slightest hesitation we here express the opinion that it is one of the best modern works upon the subject.

Cheiro was born at 10.55 a.m., November 1st, in the south of Ireland. His mother was a Greek, from whom he seems to have inherited his gift of foreseeing future events. At the time of this wizard's birth, the sign of prophecy arose in the eastern horizon. Practically from this sign he obtains the whole of his foresight and keen perception. Sagittarius is the sign of enterprise, progression and far-seeing qualities; also reproductive ability. The natives of this sign often speak beyond themselves and marvel at their own speeches. They act more from impulse than careful thought ; are remarkable for their wonderful dreams and prophetic tendencies. The ruler of the ascendant is the benefic Jupiter, which is placed in the sign Aries, ruling the head, and in the third house, ruling the mind. We may judge from this that the intellect is the chief seat of the consciousness, and through the mind the major part of life's experiences will be gathered. It will incline the native to wander and travel, and he will love the life of travel more than a settled home-life ; this is also borne out by the movable sign in the fourth.

The character of Cheiro we judge from the position of the Sun and Venus. The Sun is elevated above all the planets in the mid-heaven and placed in the sign Scorpio, in semi-square to Venus. The will although determined and resolute, has more desire attached to it than is good for the free action of the character, yet this position gives a strong will, with much self-control. The character is tempered by diplomacy and approbativeness.

The mental qualities are not of the brilliant or studious type. All knowledge is gained through perception, objectively first, travelling and sight-seeing being the best means of obtaining knowledge through the mind. There is lack of inclination to enter into deep metaphysical subjects, and all display of ability is drawn from the store of past acquirement. The reflector, Mercury, is placed in the wisdom, or mystic sign, Scorpio, giving that peculiar inherent understanding which the perceptions are ever helping to bring out. The Moon is separating from the opposition of Mercury, and Mercury is in square aspect to Mars. These are two painful aspects, bringing sorrow and worry through impulsive and indiscreet action. Accuracy in speech will be needed to counteract its evil effects. Space will not allow us to give an exhaustive reading of this interesting horoscope. Students will observe much that the people at large have no means of knowing.

Taking a general survey of the nativity, we find the principal aspects are Jupiter trine Saturn and Mercury trine Uranus, and the most important positions the elevation of Sun, Venus and Mercury. Venus in the ninth assists the prophetic power ; in the house of Mercury it enables the character to be best expressed through the scientific tendencies turned to a business account. Financial benefit will be derived through the mind in foreign countries, or those removed from the native land.

The desires signified by Mars are occult, and generally, there is indicated a great love of all that is truly mystic.

Cheiro is unmarried, which is shown by the position of Uranus in the seventh, and judging from the opposition of the Moon to Mercury, ruler of the seventh, he has little if any inclination for the knot to be tied. Romantic love affairs he will have, as he requires them, but he will

F I

finally fall in love with a very pretty woman abroad, to whom he will become devoted and attached until the close of his life. He will marry in the early part of 1906 and gain considerably, financially, by the union.

In profession, he is best of all adapted to surgery or medicine, and the medical profession would have given him every opportunity of advancement.

The trine aspect of Uranus and Mercury from angles has caused Cheiro to become much interested in a very wonderful instrument which he is at present using for testing the will and magnetic qualities of his visitors to his rooms, in 47, New Bond Street, the most remarkable feature of this extraordinary piece of mechanism being its apparent inclination to point its needle upon the dial-plate in the direction of where the planets are placed in the horoscope at birth. The instrument registers the strength of thought and amount of will-power one possesses, and this without the slightest physical contact. Cheiro has found this of much assistance in his work, and it has proved a source of great interest to all the wizard's visitors. Cheiro's sincerity and remarkable gift of character-reading should convince the sceptics who have a tendency to ridicule the practice of Cheiromancy.

## INTERESTING ITEMS.

Twins { Female, born 11.35 a.m.  May 22, 1870, London.
        { Male      „     11.50  „        „     „      „

The female is very dark, black hair, dark brown eyes, above average height for a woman, slight impediment in her speech.

The male blonde hair, blue eyes, below average height for a man, good and fluent speaker, robust figure.

They lived together at home till 15—lived together from home till about 21—then parted. At 24 or 25 the boy went to India, the girl returned to her home permanently.

\*     \*     \*     \*     \*     \*     \*

Make no new clothes, nor first put them on when the Moon is in Scorpio especially if she be full of light and beheld by Mars, for they will be apt to be torn and quickly worn out.

\*     \*     \*     \*     \*     \*     \*

In every election let the Moon and Lord of the Ascendant be free from impediment and affliction.

# The Theoretical Value of the Degrees of the Zodiac.

## By H. S. Green.

FOR a long time past, astrologers have been familiar with the idea that each degree of the zodiac has an influence of its own, when on the cusp of the ascendant; that each one possesses some power or peculiarity more or less distinct and different from those adjacent. In the various volumes of the *Astrologers' Magazine*, descriptions were given of nearly all the degrees of the zodiac. The pamphlet compiled by " Raphael " on the same subject will also probably be known to all astrologers.

If each degree has a character and influence of its own, just as signs and houses have, the whole scheme must be governed by law. I have previously shown in the *Theoretical Basis of Astrology* that law and system underlie the apparently random characteristics and meanings of signs, houses, and aspects; and that with an understanding of the law it is possible to deduce from it many of the apparently unsystematic rules accepted by astrologers and confirmed by experience.

The influences attributed to the various degrees of the zodiac hitherto published appear, at first glance, amenable to no system or method; there seems little or no apparent connection between the meanings of any degree and those preceding or following it; and, so far as I am aware, no law underlying and guiding the whole has ever yet been announced. But assuming that different degrees possess different influences, it is surely self-evident that there must be some cause for it all, and that it must be possible to state that cause clearly and simply. It is not mere accident or chance that governs the order and influence of the signs of the zodiac; and it is impossible to imagine that such can be the case with degrees either. The problem, therefore, is to find out a method by which we can explain and classify the influences of degrees. It is worth while adding that such a search as this, by whatever way it may be approached, is strictly scientific in its object. For there are two departments in scientific study : the tabulation of tested facts, and an intelligent understanding and classification of them. The first department alone is not science : it only becomes such when united with the second.

In classifying the unknown, we can only do so in terms of the known. In this case we have to deal with three hundred and sixty degrees ; and to express their peculiarities we have the twelve signs of the zodiac and the planets, all of which are known factors. But since the planets themselves are expressible in terms of the zodiac, we must reject them as unnecessary and fall back upon the zodiac alone. That is to say, we have to express the unknown divisions of the zodiac in terms of those that are known, the degrees in terms of the signs. We have to divide each sign into a number of parts, and express the peculiarities of each part in terms of some sign or combination of signs.

After thinking over the problem for a considerable time, and rejecting a number of methods which were manifestly impossible, I have come to the conclusion that a certain one of the sub-divisions of the zodiac adopted by the Hindus is more likely to be correct than any other ; namely, that of each sign into ten parts. In the *Brihat Jataka* (edited by N. Chidambaram Iyer) pages 5 and 75, reference is made to a number of methods of sub-dividing signs; and in the *Astrologers' Magazine*, Vol. IV., page 158 *et seq.*, some account was given of these. There are thirty degrees in each sign ; and the obvious factors of 30 most in accordance with astrology are 10 × 3. These include that three-fold division which gives us triplicities and decanates, and a ten-fold division already adopted and systematised by the Hindus.

The ten-fold division is the one we must deal with first ; and it is seen in full in the accompanying " Table of Dashâmshas." Each sign is divided into ten parts known as dashamshas, each dashamsha consisting of three degrees. In the odd signs, the first dashamsha is that of the sign itself; the second, that of the next sign ; and so on in regular order. In the even signs, the first dashamsha is that of the tenth sign from the even sign ; the second that of the eleventh sign from the even sign ; and so on in regular order to the end of the even sign. This will be seen at length in the Table.

## TABLE OF DASHAMSHAS,

### OR TENTH PARTS OF SIGNS.

| | 1st. 1°2°3° | 2nd. 4°5°6° | 3rd. 7°8°9° | 4th. 10°11°12° | 5th. 13°14°15° | 6th. 16°17°18° | 7th. 19°20°21° | 8th. 22°23°24° | 9th. 25°26°27° | 10th. 28°29°30° |
|---|---|---|---|---|---|---|---|---|---|---|
| ♈ | ♈ | ♉ | ♊ | ♋ | ♌ | ♍ | ♎ | ♏ | ♐ | ♑ |
| ♉ | ♒ | ♓ | ♈ | ♉ | ♊ | ♋ | ♌ | ♍ | ♎ | ♏ |
| ♊ | ♊ | ♋ | ♌ | ♍ | ♎ | ♏ | ♐ | ♑ | ♒ | ♓ |
| ♋ | ♈ | ♉ | ♊ | ♋ | ♌ | ♍ | ♎ | ♏ | ♐ | ♑ |
| ♌ | ♌ | ♍ | ♎ | ♏ | ♐ | ♑ | ♒ | ♓ | ♈ | ♉ |
| ♍ | ♊ | ♋ | ♌ | ♍ | ♎ | ♏ | ♐ | ♑ | ♒ | ♓ |
| ♎ | ♎ | ♏ | ♐ | ♑ | ♒ | ♓ | ♈ | ♉ | ♊ | ♋ |
| ♏ | ♌ | ♍ | ♎ | ♏ | ♐ | ♑ | ♒ | ♓ | ♈ | ♉ |
| ♐ | ♐ | ♑ | ♒ | ♓ | ♈ | ♉ | ♊ | ♋ | ♌ | ♍ |
| ♑ | ♎ | ♏ | ♐ | ♑ | ♒ | ♓ | ♈ | ♉ | ♊ | ♋ |
| ♒ | ♒ | ♓ | ♈ | ♉ | ♊ | ♋ | ♌ | ♍ | ♎ | ♏ |
| ♓ | ♐ | ♑ | ♒ | ♓ | ♈ | ♉ | ♊ | ♋ | ♌ | ♍ |

Let me make it clear that this table is none of my own inventing. I have adopted it from the Hindus without alteration, and simply because it is a necessary part of my general scheme. Indeed it seems to me the only possible way of giving each degree of the zodiac a character of its own, though here I am anticipating. The references I have already given will show that the Hindus had a number of way, of sub-dividing signs; into two, three, seven, nine, ten, twelve, sixteen thirty and sixty parts; and that each of these different modes of sub-division was used for a different purpose. Published books give practically no information as to what these purposes were, and unless further material is available in the shape of unpublished MSS., the reasons for these sub-divisions will have to be re-discovered. I am here utilising the division in ten for a practical object, and I am awaiting the time when a certain well-known astrologer will consent to demonstrate to the world that the seven-fold division (saptamamshas) governs sex.

In this Table of Dashamshas, sub-division has been carried to the extent of dividing the degrees of the zodiac into groups of three. Thus the second dashamsha of Aries consists of the fourth, fifth, and sixth degrees of that sign ; all of which alike come under the secondary influence of Taurus. That is to say, the strongest influence of these three degrees is that of Aries, the sign to which they belong ; and the sub-influence of Taurus, which they manifest as a dashamsha, is distinctly inferior to that of Aries. The same rule holds good with regard to all these groups of three. The dashamsha modifies the local meaning of that part of the sign in which it occurs, but its power of modification is held in check by the general meaning of the sign. For instance, the sign Aries is movable, and its Taurus sub-division fixes it slightly, but not so much as would a fixed sub-division of a fixed sign. The whole is greater than its parts, and dominates them. A dashamsha can only modify, not contradict, the nature of the sign of which it is a part.

It will perhaps occur to the reader to ask what is the difference between the Taurus sub-division of the sign Aries, and the Aries sub-division of the sign Taurus. The reply is that in the first case Aries will be the primary influence and Taurus will be subordinate and secondary, a mere modifying influence; while in the second case the relations between these two will be reversed, Taurus primary and Aries secondary in importance. The difference somewhat resembles that between the lord of the first in the second and the lord of the second in the first. There will be a strong resemblance between the two cases, but differences in detail. In the first case Aries might be said to be no the ascendant, influenced by an undercurrent from Taurus on the second ; and in the second case, Taurus on the ascendant modified by a sub-influence from Aries in the Twelfth. If the reader will draw two diagrams to illustrate this, the meaning will become clear. All other dashamshas are to be treated in the same way with relation to the signs of which they form a part.

Dashamshas have, of course, the same meaning, character, nature and influence as the signs after which they are named; for instance, a Taurus dashamsha in any sign will slightly modify that sign to express

Taurus, so far as it is capable of doing so. It seems scarcely necessary to say much here as to what are the natures of signs, and the influence they exert, since I am now assuming some slight acquaintance with the subject on the part of the reader. Each sign has its own elemental nature (fiery, earthy, airy, watery) and its own quality (movable, fixed or common); and each governs the same department of nature and human affairs as the mundane house to which it corresponds in numerical order in the zodiac; Aries and first house; Taurus and second house; and so on. For further information upon this subject I must refer the reader to the *Theoretical Basis of Astrology*, chapters V. and VII.

Having divided the degrees into groups of three, and indicated how it is possible to arrive at the characteristics of each group, it remains to be shown how, by further sub-division, each separate degree may be allotted an influence of its own. Each dashamsha consists of three degrees characterised by the sub-influence of a sign. But every sign is divided into three equal parts called decanates; and, therefore, if a sign is allotted to every three degrees, each one of the three will correspond to one of the decanates of the sign, in the following manner.

| Dashamsha : | the second of Aries. | | |
| --- | --- | --- | --- |
| Degrees : | 4° ♈ | 5° ♈ | 6° ♈ |
| Nature of Dashamsha : | | ♉ | |
| Nature of Degrees : | 1st. decan. | 2nd decan. | 3rd decan. |

That is to say, the fourth, fifth, and sixth degrees of the sign Aries are characterised, as previously explained, by the sub-influence of Taurus. The fourth degree corresponds to the first decanate of Taurus; the fifth degree to the second decanate; and the sixth degree to the third and last decanate of the same sign.

This method of treating the subject gives a different influence to every degree of the whole 360.

Before proceeding further, it will be as well to explain that in my opinion the classification of decanates as given in the *Brihat Jataka* is superior to that given by Ptolemy and usually employed by European astrologers. The Hindu decanates (drekkanas) are arranged in the following way: The first decanate of each sign is purely of the nature of the sign itself; the second is modified slightly to the nature of the next sign of the same triplicity; the third to the third sign of the same triplicity.

TABLE OF DECANATES.

| SIGN. | 1st. | 2nd. | 3rd. |
|---|---|---|---|
| ♈ | ♈ | ♌ | ♐ |
| ♉ | ♉ | ♍ | ♑ |
| ♊ | ♊ | ♎ | ♒ |
| ♋ | ♋ | ♏ | ♓ |
| ♌ | ♌ | ♐ | ♈ |
| ♍ | ♍ | ♑ | ♉ |
| ♎ | ♎ | ♒ | ♊ |
| ♏ | ♏ | ♓ | ♋ |
| ♐ | ♐ | ♈ | ♌ |
| ♑ | ♑ | ♉ | ♍ |
| ♒ | ♒ | ♊ | ♎ |
| ♓ | ♓ | ♋ | ♏ |

Thus, the first decanate of Aries is wholly of the sign itself; the second is of the nature of Aries slightly modified by Leo, the next sign of the same triplicity; and the third is of the nature of Aries slightly modified by Sagittarius, the third sign of the same triplicity, always reckoning in the order of the signs.

The "Table of Dashamshas" will give the reader the nature of each group of three degrees, and the "Table of Decanates" that of each degree of the three; and the two tables are so simple that they can be carried in the mind without any difficulty, once the general principle of each is grasped.

(*To be continued.*)

Nothing can resist the will of man when he knows what is true and wills what is good.—MYSTERIES OF MAGIC.

\* \* \* \* \* \* \*

To will evil is to will death. A perverse will is the beginning of suicide. To will what is good with violence, is to will evil; for violence produces disorder and disorder produces evil.—MYSTERIES OF MAGIC.

# Astrological Stories.

## CHAPTER II.

IT WAS not until the guests invited to the birthday party had departed that the Squire and his wife settled down to the reading of their only daughter's horoscope, which had been written by Sapal, the Squire's wife's brother, at the time of the child's birth.

Squire Lennox was of the ordinary farmer type, but an exceptionally industrious man, of the motive temperament. Since his coming into possession of the estate, at his father's decease, he had prospered beyond even his own expectations, but this was not only due to his industry, but to the fact that he shared with his wife ambitious thoughts with regard to his child's future. Although inclined to be somewhat superstitious, he could not bring his mind to believe in the star-lore of his brother-in-law, Sapal; a religious instinct that was far too strongly tinged with the orthodox prevented him from overcoming the prejudices of himself and his associates. He had narrowed his mind to that extent that he rarely, if ever, thought on any subject beyond those which appealed to his five senses, and all the arguments of Sapal to suggest the possibility of subjective thought, and a higher and more sublime condition of consciousness, had proved unavailable; the Squire was too satisfied with his physical conditions to trouble himself about that which required the effort of thinking and reasoning, and he accepted the written delineation of his daughter's horoscope with a good-natured smile, and a shrug of his shoulders, with the remark that time perhaps, would prove that neither he or his daughter were amenable to the starry influences, simply because the stars were too far away to affect anyone. "But," he observed, as he took the papers from Sapal's hand, " if I see the slightest chance of any of your predictions coming true, I shall consider that, after all, there may be a grain of truth in what you so strongly assert."

And so they parted, these two men, so strangely different in temperament and thought. Sapal was tall, thin and bony, with a face that was always grave and solemn, but out of which there gleamed two orbs that seemed to burn like a living fire; they were remarkable eyes, as black as jet, around which the white seemed doubly white by the contrast. The earnest and intense gleam in those eyes seemed to carry conviction itself. Several years spent in India had coloured his skin a tawny brown hue, and gave to his face a peculiar expression which was unmistakably characteristic of the mystic that no one would have been the least surprised to find that he was what he looked—an *Astrologer*

The Squire was not tall, but slightly above the medium height, with fair hair, and florid face, and with the exception that he spoke quicker than those of his class were wont, he was all one would imagine the typical farmer to be. He was a noted horse-breeder; and was the most successful horse-dealer in his county, and at the time at which our story begins he had begun to take great interest in the animal, whose ruling planet Sapal once told him was Jupiter. He had recently been victorious in the county races, the event bringing him into contact with those moving upon a higher social scale than himself, of which he took advantage seeing in it an opportunity for his daughter's future welfare. The Squire had one fault, if fault it could be called, he was generous to excess.

The event of his daughter's tenth birthday had given him the opportunity of being more than usually liberal, and through this generosity he had been prompted in his impulsive way to allow Willie Arter to come to the party. But his wife's discretion had made ample provision for a kitchen-party, which afforded Willie more freedom than he would otherwise have had, if placed with those above him in his station in life. The Squire had invited several of the poorer children in the village, to whom the great Hall kitchen was that night specially devoted. The strange fact of two children being born on the the same day had caused him to remember his own child's horoscope, and it suddenly occurred to him that here was at least a proof that the assertions of the Astrologer could not be true, and he hit upon the idea of watching Willie Arter, so that he could judge if any similarity existed between the labourer's son and his child; also that he might question Sapal and obtain his opinion of the coincidence.

Physically, the Squire and his wife did not appear to be well mated. Mrs. Lennox was tall, thin, and very refined; her face was filled with a gleam of life that seemed ethereal in its expression. She was mental in temperament, and as devoted to her husband as any woman of the vital qualities would be, but her devotion was of the mind, being thoughtful as to her husband's interests to the highest degree. She was very prophetic, having come from a family of seers and mystics, of which faculty or quality her brother, Sapal, seemed to be endowed with more than the ordinary share. Like his sister, he was intensely mental, and between them there existed a friendship that was ideal in the extreme. She knew his power and wonderful gifts, and shared with him an intense love of all that was occult and mystical, but she concealed her passion for mystery and the metaphysical simply because she could find none, save her brother, who could understand her. It was at her request that Sapal had cast her only child's horoscope, but all their united efforts to convince the Squire of its value had proved futile, simply because he could not understand that which did not appeal to his objective vision. The subject dear to the heart of both brother and sister, had long since been shelved, and it was discussed only when they were alone and the Squire beyond hearing. Seven years had passed without reference to the matter, and, but for Willie Arter's appearance upon the scene, the horoscope might have been entirely forgotten. But now his slumbering mind seemed to have a conclusive proof that such a thing as planetary influence could not exist.

The last of the departing guests had left the Hall when the Squire and his wife settled down in their private room to read Bessie's chart. Placing the bulky document upon a small round table, the Squire filled his pipe, and made sundry preparations for his physical comfort before giving himself up to the task of listening to his wife, who was to read Sapal's judgment to him.

"It looks very much like Greek, my dear," he said after adjusting his spectacles and examining the first page. " The nearest thing to it I have ever seen is the drawing of the cart wheels in Benson's Catalogue, but I suppose you understand with your clever brain, my dear," as he handed the paper to his wife.

"Yes," she replied; " I think I can understand Sapal's strange figures, although years have elapsed since he taught me his mystic lore. If all the wise men say be true, each life is but a chapter in one great horoscope, the pages of which roll up with time, to be unfolded when the great scheme, which originated in the Divine mind, is fulfilled. At school we re-wrote the mottoes in our copy-books, and we are still at school, but now we choose the mottoes which we prefer to copy from the Book of Life, and this is but the prophet's knowledge of the plan and the scheme into which this young life has fallen. As a chart it may guide her aright; to us it comes in time and season. Let us profit by its study." So saying she began to read, first laying the map upon the table.

*(To be continued.)*

---

Revolutions may produce effects happening in the years following, either because one year is preparative to another, or because the nativity decrees what the revolution perfects, or by reason of the greatness of the event as death, or of the causes, as when the Sun is exactly in opposition to Jupiter.

\* \* \* \* \* \*

When Mercury is under the earth he has greater efficacy in relation to giving arts and sciences, but in respect to eloquence he is best when above the earth.

\* \* \* \* \* \* \*

A native of a city having the same sign and degree ascending with that city, shall in that place, by that alone grow great and eminent.

\* \* \* \* \* \* \*

Saturn, lord of the year and in Scorpio signifieth abundance of rain and increase of waters both in rivers and fountains: also that they shall be corrupt; and if he be meridional he shall denote a scarcity of provisions appertaining to the life of man, especially such as are produced by the earth. If he be oriental there shall be many dissensions, quarrels and wars between Kings and Great Men; if retrograde it shall go ill with all manner of men and their affairs; if he be direct, travellers both by sea and land shall be successful.

Saturn is lord of the year, as shown by the figure for the Sun's entry into Aries this year.

# Calendar for ♍ September.

" Therefore, to whom turn I but to Thee, the ineffable name ?
Builder and maker, Thou, of houses not made with hands ! "

SEPTEMBER was the seventh month of the Romans, counting from March when the sun entered Aries. It became the ninth month when January and February were added to the year of Numa, 731, B.C.

During the early part of this month the Sun is in Virgo, entering Libra on the 23rd. Three parts of this month are under the Mercurial influence. The gems for the month are pink, jasper and hyacinth. The ruling colors gold and black, speckled with blue dots. The Moon holds the following positions this month.

| D M | D W | Moon at Noon. ° ′ | APPROXIMATE TIME OF LUNAR ASPECTS. |
|---|---|---|---|
| 1 | W | 6♏27 | □ ♀, 0 32 a.m., ⚹ ⊙, 5.5 p.m. |
| 2 | Th | 20 ,, 46 | ⚹ ♃, 8.a.m., ☌ ♄ ♅, 7.30 p.m. |
| 3 | F | 5♐ 2 | △ ♀, 7.30 a.m., ⚹ ♂, 1.10 p.m., ⚹ ☿, 3.5 p.m., □ ⊙, 11.13 p.m. |
| 4 | S | 19 ,, 12 | □ ♃, 11.20 a.m., ☍ ♆, 5.30 p.m., ☽ ⚼ ♀, ♀ ∠ ♃, P. ♅. |
| 5 | S | 3♑14 | □ ☌, 6.50 p.m., □ ☿, 8 p.m., ⊙ Q. ♄, ♅. |
| 6 | M | 17 ,, 7 | △ , 6.25 a.m., △ ♃, 3.45 p.m. |
| 7 | Tu | 0♒50 | ⚹ ♄, 2,32 a.m., ⚹ ♅, 2.40 a.m., ☿ ☌ ♂, 7.15 a.m., ☽ ⚼ ♃, ♆, ⊙. |
| 8 | W | 14 ,, 23 | ☍ ♀, 0.26 a.m., △ ☿, 1.15 a.m., △ ♂, 1,45 a.m., ☿ ⚹ ♀. |
| 9 | Th | 27 ,, 45 | △ ♆, 2.35 a.m., □ ♄, 8.5 a.m., □ ♅, 8.5 a.m., ♄ ☌ ♅, 9.54 a.m., ♀ ⚹ ♂. |
| 10 | F | 10♓54 | ⊙ Par. ♃, ♀ Par. ♄. |
| 11 | S | 23 ,, 51 | ☍ ⊙, 2.12 a m., ☍ ♃, 5.10 a.m., □ ♆, 9.35 a.m., △ ♅, 3.25 p.m., △ ♄, 3.30 p.m. |
| 12 | S | 6♈34 | ☍ ☿, 2.30 p.m., ☍ ♂, 10.10 p.m., ⊙ Par ♂. |
| 13 | M | 19 ,, 3 | △ ♀, 0.45 a.m., ⚹ ♆ 6.52 p.m., ⊙ ☌ ♃, 6.39 a.m. |
| 14 | Tu | 1♉19 | ♂ Par ♃ |
| 15 | W | 13 ,, 24 | □ ♀, 7.15 p.m., ⊙ □ ♆. |
| 16 | Th | 25 ,, 20 | △ ♃, 3.55 a.m., △ ⊙ 8.45 a.m., ☍ ♅ 1 p.m., ☍ ♄ 1.30 p.m. |
| 17 | F | 7♊12 | △ ☿, 7.30 a.m., ☿ ∠ ♀ |
| 18 | S | 19 ,, 3 | △ ♂, 4.30 a.m., ⚹ ♀, 2.30 p.m., □ ♃, 5.35 p.m., ☌ ♆, 7.5 p.m., ⊙ ⚹ ♅, 2.10 p.m., ⊙ ⚹ ♄ 11.18 p.m. |
| 19 | S | 0♋59 | □ ⊙, 2.51 a.m., □ ☿, 4.15 p.m. |
| 20 | M | 13 ,, 4 | □ ♂, 8 p.m. |
| 21 | T | 25 ,, 24 | ⚹ ♃ 6.15 a.m., △ ♅ 1.15 p.m., △ ♄, 2.5 p.m., ⚹ ⊙, 6.55 p.m., ⚹ ☿, 9.30 p.m., ♃ □ ♆, 7.32 p.m. |
| 22 | W | 8♌ 3 | ⊙ ☌ ☿, 11.40 a.m., ☽ ∠ ☿ ♃ ♆. |
| 23 | Th | 21 ,, 5 | ⚹ ♂, 7.45 a.m., ⚹ ♆ 2.40 p.m., □ ♅, 9 p.m., □ ♄, 10 p.m., ☌ ♀, 10 p.m., ♀ □ ♄, ♅. |
| 24 | F | 4♍32 | ☽ ∠ ♂. |
| 25 | S | 18 ,, 25 | □ ♆, 7 p.m., ☌ ♃, 8.30 p.m., ☿ ⚹ ♄. |
| 26 | S | 2♎40 | ☌ ☿, 1.5 a.m., ⚹ ♅, 1.15 a.m., ⚹ ♄, 2.30 a.m., ☌ ⊙, 1.46 p.m., ☿ ⚹ ♅. |
| 27 | M | 17 ,, 12 | ☌ ♂, 7.20 p.m., △ ♆, 8.45 p.m. |
| 28 | Tu | 1♏55 | ⚹ ♀ 0.30 p.m. |
| 29 | W | 16 ,, 40 | ⚹ ☿, 11.45 p.m. |
| 30 | Th | 1♐20 | ⚹ ♃ 0.30 a.m., ☌ ♅, 3.19 a.m., ☌ ♄, 5.15 a.m., □ ♀, 5.55 p.m., ⚹ ⊙, 11.2 p.m. |

## THE GENERAL INDICATONS FOR SEPTEMBER.

The very good days this month are the 6th, 13th, 21st and 26th ; the evil are the 9th, 12th and 23rd. The following days are especially good otherwise in connection with the various headings used.

### BUSINESS ENTERPRISE.
#### Travelling, Correspondence, &c.

| Good for : | | Not Good : | |
|---|---|---|---|
| 3rd, p.m. | 23rd, a.m. | 5th, p.m. | 12th, p.m. |
| 17th, a.m. | 25th and 26th. | 19th and 20th, p.m. | |
| 18th, a.m. | 29th, p.m. | | |

### FINANCE.
#### Love Affairs and Pleasure.

| Good for : | | Not Good : | |
|---|---|---|---|
| 2nd, a.m. | 18th, Afternoon. | 1st, a.m. | 14th and 15th. |
| 3rd, a.m. | 21st, a.m. | 4th, ., | 18th, Evening. |
| 6th, p.m. | 28th, p.m. | 8th, ,, | 23rd. |
| 13th, a.m. | 30th, a.m. | 11th, a.m. | |
| 16th, a.m. | | | |

### LAND AND HOUSE.
#### Elderly Persons and Oddities.

| Good for : | | Not Good : | |
|---|---|---|---|
| 2nd, | 18th, p.m. | 9th, a.m. | 16th, p.m. |
| 7th, a.m. | 21st, ,, | 23rd, p.m. | |
| 11th, p.m. | 25th and 26th | | |

### HONOUR FAME AND POWER.

| Good for : | | Not Good ; | |
|---|---|---|---|
| 1st, p.m. | 16th, a.m. | 3rd, Evening. | 11th, a.m. |
| 6th, a.m. | 21st, p.m. | 13th. a.m. | |
| 13th. | 30th, ,, | | |

## Birthday Anniversary Prospects.

ALL persons born in the month of September between the 1st and the 23rd come under the sign of the Virgin, Virgo. If born after the 23rd they partake of the qualities ruling next month. All persons coming under the influence of the sign Virgo are Mercurial in quality they are quick and practical ; very perceptive and intuitive.

Their highest powers are " Circulation and Vibration." They are very orderly and methodical, generous and solicitous about others' affairs and welfare. They can keep secrets, are capable, efficient, and possess good intellectual discrimination; have great aptitude and endurance. Their mental powers fit them for musicians, doctors, chemists, or book-keepers. Their health will always be good if they never take drugs. Their marriage partner should be born about the same time as themselves or the early part of December.

## TRANSITS.

The benefic influence of Jupiter's passage through their ruling sign will benefit all persons born before the 23rd. New ventures and undertakings may be started successfully, and business pursuits will prove profitable and beneficial to health. Advancement and progress will come from the position of Jupiter, and very little real harm need be feared during their next year of life.

## THE SOLAR REVOLUTIONS.

The Sun upon its return each year to the place it held at birth has been found to afford a clue to the next year's directions. This month, until the 23rd, Virgo stands as the centre or ruling sign, and from it the following lunar influences are judged. On the first the Moon is in the third from the first (♍) and on the 3rd in the fourth from this position of Virgo and so on.

### BIRTHDAY INDICATIONS.
#### Sun in Virgo.

The sign Virgo rules the solar plexus, the brain of the stomach. All persons born under the influence of Virgo act from the practical and materialistic side of life. They are fine discriminators and have commercial instincts beyond the average. They view life from the plane of use and service; and are more engaged in developing the physical and practical side of life than the theoretical and speculative. The following judgment will apply to them in a general way, more or less, according to the day of September on which they were born. Those born on the :—

1st.—May expect to hear of the death of relatives, troubles through

G

brethren, financial loss through them, and travel. Those born in the morning will suffer more than those born in the afternoon. Care should be taken to avoid drugs of every description, as there will be dangers to be apprehended through poison. Drains should be seen to, and infectious places avoided.

2nd a.m.—Gain through the death of relatives. There will be some short journeys, and much correspondence; satisfactory legal transactions, and a higher train of thought during the year.

2nd p.m.—The year will produce some sudden changes and some heavy sorrow. Aged relatives will die, and there may be vexatious journeys through relatives. The mind will be depressed, and the will should be exercised to overcome all fits of depression. Avoid bathing; be careful in diet and be prepared for sudden events.

3rd.—This is a fortunate birthday. There will be good news from abroad, and domestic affairs will be peaceful and good. To the married an addition to the circle is probable. Generally speaking, all things will go well this year.

4th.—The influences are not good. Guard against dishonesty in the home circle, and avoid waste and extravagance. Make only those changes that are necessary. You will have prophetic tendencies, and will see ahead more than usual. Have no disputes with religious persons, and be careful in speech.

5th.—Be on your guard against thieves; look after your possessions; avoid all speculations and spend the year quietly, steering clear of all disputes. Mercurial-Saturnine and Martial persons will do you harm. Females are warned against the possibilities of losing their honour this year.

6th.—The influences are good. With tact and perseverance, the year will be a very successful one, and prosperity will attend your efforts. You may rise to a greatly improved position by making use of all the opportunites that will come in your way. Single persons will become engaged.

7th a.m.—The influences are good, and much of the foregoing remarks will apply. Those connected with business pursuits, particularly agriculture, will prosper.

7th p.m.—Keep the blood pure this year, watching diet. Avoid all damp and marshy places. The health will require attention, otherwise the influences are good.

8th.—Males should be very cautious in dealings with the opposite sex. Servants will cause annoyance to employers, and females will have disappointments. This will be an active year, there will be much correspondence and, generally speaking, the year will be prosperous, successful and happy. There will be losses amongst uncles and aunts.

9th.—This will be an unfortunate birthday. Health will suffer; the circulation must be attended to, the blood and eyes will be liable to affections. Sudden events will happen; there will be unfortunate changes, and deaths amongst the mother's relatives.

10th.—This will be an uneventful birthday anniversary. There will be little success in love affairs, and some disappointments may be expected. The desires of the year will be towards economy.

11th.—Those who are married will experience trouble in the domestic sphere; some peculiar experiences will be realized. All persons who were born on this day should avoid law and control all irritable feelings.

12th.—This is a very unfortunate birthday. Deaths will occur in the family circle; impulse and rash acts must be avoided, and all danger of accidents guarded against. It will be an unpleasant and disastrous year. Evils arising out of careless and thoughtless action may be expected.

13th.—You may gain by will or legacy this year. Some benefits will come through co-workers, shares, etc. It will be a year of financial gain from others.

14th.—Be careful in money matters, and avoid becoming surety for partners and relatives. In the main the year is uneventful.

15th.—You will have disappointments in love affairs, financial losses, and unpleasant news from abroad. Take heed lest it be a very unfortunate year; avoid all inclinations toward obstinacy and self will.

16th a.m.—The year will be fortunate. Be careful in all correspondence, and keep the mind free from sarcasm and over criticism.

16th p.m.—Avoid all long journeys and finance in connection with foreign countries. Protect the throat and avoid taking chills. The year on the whole will be troublesome.

G I

17th.—Young people will make educational progress. Literary work will be successful and the mind will be more than usually active. Correspondence will be good.

18th.—Some advancement is promised, and there will be improvement in professional matters, but some financial loss is threatened by litigation; avoid law if possible and push all business affairs.

19th.—There will be unfortunate changes, and the year will contain many worries and anxieties. Hopes and wishes will bring disappointment. Keep very quiet throughout the year and don't worry if possible·

20th.—Loss and trouble through friends and acquaintances is threatened; changes in the home-life that should eventually prove beneficial.

21st.—The year will be a very active one, bringing success and advancement; travel and beneficial changes, and probably fame and honour.

22nd.—Many petty worries and trouble that can be banished by a hopeful attitude is the meaning of this birthday influence. Curb the emotions and study self-control.

### The Sun in Libra.

23rd.—The Sun has now entered Libra, the Seventh sign. Those born before noon have a good birthday anniversary, indicating a pleasureable year. Those born in the afternoon and evening will have some sorrows and unpleasant experiences; be prepared for sudden and unexpected changes.

24th.—An uneventful year. Avoid disputes, and try to realize that peace is preferable to warfare.

25th.—Gain through the help of others, with some increased success in general affairs.

26th.—This will be an important year; it will bring fame, success and much improvement in all affairs. To a politician it means great success. Artists will become popular, and all persons whose birthday this is will find their affairs proceed to their entire satisfaction.

27th.—This will be a fortunate birthday. Financial gain is indicated, as well as general activity in all business and outside affairs.

28th.—A good year for finance, but probability of death of partners and co-workers. The year will have some worries.

29th.—An eventful and prosperous year. Gain through correspondence and literary and artistic pursuits.

30th.—The year will be mixed with blessings and sorrows, pleasure and pain. Mental troubles will come, but amid it all the end will look clear and bright; out of sorrow will come joy.

# Editorial Comment.

HERE is a small pamphlet issued by a person whose name is probably " A. J. Pearce," and the title of which is *Star Lore*. If he *is* the editor of *Zadkiel's Almanac*, then we are surprised at his treatment of a matter that did not concern him. The whole of the article on " Two Remarkable Horoscopes," which appeared in the August number of that pamphlet, the major portion of which is copied from our July number, shows the keen jealousy and irritating envy that must be felt at our success. The following conclusion to the article will speak for itself :—

" Nevertheless, certain self-styled ' Modern ' Astrologers still present a hotch-potch of natal and horory astrology mixed up together, and reject heredity as of no consideration, thereby misleading students who are induced to begin under their tuition, and bringing Astrology into disrepute. The superstitious nonsense in " MODERN ASTROLOGY," and certain guides is nauseating ; and, it is lamentable that it should lead some students away from the true science taught by Placidus and Zadkiel I. Certainly no one of good education, breadth of mind, and clear intelect, could be attracted away from the great masters."

The person who wrote this evidently considers that the mantle of Captain Morrison (Zadkiel I.) has fallen upon his shoulders and that he is the only Astrologer living in the world to-day. If anything is nauseating it is the silly jealousy and petty quibbling of the vain " A. J. Pearce," but it is the case of the dog in the manger over again. Galled to excess at the success of a publication that has lived over seven years, while each attempt he has made has failed, he attacks in the hope of getting a cheap advertisement for his valueless pamphlet, which can probably boast no more than a hundred readers. He thinks he is an authority on a science that can now be read by all, without addling the brain with a lot of useless figures. If " A. J. Pearce " will spend more time in improving his judgment he will do some good, but until this happens he had better stick to the tracks of his predecessor and copy his rules for mundane predictions.

To prove that we realize what this means we shall shortly publish a Nativity with "A. J. Pearce's" delineation. The judgment is as wide of the mark as any novice could possibly reach, and yet he wishes all students of Astrology to look upon his personality as the only authority. What conceit! But it is another instance of the " pulling down element; " it is easy to destroy, but not so easy to build up again.

We would gladly welcome any co-workers in this great science of Astrology, and when we find a more useful publication than our own, we shall with pleasure draw the attention of every one of our supporters to it; but we regret that it is not possible to recommend students to waste their money on a pamphlet which is evidently published in order to keep alive and rehabilitate the waning interest in *Zadkiel's Almanac,* which has deteriorated both in quality and value since " A. J. Pearce " has been editor therof. Our attitude and feeling toward those, whom we cannot help observing are our enemies, has always been friendly and sympathetic, but the conduct of this writer is mean, paltry, contemptible and unworthy of one who at least, claims to be, a student of Divine Law. No motive but that of pure love for an ancient science, which needs a modern interpretation has induced us to attach ourselves to an unpopular and pecuniarily unprofitable subject. If it were not for the encouragement that we are daily receiving, we often should wish our work had fallen into other hands. We know that our labours will be appreciated when the life has left the form. If we are misleading students by our work then may the Divine powers, forgive us, for it is entirely unintentional, and is the result of our reason, as well as the intuition. With regard to this unkind person who sees fit to attack us without cause, in season and out of season, we would ask him to either hold his peace or display a little more of the tact and talent he would have us believe he possesses. He can at least be truthful, if nothing else, and we leave it to his good taste to apologize for his unjust and unwarranted remarks upon a subject that did not concern him in the least.

# Letters to the Editor.

Letters of general interest only are inserted.  Correspondents desiring reply must please enclose a stamped addressed envelope.
All correspondents should give full name and address, not necessarily for publica tion, but as a token of good faith.
N.B —Writers of signed articles are alone responsible for the opinions contained therein.

SIR,—Prof. Henry's letter on page 48 is interesting, but seems to have been written under a misconception.  I had not the slightest intention of "rapping over the knuckles" either the Professor or any one else to whom I referred in my paragraph on page 429 of the last volume.  Prof. Henry's original letter (page 252) I took as a complaint against the many different systems of Astrology that have been springing up recently; and he himself used the words, "matters are beginning to get very much mixed."  I sympathised with this complaint, and intended my comment to read as supporting it from my own point of view.

Again, when I wrote that Kabalistic Astrology was not astronomical, but a divinatory system comparable with cartomancy, I was simply stating a bald fact ; and it never occurred to me that any one would suppose this to be an expression of opinion adverse to either system.  I hold no such adverse opinion.

"The Tarot of the Bohemians," I purchased and read several years ago, but I was informed by a well-known learned Kabalist and Rosicrucian that the system of interpretation advanced in the book is not the correct one.  A similar expression of opinion will be found in the review of the book in the *Future* (April, 1892).  "The Tarot" is undoubtedly very interesting.

Yours truly,

H. S. GREEN.

## SECONDARY DIRECTIONS AND "STAR LORE."

SIR,—I cannot see that the cause of Astrology can be advanced by importing into our discussions personalities, which are, in my humble opinion, always, to utilize a slang expression, rather "bad form," whilst, amongst lawyers, much of whose time is passed in argument, it is considered an infallible sign of a weak case to abuse the other side's attorney.

I am, individually, exceedingly anxious that good feeling should be preserved amongst all Astrologers, and I earnestly entreat them, as they respect the cause they advocate, to abstain as far as possible from the *argumentum ad hominem*, and to confine themselves to sober argument, which alone can avail to smooth the difficulties we all have to contend with in the search for truth.

Having, then, these ideas, it was with extreme regret I noticed in the July number of *Star Lore* the remarks made by the able editor (who has undoubtedly done great service to the cause of Astrology) as to Secondary Directions, and, more especially, the statement put forth as regards " Modern Astrologers," whom he thought fit to describe as, "almost without exception imperfectly educated and incapable of grasping and appreciating the Placidian system." The editor, I fear, must have been suffering from the effects of the hot and close weather of June, when he ventured to allow himself to pass a judgment of this description on persons he is barely acquainted with, and of whose educational status and capacities, he clearly, by the statement he makes, is quite ignoraant.

The Placidian System is, after all, not so very abstruse, nor is it a branch of the higher mathematics! It is really easily mastered by anyone of average ability, as the editor of *Star Lore* himself admits, when he says that some lazy astrologers " will not take the *trouble* to master the semi-arc system." So that it would appear, upon the admission of the editor of *Star Lore* himself, it is only a little *trouble*, and not great talent, that is necessary to master the Placidian system of directing. I quite agree with this last statement, that the system of directing is easily learnt, and I only wish that it were as easy to form a correct judgment as to the effects of such direction; but *that* is an entirely different matter. I venture to hope that " Modern Astrologers " have amongst them many capable of mastering the Placidian system of directing; but even were this not so, I entirely fail to see what is gained by publishing statements of the above description !

There is one other matter to which I must refer, and that is contained in the concluding words of the article, which are as follows :—

" Students are earnestly advised not to waste their time on secondary directions."

These words are, in my opinion, calculated to check enquiry and experimental research. Whilst, with regard to the advice given, I must submit to the Astrological world that the able editor of *Star Lore* is not justified in putting forth such a statement, and for the following reasons :—

He cites as his authority for relying upon Primary Directions, Placidus de Titus. Does he rely upon all the doctrines of Placidus in their entirety, or does he consider himself at liberty to pick and choose from those doctrines, to take those that suit him, and to reject the others? Of course, if he reserves this right to himself, there is little more to be said. But to those who value, and in my opinion with excellent reason, the doctrines of Placidus, I would submit that Placidus himself attached vast importance to Secondary Directions. He held the view, in which I also humbly concur, that the Primary Directions alone are not sufficient, but that these must be interpreted together with the Secondary Directions, Progressions, Ingresses and Transits. In many of his famous " Thirty Nativities," Placidus takes the greatest care in calculating and tracing the effects of Secondary Directions, and, to my mind, the numerous examples he gives amply suffice to establish the power and efficacy of Secondary Directions.

How, then, in the face of such evidence, given by Placidus himself, can the editor of *Star Lore* venture to advise Astrological students to ignore

Secondary Directions, and "not to waste their time" thereon? If, in his article, he had been contented with the statement he previously makes, that Secondary Directions are only "supplementary" to Primary Directions, I should not have thought it necessary to refer to the matter at all. Although perhaps, a statement that a thing is, at the same time "supplementary," and "scarcely worth consideration," is hardly to be commended for its consistency! He, however, does not allow the matter to rest even in that position, but seems to me to go rather out of the way to make the definite statement, in the last lines of his article, to which I have referred, and which in my opinion, for the reasons I have stated, is not justified, either by fact or experience, and certainly not by Placidus, upon whom he professes to rely!

He seems to forget, too, the words of Placidus, who says that:—

"The particular time of their (i.e. Primary Directions) effects may depend "upon other motions . . . . for which reason the times of these subsequent "motions of the causes (i.e., Secondary Directions) demand our greatest "attention."

So that the able editor of *Star Lore* is of opinion that the study of Secondary Directions is "waste of time," whilst Placidus says distinctly, they "demand our greatest attention!"

And not only does Placidus say this, but he supports his assertion by numerous examples in the "Thirty Nativities," which, without doubt, justify him

Again, it must not be forgotten that, although the able editor of *Star Lore* cites Placidus as his authority, yet he does not follow him by any means in all things, and it is not fair to represent that the system taught by the editor of *Star Lore* is identical with the Placidian system of direction, because it is not. One very important difference is the method of equating the arc of direction. In this, the system of Placidus differs considerably from that of the editor of *Star Lore*. I am not now discussing the question as to which is the most satisfactory system, I am only affirming that they differ.

Whether Placidus would have approved of some portions of his system being adopted, and others rejected, I cannot say; but this is what has been done. Any man has a perfect right to take any portion of any system and use it, but he must not, unchallenged, be allowed to call that part the whole!

It is, therefore, to be hoped that the editor of *Star Lore* will see fit to qualify the statement he has made—perhaps rather hastily—as to the study of Secondary Directions being a waste of time, and that he will once more fall into line under the banner of Placidus, and use his great astrological abilities in unison with many other earnest students of Astrology, who, although they may not agree entirely with one another upon the question of Direction, are, or at least should be, united in the desire to ascertain truth, and advance the cause of Astrology.

In regard to Placidus, if I may be allowed to offer a suggestion, I should advise all students to make a thorough study of the "Thirty Nativities." I feel sure they would derive great benefit from such a study, and would perceive how the Primary and Secondary Directions, and the Progressions, Ingresses, and Transits, work together to bring about the different results. Especially as an evidence of the power of Secondary Directions, I would advise anyone who may possess the " Primum Mobile " of Placidus, to refer to Nativity No. XVI. of Antonio Maria, Cardinal de Salviatis, and they will there see how wonderfully the Secondary Directions coincided with the event, even to the day, at the time of his being made a Cardinal. Placidus himself seems delighted at the admirable way in which the event coincided with the aspects.

In the present state of our modern Astrology, when we have undoubtedly lost much of the knowledge once possessed by the Chaldeans, it seems in the highest degree unwise to reject any system of direction entirely; rather should we thoroughly investigate *all* the systems put forward, as, in all probability, each possess some germ of good which we may do well to preserve, and, in course of time, and with the aid of experience, we may perhaps be able to found a new system of direction, based upon the good points derived from some, or all, of the numerous systems with which we are now acquainted. Above all, we must not dogmatise, or lay down any hard and fast rules derived from the experiences of only one life term, for the space of five lives of, say 70 years each, would, in my opinion, prove all too short to solve the various problems to be met with in the study of Astrology.

Placidus seems to teach that the Primary Directions indicate the nature of a coming event, and the time generally. Then the Secondary Directions, Progressions, Ingresses and Transits fix the time more accurately, and define the event more definitely, the time being, in most cases, indicated by the Secondary Directions to the month, and often to the week, or day.

Of course there is great labour involved in working out the Directions of a Nativity as Placidus worked them out, but I have every reason to believe that his system, in the main, will well repay any labour conscientiously expended upon it. There is no royal road to a knowledge of Astrology. By hard, steady, and discriminating work alone, can we hope to compass the journey.

Yours faithfully,

August, 1897.                                    "AQUARIUS."

———

DEAR SIR,—I am sorry you have ceased to interpret the monthly figures, as, although I could not always follow Leo's reasonings, his remarks were very suggestive.

We need a thorough re-examination of the aphorisms of Mundane Astrology. Take, for instance, the statement that the malefics rising cause strikes, etc. Raphael's predictions for May have failed signally, although based on this maxim as the malefics are just rising. Leo's principles throw some light on this difficulty. According to them, the position must be compared with the quarterly figure, and we obtain as the correct prediction " great excitement concerning foreign affairs." This was verified, to some extent at any rate, by the public interest in Greece and the Transvaal.

At first sight, the Paris disaster appears to be a signal proof of the method, but it does not bear examination, for the figure for Paris is nearly the same as for London, and hence the excitement must refer to countries foreign to both. I wish that Mr. Green would say what, in his opinion was the aspect that indicated the Paris fire.

Yours truly,

J. W.

———————

Dear Sir,—Leo's letter on the " Horoscope Revised " in your February issue, and his comments on my remarks re the twin births on p. 337 of same, call for some reply, in which I desire to be as practical as possible.

I need scarcely refer at length to the individual cases already dealt with. No amount of allowances will make them fit the persons so well in the modern way of working as they do by the equal division. I may state in regard to the Queen, that she is, of course, Mercurial, because that planet ascending in Taurus just below the cusp (in the equally divided horoscope), lends its character to the face. Her generally known qualities agree entirely with this position. The other cases are equally distinct in this way, as I have clearly shown, and so, for the time, I will pass them.

Leo calls my rectification of the twin horoscopes a " private distortion," which is rather an unkind cut, but the same remark might equally apply to the opinions and methods of all persons who happen to differ through honest conviction from others.

In my notice of the twins referred to, I do not conclude " that the surgeon was twenty minutes out in his observation of the first birth, and yet that he was correct in giving the interval between the two births as fifteen minutes ;" neither do I ignore the difficulty of rectifying the second birth. I do not for a moment question the timing of the observed phenomena relating to the births, but I know the sensitive astral moment does not always immediately coincide with these physical manifestations, which result therefrom, and the " first breath " happens a little later (varying from a few seconds to several minutes) than the moment obtained by the rectification. This is but natural, for the cause of a physical effect generally precedes the actual exhibition.

My statement was quite correct with regard to the position of Uranus at these births. The planet was just below the cusp of the Celestial Ascendant at the first birth, and crossed the cusp during the interval between the two births. This in no way ignores the fact that the tumour " existed before birth," but rather indicates it, for when the birth was complete, Uranus afflicted by ☌ ♃ from ♉, had risen above the ascendant.

If the conditions observed in other twin cases referred to in my former letter are resolvable into a general law, these positions are fully significant of the effects noted.

I am continually meeting with persons who *agree in type*, according to the ancient traditions, with the ascendant of the *equal* horoscope, who do not reasonably accord with the usual form without resorting to complicated dove-tailing of positions not usually considered.

I desire to deal with the technical and practical application of the method by equal division, as compared with the unequal horoscope by oblique ascension, and if I unintentionally prove somewhat lengthy in my remarks, it is the great importance of the subject which demands it.

Leo challenges my figures in " The Horoscope Revised," which he says are " altogether erroneous," but he is mistaken. They are quite correct from my standpoint, though not so from his. He states that " the ascendant of every horoscope is at right angles (90°) to the Meridian, and never other-wise, whatever the difference in longitude may be." This depends entirely upon the method employed in making the measurement. From the actual mid-heaven or zenith of any point to the visible horizon may be 90° at any time, I admit; but the Zodiacal positions as given in the orthodox western horoscope do certainly not give this; neither does any horoscope (unless for a place situated under the Zodiac), give the real mid-heaven or zenith. On the same principle, the horoscope does not, from my standpoint, and from that of ancient custom, necessarily give the visible horizon. It is a *matter of projection* along a given longitudinal line running parallel with the poles at *right angles to the earth's equator*. This is evident from the fact that the real mid-heaven, say, of London, can never be any part of the zodiac. And how can, say, the 1° of ♑, which extends to about 20° south latitude, ever become the mid-heaven in Greenland? Yet we know it may be so Astrologically considered, and the peculiar qualities of ♑ are in such cases directed by projection along the Meridian or longitudinal line, which extends from such a place, and cuts through that degree of the zodiac, however remote it may be. It is quite similar with regard to the Celestial ascendant, when measured by 90° of longitude from the meridian. I cannot supply a diagram just now to illustrate exactly what I would describe, but, by the aid of a large globe, I am fully satisfied with my position.

The point of this Celestial ascendant is well defined by natural evidence; it is the place occupied by the sun daily, throughout the year, at 6 a.m. solar time. The Celestial circle, containing 360°, represents twenty-four hours, and from one cardinal point to the next is six hours uniformly. There is no imagination or " private distortion " about any of this; it is an undeniable fact.

I commenced my Astro study in 1873, and always employed the usual method, with tables of houses, until 1895; therefore, I am no chicken in the matter, but I am bound to confess that I find more uniform succcess by the equal division, and continued investigation only confirms my views.

It is the circle of the heavens, *measured parallel with the equator* from the point exactly overhead—the zenith—which must be taken as the horoscope in its real meaning. The mid-heaven and the ascendant being projections along given lines of longitude, the one, extending from the actual zenith, the other at 90° to the east in the exact circle of latitude.

If any reader desires to try the difficulty attending the orthodox method, let him set a horoscope for Fahlum, Sweden, on any date, Lat. 60° 38′ N. Long 1 h. 2 m. 40 s. E., and place ♑ 0° to the meridian. In doing this, let him employ a good globe, when he will find the *whole circle* of the Ecliptic runs parallel with the horizon of the globe, giving no ascensions of any kind, either oblique or otherwise. In this case the ascendant and M.C. can only be projections along certain longitudinal lines, measured from the zenith in the circle of latitude, and running parallel with the poles *to the equator*, which is the focus of all these forces, and from whence they radiate both north and south.

With regard to an ascendant by oblique ascension being the starting-point of measurement advocated by ancient Hindu Astrologers, as, for instance, in the *Brihat Jataka*, I do not find it so. There is no reference whatever to an ascendant by oblique ascension given by the author, and what is supplied on this subject is given entirely by the translator, and is quite modern, forming no part of the original work.

Yours faithfully,

"ZARIEL."

---

DEAR SIR,—Press of work and consequent lack of time has for several weeks prevented me from addressing you in regard to a point suggested to me by a correspondent in the "Student's Corner" of your magazine, Vol. II.

I know of no journal in whose pages I find such profit and pleasure as in those of MODERN ASTROLOGY. In your own thought I meet an interior perception of the qualities and laws of the great life-currents of the universe that goes far toward redeeming the science to which you are devoted, from being, what it has so generally become, one of hard mathematical deduction of results from certain dry formulæ, handed down from a time when men *knew*, and did not merely theorize. Knowledges of these things can only be a consciousness of facts, actual experience; it can never be conclusions reached from premises of which the reasoner has no *experience*, and, therefore knows nothing. And Astrology will never become a vital science until the realm of causation, that of the great currents of solar and planetary life, becomes to the student a world of actual experience, and the changing events which transpire there as real to him, as much a part of his every-day life, as he now finds the world of effect.

My development upon occult lines has been a matter of less than **three years**, and, consequently, I am only on the borderland of this ideal life of (or in) the heavens; and yet, when the Sun and Moon change their positions, passing into another sign, I have no language by which to convey to you the entire change in my own consciousness, and in the consciousness of the qualities by which I find myself surrounded—the mentality, the emotional nature, physical sensation—all are changed, and I feel and know that I have entered a new world. A favourable aspect will create vibrations upon which will roll into the soul a delight of a character and intensity of which I shall not attempt to speak. I have been interested in studying just when these conditions are active and their nature. But as interesting as all this is to me, I must not impose further upon your kindness, which on a former occasion I so much appreciated, but proceed at once to the real object of my communication.

In the February number of MODERN ASTROLOGY, page 344, a corres-pondent cites the case of a cripple, born June 16th, 1882, 9.30 p.m. at St. Mary Church, Torquay. On examining this nativity I find Capricorn rising —that the body is characterized by the Capricorn qualities. Now, Pisces is the common, or expressing sign, of the trinity (one of the four grand divisions of the Solar Man, taking the signs in regular order, as Aries, Taurus, Gemini), of which Capricorn is the head, and for which it gathers; therefore, the ex-pression of his physical nature is characterized by the planets found in the sign Pisces.

According to Solar Biology, Uranus and Mars are both found there. "The "influence of Uranus is entirely of a metaphysical character, and its real "nature and influence cannot be fully expressed by any organism on this "planet; therefore, it produces strange effects upon the life, as it serves as a "depolarizer, turning the forces away from the animal instincts, towards the "spiritual." We readily see the effect, if this planet characterizes the physical organism in its expression, we might expect almost anything ab-normal; and when Mars in Pisces still further leads out the physical nature of this boy, we cannot wonder that it is indeed marred, and that he is an un-fortunate cripple. In several instances I have found a defective body the result of the common sign which leads into expression the rising sign of the individual, being characterized by Uranus and Mars.

I have been much interested in the study, from a psychic standpoint, of the law by which the qualities of the cardinal or fixed signs are led out (ex-pressed) through the common signs. At the risk of making my letter an unpardonably long one, I will touch upon my own work in that direction. I find that each of the common signs lead out the qualities of, first, the fixed signs of the *triplicity* to which they belong, and, second and most strongly the cardinal signs or heads of their *trinities*. Consequently, Gemini leads into ex-pressions, first Aquarius, second Aries.

When I first opened into the astral life-currents, with the passing of the

Sun or Moon into Gemini, I would find myself looking out over a vast ocean, whose tumbling, heaving waves seemed to be those of ceaseless mental action, and yet I did not understand why this restless activity should take the form of a vast ocean ; but some months later I saw that, in meeting Gemini, the expression of mind, the centifrugal force, the principle of unrest and dis-organization, I had gazed out upon the great ocean of unrest over which Aquarius, " the water-bearer," presides—Aquarius, the ultimate of the mental triplicity. Again, Gemini is the principle which rules mental formation, or the words, and, as such, its ultimate and strongest expression is found in Aries, the head of its trinity. It is the word, the formation of mental activity.

It would be a lengthy undertaking to carry out this thought in connection with all of the common signs, but a word in regard to Sagittarius. The function of Sagittarius is that of focalization—the arrow-point. In its relation to the triplicities, it leads the Leo into expression, and in the trinity we find it the expression of Libra, " As above, so below," and we may observe the manifestation of the Sagittarius function upon the animal plane. It most forcibly appears in the expression of the psychic, or snake-qualities (Libra), which is the form of the embryo, or primal animal life. Accordingly, the snake or psychic qualities expressed by means of focalization draws its prey to itself with the eye, the snake " charms " to itself. The highest form of animal life is found in the lion, the king of the forest, who belongs to the cat family. Again in this family we find the cat focalizing upon its prey, " charming " to itself as it did when a snake upon the first round of the ascent of animal life. So the snake and the cat family (lion) are true to their normal expression through focalization—Sagittarius.

Upon a higher plane, we know that Libra works through the psychic perception, or focalization through the eye.

Now, as regards Leo's manifestation through Sagittarius. The power of Leo lies in that relentless, almost cruel will. It moves quietly but resistlessly and knows no failure. The will is the ultimate of all a man's intellectual conclusions, it is the focal point of the entire action of his life qualities, the ultimate of the man ; and that focalization finds expression in Sagittarius, the arrow-point : through this focal point he conquers all resistance. As through Sagittarius, the primal currents of his life (Libra) found expression, so through the same sign does he express the ultimate conclusion of all his being.

The priestly sign, Sagittarius, meets the Deity as the server of the great primal life-currents—the mystic darkness of the Libra life ; and again it meets him as the server of Leo, who, after mounting life's ascending spiral, again returns to the God whence it came. Thus upon the animal, upon the mental, and upon the priestly plane, we trace the functions of Sagittarius, the principle of focalization, the priestly sign,

Yours, etc.,

" LANDON FAUNTLEROY."

# Questions answered by the "Astrologer."

No. 27.—*T.P., m, 8.30 a., April 29, 1863, Kent. Mother died October, 1894. Q.—Should I be in business for myself or the employ of others?* A.—You will succeed best in life in others' employ.

No. 28.—*Loyalty, m, 8 a, November 28, 1866, Reading. Q.—Am I likely to make an important journey in 1898?* A.—The year 1898 will be important successful, and eventful; but there is no sign of a journey.

No. 29.—*Bothered, f, 7.30 a, March 21, 1856. Q.—What time this year shall I lose a female relative?* A.—At the close of the year, or just before your next birthday.

No. 30.—*Roslyn, f, 5 to 7 a, November 28, 1869, Yorks. Q.—Marriage Partner?* A.—Middle stature, stout well-set body, strong and compact. brown curling hair, free and generous, fond of good living and the opposite sex.

No. 31.—⊙ *in ♉, f, 11.30 a, April 29, 1867, Selby. Q.—Shall I be successful through a domestic registry in a certain town?* A.—No, postpone the idea until next year. Apply again.

No. 32.—*C. C. L., m, 5 p, September 5, 1881, U.S.A. Q.—Trade or profession?* A.—Private Secretary. Fruit or grain grower, or travelling agent and salesman.

No. 33.—*W. E. J., f, 3 p, November 21, 1840, London. Q.—Shall I marry again?* A.—You will.

No. 34.—*Lassie, f, 3.40 p, May 6, 1872, Surrey. Q.—Shall I succeed better in a foreign land?* A.—Yes, you would do well abroad.

No. 35.—*Chihua, m, 6 a, September 4, 1842. Liverpool. Q.—September 21, 1896. Venus trine Mars, result?* A.—A legacy from abroad.

No. 36.—*D. W., f, 11.45 p, June 29, 1863, Portsmouth. Q.—Marriage. A.—* Late marriage indicated, probably after forty.

No. 37.—*November.*—Take the one born in March.

No. 38.—*Greece, m, 10. 50 p, April 28, 1861. Q.—Death?* A.—In five years' time.

No. 39.—*Nix, f, 0h 0' 52'' a, February 19, 1858, Lat 40. Q.—Does the horoscope indicate journeying about, desired so much?* A.—Yes.

No. 40.—*Sun in Leo*—Not so soon as you expect.

No. 41.—*Isabel S. Wight, f, 2.30 p, October 18, 1870, Boston. Ovaries, Particulars of 1899.*—She will undergo the operation, and live.

No. 42.—*L. F. Bassett.*—Not a great deal unless much time and labour is expended, and unusual care is given to the matter, which is rarely, if ever, paid for.

No. 43.—*Libra, m, 4.30 a, November 11, 1868, Colombo, Ceylon. Q.—Date of Death?* A.—Your death will be sudden in the 60th year.

# Modern Astrology

Edited by
ALAN LEO, P.A.S.

The Official Organ of the Astrological Society.

Vol. 3, No. 3.　　✳　OCTOBER, 1897.　✳　Price 1s.

## Predictions.

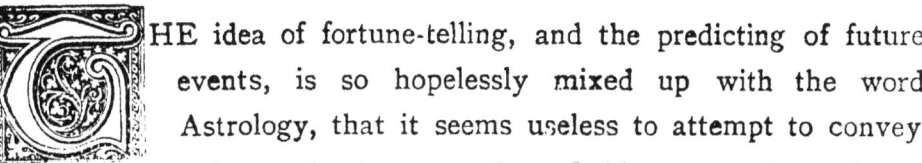

THE idea of fortune-telling, and the predicting of future events, is so hopelessly mixed up with the word Astrology, that it seems useless to attempt to convey to the world at large, the true meaning of this very ancient science. That within its wide range, there is the clue to the future and its happenings we have no wish to deny, having certain knowledge that the future can be foretold with an accuracy and precision, that is at times startling, even to those who are familiar with its power of prophecy. But this is by no means the most wonderful side of Astrology, as those who have investigated its esoteric side can testify, for the latter is the key to the mysteries, affording an explanation with regard to matters that are not concerned with the ever-changing and fleeting material world, for esoteric astrology deals with the permanent and spiritual side of universal laws.

It is only when the science is seriously studied that one begins to realize its possibilities, and the predictive feature begins to lose its charms. The anxiety which all beginners feel is exhibited in their mad rush into predictions, with the hope of convincing sceptics, and more harm than good is often done thereby, the old adage, applicable to the case, aptly putting it, that to " Convince a sceptic against his will, he will be of the same opinion still." There are, however, exceptions to

H

every rule, and sometimes a prediction may arrest the attention of a thinker, and give him the incentive to investigate the subject for himself.  If we were to publish all the successful predictions that we have made, we should have a weight of evidence on our side that even the most perverse critic might hesitate to pass an ofthanded, and we might say malicious, expression as to Charlatans, quacks and humbugs.

Owing to a certain lack of self-esteem we have not been anxious to parade our successful predictions before the world, believing as we do, that the predictive tone should be lessened, and the part which teaches self-knowledge encouraged instead, having more love for the science in its entirety, than a specialization of any one of its parts.

It was owing to the predictive portion called Horary Astrology, that the science became degraded, and declined in the Roman era, just as the true mythologies have been ruined by the Greeks.  Even to-day the ancient science as handed down in books is so tainted with the horary feature, that it has become a life's task to separate them, predictions coming from this branch alone.  By no means do we wish to imply that Horary Astrology is false and valueless.  As a matter of fact when Horary Astrology is properly understood ; it is valuable, and thoroughly reliable.  But it must have nothing to do with frivolous and nonsensical questions.  To prove this we will give one out of the many successful horary predictions that we have made, and if any of our readers who have obtained successful predictions from us, will allow us to publish their names and addresses, with the facts, we invite them to send the particulars to us as early as convenient.  Apart from this we could publish scores of instances where the fulfilment of predictions have proved the truth of Astrology, but hitherto our own conviction has been sufficient warrant for our spreading its truths.

On June 3rd, 1895, we received the following letter.  Critics and others may take it for what it is worth, but they will find facts stubborn things to deal with, no matter how they criticise :—

> Temple Chambers,
> Falcon Court,
> Fleet Street, London, E.C.
> June 3rd, 1895.

DEAR SIR,—It has occured to us that you might be willing to erect a horary figure of the *Unknown World* which would give us some indications as to its future prospects, while at the same time, it would be advantageous to print same in our next issue. We shall be glad to give any particulars that may be necessary. The first number of the Magazine was published on August 15th, 1894, but had been projected more than three months previously. If you can assist us in this way we shall be much obliged.—Yours faithfully, James Elliot & Co.

This letter was read at Bouverie Street at 9.30 a.m., June 4th, 1895, for which time the following map was erected.

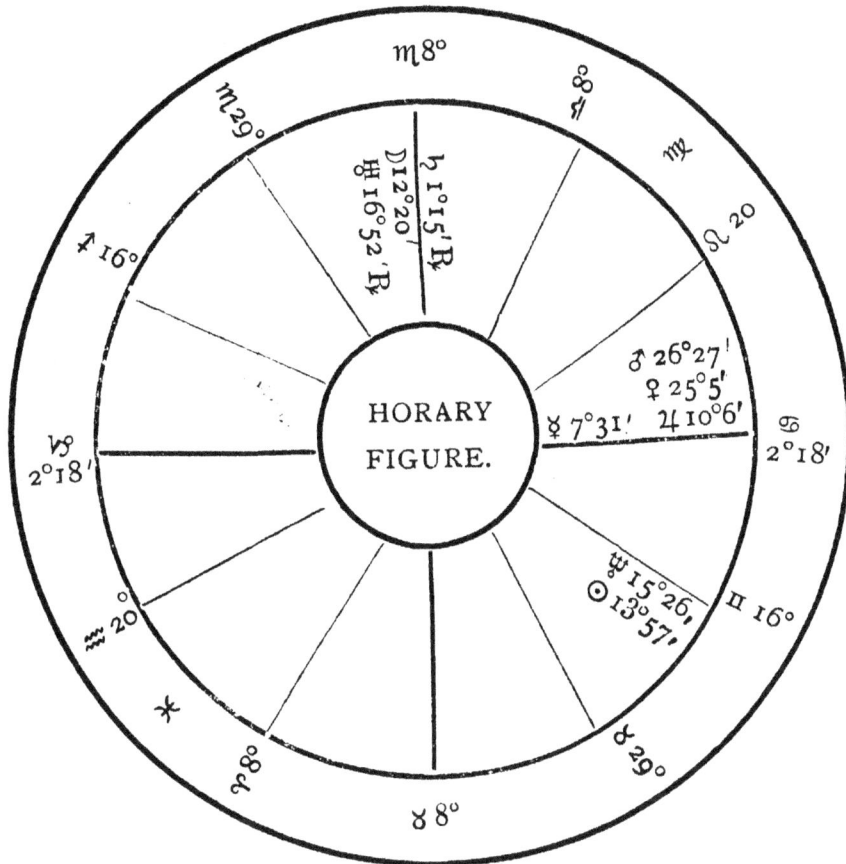

The answer sent to the above was clear and concise, and to the effect that the magazine would expire *suddenly* whenever the time came, and the Astrological indications were, that the time was very close at hand. The judgment was based upon the position of the Moon in her fall, placed between the two malefics Saturn and Uranus, having application to the later, and applying to house of the benefics; also Mars and Venus applying to the Square of Saturn, thus supporting the aspects on the date of publication, August 15th, 1894, *Moon Square Uranus.* In all probability the idea had been projected about the 18th of May, 1894.

Now this prediction was verified by the non-appearance of the twelfth number of the *Unknown World,* a fact lamented by all of its subscribers and readers, indicated by Jupiter and Mercury in the Seventh. *Pall Mall Gazette* and other scoffers what have you to say to this? It would be better for some editors to copy the plan of the editor of *Hearth and Home*, who in reviewing our work is not afraid to speak the truth, as the following quotation from his interesting paper proves: " Unfortunately I know nothing of the subject, and cannot therefore, speak with any authority on the merits or demerits of the book ; but it is evident that the author knows his subject; and is a believer in what he teaches. I therefore recommend the book to any one who wishes to study the subject."

The intolerance and wilful ignorance of such writers as the person who reviewed " Practical Astrology " in the *Pall Mall Gazette* is sinful, because opportunities are now offered by the activity of Astrologers for any one to study or investigate the science for themselves. This foolish man has a book sent to him for review, and after making several nonsensical remarks he ends by disrespectfully calling the writer of a work, that he cannot understand, a quack and a Charlatan. We can forgive him for his unkind remarks about our personality, but we cannot but deplore the lack of gentlemanly courtesy which one naturally expects from a person in his position. But we take a hint from his remarks that Astrologers "invariably fail to predict any thing," and the subject of predictions shall receive our attention ; and the first is that the *Pall Mall Gazette* will be forgotten, and its name obliterated from the memory of man as a thing that never existed, when the science of Astrology will be in the minds, and its wonderful works in the mouths of every man. The best he can ever do is to copy the opinions of others, therefore the science of Astrology is not for him.

Seriously considered, predictions bring with them grave responsibilities to those who do not speak idly, with full consciousness as to their import. For instance we see great earthquakes, and very serious disasters for England, and the great powers in the middle of next month, November. England will make great preparations for war, if not actually engaged in serious warfare before the month is out. For America the outlook is also very grave, and history will be made at a rapid rate during the close of the present year, and the end of 1897 will be the most eventful period we have ever known. Earthquakes on the ninth of November, which is a serious birthday anniversary for the Prince of Wales; great gales about that date, until the 16th. Snowstorms and hurricanes; many serious wrecks and grave calamities on the 21st. The whole of November will be gloomy and distressing. There will be many sudden deaths and deeds of violence, murders and suicide about the 18th, and the newspapers will be more concerned about the physical expression of the malefics than the great causes that lie behind the manifestation.

Turkey will begin to realize her position in Europe this month. Africa, Egypt, Spain, and America will suffer severely. There is only one faint hope of the peace of Europe being preserved, and that is the presence of Jupiter in Libra, which at least means that amidst it all, there will be JUSTICE.

It is not a pleasant position to be blessed with abnormal hope, and yet have to predict disasters, and often the fear of being considered alarmists, has kept us from speaking of things to come concerning which we have Astrological knowledge. However, we will turn our attention to the predictive side of our science, and in the near future shall publish as many definite and distinct predictions as it is deemed advisable. We have already said sufficient to claim the title of prophets, and whether false or true, remains to be proved in the very short period that will elapse betwen the publication of these predictions, and their verification. We write fully three months before any of the events are due, and to emphasise our remarks, we repeat that November 1897 will be noted for sudden events, such as gales, deaths, murders, suicides, wrecks, wars, diseases, and a commencement of troubles in the religious world, amidst which there will be a steadily increasing marriage record. Crime and bloodshed will be the prominent features of the month. We are on the eve of a great and serious struggle, the culminating point of which we shall not reach until the beginning of the year 1900, when the spring will bring the dawn of a new era, full of prosperity and happiness. Mark well this prediction. Those who survive the next three years will have passed through a crisis, the like of which has not occurred during the present century, the cause of the whole springing from the intense selfishness of a few personalities, the representatives of the selfish portion of humanity.

" TEMPUS OMNIA REVELAT."

# A Simple Method of Instruction in the Science of Practical Astrology.

BROADLY speaking, we may class humanity into three groups, the poor, the middle class, and wealthy, so far as finance is concerned. We may also extend the classification to the mental conditions, as ignorance, knowledge, and wisdom, not for a moment implying that the poor are always ignorant, or the rich wise ; although in a measure, we shall find that poverty often arises from a lack of knowledge, and riches from perverted intellect. Extremes meet in the rich, and the poor, while the middle classes may be generally considered as the balance. It may easily be seen that mental culture must tend to improvement of environment. Those who cannot appreciate artistic and harmonious surroundings, are often content to remain in surroundings in which others could not possibly exist, the more sensitive, and refined the nature, the more effort is expended to secure harmonious surroundings. Those who linger in the animal conditions, under the rule of Mars, can never appreciate the refined tendencies of the saturnine element. Probably the best means of judging the environment would be that offered by the signs of the Zodiac. The summit of physical refinement would be reached in Capricorn, this sign giving ambition, love of beautiful surroundings, and external grandeur, while the mental culture, and refinement would find best expression through Aquarius. In this sign we have all the indications of a refined mind, and a great life of mental harmony. In Pisces we may look for emotional refinement. The luminaries in the sign Capricorn, never fail to give an intense desire for perfect physical surroundings in the home life, the Sun building it as the ideal of physical existence, while the Moon takes steps to give it expression at the first opportunity. Those who have the ruling planet placed above the earth in the South-eastern portion of the map, rise in life, to a better condition ; if in the twelfth house, by much labour and the overcoming of obstacles, and often by the help of enemies ; in the eleventh, through the assistance of friends, which they never lack ; while in the mid-heaven, by their own industry, and strong moral character. The progress of the ruling planet will always show the improving condition of the environment. Its position in the ninth may indicate improvement by voyage to foreign lands, the church, etc. The eighth through wills, legacies, and finance of marriage partners, and the seventh through strangers, law, and marriage or partnership. When the ruler is below the earth progress is uphill work, and comes only late in life, but to the ruling planet, all changes in environment must be referred, and the position, aspects, and condition of the Moon also, the latter being the expression of all the influences she collects. To illustrate some of the foregoing remarks we produce the following horoscope

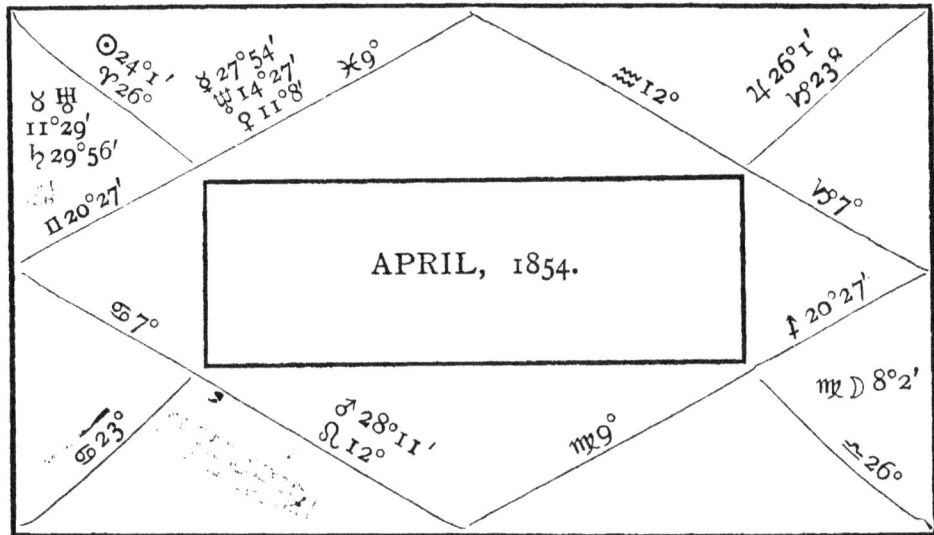

APRIL, 1854.

This gentleman was born into a poor environment, so far as finance is concerned, but now holds a position in which he commands respect and associates with persons of culture and refinement. He has always been helped on in life by his friends, and those particularly connected with science and religion. Jupiter in the ninth sextile to his ruling planet Mercury, in the eleventh, a common sign rising, and the ruler in a common sign describes the environment at birth, as also the position held through life, notwithstanding the aspect of Jupiter. Through the help of friends he holds a position that he could not have obtained without their aid. He is highly mediumistic, having at one time been what is called an inspirational speaker. He should seize every opportunity during the middle portion of life to avoid a return to the conditions indicated by Mars in the fourth, square to Saturn. Another case may be taken to illustrate environment : a female born at 6.30 p.m., April 17, 1868, Hants. This person is a dressmaker who works for a mere pittance, spending a week or so in different houses for a few shillings per week and her food, a position from which she seems incapable of rising. Her ruler, Venus, is in the common sign Gemini and in the western position of the heavens at birth. The environment is respectable, but very ordinary. Now contrast these with the horoscopes of Napoleon I. and III., and the rules may be obtained for judging environment.

There is now one very important consideration with regard to one's environment. A retrograde ruler may retard one's progress, and delay progress for some wise purpose, but we may also be greatly helped by contact with another individual whose ruler and ours is in harmony and sympathy. Those persons signified by the afflicted planets in the Nativity cannot be helpful to us, excepting through the pain and sorrow that they cause. On the other hand, we have known lives that were latent and inactive, become stirred into life and enthusiasm through the benefic influence of those signified by the planets in harmony with their ruler.

Take Napoleon's Josephine. Through her, his star shone bright nd reached its greatest brilliancy, and through her it also set. The whole is well borne out by the seventh house which not only indicated his wife, but also the public, which are governed by the Moon. Again we have this illustration in the horoscope of Mr. Gladstone. A gentleman born in the north at 11.40 a.m. May 10, 1857, into a very indifferent environment, was helped by a friend who took a fancy to him when a lad, and from that start he has risen to a very comfortable position in life, from which, by energy and a strong will, he may acquire a fortune. Mr. S. was born at 11.45 p.m. February 22, 1843, London, into a very good environment. By gradually buying house property he has placed himself in a splendid financial condition, but he cannot obtain political fame, note Mars, ruler, square Sun. Mr. E. G. C. was born at 2 a.m. December 23, 1862, into a poor environment, but very respectable, do what he will he cannot rise above a poor respectability

Within the limits of the ruling planet we have the power to alter our physical and material environment, and from the position and aspects to this planet we can predict the whole of the future life.

The fourth house and its ruler, in all probability, indicates the close of the past life, while it has the tendency to show the end of general affairs in this. It is the magnetic point to which all the influences in the Nativity are drawn. In a general sense the Moon as ruler of the natural fourth, in the order of the signs from Aries to Pisces, indicates the kârma, or fate, of the past and present; her applications indicating what has to be gone through, and her separations that which is brought over from the past. The Sun marks the hours of the greater cycles, and the Moon the minutes or lesser cycles, while Mercury, the winged messenger between the two, preserves as memory the experiences. And what is the meaning of it all, why the environment? When the Sun, ruler of the heart, illuminates the brain, then is the Solar orb truly exalted in Aries, the sign of the head. And when the Moon, ruler of the stomach, into which the food is collected for digestion, rises into Taurus the sign next to the Sun's illumination, then the speech is directed by the Sun's illumination, becoming silver as compared to the silence which is golden. The life's work of that individuality which holds these positions is nearing completion, and it may be that we, too, have to pass through many Moons, to our one Solar cycle thus giving several lives to the one Solar experience. Whatever the sun has in ideality, that will be the expression needed by the Moon. It may be, when the life quickens, that only one lunar cycle may be needed to complete the Solar experience. Of this we cannot say, but this is quite certain, more than one earth life is needed to know the qualities that may be expressed by each sign. If the primal quality of the Sun is fire, then it will be best expressed by fire or air, certainly not earth or water. Lives of the concrete nature are needed to acquire soul qualities, no matter what the nature of the environment may be, there is always opportunity to gain the required experience. The ideal must be made manifest. We are the builders of our own character, and with each thought we weave our future environment. The liquid mercury is ever being moulded by the one desire and will, but the desire must give way finally to the will, and the Moon must collect the perfume from the choicest flowers before perfection can be gained. Between Aries, and the culminating Capricorn, there is ample scope for all desires, but the true desires are those of the Uranian eleventh. Between Mars and Saturn lies the whole range of the personality and when the former is exalted the fullness of the latter is attained. Here is wisdom; search well its inner meaning. We are governed by a Divine law, and the aim of our lives should be to attune our consciousness to that of the Divine Ruler, and expand the limitations of the Personality until we are one great Individual Star.

Before leaving this interesting subject of environment, a word or two may be said in conclusion as to what it is that is limited by it. The Personality is that part of the Individuality that is focussed and expressed through the ascendant, and its progress is seen by the ruling planet, be that planet what it may. In judging any horoscope it would be safe to look for expressions of the personality in the ruling planet, Mars and the Moon, while the individuality would be denoted by the Sun, Jupiter and Venus. These two phases of expression will be conveyed into Mercury, Saturn, and Uranus, the whole to some day have but one expression through Neptune.

In judging the environment never fail to tabulate the position, sign, house and aspect of the ruling planet. The horoscope of Napoleon III. is well known to students, and it will serve as a final illustration of environment. The sign ascending is Capricorn, the head of the serving trinity, a cardinal sign of personal power and ambition. The ruler is Saturn, in the mid-heaven, exalted over all the planets, in the sign of pride, determination, and tenacity, partaking of martial qualities. The Moon is in the sign of mental refinement, firmly fixed in the ascendant, while Mars also ruler of the personal and physical conditions, is united to the Individual Sun. Again Venus Individual, is linked to Mercury, the bridge between the I and P, and Jupiter stands alone. No matter how limited and cramped the environment may be, it can be expanded into either the Sun, Jupiter or Venus, in a greater or lesser degree. To deliberately cut oneself off from the influence of love, and the spirit of compassion, is to become spiritually wicked, almost an impossible thing for the majority to do. We can all expand to love, and if we will learn from our experiences we may all some day be wise. When the limitations of Saturn are overcome, and doubt makes way for hope, then comes the faith that leads to charity. Be wise in time, and overcome the personality that it may be a fitting servant of the real, and true individual Man or Woman.

# The Theoretical Value of the Degrees of the Zodiac.

### By H. S. GREEN.

It will be seen from this classification that there are degrees in different parts of the zodiac that possess, somewhat similar influence. Thus, the second degree of Aries will be not unlike the fifth dashamsha of Aries, and especially the 13th and 15th degrees of it.

| Degree : | 2°♈ | 13°♈ | 15°♈ |
|---|---|---|---|
| Dashamsha Influence : | ♈ | ♌ | ♌ |
| Degree Influence : | ♌ | ♌ | ♈ |

But in each case although there is a resemblance there is also difference. The second degree of Aries is almost wholly Aries, with only a very faint undercurrent of influence from Leo. In the thirteenth degree, the influence of Leo is very much stronger, about double as strong as in the second degree ; this might be represented by the Sun rising in Aries, Leo being in the fifth house. In the fifteenth degree, Leo is still nearly as strong as in the thirteenth, but Aries gives a very faint modification for the degree ; which might be represented by the Sun rising in Aries, Mars being in Leo in the fifth house.

The strongest influence is always that of the sign to which the degree belongs ; the next, which is weaker, is that of the dashamsha ; and the last, which is weakest, is that of the degree.

Not only are there degrees within the same sign bearing some general resemblance to each other, but degrees in different signs may also approximate some common type. Here, however, no matter how strong the apparent resemblance, it is easy to draw a distinction Contrast, for instance, the Sagittarius dashamsha of Aries, with the Aries dashamsha of Sagittarius.

| Sign : | Aries. | Sagittarius. |
|---|---|---|
| Dashamsha : | Sagittarius. | Aries. |

The first of these would be represented by Jupiter rising in Aries, Sagittarius being in the ninth house. The second by Mars rising in Sagittarius, Aries being in the fifth. In both there is a mixture of Aries and Sagittarius, but the proportions of the mixture vary, Aries preponderating greatly in the first and Sagittarius in the second. The same kind of symbology may be used to distinguish degrees as well as dashamshas, in instance of which we may take the second dashamsha of Gemini, which includes the Queen's ascendant (5° ♊ 41′).

| Sign and Degres : | 4° ♊ | 5° ♊ | 6° ♊ |
|---|---|---|---|
| Dashamsha : | ♋ | ♌ | ♋ |
| Degree : | ♋ | ♏ | ♓ |

The fourth degree might be symbolized by the Moon rising in Gemini, Cancer being on the second ; the fifth would be the same, but Mars would be in the second and Scorpio in the sixth ; the sixth degree (the Queen's ascendant), would be the same as the fourth, but Jupiter would be in the second and Pisces on the mid-heaven.

SYMBOLICAL DIAGRAMS OF DEGREES.

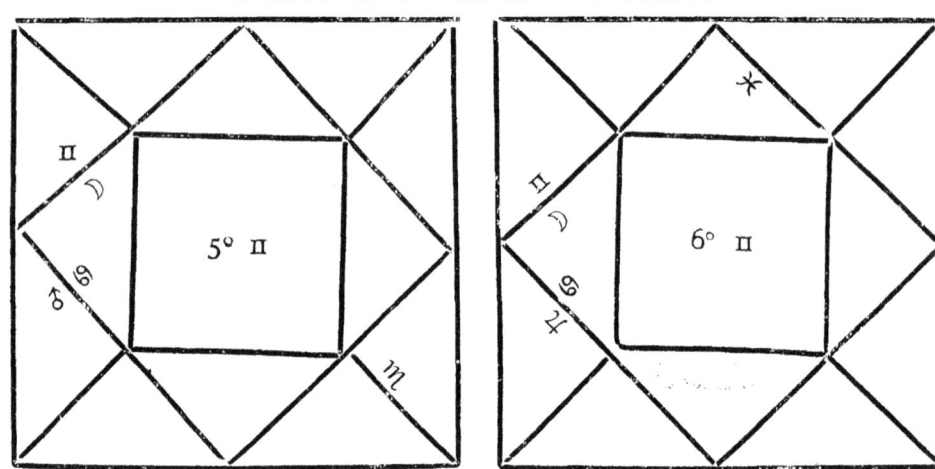

It is necessary to add a word of caution here, lest the reader should attach too hard and fast a meaning to what is only intended to be symbolical. The Moon rising in Gemini merely means that a ray from Cancer in the second house is thrown into Gemini in the first. Mars in Cancer in the second house only signifies that a ray from Scorpio in the sixth is thrown into Cancer in the second. This " Mars " is only a ray from Scorpio ; it has nothing to do with Aries, and carries with it no influence of Aries ; so that it is not the ordinary Mars of the choroscope and must not be interpreted as such or it will lead to onfusion. In just the same way, in the diagram of the sixth degrees, the Jupiter in Cancer means that a ray from Pisces in the mid-heaven is thrown into Cancer in the second house. This " Jupiter " is wholly Pisces, and carries none of the Sagittarius influence. Let the reader bear these distinctions in mind when drawing diagrams of other degrees.

In interpreting such a diagram as that of the sixth degree, we proceed in this order .—

(1.) Gemini, the zodiacal third, is rising.

(2.)  It is modified by the influence of Cancer, the zodiacal fourth.

(3.)  Cancer is here relatively the second, and qualifies the meanings of the second house.

(4.)  Pisces, the zodiacal twelfth slightly modifies Cancer (being its third decan).

(5.)  Pisces is relatively the tenth to Gemini.

It is easy to see that the influence of a degree is far more complicated than would be supposed from an inspection of the published interpretations of the meanings of degrees. To write down all the possibilities resulting from the diagram of the sixth degree of Gemini would be to produce a lengthy paragraph or two. Therefore, to simplify the testing of the scheme here put forward, the reader should confine his attention at first to the modifying influence of the dashamsha upon the sign, and leave the question of separate degrees until later on.

It has usually been supposed that the influence of degrees bears principally upon the degree on the cusp of the ascendant. It seems far more probable to suppose that it relates more or less to every degree occupied by a planet, and especially to those of the Sun and Moon. As a matter of course the cusp of the ascendant cannot be properly tested unless the *exact* time of birth is known.

From a few observations I have made, I am inclined to think the dashamsha of the ascendant not only influences the character and fortune but also the *personal appearance* of the native. The Queen's rising sign Gemini, which has a sub-influence from Cancer and the Pisces decanate of Cancer, is an instance of this.

There is a curious coincidence to be noted between the scheme here outlined and a statement concerning Hindu astrology made by Mr. Chidambaram Iyer, the translator of the *Brihat Jataka*, and other works. On page 32 of *Fate and Fortune* he says, respecting certain famous Hindu books :—" The influence of the Lagna (the part of the ecliptic rising at the time of birth) is given for every six minutes (of space) or one tenth of a degree of the zodiac, irrespective of the planetary places. The influence is so great, and given in such detail, that all the more important events of life can be predicted from the Lagna alone."

In the scheme given in this paper it will be seen that each dash-amsha corresponds to three degrees; that each decanate of the dashamsha corresponds to one degree; and consequently that, as a decanate contains ten degrees, each one of these degrees will correspond to six minutes of space, which is the exact amount mentioned by Mr. Chidambaram Iyer. The following table will make this clear.

$$\text{One dashamsha or sub-sign} = 3°$$
$$\text{One decanate of the sub-sign} = 1°$$
$$\text{One degree of the sub-sign} = 6'$$

This is a curious agreement, and certainly looks like something more than a coincidence. It seems to indicate that this sub-division of signs into tenth parts was really the method used by the ancient Hindu astrologers to arrive at the influences of degrees and parts of degrees. But whether or not this was so it is quite out of the question at our present stage of acquaintance, or lack of acquaintance, with the subject, to pretend to go into such a minute sub-division as six minutes of space. Considering how seldom we can rely absolutely upon any estimated time of birth, the task of proving or disproving the alleged influence of dashamshas is quite complicated enough for the present. When experience has justified this method of sub-dividing signs, it will be time to proceed further. So far as my own investigations go they tend to confirm the theory of dashamshas; but I recognize what an immense volume of special research will be necessary before a confident verdict can be pronounced. There is a sufficient number of astrologers capable of estimating the modifying effect of one sign upon another to render unnecessary the insertion here of the influence of the one hundred and twenty dashamshas in the zodiac, to say nothing of the whole 360 degrees, even if a writer were not justified in shrinking from the task of elaborating such a list. It is also quite unnecessary to compare the characteristics of the degrees resulting from the scheme here put forward with those that have previously been published. Some agree and many do not. One or two curious coincidences may be mentioned. According to " Charubel," the last degree of Pisces " is in sympathy with the sign Taurus." This is the Taurus decanate of the Virgo dashamsha of Pisces, so that " Charubel's " clairvoyant method and the one here given, based upon the Hindu, meet curiously in this degree.

14° ♈, according to "Charubel," is "a true solar" degree. It is part of the Leo dashamsha.

16° ♈, in the same interpretation, has for its symbol, " A man with a sheaf of corn under one arm and a sickle under the other." It belongs to the Virgo dashamsha of Aries.

18° ♊. "The number six rules this degree," says "Charubel." The reader will see that it belongs to the sixth dashamsha of Gemini.

30° ♊. "Symbol, an execution." This is the Scorpio degree of Pisces dashamsha.

For convenience of reference, I append the ascending degrees of several persons whose horoscopes have been published.

| Name and Ascendant. | | Sign. | | Dashamsha. | | Degree. |
|---|---|---|---|---|---|---|
| Queen Victoria, 5° ♊ 41′ | ... | ♊ | ... | ♋ | ... | ♓ |
| Lord Rosebery, 28° ♓ 3′ | ... | ♓ | ... | ♍ | ... | ♑ |
| Napoleon III, 13° ♑ 2′ | ... | ♑ | ... | ♒ | ... | ♊ |
| " Charubel," 13° ♏ 28′ | ... | ♏ | ... | ♐ | ... | ♈ |
| Beaconsfield, 27° ♏ 40′ | ... | ♏ | ... | ♉ | ... | ♉ |
| Princess Beatrice, 0° ♍ 54′ | ... | ♍ | ... | ♊ | ... | ♊ |
| Kaiser William I, 18° ♌ 51′ | ... | ♌ | ... | ♒ | ... | ♒ |
| Sir Henry Irving, 1° ♏ 38′ | ... | ♏ | ... | ♌ | ... | ♐ |
| Prince Rudolf, 9° ♊ 23′ | ... | ♊ | ... | ♍ | ... | ♍ |
| " Sepharial," 24° ♐ 32′ | ... | ♐ | ... | ♌ | ... | ♌ |
| Alan Leo, 27° ♌ 34′ | ... | ♌ | ... | ♉ | ... | ♑ |
| Shelley, 26° ♐ 26′ | ... | ♐ | ... | ♌ | ... | ♈ |
| Swedenborg, 24° ♐ 56′ | .. | ♐ | ... | ♌ | ... | ♌ |
| H. P. Blavatsky, 12° ♋ 24′ | ... | ♋ | ... | ♌ | ... | ♌ |
| Tennyson, 22° ♊ 13′ | ... | ♊ | ... | ♑ | ... | ♉ |
| Byron, 2° ♋ 44′ | ... | ♋ | ... | ♌ | ... | ♐ |
| Gladstone, 2° ♑ 29′ | ... | ♑ | ... | ♎ | ... | ♊ |
| Mrs. Besant, 1° ♈ 40′ | .. | ♈ | ... | ♈ | ... | ♌ |
| Col. H. S. Olcott, 23° ♎ 47′ | ... | ♎ | ... | ♉ | ... | ♑ |
| " Raphael," 4° ♈ 30′ | ... | ♈ | ... | ♉ | ... | ♌ |
| W. Q. Judge, 19° ♈ 3′ | ... | ♈ | ... | ♎ | ... | ♒ |
| Huxley, 13° ♋ 11′ | ... | ♋ | ... | ♌ | ... | ♐ |
| Kaiser William II, 20° ♋ 19′ | ... | ♋ | ... | ♎ | ... | ♊ |

Our flesh is but our swaddling clothes, used by the soul during the process of developement.

# Christian Astrology.

By ♎.

T must often have struck us when reading the Revelations that among those wonderful beasts and dragons presented to our imagination there might be many Astrological references and allusions.

We will first begin with the book sealed with seven seals, which seals are the seven planets, and we will call the book "The Book of Life," because it is the book of physical manifestation whereby we come under the astral influence. But no one is found worthy to open this book except Aries, representative of Christ, the real Pascal Lamb. The horns and eyes which are the seven spirits of God, show that He had put Himself under the astral influence, and as the proverb has it had "ruled his stars." No one else in Heaven or in Earth had so far done this. Those in heaven had had no trial ; those on Earth were yet bound by the planetary chain : only the Lamb had overcome to open the book and to loose the seals thereof.

Let us look at the first four seals, which astrologically represent the four cardinal signs (♈, ♋, ♎, ♑), and their rulers. The white horse, or Cancer, comes first, and "him that sat on him had a bow," the silver bow of the crescent Moon. This is the peace-maker bringing peace to the Earth, he goes forth "conquering and to conquer." The next and second is Aries, the day house of the planet Mars. To the rider of the red horse is given a great sword and the power of the infliction of death. Then comes the black horse whose rider carries a pair of balances in his hand. This will be easily recognised to be the sign Libra, house of Venus. Lastly, of the four angular seals we have that of Capricorn, whose ruler is Saturn, the planet above all others which influences old age, sorrow, fear, and the dissolution of that part of us which is material. The four horses may be considered to stand for the four cardinal signs, and the riders with their insignia for the planets, lords of those signs.

The four Beasts also have the right to an explanatory note, being the four fixed signs of the Zodiac—Leo the lion, Taurus the calf, Aquarius with the face of a man, and Scorpio the flying eagle. These, ít will be seen, invite the Evangelists to "come and see," or as it is simply translated in the revised version " come," we may take it to mean " come forth." Taurus the calf, and second Beast, saying come forth to Aries, the red horse, and second seal, and so on.

We have now accounted for four out of the seven planets, the Moon, Mars, Venus and Saturn, and we have three remaining, Jupiter, Mercury and the Sun. I have given the fifth seal (the souls under the altar) to Jupiter, and to Mercury the sixth seal, on the opening of which the Sun and Moon become darkened and the stars of heaven fall to the earth; because, on referring to Genesis I, 14 to 18, we see that on the fourth day, Wednesday (the day of Mercury) the Sun, Moon and Stars were created; therefore Mercury would seem to rule the firmament and the sixth seal.

The planetary influence and all material things are here done away with, followed by the sealing of those who have overcome all earthly longings.

Then we have the opening of the seventh seal, " and when he had opened the seventh seal there was silence in heaven about the space of half-an-hour."

No explanation of this is given, and, therefore, this seal may be veiled in mystery and beyond our physical horizon. If any student can throw light on this it will give me much pleasure.

I have yet a few words to say about another part of Revelations —that part which might be called the allegory of the birth of Christ, and his victory over death and sin. We will turn to the twelfth chapter, and this time we shall deal with the constellations Virgo, Libra, Scorpio and Sagittarius. To make it more clear we will imagine St. John standing under the open sky : it is night and myriads of stars are above his head. He beholds a great wonder in heaven, a woman clothed with the Sun, and behold another wonder, a great red dragon who is going to devour her child as soon as it is born.

These are the signs Virgo and Scorpio, Virgo the woman; Serpens in Scorpio, tthe Dragon. Those readers who have illustrated maps of the constellations will do well to look at them, and they

J

will see that Serpens stands near to Virgo, his mouth is open and above his head is Corona Borealis or the Northern Crown, composed of seven stars.

The child is Spica, in the ear of corn, and this star will be found in the ascendant of "Our Lord Jesus Christ's" horoscope as given in the Astrologers' Magazine, Vol. I.

Then comes the war between Michael, angel of the Sun, the spiritual man or immortality, and death, ignorance and sin, as signified by the dragon, the eighth sign, the latter being cast forth to torment the earth. The child is caught up to God and to His throne.

Passing over the next few chapters we will follow up the fate of the Dragon. In the nineteenth chapter, Christ is represented as coming on the white horse of Sagittarius, the archer, to fight against the Beast and his army, who finally are cast into the lake of fire.

On again referring to our maps, we shall see that Ophiuchus struggling with Serpens and trampling on Scorpio will well stand for the angel binding the Beast or Dragon for a thousand years.

Virgo, then, is the woman; Scorpio with Ophiuchus binding him is the Dragon; the King of Kings is represented by Sagittarius, with his arrows making war against the Beast and his army.

---

There are two poles of generation, the mental through the head and brain, the physical through the generative organs, while between the two is the heart as grand centre. The centre of the triplicities, Intellectual, Maternal and Productive are vital points governed by Taurus, Venus, Leo, Sun, Scorpio and Mars. The sting must be extracted from the latter before the centre of the centres can act.

\*　　\*　　\*　　\*　　\*

Antipathy arises from the discordant vibrations set up by opposite magnetisms, but when we have passed through the seven rays or colors and harmonized our Soul with them, then are we in sympathy with all the world. Love is the highest vibration, to reach which we pass through all vibrations. Love is harmony, and its essence brings the peace that passes understanding.

# The Horoscope for the Month.

## MADAME MARIE BASHKERTSEFF.

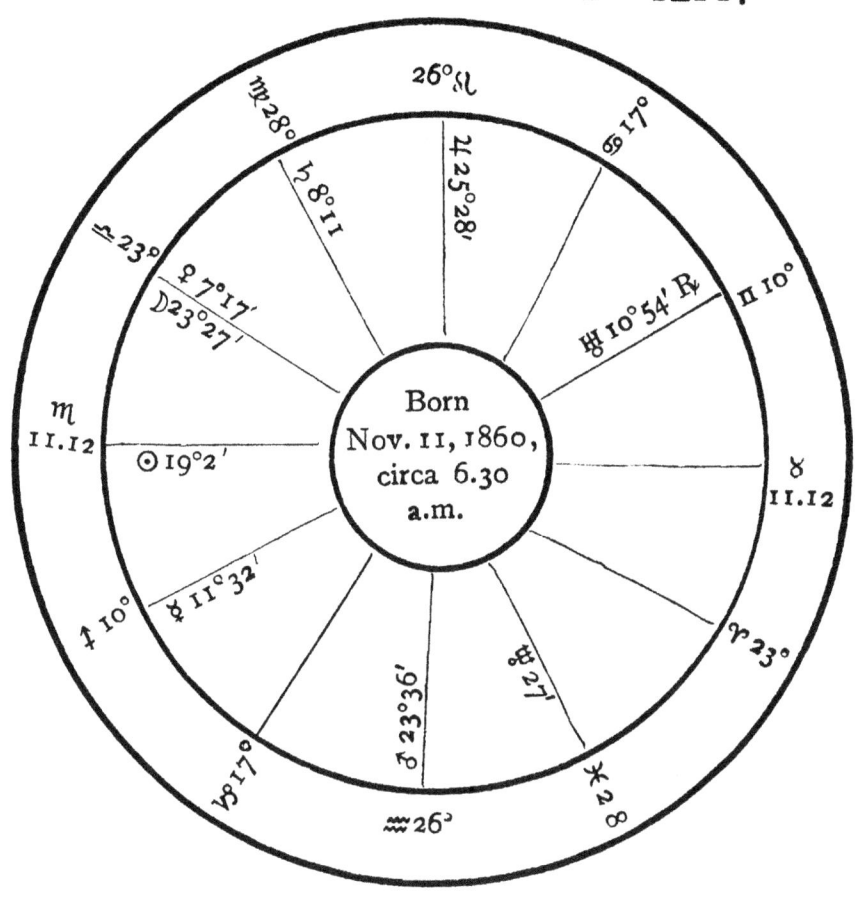

Common, 4.

Cardinal, 2.

Fixed, 3.

Exalted, 0.

Fire, 2.

Earth, 1.

Air, 4.

Water, 2.

| Planet. | Sign. | House. | Declin. | Lat. | General Aspects. |
|---------|-------|--------|---------|------|------------------|
| ☉ | ♏ | I | 17 S 29 | — | □ ♂, ∠ ♀ |
| ☽ | ♎ | 12 | 13 S 59 | 5 S 50 | ✶ ♃, △ ♂, ⊡ ♅, ∠ ♄, ∠ ♀, P. ♃ |
| ☿ | ♐ | 2 | 24 S 42 | 2 S 35 | ⌐ ♄, 8 ♅, ✶ ♀, ☌ ♂, ∠ ☽ |
| ♀ | ♎ | II | I S 33 | I N 41 | ✶ ♂, △ ♅, ⊡, ♀ ⊙, |
| ♂ | ♒ | 4 | 15 S 57 | I S 48 | 8 ♃, △ ☽, □ ⊙, ⊡ ♀ |
| ♃ | ♌ | 10 | 13 N 46 | 0 N 45 | 8 ♂, ✶ ☽, ∠ ♀ |
| ♄ | ♍ | 18 | 9 N 56 | I N 32 | □ ♀, ♅, ∠ ☽ |
| ♅ | ♊ | 8 | 22 N 43 | 0 S 3 | □ ♄, 8 ♀, ⊡ ☽ △ ♀ |
| ♆ | ♓ | 5 | — | — | □ ⊙ |
| M.C. | ♌ | — | — | — | ✶ ☽, 8 ♂, ☌ ♃ |
| Ascen. | ♏ | — | — | — | ✶ ♄, ⊡ ♆ |

# THE HOROSCOPE OF MARIE BASHKIRTSEFF.

## By Henry Durrant.

ARIE BASHKIRTSEFF was born at Poltava, in the Ukraine district of Russia, on the 11th of November, 1860, at or about 6.30 a.m., consequently she belongs to the Scorpio department of human life. The 12th degree ascended of the 2nd decanate, the latter being under the positive sub-rule of Jupiter. Mars, the ruler of the nativity, is in the sign Aquarius, near the cusp of the fourth house. The Sun ascends in the natal rising sign, and the majority of the planets will be found on cusps of houses.

Scorpio is a feminine, moist sign with perhaps the most thoroughly distinctive physical characteristics of the whole twelve, and as a rule the astrologer finds no difficulty in recognising its subjects either from a personal inspection, or from a photographic or other presentment. The first face of the second decanate, that is, the intercepting degrees between 10° and 15° inclusive, gives a "middle stature; well proportioned, fair and open; fair hair; eyes of greyish colour. Characteristics:—thoughtful, discreet, generous, of good disposition; fond of art and science; creditable ambition; of fixed purpose." The whole sign is remarkable for its strong will power, its intense loves, hates, and its severe and sarcastic criticism.

Personally, Marie Bashkirtseff was of a medium height, with a finely developed figure, and a brilliant complexion of the kind that usually attends consumptives. The hair was of a fine shade of golden red, and the eyes deep grey in tone, while the face was full of fire and energy, and the two fore teeth were a little apart. Such she was while enjoying her brief womanhood.

As to her powers they were no doubt intense—indeed everything she did, possessed an element of vigour and vitality remarkable in one so afflicted in health. Her personality however is difficult to understand—at all events from the literary legacy she has bequeathed us, for as she appears therein she attracts irresistibly one moment, but to revolt almost in the same breath. Hers was indeed a peculiar temperament, combined with a strong will—the *I* at all costs even to one's self—a thwarting of which nearly always resulted in nervous prostration, a fairly safe indication of her want of balance and control. She was proud, aristocratic, patronly, egotistical, ambitious, envious, dissatisfied. Half-repellent, half attractive, she stands out from her diary, with an abnormal talent for most things, and real genius for a few. If the curb had been judiciously applied she might have written more than one excellent imaginative work for her bent of mind betrayed a decided leaning to dramatic completion. At twelve years old she commenced to write her diary, and in her own words " it begins to have some meaning from the age of fifteen or sixteen." It is curiously difficult to understand when Marie's childhood occurred, for there is small indication of any infantile condition having obtained in these years, early though they be. At twelve or thereabouts she had fallen in love with an English duke, and for a time her entries bear much upon this *affaire du cœur*. She prays that God will make her a present of this particular member of Albion's aristocracy, promising that she will make him a good wife, and never occasion him cause for regret. But this premature *amour* was speedily crushed irrevocably by the marriage of the Duke himself—and not to Marie. She is always philosophizing, not puerilely, but with a consistent grasp; yet her quick intuition comes at times perilously near overthrowing her *petite* logical structures. As a psychologist she is frequently very striking, always original with her semi-christian, semi-pagan and fetishtical beliefs, but along these lines there seem to have been a hazy doubtfulness and temerity which barred her way like Ibsen's Boyg and forced her to go "round about." Her romantic nature was ever in quest of strange forms of excitement, evident from Neptune's position on cusp of fifth in her horoscope. She possessed a mad craving for power, wealth, exaltation. It amounted almost to a disease. Writing under date of March 31st, 1870, she says :—"I have no faith in any one . . . . . I am ambitious—that is my misfortune . . . . I want to be Cæsar, Augustus, Marcus Aurelius, Caracalla, the Devil, the Pope! I want—and I am nothing."

She had the possibilities of artistic expression in many ways, by literature, music (she possessed a splendid voice until her fatal disease ruined it), painting, sculpture. She was a linguist, no mean stndent, and chemistry attracted her (note the Sun rising in Scorpio).

The fatal disease however followed her spectre-like from birth. Writing in the April of 1876, she records a strange whistling in the chest, a cough and a redness of the nails. She has an idea she is going to die, but the symptoms leave her for a while. Soon, however, she experiences renewed attacks, sometimes very terrible. Her beautiful voice goes, but her buoyant spirits remain to the last. In the year 1884 her painting " Le Meeting," is a striking artistic success, she enjoys the closest friendship with Bastien Lepage, she is very busy indeed, and her diary entries become shorter. On October 20th they cease for ever, and by the 31st of that month, so far as her personality is concerned, she is no more.

Examining the indications in her horoscope we find that she was a Sun in Scorpio person. The luminary being so close to the cusp of Ascendant rendered her arrogant, to which defect the opposition of Mars and Jupiter also contributed, both planets being in houses ruling the attitude of the mind. At the same time it inspired her with unlimited ambition, and a full share of pride. The same position inclined her to dabble in chemistry, and gave her a magnificent carriage and deportment. The solar orb having its *locus* in Scorpio is well known to endow the nature with a firm but delicate touch, so necessary in the painting, art and surgery. Besides this it imparts a power of healing by physical contact, and the electro-magnetic force which resides in the whole body in such cases is frequently enormous. The proximity to these people is a tonic in itself. They are able to perform cures by the laying on of hands. The angular position of the orb in the tenacious sign Scorpio is also responsible for much spirited determination and executive power generally. We see however that it bears a square from Mars inciting her to rash actions, provoking much ambition and marked vanity, infusing irritability and courage, but at the same time depreciating the vitality. Four planets are in airy signs, consequently her temperament was of the mental order, but the positions of the individual modifying factors do not warrant a balanced mind.

Regarding the natal figure more closely, we find that there is a superabundance of the angle of sorrow, viz. :—the square and others based thereon, but these aspects do not lessen the influx of power on that same account. In the most brilliant geniuses they will obtain rather than the soothing trines and sextiles, for they destroy conventionality and orthodoxy, two stockades ever in the way of the soul's advance. It will be noticed also that most of the planets are on cusps of houses, which renders them particularly strong. In addition to this the Moon and Uranus are in mundane sextile to the M.C., and these are very powerful, particularly from cusp of twelfth.

Mercury, as ruler of the mind, is on cusp of second house in Sagittarius, the sign of introspection and the natural triginta of degrees dominating philosophy, science and religion. It is in the positive face of the decanate of ♂. The principal aspects to this point? are the square of Saturn, the opposition of Uranus and the sextile of Venus. Thus with Mercury in the position previously tabulated and Mars opposition Jupiter ninth and third, questions of religion and philosophy were bound to enter into this subject's life scheme. As the positions warrant they were chiefly of a dogmatic and polemical character. A certain amount of bigotry would emanate from the same influences. The opposition of Uranus and Mercury would render her too dogmatical, critical, cynical and untrammelled, while the square of ♄ would convey an amount of stubbornness. These positions would give originality but would cause her to be wilful. She would have her own way and think for herself, She could not be dominated, and must frequently have shocked goody-goody people.

The sextile of Mercury and Venus endowed her with artistic musical and literary talent—sensuousness—and the trine of Uranus increased and stamped it with the brand of originality. The square of Saturn to Mercury gave her philosophical tendencies and steadied the opposition of Uranus.

As her diary shows she had peculiar ideas anent the grand passion born out in her horoscope by the trine of Venus and Uranus, which aspect also contributed to provide her with a fascinating demeanour. Many little romances are traceable to this origin. For her lavishness and extravagance we look to the opposition of Mars and Jupiter which impressed her besides with a scornful spirit, marked vanity and a candidness little removed from discourtesy, all of which traits were accentuated by the constitution of the ascendant &c.

But the figure is sealed with Phthisis. The common signs are heavily afflicted. On the cusp of the eight house, that of death, on the sign Gemini ruling the lungs is posited Uranus. It receives the opposition of ☿ the ruler of Gemini posited in Sagittarius, also with Virgo and Pisces ruling the lungs, and the square of Saturn from Virgo and the Sesquiquadrate of the ☽. Mars, the natural ruler of the eighth, is in third house the latter having the nature of the zodiacal Gemini. The Sun is in affliction by squares thrown from Mars and Jupiter and this must have considerably weakened the heart, seeing all three are posited in signs ruling the vital centres. At the time of death the Sun by secondary motion had attained the parallel declination of Uranus in radix, but there were other directions in force too.

In conclusion this horoscope may advantageously be compared with du Maurier's given last month. Many points of resemblance exist for the student, and are very interesting indeed.

---

WHY IS MARS RED? "*Scraps,*" *Sept.* 11*th*, *1897.*—The brilliant red colour of our neighbouring planet has long been a question to astronomers Under a strong telescope the whole of its surface, except the white ice-caps at the North and South Pole and the grey-green oceans, is of a strong ochreous hue. For long it was supposed the atmosphere of Mars must be red, but this has been disproved. Truly, a red sky instead of a blue one would look a trifle peculiar. But now the idea is that all the grass on Mars is red, and the leaves of the trees of the same colour. What conditions could produce such a result no one on this earth can say, but it is the only explanation that meets the case. No doubt to the Martians our earth appears of a beautiful green.

# Astrological Stories.

## THE NATIVITY, by Sapal, Astrologer.

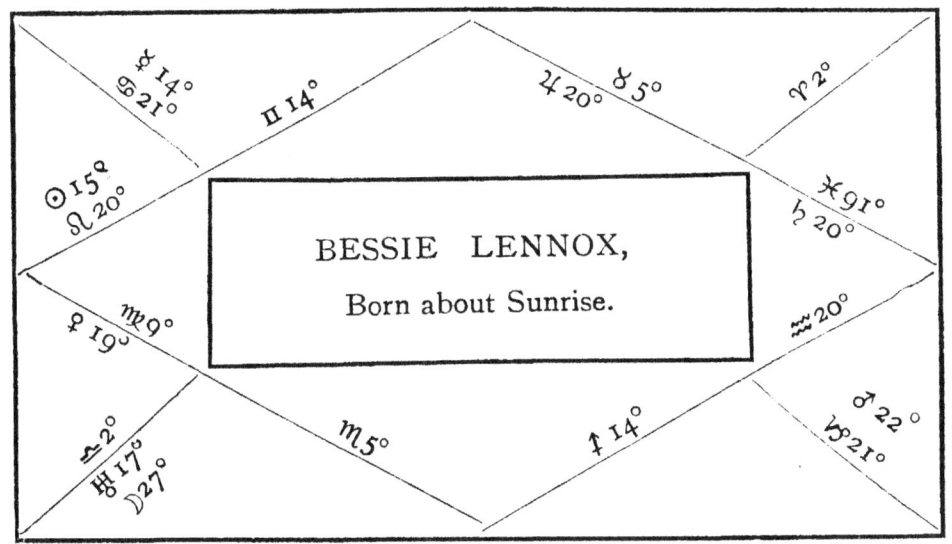

BESSIE LENNOX,

Born about Sunrise.

☉ ✶ ♅ □ ♃ .        ♀ ☌ ♄ △ ♂ ✶ ♅ .        ♄ ☍ ♀ ⚹ ♅ .

☽ □ ♂ ⊡ ♄ .        ♂ □ ☽ △ ♀ △ ♃ □ ♅ .        ♅ ✶ ☉ □ ☿ .

☿ □ ♅ ☍ ♂ △ ♄ .        ♃ △ ♂ △ ♀ .        Asc : □ ♃ ✶ ♅ .

" T is my pleasant task, to express my judgment upon the effects of the planetary positions and aspects of the heavenly bodies at the physical birth of my niece Bessie Lennox. From birth to what we all call death the wheels of life revolve unceasingly. Each life is within a transparent globe coloured by the ever changing colours that flash forth from its potent centre ; each globe is a miniature Sun moving within the greater solar sphere. Millions of these globes, in miniature, hang from the parent flame, separate in its own special quality, yet united by the ever flowing ocean of love in which it is bathed. Around the central flame are the seven spirits before the throne, whose influence pours through the seven planets in our solar system, each planet circling in its own ring, having its own colour and influence, but operating differently. Within one of these rings, our earth is revolving, giving and receiving the solar rays in altered conditions, changing color and vibration. This is the soul of astronomy, a science the most wonderful and profound that the mind of man can understand. At each physical birth a portion of the individual, which overshadows and encircles the form, tries to manifest itself through the body, and as the child grows from infant to youth, into manhood or womanhood, the individuality gains more and more a hold upon what is its personality, expressing to the best of its ability, the qualites it has acquired by other contact with forms, and seeking the experience required to acquire other powers and virtue. It is like the bee sucking honey from the flowers, each personal life is a flower, some sweeter than others, but each yielding its share of the honey. On the day this child was born the planets were well distributed in the heavens, and the aspects of the heavenly bodies of a very mixed nature. At the time of her birth the twentieth degree of the celestial sign Leo ascended in the eastern horizon. The Sun and Mercury had risen, Jupiter was in the meridian, Saturn and Mars sinking in the west, Venus, Mars and the Moon rising, four planets were above the earth, and four below, four held cardinal positions, two common and two fixed. One planet held a fiery station, three earthy, two watery and two airy ; these are the qualities expressing their virtues. The Sun alone was in his own house ; Mercury was in the house of the Moon ; Venus the house of Mercury ; Mars was exalted in the house of Saturn ; Jupiter in the house of Venus ; Saturn in the house of Jupiter ; and Uranus with the Moon in the day house of Venus—Libra. In considering all these factors I judge the child will reach maturity, be well formed in the upper parts of the body, having a clear skin, fair hair, with brownish blue eyes changing to hazel. She will be strong-willed, aspiring, and ambitious; of a free and independent spirit; courageous, loyal, pure and faithful.

Her very nature is sympathy, and for all that lives and breathes the breath of life, she will feel, for she has the tenderness of a woman with the inherent wisdom of the man. Her dominant key-note is " Faith and self control." Hers is no ordinary natus, for mark, she brings over from other births both intuition and reason. Note the Moon, or personality, in that sign is balanced, in the house of the balance, and

Herschell the mystical, gives that inner perception, or soul sight which senses rather than thinks, realizes and knows.

She is born under the royal sign Leo, and is a child of fire, and the spiritual fire is in its central focalizing spot, the heart, and finds its best expression in that sheath, which is the " Throne of the Sun." She has a fine, sensitive love nature, which causes her to live to a great extent in an ideal world. She will be liable to be misunderstood and her motives misjudged by the practical selfish world. Her nature is open, frank and noble, she must be taught early the value of silence, and caution. Her will is enduring, and if she undertakes any mission she will carry it through at any personal cost or self sacrifice, as long as it is honest and just she will die for her principles, she will not argue about them, she will *act*. Great endurance, force and compassion are the main qualities shown in this map. The mind is very receptive, retentional and inspirational.

So much for the character and mind. Now let us mark the events of the unfolding life ; its sorrows and its joys ; considering marriage, wealth, health and the evolution of the soul by its various experiences. With Jupiter lord of the tenth house, no dishonour can ever fall upon the native, for her morality and virtue is dominant, she does not suffer personally, but the troubles of others fall heavily on her young shoulders, and her tender heart suffers in others lives. The planet of force is in the house of service, and cradled in luxury, born into wealth and position, she will become a server of others.

Her constitution is a good one, with great inherent vitality, yet she will once be near losing her body by a dangerous fever and be in danger of a severe accident by fire ere the first ten years have passed, through the carelessness of a servant, yet she will live for she is a strong soul with a mission to fulfil.

At seventeen a severe shock falls upon her, and a change of residence is denoted, Mars square Herschell and Venus opposition Saturn, now acts, and the shadows of Saturn fall upon the native—a cloud before the Sun, home troubles, pain, loss—then, Mercury square Herschell and opposition Mars—fall out and the mind is distracted and torn, but be ye not afraid nor discouraged, for behind the clouds the Sun is shining, and in this very shock the soul's awakening will be accomplished. Look at the seeds growing : first the sunshine and then the rain, and lo ! the flower is there.

The next point I have to remark upon is peculiar: for no ordinary marriage is shown by this figure, she will marry rather late in life to a man of great position, holding a very influential post, a perfect marriage—the union of souls. A true marriage is a union of similar tastes. In unity not in dissimilarity, is happiness found. She will mate with a child of fire, born under the same ruler. Her courtship will be a foretaste of heaven, and mark the ruler of her fifth house is in trine to Venus, Jupiter restores what Saturn took away. The ruler of the seventh is in the third,—her seventh by sign—thus she will need a man of wisdom, peculiar and unorthodox in views, beyond the average of humanity. It is a union brought over with all its peculiar and romantic features. Their ages will be identical and she will meet him first in early girlhood, but the storms of life will beat on both ere they meet again. In the same month, they were both born, nay, the figure I have taken gives the same day. Help-meets and companions, amidst the crash and din of a serious catastrophe they meet again, in different bodies and of differing sex, but the same souls. Bessie will know poverty and affluence, joy and sorrow, death, sickness and pain, a life crowded with experience, for she has desired in some other life, the rulers of the spheres to let descend upon her all her past misdeeds in punishment, to be free from the web of illusion, she herself has woven so as to minister to others, "Freedom and time for service." Another stood by her in that moment and dedicated *all* to the *use* and service of humanity, and the rulers of the spheres gave these children of fire their desire, for as gold is purified by fire, so is the heart by pain.

The innate nature of these twain are similar, for many lives they have grown side by side. This life is a completion for them of a certain cycle. She learns to strengthen her character, he comes to purify his, he to hold his senses once again captive, she to gain the mastery of mind. Bessie has a grand spiritual nature, she will develope—the possibilities before her are enormous ; and the gifts I hold to-day are hers in the near future— she too was an astrologer in her past life. Her significator has the sextile of Herschell. I have not said all I might, because others are concerned and the value of silence I have long learned to appreciate.

Farewell! when you need me, you will find me.

                                        SAPAL."

*(To be continued).*

# How to Calculate Foreign Horoscopes, with Rules for South Latitudes.

## PART II.

### To find the Planets' Places.

N the ephemeris, the places of the planets are given for noon at Greenwich; and when an astrological figure is erected for some distant place, it is necessary to take the difference of longitude into consideration.

The longitude of the birthplace in time will already have been ascertained in Part I. Add this to the time of birth if West of Greenwich, but substract if east. The result will give the time for which the planets' places must be calculated from the ephemeris. They are then inserted in the map in the usual way.

Example V.—A child was born at Dublin at 2 p.m. any day. For what time on that day must the places of the planets be calculated in a Greenwich ephemeris?

Dublin is 6° 17' W; and when turned into time this amounts to 25 minutes. As Dublin is west, this must be added to the time of birth, 2h. 25m. p.m. will be the time for which the positions of the planets must be calculated.

Example VI.—A child was born at New York at 10 p.m. on January 1st in any year.

| Longitude of New York | ... | ... | ... | ... | 74° 0' w |
| Equivalent in time | ... | ... | ... | ... | 4h. 56m. |

Add this to the birth time, and the result is 2h. 56m. a.m. on the *next day*, January 2nd.

Example VII. A child was born at Paris at 9 a.m. any day.

| Longitude of Paris ... | ... | ... | ... | ... | 2° 21' e |
| Equivalent in time | ... | ... | ... | ... | 9m. 24s. |

As Paris is east, subtract this from the time of birth, and (ignoring the seconds because less than half a minute) 8h. 51m. a.m. is the required time for calculating the planets' places.

Examples VIII.—A child was born at Athens at 1 a.m. on May 1st any year.

Longitude of Athens     ...    ...    ...    ...     23° 41′ E.

Equivalent in time    ...    ...    ...    ...      1H. 35M.

As Athens is east, subtract this from the birth time. The required time is then found to be 11h. 25m. on the *previous day* April 30th.

## PART III.

### SOUTH LATITUDES.

In the ordinary horoscope for a place north of the equator, the cusp of the ascendant is on the left hand side of the figure and that of the seventh house on the right. That is to say, if the reader faces due south, the ascendant of the heavens will be on his left, and the stars will set on his right. In the southern hemisphere this will be reversed. He would there stand facing the north (because the Sun is in the north at noon) and the ascendant will be on his right and the descendant on his left. Consequently, in transferring this to paper, that which in a horoscope for north latitude would be the cusp of the seventh is the cusp of the southern ascendant, and the rising sign with its degree and minute are marked there accordingly ; that part which is the northern sixth house being the southern second ; the northern fifth, the sonthern third ; and so on. Two figures drawn in this way will be found, one in the *Astrologers' Magazine*, Vol. IV., page 59, and the other in Mr. Pearce's *Text Book*, Vol. I. page 57.

But convenience and common sense justify the advice given by Mr. J. C. Dalton, in his *Spherical Basis of Astrology*, page 6.; and we advise the student to draw the southern horoscope in exactly the same way as the northern, so far as the mere position of the houses is concerned. " Make the figure with ascendant on the left as usual. To reverse it, though correct in idea, causes endless confusion to one accustomed to the common position."

To ascertain the cusps of the houses in a figure for south latitude, proceed as follows :—Turn to a table of houses for the same latitude *north* as the horoscope is south. Knowing the sidereal time of birth (or right ascension of the mid-heaven in time) as found by Part I. turn to the proper column and write down the sign and degree on the cusp of the *tenth house* just as given there. Then add 12h. to the sidereal time of birth, turn to the proper page, and note the degrees for the cusps of the 11th, 12th, 1st, 2nd and 3rd houses, and write them in the figure ; only instead of the signs there given use the opposite ones.

Example IX.—For the sake of convenience and simplicity, let us suppose a child is born in latitude 51° 32' S., which will be just as far south as London is north. We will also suppose that the sidereal time of birth has been found to be 16h. 12m. 13s. From the table of houses for London, the reader will easily see that the cusps of the houses will stand as follows :—

| 10th. | 11th. | 12th. | 1st. | 2nd. | 3rd. |
|-------|-------|-------|------|------|------|
| 5° ♐ | 12°♑ | 15°♒ | 11°♓2' | 2°♈ | 0°♉ |

Then calculate the places of the planets according to the directions in Part II. and fill them in the figure,

———

For Psychologists.—Mr. J. Cotteral, of Guelph, fell asleep at four o'clock one afternoon, and in a dream saw a dead body covered with a white sheet, and on lifting it recognised his son. He awoke with a start, and related his dream to a friend. That night he was aroused by a telegraph messenger, who brought a telegram informing him that his son had been drowned at Hamilton. The dream and the drowning occurred at the same time.—*Guelph Advocate* (Canada).

\* \* \* \* \* \* \*

The " Theosophical Review," 1s. 6d., The Theosphical Publishing Society, Charing Cross, W.C.

" Lucifer " has changed its name, and now goes forth to the world as " The Theosophical Review." The contents of the first number under the new title are full of interest and valuable instruction, with the change of form, we welcome a quickening of the life. Mrs. Annie Besant writes a splendid article upon the Theosophical movement, in which she alludes to the great conjunctions of the planets in the sign Sagittarius marking off the end of the cycle in 1897, 1898 and 1899. Mr. C. W. Leadbeater commences an article upon The Christian Creeds, which is unique in its explanation of some of the doctrines of Christianity. From cover to cover the Magazine is full of interest, and we cannot do better than recommend every one of our readers to become a reader of the Theosophical Review.

# Calendar for ♎ October.

"Oh live, and love worthily; bear and be bold."

OCTOBER was the eighth month in the year of the Romulus, as its name implies, and the tenth in the year of Numa 713 B.C. October still retained its first name although the senate ordered it to be called *Faustinus*, in honour of Faustina, wife of Antoninus, the Emperor; and Commodus called it *Invictus* and *Domitianus*. October was sacred to Mars.

During the first twenty-two days of October the Sun is in Libra, and under the influence of Venus. The gems for the month are diamonds and opals; the ruling colours are crimson and light blue. The following are the approximate aspects and positions of the Moon for October.

| D M | D W | Moon at Noon. ° ' | APPROXIMATE TIME OF LUNAR ASPECTS. |
|---|---|---|---|
| 1 | F | 15♐49 | ☍♆ 11.20 p.m.; Mercury Stationary |
| 2 | S | 0♑ 3 | □☿ 1.10 a.m., ✶♂ 2.45 a.m., □♃ 3 a.m. |
| 3 | S | 14 ,, 1 | △♀ 1.5 a.m., □☉ 5.32 a.m., ☿ P♃, ♀ P♂. ☽ First Quarter |
| 4 | M | 27 ,, 42 | △☿ 6 a.m., △♃ 7.45 a.m., □♂ 9.15 a.m., ✶♅ 10 a.m., ✶♄ noon, ☽⊡♀ |
| 5 | Tu | 11♒ 8 | △☉ 2.45 p.m., ☽⊡☿, ♃, ♆ |
| 6 | W | 24 ,, 20 | △♆ 8.45 a.m., □♅ 4.22 p.m., △♂ 6.15 p.m., □♄ 6.30 p.m., ☽⊡☉, ♀☌♃ 0.4 p.m. |
| 7 | Th | 7♓19 | ☍♀ 11.55 p.m., ☽⊡♂, ♀✶♅ P. ♃ |
| 8 | F | 20 ,, 8 | □♆ 4.30 p.m., ☍♃ 11.30 p.m., ☿✶♄ 11.55 p.m. |
| 9 | S | 2♈46 | △♅ 0.40 a.m., △♄ 3 a.m., ☍☿ 3.20 a.m., ☿ P. ☉ |
| 10 | S | 15 ,, 14 | ☍☉ 4.42 p.m., ☽⊡♄, ♅. Full Moon. ♂ enters ♏. |
| 11 | M | 27 ,, 31 | ✶♆ 2.10 a.m., ☍♂ 7.5 p.m., ☽⊡♀. ☿ enters ♎. |
| 12 | Tu | 9♉40 | ☽⊡♃, ♃✶♅ 6.52 p.m. |
| 13 | W | 21 ,, 40 | △♀ 9.50 a.m., ☍♅ 10.55 p.m., △♃ 11.10 p.m., ☽⊡☿ |
| 14 | Th | 3♊33 | ☍♄ 2 a.m., △☿ 4.15 p.m., ☽⊡☉ |
| 15 | F | 15 ,, 23 | ☽⊡♂, ☉△♆, ♀□♆ |
| 16 | S | 27 ,, 12 | ☌♆ 2.25 a.m., △☉ 3.35 a.m., □♀ 5 a.m., □♃ 1.5 p.m. |
| 17 | S | 9♋ 5 | △♂ 3.15 a.m., □☿ 2.30 p.m. ☽⊡♄, ♅ |
| 18 | M | 21 ,, 7 | □☉ 9.9 p.m., ✶♀ 11.55 p.m., ☿ P. ♀. ☽ Last Quarter. |
| 19 | T | 3♌23 | △♅ 0.25 a.m., ✶♃ 2.5 a.m., △♄ 3.45 a.m., □♂ 6.2 p.m. |
| 20 | W | 15 ,, 59 | ✶☿ 10 a.m., ✶♆ 11.55 p.m., ♀☌♃ 1.10 a.m., ♀✶♃ |
| 21 | Th | 28 ,, 59 | □♅ 9.10 a.m., ✶☉ 10.45 a.m., □♄ 0.45 p.m., ♀ P ♃ |
| 22 | F | 12♍27 | ✶♂ 4.30 a.m. |
| 23 | S | 26 ,, 25 | □♆ 5.5 a.m., ✶♅ 2 p.m., ☌♃ 4.42 p.m., ✶♄ 5.15 p.m., ☌♀ 11.36 p.m. |
| 24 | S | 10♎51 | ☿△♆ |
| 25 | M | 25 ,, 40 | ☌☿ 8.4 a.m., ☌☉ 11.28 p.m. |
| 26 | Tu | 10♏44 | ☌♂ 0.47 p.m., ☽⊡♆, ♀ P. ♃ |
| 27 | W | 25 ,, 52 | ☌♅ 3.5 p.m., ☌♄ 6.33 p.m., ✶♃ 6.40 p.m., ♃✶♄ 11.31 a.m. |
| 28 | Th | 10♐56 | ✶♀ 8.30 a.m. ♃ enters ♎ |
| 29 | F | 25 ,, 45 | ☍♆ 6.20 a.m., □♃ 7.55 p.m., ✶☿ 8 p.m. |
| 30 | S | 10♑13 | ✶☉ 6.55 a.m., □♀ 2.10 p.m., ✶♂ 7.40 p.m. |
| 31 | S | 24 ,, 18 | ✶♅ 6.35 p.m., ✶♄ 10.55 p.m., △♃ 11.30 p.m. |

## NOTES ON THE MONTH.

The New Moon for the month occurred on the 26th of September, and may be considered the map for the Autumnal quarter, when taken in conjunction with the quarterly figure. The following are the

## NEW MOON FIGURES FOR LONDON AND NEW YORK.

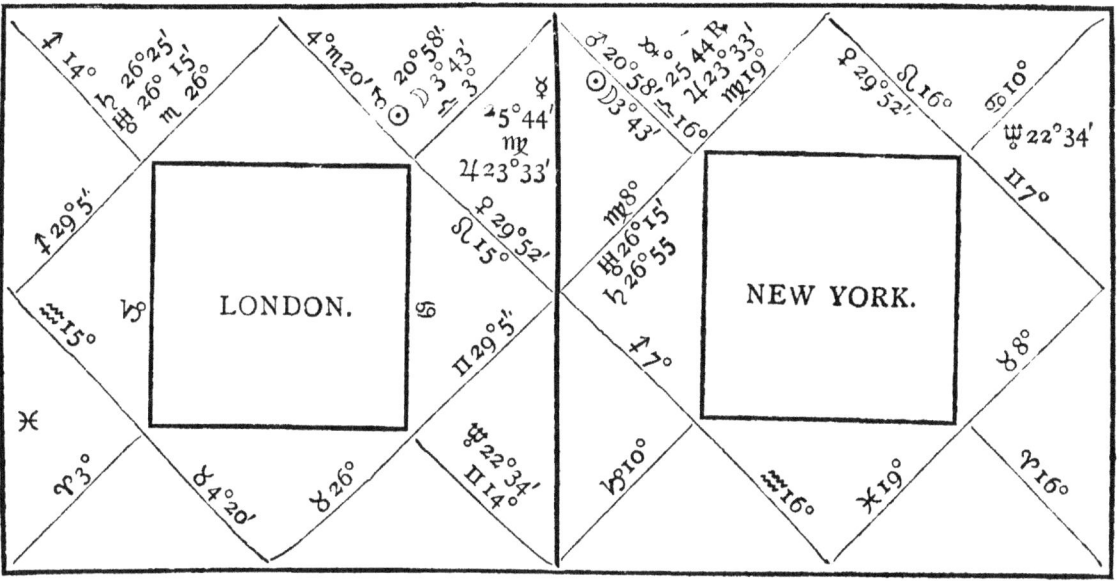

The value of Mundane Astrology lies solely in the *Judgment*, the predictions requiring that careful foresight which can come only by practice. To become really clever at Mundane Astrology a wide knowledge of the world's affairs is required, so that the artist may be able to forecast the direction in which the events will fall. There are few real Astrologers who can spare the time necessary to successfully interpret this especial branch, and fear of failure keeps many from venturing any predictions worthy of notice. We propose risking failure for the purpose of gaining experience, and the following is our judgment of the maps for London and New York.

To London, the great city of extremes, which is practically the centre of the world, all eyes are turned, from thence to the city of the coming race, New York. The figure for London shows the last degree of the sign Sagittarius ascending; the influence of Jupiter waning, and that of Saturn increasing. Mars, the ruler of England, holds the position held by the Moon at the Vernal ingress, at the birth of the

K

year. This will affect the health of the nation, being supported by the ruler of the sixth in the above map, falling in the eighth, in conjunction with Jupiter, ruler of the first. Bowel complaints will be prevalent, and many victims carried off, especially amongst young children. October will produce much infantile mortality, particularly about the 8th of the month.

Foreign affairs will cause excitement, and rumours of war with a foreign nation will be in the air. India will cause trouble while her ruling planet is in Scorpio and in conjunction with Uranus; and we may expect to hear of troublesome times in Australia. We judge from the intercepted sign, Capricorn, in the Ascendant of the map that India will attract to herself the attention of all Europe, in a marked degree, and her troubles will be alarming. Our government should watch every move of Russia. It will be interesting to note events about the 16th of this month. Coming events cast their shadows before, for which the month will be notable. The ruling star of Great Britian is in its fall. We must be prepared for reverses.

NEW YORK.—The Ascendant for America at the time of the New Moon is Scorpio, which contains Saturn and Uranus. The goverment of America will have their hands full, and will hold an unenviable position before the world. Their opponents will be strong, and sorrow and affliction will fall upon the land, affecting the people grievously. There will be many sudden deaths and much crime. The President will be in danger; sorrow will come to him and he will require more than usual protection. He will have good intentions but suffer through the conduct of those holding power and authority. There will be much activity in the money market, and business affairs will be prosperous during the month. America's ruling planet is retrograde, and she will be fortunate if she escapes war, there is every probability of war between Spain and America.

Students should notice the rising and culminating places of Saturn and Uranus

--------

The law is both merciful and just. Mercy and justice are only opposite poles of a single whole, and mercy without justice is not possible in the operations of the law. That which man calls mercy and justice is defective, errant, and impure.

# Birthday Happenings
## OCTOBER.

E are all more or less anxious to know what the coming year has in store for us, and even if we do not confess it, we would be glad to have some intimation as to whether the Sun will continue to shine upon us, or the clouds break and the sky brighten, metaphorically speaking. We cannot help this, for, look upon it how we will, the major portion of one's life is held by fate, and this fate can only be broken or altered by the will. We may change the direction of a ball once set rolling, but roll it will when once set going, until the energy expended in sending it forth is exhausted. Who can say what to-morrow may, or may not, bring forth? And who can foretell what our attitude will be under any given circumstances. We will act in accordance with our radical nature. To be forewarned is to be forearmed; therefore, having knowledge we may alter the current of our fate, aud direct the energy by our will into a groove whereby the forces may break without serious disaster.

During the first twenty-two days of October the Sun is in the sign Libra, the sign of the Balance, indicating the principle of Justice. This is the internal keynote of all born this month. They have in ideal this principle of justice, and they seek their own when they seek harmony, peace and equilibrium. It is said that their highest powers are PERCEPTION and INSPIRATION.

In the following remarks upon each day's influence during October, it must be understood that the forcast of the year is *general* and not in anyway definitely particular. The greatest care is taken to give the best judgment based upon the Solar and Lunar indications, but in all cases the nativity is the root, and should be consulted whenever it is possible. We will gladly explain the modifying or extreme aspect in the nativity of any new subscriber, who remits a year's subscription this month to Modern Astrology.

INDICATIONS FOR THE ENSUING TWELVE MONTHS OF ALL PERSONS
BORN DURING THE MONTH OF OCTOBER IN ANY YEAR:

1st.—This will be an active year. There will be some travel, many short journeys ; gain through relatives, and much excitement over their affairs. The mind will be more than usually engaged with deeper thoughts, and married persons will gain through their partners. It will be a good year bringing peace and prosperity.

2nd A.M.—There will be some financial losses during the year. The home-coming of some distant relative will disturb, or trouble will come through correspondence. Be very careful in signing papers, and avoid becoming surety for anyone. There will be gain and loss through speculations, and to the married an addition to the family circle.

2nd P.M.—Employment will be insecure, and there will be some domestic trouble, producing some improvement and prosperity later. Care must be exercised in all general affairs during the first six months, but during the last half of the year there will be much improvement.

3rd.—Avoid all disputes with persons who are your superiors in any way. Do not travel unless it is necessary. Avoid chills and keep the circulation active. With care the year may end satisfactorily.

4th.—Avoid all disputes and litigation, and anxious affairs. The year will bring some fame and success, but beware of sudden changes. Literary work will prosper, and the social life will bring joy and happiness, if hope is cultivated.

5th.—Financial loss is indicated. The blood will require attention, yet with care the year will turn out successful.

6th.—You will have a successful year, if travelling is avoided. Steer clear of aged persons and those of peculiar and Bohemian habits. Keep away from the water, and have nothing to do with speculations. There will be a mixture of joy and sorrow.

7th.—Finance will suffer, and health also if care is not taken to avoid taking cold at the feet, therefore, keep them dry and warm. The single may expect disappointment in love affairs, and males should avoid the opposite sex, or sorrow and trouble will follow.

8th.—This is an unfortunate birthday. Health will suffer, probably through damp clothing. See to the health ; live moderately. Voyages will not be successful.

9th.—Nervous complaints are threatened, and you will suffer from headaches, but you will gain in some unexpected manner. Subordinates will trouble you, and opponents will be strong. The year is good for occult study.

10th.—This is an evil birthday. The single should avoid marriage, and the married, law. Persons born this day will suffer through headstrong and impulsive action, and meet with many opponents, and some peculiar and uncommon experiences.

11th.—You may come prominently before the public, for there is danger of notoriety. Avoid law and all disputes, as well as love, courtship and marriage.

12th.—Gain by legacy is indicated, with some financial losses. You may lose a relative or mutual companion. Sudden gain is promised with minor losses.

13th.—This will be a successful year financially ; it is a good year to court and wed, but expect some bad news from abroad, if you have friends or relatives there. By will and effort you may make this a very prosperous year.

14th.—A death will occur in the family circle, probably an aged person. It will be a good year for correspondence, but there will be some sorrow and disappointment.

15th.—You will probably travel, and gain through superiors, but suffer some temporary loss financially. The year will bring some uncommon events.

16th.—Avoid travel, partners and relatives. You will suffer financially, and have many difficulties to contend against. Health will suffer, and deaths in the family are probable.

17th.—Much trouble over writing and correspondence may be expected, but you will fearlessly fight all your difficulties, and overcome through pluck and endurance. You will be helped by others.

18th.—You will obtain some fame and honour this year, and produce enemies by your success. With care you will be very successful. Avoid over-ambition and let the tide carry you.

19th.—This is a fortuate birthday in many ways. The social life will improve and bring happiness, but all excesses must be avoided. Legal affairs may affect finance. Females must be discreet.

20th.—The year will be successful, and you will obtain many new friends. Letters from abroad will contain good news, and you may contemplate travelling. All literary work will succeed.

21st.—There are mixed influences at work. Avoid travel and elderly persons, removals, and speculation. You may obtain advancement and social improvement. Look well to health.

22nd.—This will be a good year for business pursuits, fresh enterprise, and an active period may be expected. The year may be made successful.

23rd.—The Sun has now entered Scorpio, the eighth sign of the zodiac, details of which will be given next month. This is a fortunate birthday; good for finance, new undertakings, travel and adventure. You may buy land or property and make satisfactory investments in earthly matters. For love, courtships, and marriage it will be favourable.

24th.—The influences are weak for the year, and may produce anything of the ordinary type. There is a probability of marriage for the single, but nothing definite is promised.

25th.—The year will be good and fortunate; ambitions will be realized, and there will be activity toward success. Each month should show more improvement of affairs.

26th.—The year will not be good. Deaths will take place in the home circle, and some sorrow is threatened. Courtship and marriage should be avoided during the coming year.

27th.—Sudden and unhappy events are foreshadowed, yet there will be some hopeful prospects in sight. Be careful in travelling, and take precautions to guard against accidents. It will be to your advantage to insure against accidents.

28th.—Finance will be good, and marriage prospects hopeful. Be guarded in speech and careful in action. The year may be a successful one.

29th.—Avoid speculation, wear warm clothing, and in dealing with others do more by correspondence than direct.

30th.—Removals and changes are indicated ; also increased expenditure, which will have a satisfactory result. Love affairs will be prominent.

31st.—This will be a successful year, and you will do well in all directions. All you will require is more concentration, and steady application to make the year prosperous.

## GENERAL ADVICE FOR THE MONTH.

For correspondence, literary matter and affairs connected with public servants, solicitors, booksellers, editors, collectors, schoolmasters and merchants ; also all matters connected with carriage, post office, and travel, the following days are good : 4th, 6th, 7th, 14th, 20th, 25th, and 29th, and the following *not* good : 2nd, 5th, 9th, 13th, 17th, 21st and 28th.

For finance, pleasure, theatres and concerts, friendships, love affairs, and marriage; also for dealing with actors, dressmakers, upholsterers, and musicians, the following days are propitious ; 3rd, 13th, 18th, 23rd and 28th, but *not* the 4th, 7th, 11th, 16th, 20th, 27th or 30th.

For business men, doctors, surgeons, dentists, chemists, cutlers, and soldiers, and for all matters requiring courage, skill and daring, the following are good days : 3rd, 6th, 17th, 22nd and 30th, but *not* on the 1st, 4th, 7th, 11th, 15th, 19th or 26th, there being danger of accidents on these days.

For dealing with clothiers, lawyers, judges and religious persons, also for all new undertakings and fresh enterprises and social gatherings, choose the following days : 4th, 13th, 19th, 23rd, 27th and 31st, but *not* the 2nd, 5th, 8th, 12th, 16th or 29th.

For all matters of contemplation, tact and diplomacy, careful and steady thought; also for dealing with builders, land agents, landlords gardeners, and elderly persons, the following days are good : 4th, 9th, 19th, 23rd and 31st, but *not* the 3rd, 6th, 10th, 14th, 17th, 21st and 27th.

For dealing with Bohemian, eccentric and uncommon persons, railway authorities, etc.; also travelling by rail, or seeking adventure and out-of-the-common affairs, the following days are good : 4th, 9th, 19th, 23rd and 31st, but *not* the 3rd, 6th, 10th, 14th, 17th, 21st and 27th.

YOU CANNOT SERVE GOD *and* MAMMON.

# Editorial Comment.

EVERAL of our readers have been kind enough to send us proofs of their confidence in our work, and many have expressed their sympathy with our editorial remarks of last month. It was absolutely necessary for us to speak plainly simply because the enmity displayed by those who have chosen to become jealous and envious of our work create false impressions. We claim to be pioneers of a Modern Astrology which has nothing in common with that practised by ordinary professors, modern only in its application to the present living race, and not modern in the sense of a new system. The ancient laws and rules of Astrology have ever been and ever will be the same, but we are not Egyptians or Romans, but a modern race, having progressed to a fuller, and more active consciousness ; therefore, we must fit the ancient laws to modern times. When Mr. A. J. Pearce makes the statement that our Modern Astrology is two hundred and fifty years behind the age, he displays an ignorance of our system, which can only be accounted for by an entire lack of sympathy with the vital truths of the science, in which we should be co-workers and not opponents. He has had ample opportunity of giving to the world the truth in his various attempts to run a successful publication, but they have hitherto failed. Ours alone of all the publications issued during the present century, has been successful, and that speaks volumes for the system we advocate. It is because we have put soul into our work, and give forth the truth freely as we have received it, that we flourish, and will continue to flourish until the end.

The gentleman who sent the two remarkable horoscopes which we published in the July number has very little cause for annoyance, for not one person who reads the letter there published can trace the author's identity. We have more than one subscriber in that direction, but the quotation given by Mr. Pearce will suffice. " You can make such judicious use of it, the letter, as you please, suppressing my name."

Does any of our readers known the gentlemen's name or where we have published it. ?

We need hardly state how thoroughly disgusted we are with this childish wrangling, for after all it is only concerned with personalities, and not the vital truths of Astrology. We have gathered around us those who think as we think. It is certainly not too late for any one of our friends to investigate the methods and systems of other students besides ourselves, and decide for themselves the true from the false.

We have thought it advisable to refer to this matter again but this will be the last time, and we protest against wasting valuable space over our personalities. The sole aim of the true Astrologer is to get above the personality, and only by so doing can we become the " wise man who rules his stars." It is the soul of man that is free and only when we find our souls can we find freedom. All that which is below this reality is bound, and limited, and under planetary influence. To rise above the animal and mental conditions of limitation, the concrete existence, is to taste that glorious liberty which awaits the perfect man.

## THE HALL FUND.

Additional subscriptions to the Hall Fund have been received as follows :—

|  | £ | s. | d. |
|---|---|---|---|
| Amount brought forward from June ... ... | 4 | 11 | 10 |
| Anthony James ... ... ... ... ... | 0 | 2 | 0 |
| Miss A. G. Smythe ... ... ... ... | 0 | 5 | 0 |
| Mrs. Emma Wray ... ... ... ... | 0 | 5 | 0 |
| Mrs. Wallis ... ... ... ... ... | 0 | 5 | 0 |
| T. P. ... ... ... ... ... ... | 0 | 4 | 0 |
| Miss Carpenter ... ... ... ... ... | 0 | 3 | 0 |
| Mrs. M. F. Thomas ... ... ... .. | 0 | 2 | 6 |
| Miss Howard ... ... ... ... ... | 0 | 8 | 0 |
| A. Smith ... ... ... ... ... | 0 | 2 | 6 |
|  | £6 | 8 | 10 |

# Letters to the Editor.

Letters of general interest only are inserted.   Correspondents desiring **reply must** please enclose a stamped addressed envelope.

All correspondents should give full name and address, not necessarily for publication, but as a token of good faith.

N.B.—Writers of signed articles are alone responsible for the opinions contained therein.

DEAR SIR,—It seems to me that a very important fact in the recent troubles in the East has been lost sight of by Astrologers.   It is well known that all Eastern potentates have a Court Astrologer, or Astrologers, whom they are constantly in the habit of consulting.   Do not you and your readers think it likely that the " Sublime Porte " owes its success in war and diplomacy, and its general immunity and impunity to a careful following of their advice, and a wily watching of time and seasons ?   See how everything has turned out in his favour !   He has massacred the Armenians ; he has conquered the Greeks ; he has outwitted the Ambassadors ; he has snapped his fingers at an armed Europe.   He knew perfectly well that, although the Powers were formidable enough to look at, they were made perfectly helpless by mutual jealousy.   An ordinary horary figure would have told him that.   But these Oriental artists have much more complete equipments than one simple question would furnish them with, and have, no doubt, mapped it all out for this precious Abdul, so that he knows exactly how far he may go, and when to stop ; when he may ride the high horse and take active measures, and when he had best apologise, and cringe, and eat humble pie, and sing small generally.   But, mark you, this does not often happen ; it is seldom, if ever, necessary.   He is too artful for that.   It is a damnable use to make of our science ; but there is not a shadow of doubt that he does use it thus.   To take two palpable instances :—

War was declared on April 17.   Why was it deferred to this date, pray ? Greece had been busy some time.   Your friends the journalists say that that was the date when actual invasion of Turkish territory took place, and that previous skirmishes had been regarded as isolated acts of brigandage, etc., a sort of " dignity and impudence " arrangement.   But to me there is significance in the fact that Mars (the god of war) and Mercury (lord of Virgo, which sign, I believe, rules Turkey) came to an exact sextile on that date. Jupiter had still 7' or 8' of arc to go backward, which took him about a week. To this short retrogression the Greeks owed their first successes and popularity.   All were howling at the Turk.   But how long did it last ?   Jupiter stood still in his backward march ; retraced his steps, and is still triumphantly direct in Turkey's ruling sign !   But hist !   Mars approaches : the Turk lies low.   Mark his altered tone to the diplomatists.   Why ?   Simply these little symbols, that's all :  ♂ ☌ and P ♃ (Mars conjunction and parallel Jupiter), on July 24-5, in 10° ♍ 20', or thereabouts.   But all these are only transits after all.   The Sultan's astrologers are in possession of other and more important data than these, embracing radical figures and directions for himself the King of Greece, and all the courts of Europe.

You offer a guinea, Sir, for the best suggestion.   Mine may not be the best, but I suggest that, coupons being thrown overboard, popular interest would be awakened by watching European and other courts (more especially Turkey) astrologically, and venturing to predict such changes of front on the part of the rulers and prime ministers as I have noted.

Yours fraternally,

"LUNA."

SIR,—Most Astrologers in the so-called civilized portions of the world spend much of their mental force contending against newspaper people, or book-writers who scoff at Astrology. I have spent much of my time among newspaper people. They are largely governed by the nervous, unstable planet Mercury and very susceptible to the changing opinions of those who give support to their publications. They are a jolly set of people, argumentatively combative, but are not the deep thickness of the world. The words are usually parrotty. and their thoughts largely on the surface, and they thus represent the active thoughtless moving masses or humanity. Their mental requirements are of such a varied nervous nature, that it would be almost impossible for their mind to concentrate long enough to comprehend the basis of all things, as contained in Astrology. They are mere "ink slingers," and, like humming birds, jump from flower to flower, not stopping long enough at any one to make a careful investigation. What they claim to know they are seldom sure of, and would have to go to some one in the line of their investigations to find out, and then according to their temporary bias, on a commercial basis, would swear to it, or deny it, and then admire themselves in the mirror for the stock of knowledge which some one else has displayed through them. They have a power in moulding opinion among the unthinking masses, but the thinking minds move on without their assistance, and finally drag them unwillingly after them. It is like wasting breath to contend with them. People who think by newspaper rule are not the pioneers in the thought-world. They are only the garrison that hold places conquered by the advance troops; who feed on the stores captured by others, while those others are still in advance foraging for more.

As an Astrologer, scientific and philosophic, and a student of world-lore for over half a century, I have no apology to offer for Astrology. So far as I am concerned I care not whether others believe or disbelieve it. I judge of the quality of my pudding by the way it appeals to my taste, and if others wish to eat what to me would be stubble, I certainly have no fault to find with them, and I would no more appeal to them than I would to a dog to enjoy my salad and forsake his dirty bone. I happen to be born, however, with boldness enough to say, that any man who scoffs at Astrology is an ignoramus, even though he may have been educated in all the colleges of this civilized world.

Yours, etc.,

"PROF." HENRY,

Salem, U.S.A.

[NOTE.—"Prof." Henry is Editor of the Radix, published in Salem. We can recommend Americans to procure a copy and judge of its merits. ED.]

SIR,—Kindly allow me to enter a protest against the supposed malefic influence of the Planet Neptune. In my nativity, as the majority of your readers are aware, Neptune is rising inside the first house, in opposition to Mercury just inside the cusps of the seventh, and in mundane square to my Moon in the fourth. It has been close to my Moon since September 1891. In June 1892 it was on it, and in December of the same year it was there Heliacentrically till May 1893. In February 1894 it was but one degree past the Moon's place, and within orbs for years, a rather long period by the way. It has also transited my Venus, and is now on my Mars, and I still live, despite all the imaginary evil influences. During the time my aged mother (80) or wife (60) have not died; I have not become insane, nor have I had any especial worry, trouble, or anxiety solely attributable to this transit. Whatever has taken place has been correctly shown by other positions and influences.

Yours, etc.,

R. H. NEPTUNE.

SIR,—A clergyman who is justly celebrated in his own city was once heard to say that, " if people only would study the Bible as they studied Shakespeare or Browning, instead of construing it like Mother Goose, there would be much less of theological differences." This lesson might well be taken to heart by many of our so-called learned men in their attempts to solve the Greek Mythologies. So far as the writer of this article has been able to trace it, the Greek Mythology all turns on the planets, their motions, and their influence on the earth and its inhabitants. In no instance is this more clearly shown than in that very clever work by Ignatius Donnelly, " Atlantis," and it is a matter of regret that the learned writer did not add a knowledge of Astrology to his other numerous accomplishments.

From the earliest history or tradition of that remarkable continent, it is learned that it first began to be a power under the rule of a king called Uranos (Uranus), of whom Berosus says, he taught the ancient Chaldeans letters and arts of all kinds; he taught them how to construct cities, to found temples, to compile laws, and explain to them the first principles of geometrical knowledge. Here we have a key, to some great extent, of the influence of the mysterious planet Uranus. His influence on art and letters is well exemplified in the recently published horoscope of du Maurier, and his great influence on legislators and legislation is as well known as that over inventions and geometry.

To imagine these kings of Atlantis to have been simply individuals, would be to crowd an immense progress in science, arts, and civilization into an impossible space. We are, therefore, thrown back upon the hypothesis that it was the rule of the planet Uranus which is here referred to. During this rule of Uranus it is not improbable that the Sun was progressing through some sign in the great zodiac by which the planet is best enabled to manifest its influence. The sign Aquarius has been by some assigned to Uranus, and

I am inclined to think correctly, as I shall endeavour to show. As the Sun has but recently entered that sign, and allowing (about) 2,500 to each sign, it would have been (about) 30,000 years since this great kingdom began to make its history; (If I am wrong in this calculation, I stand ready to be corrected by any one). That is, supposing that only one revolution of the grand zodiac has taken place since that time.

Additional proof that the previously stated hypothesis is correct, is found in the chronology of the later " Kings " of Atlantis. Uranos was *deposed*, and succeeded by his son Chronos, which we all recognize as a name of Saturn. Chronos was called, (says Donnelly), the ripener, the harvest god, and was probably identified with the beginning of the " Agricultural Period." The connection of Saturn and its sheath, Capricorn, with agriculture and earthy employments, is too well known to be dwelt upon. Chronos was said to have visited Italy and taught its inhabitants agriculture, gardening, and how to tend and cultivate the vine.

Some light might be had, by this, on the parts of the earth under the rule of Saturn, or Capricorn. The legend of Chronos swallowing his children has been said to refer to the appearance and disappearance of the rings of Saturn, according to the relative position of the earth. The fact that this King directly followed Uranus, (Aquarius) can hardly be called a coincidence in view of the order of succession of the signs in the Grand Zodiac.

Chronos also was *deposed*, and his successor was his son *Zeus*, whom we all know as Jupiter, or Jove. He was called the thunderer, and was always represented with thunderbolts in his hand. The similarity of the bolts of Jupiter, with the bolts of the Archer, Sagittarius, the sheath of Jupiter, is very striking. The character of Zeus also corresponds very closely to that which Astrology gives to Jupiter. He was recognized as the father of the whole world; he everywhere rewarded uprightness, truth and kindness; was merciful to the poor and punished the cruel.

The most interesting part follows here :—

The Kingdom of Atlantis was now divided, (note Sagittarius, a double-bodied sign), the ocean, the islands, and the navigable rivers falling to Poseidon, or Neptune. Poseidon was the first to train and employ horses. (Sagittarius people are all more or less " horsey.") He was worshipped in the island of Tenos, in the character of a physician. Homer makes Neptune the ruler of the seas.

That Poseidon answers to the planet Neptune there can be no doubt, but it is doubtful if he has ever been thought to have any connection with Sagittarius. His watery nature is well shown in Scorpio, and it might well be enquired if the symbol for Scorpio (♏) be not a remnant of the three-pronged trident of the sea-god. His being worshipped as a physician, indicated his unquestioned influence through Scorpio, that sign being such a favourite one for doctors and surgeons. Further on the history becomes so intricate and so intermingled with individual acts as to make it an almost interminable study, but enough has here been given to throw a glimmer of light on the great truths which the "superstitious" Greeks endeavoured to teach through their poems. Their history was so closely identified with the planetary revolutions as to be practically inseparable.

I venture this opinion or theory of the nature of Neptune, and as to its sign or sheath, with some misgiving. The veriest tyro in Astrology, I hesitate to bring my views before that august body, the Astrological Society. I place them here, however, for what they are worth, and shall be more than gratified if they call forth any comment.          Yours, &c.,

G. C. McINTYRE.

# Reviews.

"Volo, or the Will." What it is; How to strengthen and how to use it. By Arthur Lovell. London: Nichols & Co., 23, Oxford Street, W., 1897. Price 3s. 6d.

This volume of 148 pp., is the second of the "Ars Vivendi" series. As the title of the series denotes the object is to make clear a method of living which shall commend itself to the common sense of every thoughtful and practical man. The system set forth "subordinates all knowledge what-soever to the education and welfare of the spiritual man." In Volo, Mr. Lovell enlarges on these topics with a fair amount of originality and force, and in doing so endeavours to show " that it is possible for man to build a lasting edifice of mental and bodily vigor they will be impregnable to the assault of disease." This cry of man for health of body and mind, re-echoed for ages, can, the author affirms with confidence, be satisfied. By unifying and consolidating the knowledge and the powers of the individual into a self-consistent whole, thus making the will an unit of force and supremacy, he contends that it is possible to accomplish the desired end. The volume is divided into two parts, the first for whoever is about to take self-culture or self-discipline into hand seriously; and the second for those who are determined to advance along those lines. The book is worthy of a serious and painstaking perusal by all who wish above all things to learn how to know, and knowing, to make all they can of themselves.

"Almost a Woman," by Mary Wood Allen, M.D. London: L. N. Fowler & Co., 7, Imperial Arcade, Ludgate Circus, E.C., Price 1s. 2d. Mothers who contemplate revealing to their daughters the mysteries of sex, and of their especial function will find the booklet very helpful. It reduces the medico-scientific theories to a very simple basis, and in pure but plain terms unveils with a loving heart and firm hand the dangers that beset one who is just entering womanhood. The ideas of the author are excellent in reference to purity in thought and action and of the responsibility of mothers o daughters who are just—

"Standing with reluctant feet
Where the brook and river meet
Womanhood and childhood fleet !"

By the same author, " Almost a Man " is unique in literature, but worthy of the earnest attention of thinkers on the vital questions of heredity, sexual morality and methods of reforming the race by transmitted traits ; and of the responsibility to the race and to womanhood, of one who has received the divine gift of manhood, *i.e.*, " potential fatherhood." A novel feature of both these booklets is the formulated pledge for furthering purity. That for young women of over twelve years of age is " The White Shield Pledge," and advocates the recognition of purity as equally binding upon men and women ; modesty in dress and demeanor, avoidance of conversation, amusements and books tending to produce impure thought.

" Ye White Cross Knight " is required to treat all women with respect, and endeavour to protect them from wrong and degradation," to maintain the law of purity, and to guard and instruct younger or more ignorant boys, etc. Both are couched in reverent but concise terms.

---

" INTELLIGENCE," the foremost metaphysical magazine published in the States is devoting much of its valuable space to Astrology, the last three numbers having articles on the subject. The August number contains " An Astrological Prediction on President McKinley's Administration," by Mr. Julius Erickson. This is not the first time that Mr. Erickson has come to the front with predictions on the outcome of presidential administrations. He made a forecast of ex-President Cleveland's first official term, which was verified almost to the letter. He followed this up with one for Mr. Harrison's term, and then another for Mr. Cleveland's second term, and now be comes forward with predictions concerning Mr. McKinley's administration. Mr. Erickson's prophecies have, thus far, been very accurate. His reading of the horoscope for the time of the inauguration last March covers a great deal of ground, as it is not confined to the events which will effect the White House directly. Pisces 29° culminates, and Cancer 16° 48′, ascended at the time the inauguration took place, with the Sun and Moon in the Ninth, the latter carrying the influence of the tenth ; Mercury in the eighth ; Venus in the tenth ; Mars and Neptune in the twelfth ; Jupiter in the third, and Saturn and Uranus in the fifth. The Moon being elevated in a sign congenial to her nature and ruling the Ascendant, Mr. McKinley will, Mr. Erickson claims, triumph over his enemies, which, though numerous, will be unable to over-power the President. We will comment on the figure in the next number of MODERN ASTROLOGY. The other contributions in August " INTELLIGENCE " are of interest to Astrologers as well as to all other students of advanced thought.

---

### RECEIVED.

" Intelligence," " Esoteric," " Theosophist," " The Theosophical Review," " Vegetarian," " Light of the East," " Notes and Queries," " Knowledge,'- " World's Advance-Thought and Universal Republic," "Phrenological Magazine," " The Hermetist Mind," and " Sepharial's latest works on Magic, Cards," " The Crystal," and " The 20th Century Astrologer."

# Questions answered by the "Astrologer."

*(See August Number for Particulars).*

*Enclose Twelve Stamps for Post Answers.*

---

*No. 44.—G. Adcock, m. 10.50 p., October 21, 1876.*  *Q.—When shall I regain the hearing I have partly lost ?*  *A.*—You will not get worse, but we see no signs of your ever getting better.  Your deafness comes from the throat, Uranus on the cusp of the second.  Never get the feet wet or damp.

*No. 45.—TAROT, m, 7.35 a., August 28, 1883, Oldham.*  *Q.—Shall I be successful as a butcher ?*  *A.—*Yes.  You must be very careful of a bullock, *some day.*

*No. 46.—T. B., m, 8.30 a., April 29, 1863, Hythe, Kent.*  *Q.—What are weak points in my character ?*  *A.*—Irresolute, not firm, too easily psychologized, too sensitive and too approbative.

*No. 47.—J. H. H., m, 8.25 a., December 23, 1843, Oldham.*  *Q.—Which has been or will be the most successful part of my life (financially)?*  *A.*—The close.

*No. 48.—S.A.B.F., f. 1.30 a, November 26, 1839.*  The future will be moderate.  If you enter business do so on your own account and by yourself.

*No. 49.—Ajax. m. 6.30 p., November 7, 1879, Lond.* Earthy employment, and I would recommend the greengrocery business, and as a fruit salesman you would succeed.

*No. 50.—R, Ayers. m.*  Let me have full particulars of the first fit when we will advise you.

*No. 51.—Gideon f. 12.28 noon, August 12, 1877.*  She will marry at **25**, but I fear her partner will be a drunkard.

*No. 52.—Mabel D. B, f, 5.10 p, June 10, 1871, N.Y.*  Between **37** and 4o the troubles will occur.

*No. 53.—Capricorn f, 6 p, August 3, 1859, Walsall.*  Business, furniture or antique articles, curiosities, &c.

*No. 54.—A. Wright, f, 1.50 a., December 21, 1831. Bristol,*  You will live to a very old age.

*No. 55.—Sun in Leo, m, 8 p, August 5, 1850, Salop.*  Yes, start next spring.

*No 56.—T, P., m, 8 29 a, April 29, 1863, Kent.*  Trade, printer or bookbinder.

*No. 57.—Ghislame Libra, f, 4 p, September 29, 1846, Brussels.*  I would advise you to seek a mental employment where your head would be engaged more than your hands.

---

LONDON :

Printed by the Law & General Printing Co., 1 & 2, Bouverie St., & Camberwell ; and Published Monthly by the Proprietor, Alan Leo, at 9, Pleydell St., Fleet St., EC.

Edited by
ALAN LEO, P.A.S.

The Official Organ of the Astrological Society.

Vol. 3, No. 4.    ✳    NOVEMBER, 1897.    ✳    Price 1s.

## Astrology and its Professors.

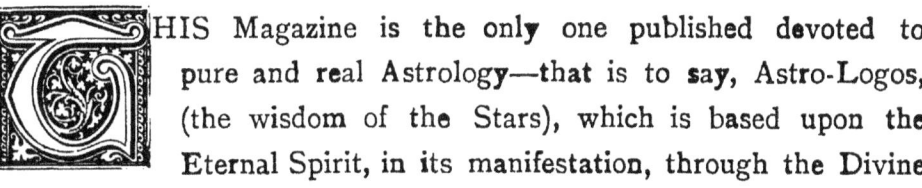

THIS Magazine is the only one published devoted to pure and real Astrology—that is to say, Astro-Logos, (the wisdom of the Stars), which is based upon the Eternal Spirit, in its manifestation, through the Divine Logos of this Solar System, as the law, which guides; directs and governs the workings of NATURE. It seeks to explain the laws of action, and re-action, which is expressed in the Re-incarnation of Theosophy. The Kârma, of the Hindus, and the Fate, spoken of by Astrologers.

There are two other Magazines, one is partly Astrological, and claims to be "the only one of its kind in existence." The other, so far as we can judge, is concerned with trying to make its readers believe, that it is the only one in existence that knows anything at all about Astrology, and that all the others are, fools, and pretenders, simply because they do not happen to continually advocate certain text-books, and swear by Ptolmey, to the exclusion of other teachers and systems.

To exclude Esoteric Astrology, which is our especial study, from

L

the science, is to show that the real and vital point as a student has not been reached. This pure esoteric side of Astrology, has been corrupted by those who are more anxious for fame, which they hope to gain by the predictive, and materialistic side, and their own conceit, than a study of its spiritual nature.

If Astrology were accepted in its true Spiritual light, then its preservation, through all the cycles, races, and nations would be assured, and instead of corruption in religious systems, we should have all nations recognising the wise Hand of Divinity working with a harmonious law as indicated by Planetary influence.

The planets as we see them are the physical bodies of great Spiritual Intelligences, and we believe the Sun to be the body or vehicle of the God of our solar system. It is by ignorance and abuse of the law that we come under what we believe to be Fate, and our aim is to show fellow-students how they may overcome their fate, by a knowledge of the good law.

It is no wonder that the scientific men of to-day ignore the study of Astrology, when we come to look upon the way its teachings have been presented to the world by those Astrologers who have not understood their own science, and who were entirely deficient in their knowledge as to the working of the law.

For no other purpose than that of producing harmony amongst Astrologers, was the Astrological Society formed, yet not one of these so-called astrologers have even once attended, or offered it their support and help. Perhaps this is why the Society is steadily increasing, and becoming more and more appreciated by students. It is undoubtedly a splendid thing to possess mathematical ability; but when the energy expended upon the mathematics robs the judgment, and the esoteric side is not considered, then less figures, and more reason would be beneficial. All argument is unworthy of the Astrologer, to say nothing of childish abuse, and personal disrespect. We are all nothing more than students, and when our consciousness expands to the point where we can see truth in all systems, and by tolerance we can respect every one for their opinions, then we may claim to be nearing the path of wisdom, in which the recognition of the fact that all men are brothers is assured.

We claim, and rightly too, that we are advocates of a Modern Astrology that is concerned with the real, true, inner, meaning of the science of the Stars, the only true interpretation of which, to-day, is to be found in the Wisdom religion. As students of that Wisdom religion we feel grateful for the privelege of being allowed to express through the symbols of Astrology, as much of that knowledge as we have been able to assimilate. It has brought illumination into all the dark places.

---

Dare to be true; nothing can need a lie.—GEORGE HERBERT.

\* \* \* \* \*

Grumblers never work and workers never grumble.—DR. WILLIAMS.

\* \* \* \* \*

They always talk who never think.—PRIOR.

\* \* \* \* \*

Purity of heart is that quick and sensitive delicacy to which even the very conception of sin is offensive.—CHALMERS.

\* \* \* \* \*

True worth is in being, not seeming.
In doing each day that goes by
Some little good, not in dreaming
Of great things to do by and by.—ALICE CAREY.

\* \* \* \* \*

Through the wide world he only is alone who lives not for another.—ROGERS.

\* \* \* \* \*

Self-reverence, self-knowledge, self-control. These three alone lead life to sovereign power.—TENNYSON.

\* \* \* \* \*

A man can never be happy unless his first objects are outside of himself.—ANTHONY TROLLOPE.

L  I

# The Special Meeting of Astrologers.

THE Astrological Society may be once more congratulated upon the entire success of its last general meeting. There was not a vacant chair on the night of the 1st of October, and although many were again unable to be present owing to the distance of their residence from London, the members were well represented.

The chair was taken by the Society's most practical helper and worker, Mr. W. A. Bishop-Culpeper, who opened the evening with the following remarks :—

" LADIES AND GENTLEMEN,

" In opening our proceedings this evening, I think I am entitled to congratulate the members of the Astrological Society upon the fact that this room is again so exceedingly well filled, and I may say that it is a source of satisfaction to the Council that the members of the Society show their appreciation of the efforts made to render these meetings interesting by appearing here in such numbers.

" Our Society, as you all know, has not yet been founded two years ; it is a mere baby amongst societies. Still, in that short time, it has made considerable progress, and has accomplished much. It has become well known to Astrologers, and there is not now an Astrologer of the Anglo-Saxon race who is ignorant of its existence. Whilst, among the general public, it is also becoming known, thanks to the kindness of the gentlemen of the press who favoured us with numerous notices, perhaps not all as sympathetic as we could wish, but certainly, never unkindly. However, we are not afraid even of abuse ; the old science which was practised by Noah and Daniel, and accepted by the gigantic intellect of Kepler, can still stand a good deal, and we all know that it is a true science. Our opponents can never meet us in argument, because they do not understand its principles. Whenever a man seriously takes up the study of Astrology, he never after opposes it, although, maybe, as in my own case, he commences the study disbelieving in it, and intending to write against it.

" Whilst I am prepared to maintain that our Society has made great progress and accomplished much, I am by no means blind to the fact that still a great deal remains to be done, and much more could be done if our funds would permit, but alas! the income at the disposal of the Council is extremely limited. The Council are continually receiving excellent suggestions and ideas from members, which, if they could b carried out, would undoubtedly greatly increase the influence and power of the Society for good; but unfortunately, the sinews of war are not provided quite as freely as the ideas and suggestions. If some Member, between this and our next annual general meeting, would suggest or devise a means of replenishing our treasure-chest, I am sure we should all be extremely grateful.

"Now, as I have expressed myself so strongly as to the work we have accomplished, it will not quite do for me to ignore some few remarks made by our friend Raphael in his Almanac for 1898. Raphael, as you know, is a vice-President of this Society. Unfortunately he does not agree with me, and appears to think the Society has not done as much as it might have done. I may say I was rather astonished at reading these remarks, and just at this time too, because in his Almanac for 1897 he had given us ungrudging praise, and had exhorted all Astrologers to join our Society, and thus help in disseminating truth, and he mentioned that he would like to see the Society "tackle the many humbugs who pretend to understand Astrology and deceive the public." He has also expressed the opinion, I believe, that our Society should afford assistance to genuine Astrologers who are wrongfully prosecuted. Well, directly we adopt his suggestions, and attempt to carry them out by forming an Institute of Astrologers, and founding a Legal Aid Fund, he chooses that very time to come down upon us, and says we are doing nothing! Now, ladies and gentlemen, I think you will say this is hardly consistent. To me it appears most inconsistent, and I am entirely at a loss to account for it, except by supposing that our friend, although a great prophet, is still, like the rest of us, only mortal, and perhaps at times suffers from fits of depression, and imagines all is going wrong; whilst, as a matter of fact, everything is going right! I am sure that if he would only interest himself more in the affairs of the Society, and would attend some of the Council meetings, which, as Vice-President, he has a right to do, and would enquire into all the 'ins and outs, and especially aquaint himself with the amount of funds at the disposal of the Council, he would see and admit that we are really doing our best, and, gifted as he is with strong common sense, he would be one of the first to say that we 'cannot make bricks without straw!' I am sure the Council would treat any suggestions he might make with the greatest consideration. I hope he will see his way to accept this invitation, and attend our next Council meeting. I must say I do not think Raphael intended his remarks to quite bear the meaning they appear to bear; but he simply used his words as a horseman uses a spur, in order to spur us on to still greater exertion. But a good horse, he must remember, can be driven to death, which in our case would be bankruptcy, if we go too far or too fast. I am bound to tell you that Raphael has been a most generous contributor to the funds of the Society, and a valuable and valued supporter in the past. I therefore have every reason to believe that, in the future, he will be only too pleased to re-consider his remarks, and, making the *amende honorable*, will head the subscription list for the Legal Aid Fund with a handsome donation.

" There are one or two other matters to which I should like to refer. First, I desire to call your attention to the fact that an Institute of Astrologers has been founded. It is an outcome of this Society. All members must be duly qualified Astrologers. The terms of subscription are somewhat more onerous than those of this Society. The annual subscription will be One Guinea, and candidates for election must submit themselves for examination, in one branch of Astrology at least. When they have satisfactorily passed the examination they will receive a diploma, or certificate of efficiency, which will entitle them to become Members of the Institute. A Board of Examiners has been appointed by the Council, and particulars as to time and place of examination can be obtained upon application to the Honorary Secretary of this Society. At present, the examinations will be held in London. We have received applications from several candidates in different parts of the Empire, but as we are unable at present to constitute a board of itinerant Examiners, we are obliged, regretfully, to tell these candidates they must come to London.

"The public can now safely deal with members of the Institute, and be sure of getting sound astrological advice. If, therefore, in future they consult non-qualified predictioners, they will only have themselves to blame.

"The second matter is one in which I take great interest, and that is—the Legal Aid Fund. You have all seen the appeal issued by the Council for subscriptions. I surely need not urge the great necessity which exists for establishing such a fund, and I ask you all to subscribe something at least towards it. From recent decisions, and considering the position Astrology now holds, and having especial regard to the case of Jane Smith, decided on appeal by the Lord Justice Clerk, Lord Young, in Scotland, when a conviction for fortune telling was quashed with costs, I am of opinion that no conviction will be obtained against a genuine Astrologer, if his defence is properly conducted. For this purpose, however, funds are necessary, and I hope that soon the Legal Aid Fund will be in a position to provide them.

"Thirdly, I wish to mention to the members that now, in consequence of the great kindness of Mr. Alan Leo, we have the privilege of holding smaller meetings of our Society at his house—9, Lyncroft Gardens, West Hampstead, so that we have really a *pied a terre* for the Society. I think you will all agree with me that a hearty vote of thanks is due to the President for his great kindness in this matter.

"Now, Ladies and Gentlemen, I will not detain you any longer, as doubtless, you are all more eager to listen to the lecture about to be delivered, than to listen to me begging for funds, and urging you to put your hands in your pockets, but you really must excuse me, for you all know as well as I do that if I do not ask I shall not receive!"

The Chairman then called upon the President, Mr. Alan Leo, for his lecture—"Is it wise to study Astrology?"

Mr. Leo began by stating that the constitution of the Institute of Astrologers had impressed the importance of its responsibility upon him, and for this reason it was an important subject to consider. What was the nature of the word Astrology? It was derived from

Astro—Star, and Logos—Wisdom; the value of its name was seen as the wisdom of the stars, and its full meaning meant the law of the solar system. This was the soul of Astronomy, and its antiquity could be traced in the earliest records of human learning. It was the first religion, and it would be the last. In its esoteric side it embraced all religions, and from the knowledge of the wisdom religion, from which the ideas of the esoteric side were obtained, we could see that we were studying the soul of the planets; for it was the spiritual intelligence behind the planets that poured down the influence, and not the bodies of the planets only, they were all under the guidance of the one white light from the Sun, and under that Sun were angels, lords and governors. Then from a very high and lofty view of the subject, the speaker came down to its lower interpretation, in the lords and rulers and their sub-influences; their cycles, major and minor, and their government over the year, day, hour and minute; also the relations to the positive and negative, ending in the life and form, with its vibrations, as Mars ruling from gross deep red up to the finest rose pink, having various grades of the seven colours. It was the abuse of this martian influence; which gave strength and energy, that caused all the so-called evil, ending often in violence and murder—nothing but the abuse of a great principle. Where do you get your energy from, said the speaker with emphasis, but from the spiritual ruler of Mars; therefore, why abuse this great gift of strength and energy? It was so with all the planets. Saturn was the principle of Justice—the great individualizing planet; its abuse was limitation and selfishness, producing hatred, but in itself it gave the contemplative and meditative powers. Then there was Venus, blue, whose influence was Love, but its abuse lust and sensuousness; Jupiter—representative of compassion. From this point the speaker took up the national side, in which he described the great conjunction of Uranus and Saturn, and its disastrous effect upon India, as ruled by Saturn. This indicated the breaking up of the personality of that once great nation; the life had reached its height, and now the form side must be slowly broken up to make way for new conditions.

Then, passing to the national ruler of Great Britain, we had British pluck portrayed by Mars, England's ruler; and we were able to trace the progress of that wonderful country, America, by her ruler, Mercury. This led Mr. Leo into the various causes of disaster—such as wars, epidemics, etc., and from which he made an earnest appeal to the members of the Society to realize that it was the life, and not the form, that was of the greatest value, therefore the wise ruled their stars and the foolish were smashed up by their own destructive energy.

## A Study of Astrology.

Here the lecturer made the statement that he was only a student, as all other members of the Society, but, he added, there were those who were fatalists, and those who believed in the will being free. Then he explained how we became fated; the ideals were built by the soul, and this soul was weaving the future nativity. In the Soul, or ideal, we were free, but we came back to reap our own sowing, for thoughts are things, and as our thoughts were linked to desire so were we bound to the concrete. We are always free in thought, but limited in action to those thoughts, our aim should be to make our will harmonize with the Divine will; and to do this we must study God's law, as shown in the stars.

Passing through some lofty thoughts upon moral ethics, Mr. Leo spoke of the great blessing he had obtained from a knowledge of the wisdom religion, which had awakened his soul, and without which knowledge, Astrology had no charm for him. In this lies the wisdom of the study, he said. In Astrology there are no personalities, no books or creeds; but its story is written in the skies for all to read, and there we should find the history of the world. And what was the object of it all, this great and wondrous evolution?—That we might become the perfected sons of the Logos eventually, and great masters of wisdom ourselves; then we should have the perfect nativity. The lecturer laid great stress upon man's will being *superior to steller ruling*, and how our place in evolution should be upon the upward arc, so overcoming the impelling force downward. Esoteric Astrology was the spiritual side of the science, but as the Christians had taken their Bible literally, so were Astrologers taking their science literally. But after all, the ture

Astrologer was the true Christian, for in them both **was Divine Theosophy.**

The next speaker was the Secretary, who dealt with the great value to be derived from the science, as a means of self knowledge. To keep the law, you must first know that law, and as each person was a law unto himself, he must learn to know himself—to realize what forces he has, and how to direct them; and if any man, or woman, studied their own horoscope, they would see themselves reflected as in a mirror, and realize which side of their nature was weak, whether the moral, the emotional, or the intellectual, and would thus be able to guide and train themselves, so becoming more useful to themselves and others and a greater force in the world for good.

The next point taken up was the usefulness of Astrology as a practical help to mothers, and fathers, and tutors, in the training of children. To know just the faults, and the strength of the child's nature, so as to train it wisely, to assist its growth, and to help its evolution. She remarked the time was approaching when soul sight and soul power would enable us to help the young to develop in a way that was not possible with our limited knowledge of to-day, but that time was in the future —very much in the future for many. But this self-knowledge was to be obtained by study, through the intellect; and those parents who had not, either time or inclination for the study of Astrology themselves, could not do better than get their child's nativity cast by a capable Astrologer, who would direct them how to train their children in the best possible way, and what occupation or profession was best adapted for them, when their school days were over, thus saving much of the pain the boy or girl feels, in being placed in occupations distasteful and uncongenial, and, for this reason, often unsuccessful. She would have this science, or this practical and useful side of the science, more generally known, for the young of to-day would be our future men and women, and our duty to them was of paramount importance.

She next dealt with marriage, congenial and otherwise, and said in India where they studied Astrology, there was no divorce, also remarking that any two badly mated, should strive hard to discover their points of agreement (which could be seen by a study of their charts or character) with a view to lessen disharmony, and produce unity, and accord.

The Secretary, in conclusion, said she thought it was wise to study Astrology as a means of "self knowledge" and as being "helpful in helping others." She then closed with some very sound advice to the members of the Society.

Mr. Robert King then followed with the side he had specially taken up—"Medical Astrology"—and showed the birth figure would give the cause of the disease, as well as the effect, and gave the different signs of the Zodiac in their relation to physical disease, etc., after which the meeting was brought to a very satisfactory termination. There was very little discussion or argument, and the proceedings were from beginning to end of a very harmonious and instructive character.

The following is the *peculiar* report from the *Daily Chronicle* of the following day :—

" ' Is it wise to practice vegetarianism ? ' ' Is the public house a curse ? ' ' Are newspapers demoralizing ? ' These are questions which you might just as well expect vegetarians, publicans, and journalists to ask themselves as for a special meeting of Astrologers to entertain the query, ' Is it wise to study Astrology ? ' This, however, was gravely discussed at the Memorial Hall last evening, when Mr. Alan Leo, the president of the Astrological Society, whose name suggests a haunting reminiscence of that of Mr. Dan Leno, and who was born eleven minutes to six a.m., August 7th, 1860, London, delivered a lecture with this title. The meeting was small and select, and the proportion of ladies in it was about seventy per cent. It is popularly supposed that Astrologers place an almost ludicrous value upon minutes and seconds. This was not the case last night, for although the Congregational worthies, whose portraits adorn the board room looked down upon well-filled seats at seven o'clock, it was not until twenty-one minutes 2.05 seconds afterwards that the proceedings began.

SOCIETY AND INSTITUTE.

" Mr. W. A. Bishop-Culpeper presided, and in his opening remarks said that their society was a mere baby among societies, for its birth had only occurred some two years ago. Yet he was prepared to maintain that during that time they had accomplished a great deal. It was only those people who were entirely ignorant of the science, which had been practised by Noah and Daniel, who had anything to say against it, and he was glad to say that now there did not exist any astrologer in Great Britain who did not know of the Society's existence. If they had more money they might do more work, especially in the direction of defending astrologers who were wrongfully prosecuted. He might announce that they had founded an Institute of Astrologers. All the members of this would be duly qualified astrologers, and would have to pass an examination.

## OLD MOORE AND THEOSOPHY.

" Mr. Alan Leo's lecture was a queer combination of Old Moore's Almanac and a treatise on Theosophy. He is a high priest in the craft, and rather looks down upon the people who cast horoscopes for ten shillings. In fact his work is principally concerned with the purifying of Astrology. He does not countenance the degradation of this ancient science to the purpose of forecasting the winner of the Derby or even the weather. (By the way, has an Astrologer ever ' tipped ' the winner of the Derby ?) It is with him a religion and he he is an esoteric astrologer, as one might say an esoteric Buddhist, though he frankly admits that he is only a student. Yet, while the planets rule the earth you are fated, but you are free within that fate ; in fact Mr. Leo's motto is, " The wise man rules his stars, the fool obeys them," and he might have added the lucky man thanks them. Thus, a man can change by his iron will the fighting tendency of Mars into the soft influence of Venus. How it was to be done Mr. Leo did not condescend to mention, but a blush went round the room when he referred to the beautiful planet Venus, which poured down upon the earth ' love.'

## CELESTIAL BODIES AT WORK.

" Then, dropping into the Old Moore vein, the lecturer drew attention to the fact that Saturn, with the help of Great Britain, governed India, and this planet in conjunction with Uranus had been responsible for all the troubles which have beset that unhappy country. It is a common-place to say that the ruling planet of Great Britain is Mars, and that Mercury takes care of America. It is pretty certain, though Mr. Leo did not mention it, that Mars and Mercury have been in opposition a good deal lately. But the chief point which he wishes to impress upon his audience was that by gradually climbing up the moral ladder by means of astrology they might ultimately, after many incarnations, attain a perfect nativity, in which the ego has overcome all the influences which have hitherto kept him down.

"After all, it was an interesting lecture, and Mr. Leo is evidently an enthusiast. An enthusiast has been defined as one believing ten times as much as he can prove, and proving ten times as much as anybody else will believe."

---

Life and religion must be *one*, or neither can be anything.—MACDONALD.

\*     \*     \*     \*     \*

The most beautiful thing in human life is attainment and resemblance to the divine.—PLATO.

\*     \*     \*     \*     \*

You cannot dream yourself into a character; you must hammer and forge yourself into one.—TROUCLE.

\*     \*     \*     \*     \*

Every human being is intended to have a character of his own, to be what no other is, to do what no other can.—CHANNING.

\*     \*     \*     \*     \*

Enthusiasm is the genius of sincerity, and truth accomplishes no victories without it.—BULWER LYTTON.

\*     \*     \*     \*     \*

One of the mistakes in the conduct of human life is to suppose that other men's opinions are to make us happy.—BURTON.

\*     \*     \*     \*     \*

"Can two lines teach a lesson from above ? Yes, *one* can give a *volum* 'God is love.' "—LEIGH RICHMOND.

# A Simple Method of Instruction in the Science of Practical Astrology.

### HEALTH.

TO be healthy we must be whole, or complete, and have a sound body, and well balanced, harmonious mind. It is now generally known that a healthy mind produces a healthy body; and without the mind is in a good condition, the functions of the body cannot act properly. But it is not so well known that the majority of bodily ailments and afflictions are directly and indirectly the result of the mental state; astrologically, this may be discovered by the ruler of the sixth house being Mercury, the ruler of the mind proper.

We have arrived at that part of our study where we can concentrate our attention upon the physical body, and study all the rules and methods for judging the strength of the body, its weakness, and afflictions.

It is said that, "as it is above, so it is below," we are in ourselves an epitome of the universe, each part corresponding to a part of the solar system, as follows, throughout the twelve signs of the zodiac. Aries, governs the head and face. Taurus, the neck and throat. Gemini, the arms and shoulders, also the lungs. Cancer, the breasts, stomach, and chest. Leo, the heart, back, and spine. Virgo, the bowels. Libra, the reins, loins, and bladder. Scorpio, the generative organs, and secret parts. Sagittarius, the hips and thighs. Capricorn, the knees. Aquarius, the legs and ankles. Pisces, the feet and toes.

The internal government of the body according to the signs may be classified as follows :—Cardinal signs, i.e. Aries, Cancer, Libra, Capricorn—head, stomach, ovaries, reins, liver and the skin.

Fixed signs :—Taurus, Leo, Scorpio, Aquarius —Throat, heart, generative system, kidneys and the blood.

Common signs :—Gemini, Virgo, Sagittarius, Pisces—Lungs, bowels, nervous system, and matrix.

The signs are concerned chiefly with the anatomy of the body, upon which the markings or results are indicated, and affect the external part of the structure, while the planets govern the internal, or root of the afflictions, being the cause.

The Sun governs the heart, back and all the vital springs and centres, also the right eye, if not both eyes. The Sun rules over the most vital parts.

The Moon rules over the breasts, and stomach, the lymph, and fluidic system, controlling chiefly the functional parts of the body, and probably the left eye. Mercury governs the hands, arms, tongue, brain, bowels, lungs and mouth, also the nervous system, or all that which is chiefly concerned with movement and motion.

Venus rules over the throat, reins, ovaries, the chin, and cheeks, and the venous system. It also governs the internal generative system. Mars governs the forehead, nose, sex functions, gall, kidneys and sinews; it also governs the whole of the muscular system.

Jupiter governs the whole of the arterial system.

Saturn rules the bones, joints, liver, and spleen. ⁊

Uranus governs the magnetic aura, also the nerve fluids.

In considering the nature of diseases and ill-health, it must be remembered that Saturn binds and contracts, bringing cold, and limited conditions, therefore the ailments of Saturn's afflictions will be caused by colds.

Mars is expansive, hot, and inflammatory, producing fevers, &c.

Every student can see for himself that, roughly speaking, the body is divisible into a trunk which supports the head and neck, and two pairs of limbs, the upper and the lower.

The trunk is really a large box divided by a horizontal partition—the diaphragm or midriff—about its middle into two cavities—the chest and the abdomen respectively. The upper part, or chest, has a bony framework all round, and contains one lung on each side, and the heart with the larger blood-vessels between them. The heart is practically the pump which keeps going a great system of irrigation and sewage, whereby the tissues of which the body is composed are kept bathed, like a great meadow, with the nourishing blood as it leaves the heart and goes through the various blood channels (arteries) outwards ; and by the return stream (veins) are taken up the worn-out material which is no longer of any use to the body, and has to be got rid of from the blood, on its road back to the heart, by the various excreting organs— the kidneys and liver in the abdomen, the lungs in the chest, and the skin.

The lungs consist of a series of continually dividing and sub-dividing tubes, commencing from the windpipe in the throat and ending in numbers of small cells filled with air taken in with each breath. On the surface of these cells the impure blood, containing the waste material which has found its way back to the heart through the veins, circulates in minute thin-walled blood vessels, through which a constant purification is taking place, oxygen, the life-giving gas of the air, being absorbed, which changes the dark impure blood into bright red pure blood, that again returns to the heart to be pumped out and sent circulating as a nourishing stream throughout the body ; while part of the gaseous waste material passes into the lungs and is discharged in the breath as carbolic acid and water. It is this waste material given off from the lungs which makes an overcrowded room so unhealthy.

The blood purified in the lungs and pumped out of the heart passes through a large tube—the aorta running along the backbone—straight down the trunk. It gives off branches in every direction—some upward through the neck to the head, some down each arm, some to the various organs in the abdomen, and some down each lower limb. These branches, one and all, continually divide and sub-divide, getting smaller and smaller, till at the very end, they spread out into a perfect network of small tubes, through the walls of which the blood oozes, bathing the tissues and supplying nutriment, while it is here that the waste material of which we have spoken is drawn into the vessels, which are now becoming drains ; these continually unite, becoming larger and larger, veins, going from all parts through the legs, arms, neck and body to form two big veins in the trunk, corresponding to the large arteries, and entering the right chamber of the heart. From here the blood, as we have described, passes to the lungs to be purified before going to the left side of the heart, whence it again issues in a nourishing stream through the arteries.

In the lower half of the trunk, below the midriff—the abdomen—are situated the stomach and intestines, the liver on the right side, the spleen on the left, the kidneys on both sides, at the back—tubes from which lead into the bladder, which holds the urine, formed of waste material extracted from the blood by the kidneys.

The stomach is connected with the mouth by the gullet, and the food in it is digested, that is, pulpified by its juices, and passes into the intestines. There, small vessels take up its useful liquid portions to pass into the blood, while the refuse passes through the whole course of the intestines to be discharged from the bowels.

The liver receives the blood which, having done its work in supplying and nourishing the stomach and intestines, is fouled and on its way back to the heart. It extracts from this blood the bile, so partly purifying it, and discharges the bile so extracted into the intestine, to be got rid of in that way, acting at the same time as a natural purgative and disinfectant to its contents.

The whole of this wonderful mechanism is regulated and kept going by nervous force which is supplied by the brain, situated in the skull, and by its prolongation downwards in the backbone—the spinal cord. In this wonderful nerve tissue reside the powers of will, consciousness, thought, and the sense of perception, whereby any irritation of one of the nerve-threads which ramify to and from it in all directions throughout the body, like telegraph wires to and from a central station, is translated into an act of consciousness or motion.

Although it is highly essential that we thoroughly master the practical side, by a study of the anatomy of the body, and its various functions, still we must not lose sight of the very important principle of life, behind the form. If we study the life apart from the form we must go into the abstract, or the cause plane ; and if we study the form apart from the life we shall obtain no permanent or satisfactory results. Therefore we must consider the one in conjunction with the other and not apart, but we must recognise the two as separable the one from the other.

All life comes from the Sun, in no matter what condition we see it, it must have a form upon which it may focus. All life is specialized through the media that it passes, we specialize the life as it enters us,

M

through the spleen, and in this way we may imagine how the life becomes specialized as it passes through the planetary bodies. The Sun's rays are altered by the seven planets, giving rise to colours each differing from each other. Think of the Sun as a pure white light, and then arrange the various colours according to the planets, and you will understand the planets' action first upon the mind, and then upon the body. All ideas of evil, and evil influence for the time being should be banished from the mind, and every effort should, instead, be made to grasp the idea that all is good, and that evil so-called is the abuse of good, produced in reality from a mind not at ease, disease. A time will come when disease will be treated as madness or a crime. In the natural order of the zodiac, Mercury is given as the ruler of the sixth house, clearly indicating that the mind is the root of all disease, therefore to effect a permanent cure all treatment should be mental, or magnetic. Drugs may have the affect of removing the complaint, but it is only a case of removal and not cure, nature often having to take up the work, and finally effect the cure. With proper mind control, and hygienic treatment, every one should have a healthy body.

Each individual part of the body consist largely of cells, their shape is more or less round, circular or fusiform. Living cells are masses of jelly-like material, which have the power of contracting, each cell has a separate life of its own, and a consciousness of its own quite independent of our consciousness, and we are rarely, if ever, conscious of them, unless they telegraph their needs to our brain.

It will now be necessary, before proceeding, to explain all the various diseases, and their causes, to touch upon the law of heredity, as it is called.

Every physical body born into this earth is here for the first time, but not the soul that inhabits it, that had a beginning in the far-off past, in a manner which we hope to describe in the articles upon the esoteric side of astrology. Now the body born into the world certainly comes under the law of physical heredity, but not the soul, excepting that which it takes up in affinity with its body, it is drawn to the particular environment that will afford it the necessary experience and enable it to work out that fate, which it had merited by past conduct in past previous existences.

*(To be continued.)*

# Notes on the Symbolism of Aquarius.

O sign in the Zodiac equals in interest that of Aquarius, and yet comparatively little has been written about it. It is *the* distinctly human sign as denoted by its pictorial symbol, and it is with the meaning of its glyph that I intend to deal.

One is familiar with the usual figure of the Man of Aquarius holding (carelessly to my mind) a watering-pot or pitcher by his side. On comparing this with the Egyptian and other ancient zodiacs, one is compelled to admit that the old pictorial glyph is superior to its more degenerate and modern representative.

Taking first the Esné zodiac, perhaps the oldest known in Egypt, we find the waterman apparently engaged in more active work. His outstretched hand holds a vessel from which falls a wavy stream of water.

In the temple of Denderah, of somewhat later date than that of Esné, the symbol is more complex. The man wears, instead of the burnous-like headdress, a crown adorned with five lotus buds, and instead of a single pitcher, he holds one in each outstretched hand, and consequently, two streams of water fall to the ground. In another zodiac the sign is represented by a quaint looking figure, whose body takes the form of a pitcher perforated all over its surface. Now, all these figures are intended to convey certain meanings, typified by the essential parts of the symbol, namely, the human figure and the vessel of water. It is necessary to point out that the waterman is not merely a water-holder, or a passive agent, but a water distributor, as the sign expresses the positive side of Saturn, the Sifter. Through the watering-pot, perforated vessel, or overflowing pitcher, as the case may be, passes Thought—the expression of the soul—whose symbol is water. Thus Aquarius is a thought centre, from which radiates a

luminous substance, an aura peopled by thought forms.  This idea is
more emphasized in the Mithraic glyph for Aquarius—two double-

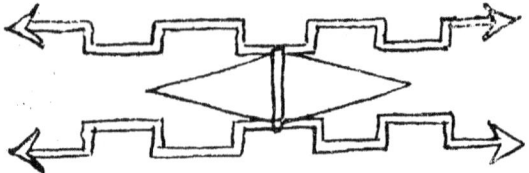

pointed arrows united by a diamond.  On the Mithraic monument this
is shown in the act of being propelled through the air.  Here the
unstable wavy lines of water are replaced by two united arrows, a
symbol fraught with deep meaning.  This sign is under the dominion
of Saturn, whose rule is well expressed by the water glyph.  The man
seeks experience through his mind, which is in constant activity,
restless as the ocean.  In his natural state he is like Reuben " unstable
as water," dimly cognisant of powers and possibilities within him,
seeking in all directions for knowledge, and knowing not that this
restless mental activity is the work of the Refiner, who " straineth all
things through his sieve, dividing the husk from the grain ; discovering
the thoughts of the heart ;  proving and purifying the spirit of man."
But it may be that the son of Aquarius, sojourning in a far country,
satiated with the husks of external knowledge, wearied with the
deceitful light of illusion, uplifts his eyes and catches a gleam from the
Star of Wisdom.  It is then his soul awakes, and his lips become
touched with the fire from off the altar.

Within the castle dungeon—powerless, forgotten, fettered—lies a
captive, the heir to a throne.  One who sold his birthright for that
which passes away.  It is he who sees that crystal ray ; and as he
drinks in the subtile essence, his fetters fall, the prison doors open, and
the captive is free.  Where there was weakness, now there is strength,
and, conscious of power, he goes forth to battle with the usurper.  So
Uranus, the wanderer, the captive, claims the throne of Aquarius, and
dons the lotus crown—emblem of his newly awakened psychic powers.
His crest is the Mithraic glyph, for his powers are united—polarised,
The arrows of his will are doubly barbed, and united by the spirit,
whose symbol is the diamond.

In the inorganic world each sand grain was once a part of a beautiful crystal of exquisite form and purity of tint, and here it lies stained and worn and broken until no semblance of its former condition is left. Yet often the microscope reveals the formation again within the grain of a crystal similar to its prototype. By slow growth, line is added to line, angle to angle, until, granting the environment is favourable, the perfect form is reached. And so it is here in the sign of Aquarius, the worn and marred soul reaches forth again to the clear and perfect crystal form who is its real self.

The reign of the mystic planet having commenced, the processes of transmutation begin. The pitcher of water withheld to the close of the feast becomes the pitcher of wine, true wine of the spirit. The dual streams of water become the united fiery arrows which strike with irresistible force. Here is the sacrifice on Elijah's altar, the body is there drenched with water, and now the fire descends to consume the offering. As one has said, " It is he that scattereth, yet gathereth. It is he that poureth out his soul unto death, yet liveth."

It will thus be seen that the Son of Aquarius has great powers if he but learns the Secret of Satan, and illumined by the Sun goes forth to battle. Long may be the strife, he may fall, yet will he hear the war cry. Though he cry " My sword is broken, my shield pierced by the evil ones," yet shall strength come to him. The darkness may cover him, yet shall he see his star above him, and to him that over-cometh there is the crown of victory.

One other thought relative to this sign, and that is the power of intuition inherent to Aquarius. The vessel of water may here among other things, be the cup of Joseph, or in Anna Kingsford's words "The Chalice of Divination, all the forms of Nature are reflected therein ; " and in connection with this, one sees that Joseph corres-ponds to Uranus in his coat of many colours, his bondage in Egypt his intuitive powers, his liberation and subsequent exaltation.

" EBN-EL-DELOU."

# "In Defence of Astrology."

IT is exceedingly gratifying to the Editor and writers of "MODERN ASTROLOGY" (a journal devoted to purifying and re-establishing the ancient science), to find that the chief occultist of the century, "Madame Blavatsky," in the third volume of the "Secret Doctrine" just published), has a special chapter entitled "The Defence of Astrology." Realizing the age in which we are living—with its materialism and sensualism; its doubt, ridicule and scepticism—she used both pen and personal influence to defend the ancient wisdom, buried under form and symbolism; to uphold the truth and realities which she KNEW lay behind what most people to-day call that absurd rubbish—Astrology.

We Astrologers are specially grateful to that "Great Soul" for helping us, and as we think it will interest our readers to see the arguments she has used and the evidence she has brought to bear in the defence of the science we love well, we purpose each month to give portions from this valuable work treating of the same.

Madame Blavatsky is no longer with us but her words remain, affecting the world's thought and a living tribute for all time. The "Secret Doctrine" being generally acknowledged by all cultured and educated minds to be the most wonderful and momentous work of this century.

"In Defence of Astrology (Secret Doctrine p. 339.)" "From the first invention of the hieroglyphics, it was *not* the vulgar but the distinguished and select men who became initiated in the secrecy of the temples into the science of every kind of "Astrology," even mark you! into its most abject kind, that Astrology which (*alas*),—the italics are ours—later on found itself prostituted in the public thoroughfares.

There was a vast difference between the sacred science taught by " Petoseris and Necessos" the first Astrologers mentioned in the Egyptian manuscripts, believed to have lived during the reign of Ramesis 11, Sesostris (King of Egypt), and the "miserable charlantary of the quacks, called chaldeans, who degraded the Divine Knowledge under the last Emperors of Rome."

" Siderial influence is dual." There is the physical and physiological influence, that of exotericiseri, and the high spiritual, intellectual and *moral* influence imparted by the knowledge of the planetry gods.

" Arago, a luminary of the nineteenth century supports the reality of the siderial influences of the Sun, Moon and planets. He asks ' where do we find lunar influences refuted by arguments, that science would dare to avow ?'

" Bailly having, in the eighteenth century, put down (as he thought) Astrology as *publicly practised,* dares not do the same with *The real Astrology.* He says,'Judiciary Astrology was at its origin the result of a profound system, the work of an enlightened nation that would wander too far into the mysteries of God and nature."

" A scientist of a more recent date, a member of the Institute of France and a professor of history, Ph. Lebas, discovers, unconsciously to himself, the very root of Astrology in his able article on the subject, in " The Encyclopediæ Dictionary " of France. He well understands, he tells his readers, that the adhesion to that science of such a number of highly intellectual men, should be in itself a sufficient motive for believing that all Astrology is not folly. While proclaiming in politics the sovereignty of the people and of public opinion he cannot admit as heretofore that mankind allowed itself to be radically deceived in this only ; that an absolute and gross absurdity reigned in the minds of whole nations for so many centuries without being based on anything, save— on one hand human imbecility, and on the other charlantary ? How for fifty centuries and more can most men have been either dupes or knaves ? . . . . even though we may find it difficult to decide between and separate the realities of Astrology from the elements of invention and empty dreaming in it. . . . . Let us repeat with Bossuet and all modern philosophers that ' nothing that has been dominant could be absolutely false.' Is it not true, that there is a physical re-action on one another among the planets?"

Is it not again true that the planets have an influence on the atmosphere and consequently a mediate action on the vegetation and animals?

Has not modern science demonstrated these two points beyond any doubt? Is it any less true that human liberty of action is not absolute; that all is bound; that all Leigh's planets, as the rest, act on each individual will; that Providence—law of cause and effect—acts on us and directs men through those relations that it has established between them and the visible objects and the whole universe. We are bound to recognize that an instinct superior, to the age they lived in guided the efforts of the ancient Magi. As to the annihilation of human moral freedom with which 'Bailly' charges their theory, Astrology, the reprobate, has no sense whatever. All the *Great Astrologers* admitted without one single exception that man could re-act against the influence of the stars. This Principle is established in the 'Ptolemæian Tetrabillos,' the *true* astrological scriptures, in chap. II and III of that book.

"Thomas Aquinas has corroborated Lebas in anticipation; he says, "The celestial bodies are *the cause of all that happens in this sublunary world*, they act indirectly on human actions: but not all the effects produced by them are unavoidable (the wise man rules his stars, the fool obeys them)—the italics are ours."

"The occulist and theosophist are the first to confess that there is white and black Astrology. Nevertheless, Astrology has to be studied in all its aspects by those who wish to become proficient in it; and the good or bad results obtained do not depend upon the *principles*, but in the "*Astrologer himself*."

B. LEO.

*(To be continued).*

---

We have only just time to announce the departure from this life of Mr. Edward Maitland, who breathed his last at 10.15 p.m., October 2nd. As far as we can ascertain he was born on October 27th, 1824, in some later issue we hope to compare this date with his death figure.

# An Essay on The Astral Forces and the Relation of the Planetary Rays to Art and Science.

### No. I.—MUSIC AND COLOUR.
### By AGAR ZARIEL.

T has often been stated, and the remark is by no means of recent date, that " Astrology " (*i.e.*, the external creative forces operating as zodiacal and planetary influence) "is the origin of every art and science known to man," and, we may add, or that ever will be known.

The electric and magnetic variations in the atmosphere, the continuous and gradual changes from day to night, the ebb and flow of the tides, the seasons of the year and alterations of temperature, times of famine and of plenty, epidemics of sickness or of crime, the births and deaths of all organized beings, the vibrations of colour, the vibrations of sounds, the different stages of life and of destiny in members of the same family, important changes and discoveries in the progressive sciences, all are due directly or indirectly to the never-ending and varying etherial vibratory forces, or Astro-magnetism, which pervades the universe, operating according to its prevailing intensity and quality upon every atomic part of the earth and all that exists upon it.

As most people are aware, there are seven primary orbs in our solar system, viz.: the Sun, Moon, Mercury, Venus, Mars, Jupiter, and Saturn. These assume various scales of inter-action according to the plane of manifestation on which their operations fall, as in the "seven ages of man," so beautifully described by Shakespeare; in the seven primary colours of the prism, naturally illustrated by the rainbow; in the seven primary sounds of the musical scale; in the seven characters of wisdom, &c., &c.

The number seven is one of great and mystic influence on human life, and this is little to be wondered at when we consider the ponderous natural forces at work around us from which the activity of this number upon mundune effects are derived.

In acute disease, the seventh day is always considered as one of the most critical to the fate of the patient.

Mr. Wynn Westcott says in his work on " Numbers "—

" After birth, the seventh hour decides whether the child will live;

in seven days the cord falls off; in twice seven days the eyes follow a light; in thrice seven days the child turns the head; seven months gives teeth; twice seven months, sits firmly; thrice seven months, begins to talk; after four times seven months, walks strongly."

"After seven years, teeth of second set appear; after twice seven years is the arrival of generative power; after thrice seven years the hair of manhood is completed; after four times seven years we cease to grow; at thirty-five is the greatest strength; at forty-nine is the greatest discretion; and seventy is the natural length of life."

Four times seven days corresponds to the lunar month; the body contains seven vital organs; and there are seven senses, &c.

The peculiar influence of this number has from the earliest ages been attributed to the influx of the seven primary orbs of the solar system in their electro-magnetic actions upon the earth, and all that breathes upon its surface.

The seven days of the week are also derived from the same source. Everything around us teems with evidence which, to the thinking mind, cries aloud in an unmistakable voice.

The successful physician is one who, whether as a result of study or by natural instinct, selects his remedies according to astral sympathies with the necessities of his patient.

The successful surgeon is one who, whether as a result of study or by natural instinct, selects such moments for performing operations which are in astral sympathy with the life forces of his patients and the nature of the operations.

The successful agriculturist is one who, whether as a result of study or by natural instinct, selects such periods for preparing the earth or sowing seed which are in sympathy with the astral conditions most suitable for such purposes.

The successful navigator is one who, by a careful observation of the astral positions in connection with his local bearings, can describe his exact place on the ocean and so guide his vessel to any part of the world.

Wherever we turn in the regions of science and art, whether of an exact or progressive nature, we find a reference in the origin of required force and action to the great celestial machinery.

The painter and musician are in constant touch with the astral vibrations on which their arts entirely depend for existence.

Heat, light, colour, and sound are intimately related, all depending upon vibratory forces for their manifestations. The vibrations of light when resolved into colour by aid of a prism, as in the rainbow, produce seven primary sensations known as prismatic colours, viz.: red, orange, yellow, green, blue, indigo, and violet.

It is the variation of intensity or rapidity in the vibrations which makes the difference in our sensation of colour. The following table by Sir John Herschel gives some interesting particulars and shows the number of etheric vibrations which affect the eye in the brief space of one second of time. Those persons whose optic nerves are not sufficiently sensitive to distinguish the difference between 458 billions and 727 billions in the velocity per second are known as colour-blind. These are the approximate limits of the vibratory forces between the extreme red of the lower range and the extreme violet of the higher register in the prismatic variations.

## VELOCITY OF "LIGHT" WAVES.

| Colour. | Vibrations per inch. | Vibrations per second. |
| --- | --- | --- |
| Extreme Red | 37,640 | 458 billions. |
| Red | 39,180 | 477 ,, |
| Intermediate | 40,720 | 495 ,, |
| Orange | 41,610 | 506 ,, |
| Intermediate | 42,510 | 517 ,, |
| Yellow | 44,000 | 535 ,, |
| Intermediate | 45,600 | 555 ,, |
| Green | 47,460 | 577 ,, |
| Intermediate | 49,320 | 600 ,, |
| Blue | 51,110 | 622 ,, |
| Intermediate | 52,910 | 644 ,, |
| Indigo | 54,070 | 658 ,, |
| Intermediate | 55,240 | 672 ,, |
| Violet | 57,490 | 699 ,, |
| Extreme Violet | 59,750 | 727 ,, |

Heat, light, and colour produce their sensations through the etheric vibration, and sound through atmospheric vibration, each bearing some affinity or relation one with the other, and with the seven primary celestial orbs, assuming different scales of manifestation according to the plane of operation, differing in degree of potency, character, and quality according to the mental or physical state.

Acting through the mental-nervous system of the human frame upon the organic functions, red is found to operate as an excitant or stimulant, answering to the martial influx. A familiar instance of this influence is the effect of this colour upon animals of the bovine species.

Orange is found to act as a tonic, answering to the Solar ray.

Yellow acts as a laxative or aperient, and corresponds to the Venus ray.

Green is a passive or mediating influence, forming a kind of link or go-between, and answers to the Lunar ray.

Blue is decidedly sedative, soothing, and melancholy in quality, answering to the cooling, meditative, Saturnine ray.

Indigo and purple is the royal colour, suggesting majesty and justice, which answers to the Jupiter ray.

Violet is a sensitive, delicate, tender hue, resulting from the highest vibrations of the colour rays, and is the mental ray of Mercury.

Like the seven primary tones of the musical scale, these colour rays have their intermediate or half-tones, representing a chromatic progression, as orange, *intermediate*, yellow, or C, *C sharp*, D.

Nowhere is this planetary, colour and tone sympathy better represented, than by the influence of sound considered in relation to the arrangement of tones, as used in the illustration of musical art, and it proves itself so neatly that the inevitable connection of colour and sound with the planetary rays is manifest, which the following explanation may demonstrate.

The musical scale, consisting of the seven primary tones used in modern composition, is an artificial arrangement which has undergone various modifications during past years in the development of this sublime art. As given to us by nature the succession of tones constitute what is known as the scale of harmonics, or harmonic chord, in the following order :—

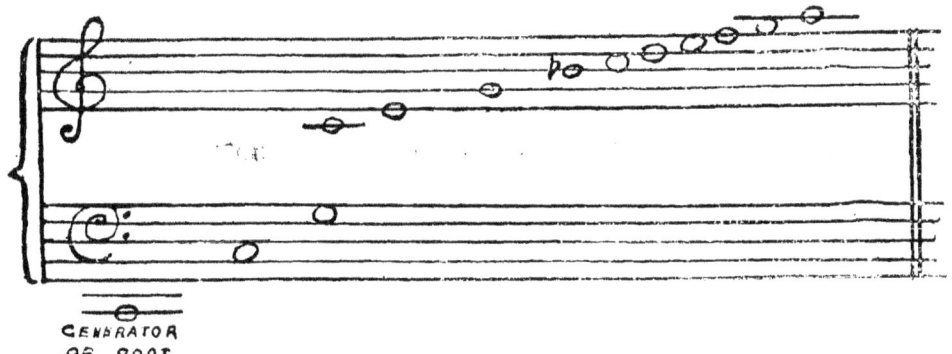

GENERATOR
OR ROOT.

In this natural series of sounds which is the same as produced by any sonorous tube, string, bell, or other tone-producing article giving the note C as a foundation or open note, there is one sound of the artificial scale missing, viz.: the B natural.

A tube or string giving C as a generating or open tone will always produce B flat amongst its harmonics, but never B natural, which indicates that though generated *on* C the tones as a whole are *in* the key of F, where the B flat finds an important place.

In order to generate a series of sounds which proclaim the key of C, we must take the note G as a root, thus:—

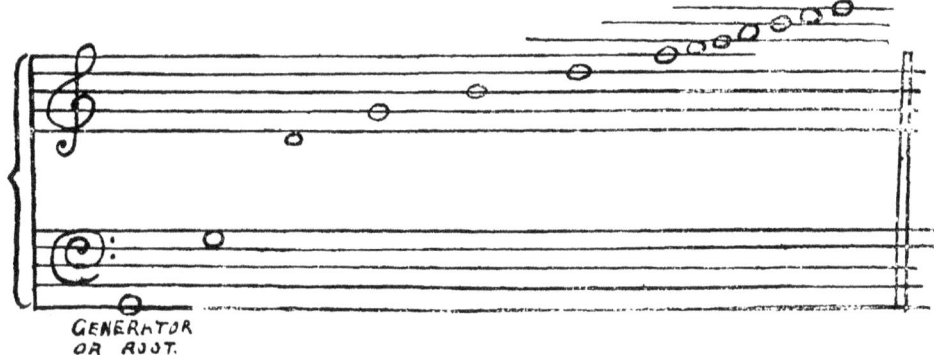

GENERATOR
OR ROOT.

In this series, though founded upon the root G, the combination of tones is unmistakably in the key of C, as my musical readers will know. The order of notation in our modern diatonic scale, say of C major, is therefore an artificial arrangement of the foregoing sounds according to certain established rules of art.

The root or generator of a series of these natural harmonic tones is called the dominant of the key, and is the fifth note of our artificial ascending scale. The note G, therefore, on which the preceding series of harmonic tones is founded, is the dominant and fifth note of the ascending scale of C in modern notation.

This key (the dominant) is beyond all question the martial sound, red in colour and dominating in force over all the others ; it serves to bind the relation of all the rest to the tonic or key-note of the scale.

The peculiar characteristics, quality, and effect upon the senses of certain notes in the scale, at once suggest their planetary and colour sympathies.

The first of the scale, key-note, or tonic on which the scale is built is the representative tone of the sun and suggests the solar orange ray of light.

The second of the scale or supertonic has a peculiar quality of romantic sentiment, having an affinity by attraction with the fifth of the scale (martial note), and a contrast of quality with the fourth of the scale. As will be shown later on, the second of the scale represents the yellow or Venus ray.

The third of the scale or mediant belongs without hesitation to the green, Lunar ray, as will prove itself by its special contrasts and affinities.

The fourth of the scale or sub-dominant is the most majestic note of the series, and as will be demonstrated, gives the royal purple or indigo ray of Jupiter.

The fifth of the scale or dominant is already described as the red, martial tone.

The sixth of the scale or sub-mediant is the most weird and melancholy tone of the series, and at once suggests the cold blue of the Saturnine ray.

The seventh of the scale, sensitive note, leading note, by its evident mental impression associates itself as the highest vibration with the Mercurial violet ray.

Now, to find the provings of this classification let us refer the tones to their successive order as used in modern art. Here follows the diatonic scale of C major, which employs the natural tones within the space of an octave :—

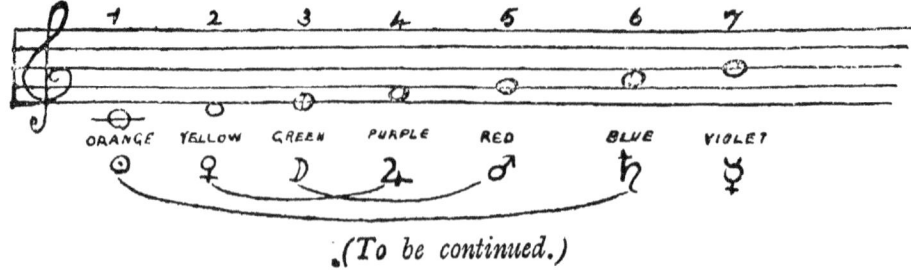

*(To be continued.)*

# Astrological Stories.

## CHAPTER IV.

WELL! Well! said the Squire, " it is all Greek to me, but Bess has surely had that fever, eh, wife, but I did not think about it at the time, but accident by fire· Eh!" "Yes! Yes!" exclaimed his wife, surely you remember the children' sparty, at Mr. Ransome's, when the decorations took fire, and Bessie's dress was all in a blaze, and his son rolled her in the hearthrug, and badly burnt his arm in the doing, while our darling had not a mark. Don't you remember now, dear?"

"Yes; how came I to forget," though it must be all five years ago. I remember sending him that cob, "Jennie" out of gratitude. Your brother is uncanny; but his power is great, and it has so far all come true; but think you it all will in the future?"

"Yes, I believe in this law," said Mrs. Lennox, gravely. "It is divine, not human, and cannot err." "But," said the farmer, slowly filling his pipe, "your brother speaks of more lives than one. In my young days, they would have said he was mad; but everything is different now. I suppose it is all education. For me, I am a plain man; what was good enough for my father and my grandfather before me, is good enough for me. But you and our little maid be different somehow. Still I shall go and see Sapal and tell him three of his prophecies are come true; and so I am bound to believe him."

"I doubt you will find him at home, my dear. In his last letters, he speaks of going to India again. May be he has already sailed, wait a few days Squire. I am even now expecting a letter."

She rose as she spoke and locked away most carefully her

daughter's chart, and then turning to her husband said, " it's just on one o'clock, my dear.   Let us sleep on it."

Some two years later, as Squire Lennox entered the breakfast-room. he was greeted by his little daughter rapturously dancing around him, " Father ! Father " she cried ! " what do you think has happened.  Willie Arter has three hundred pounds left him, and he is going to be educated, and be a doctor he says."

" Stop !  Stop !  Bessie, not so fast," and turning to his wife, he said, " what does the child mean    "

Mrs. Lennox proceeded to explain, that Willie Arter's father had a brother, who years ago, went to America, and had not since been heard of ; but that he had died recently, and left all he had to his nephew Willie, and the lawyer had written to say it was between three and four hundred pounds.

"Yes," exclaimed Bessie, "Uncle Sapal said, he would get some money, and that he must be trained for a doctor, when he came and seen us, Mother—two years ago ! ! !

Bessie's uncle had stayed a day or two with them previous to sailing for India, and had seen Willie Arter and put up his horoscope, and given advice to his parents as to the boy's training, etc.  Willie's father, though only a labourer, was intelligent, and extremely proud of his son.

" That 'ere boy will rise in life, mother," he had said many a time as he sat smoking by the kitchen fire.  " The gentleman at the house said he were to have money left un, I doant see where it be to come from, I'm sure."   Now all doubts were solved, and Willie was to go to a large public school at once !

" This is a remarkable coincidence," said Mr. Lennox.  Bessie's excitement had somehow communicated itself to him.  He rose and rang the dining-room bell.

" Jane," he said, " send Edmund down to Arter's cottage, and say I desire to speak with him and his son."

Always generous, the Squire said : " Bessie, you and Willie Arter are the same age—twelve years old to-morrow. Would you like to give him a present?" "Oh yes, father," she cried, her eyes dancing with glee. "I like Willie so much. He brought me Ruff, a tiny fox-terrier, and Dandy, a white kitten."

"Well, child, what shall we give him?" "I know, father—a watch!"

"Right you are, Bessie"; and we will have his name engraved on it, and the date. We will drive Nanny to the nearest town.—Mother, you and I, and choose it."

A few days later Willie left an environment, to which he never returned.

"How does the boy get on?" The squire would now and again ask Arter.

"He be getting on fine, sur, and schoolmaster do say as how he be a genus, whatever that mid mean."

A year or two later Willie's mother died suddenly, and soon after her husband left the farm, so Willie faded out of the minds of Squire Lennox and his wife, but Bessie remembered her playfellow, and often wondered where he was.

---

When alone we have our thoughts to watch; in the family our temper; in society our tongue.—HANNAH MORE.

\* \* \* \* \*

The years write their record on human hearts as they do on trees, in hidden inner circles or growth which no eye can see.—SAXE HOLIN.

\* \* \* \* \*

Books and magazines are but white paper unless men spend in action the wisdom they get from thought.—BULWER LYTTON.

\* \* \* \* \*

Who is powerful? He who can control his passions. Who is rich? He who is contented with that he has.—TALMUD.

N

# Calendar for November.

"Be humble, if thou would'st attain to wisdom,
Be humbler still when wisdom thou hast acquired."

November is the ninth month of the Astrological year, the Sun this month entering the sign Sagittarius. During the first twenty-one days of this month the Sun is in the sign Scorpio, the eighth sign of the zodiac, the sign of the Scorpion. This sign rules over poisons, drugs and chemicals.

---

Mrs. Annie Besant lectures at Queen's Hall, Langham Place, at 7 p.m. on October 31st, and the 7th and 14th of this month on "PROBLEMS OF LIFE AND MIND."

---

TABLE FOR THE MONTH OF NOVEMBER

| D M | D W | Moon at Noon. | LUNAR ASPECTS at GREENWICH. Before Noon. | After Noon. | General Mutual Aspects. |
|---|---|---|---|---|---|
| | | ° ′ | | | |
| 1 | M | 8 ♒ 0 | □ ☿ ⚼ ☿ | □ ☉ △ ♀ | ♀ ∠ ♅ |
| 2 | Tu | 21 ,, 20 | ⚼ ♃ □ ♂ | △ ☿ ⚼ ♀ | ♂ ∠ ♃, ♀ ∠ ♄ |
| 3 | W | 4 ♓ 22 | □ ♅ □ ♄ | △ ☿ | ♄ ♐ |
| 4 | Th | 17 ,, 7 | △ ☉ | □ ☿ △ ♂ | ♀ ⚺ ♂ |
| 5 | F | 29 ,, 40 | △ ♅ ⚼ ☿ | △ ♄ ☍ ♃ ⚼ ♂ | ♃ ♎ |
| 6 | S | 12 ♈ 3 | ...... | ⚼ ♅ ⚼ ♄ | ♂ ♏ |
| 7 | S | 24 ,, 16 | ⚹ ☿ ☍ ♀ | ...... | ☉ P ☿ |
| 8 | M | 6 ♉ 22 | ...... | ∠ ☿ | ♀ △ ☿ |
| 9 | Tu | 18 ,, 22 | ☍ ☉ ⚼ ♃ ☍ ☿ Noon. | ⚺ ☿ ☍ ♂ | ☉ ∠ ♃ ☿ ∠ ♃ |
| 10 | W | 0 ♊ 17 | ☍ ♅ | ☍ ♄ △ ♃ | ♂ ♅ ☿ |
| 11 | Th | 12 ,, 8 | ⚼ ♀ | ...... | ☿ ♅ ☿ P ♂ |
| 12 | F | 23 ,, 57 | ☌ ☿ | △ ♀ | ☿ ☌ ♂ P ♄ |
| 13 | S | 5 ♋ 47 | □ ♃ | ⚼ ☉ ⚼ ♂ ⚼ ☿ | ♂ P ♄ |
| 14 | S | 17 ,, 40 | △ ☉ ⚼ ♅ ⚼ ♄ | ⚺ ☿ | ☿ P ♅ |
| 15 | M | 29 ,, 42 | △ ♅ △ ♂ △ ☿ | △ ♄ ⚹ ♃ □ ♀ | ♀ ♏ |
| 16 | T | 11 ♌ 56 | ∠ ☿ | ...... | ☿ ☌ ♅ ☉ P ♄ |
| 17 | W | 24 ,, 27 | ⚹ ☿ ∠ ♃ | □ ☉ □ ♅ □ ♂ □ ☿ | ♀ ⚺ ♅ ♃ |
| 18 | Th | 7 ♍ 21 | □ ♄ ⚺ ♃ ⚹ ♀ | ...... | ☿ ☌ ♄ ♂ P ♅ |
| 19 | F | 20 ,, 42 | ...... | □ ☿ ∠ ♀ | ☿ ⚹ ♃ |
| 20 | S | 4 ♎ 33 | ⚹ ☉ ⚹ ♅ ⚹ ♄ ☌ ♃ ⚹ ♂ | ⚺ ♀ ⚹ ☿ | ☉ P ♅ |
| 21 | S | 18 ,, 53 | ∠ ☉ ∠ ♅ ∠ ♄ ∠ ♂ | △ ☿ ∠ ☿ | ☉ ☌ ♅ ♂ ☌ ♅ |
| 22 | M | 3 ♏ 41 | ⚺ ☉ ⚺ ♅ ⚺ ♄ | ⚼ ♆ ⚺ ♃ ☌ ♀ ⚺ ☿ | ☿ ♐ ☉ enters ♐ |
| 23 | Tu | 18 ,, 49 | ∠ ♃ | ...... | ♂ ♐ |
| 24 | W | 4 ♐ 7 | ☌ ☉ ☌ ♅ ☌ ♄ ☌ ♂ | ⚹ ♃ | ♃ ♎ |
| 25 | Th | 19 ,, 24 | ⚺ ♀ ☌ ☿ | ☍ ☿ | ☉ ☌ ♄ P ♂ |
| 26 | F | 4 ♑ 33 | ⚺ ♅ ⚺ ♄ ⚺ ♂ ∠ ♀ | ⚺ ☉ □ ♃ | ♀ ♏ |
| 27 | S | 19 ,, 16 | ∠ ☉ ∠ ♅ ∠ ♄ ∠ ♂ ⚹ ♀ ⚺ ☿ | ...... | ⚹ ♃ ♂ ☌ ♄ |
| 28 | S | 3 ♒ 36 | ⚹ ♅ ⚹ ♄ ∠ ☿ | ⚹ ☉ ⚼ ♀ △ ♃ ⚹ ♂ | |
| 29 | M | 17 ,, 29 | ⚼ ☿ | △ ☿ □ ♀ ⚹ ☿ | ☿ ♐ |
| 30 | Tu | 0 ♓ 55 | □ ♅ | □ ♄ □ ♂ | ♂ ⚹ ♃ ☿ ☍ ♆ |

The value of the foregoing table is very great to those who believe that there is a time for everything; in the August number the meaning of the symbols are explained. It will be seen from the table for November that the mornings of the 4th, 15th, 20th, are free from evil aspects, therefore these are good periods, a knowledge of the symbols and aspects is necessary for those who desire to benefit by the table, all that is required is a very little practice.

## A Strange Omission.

### NO OFFICIAL RECORD OF THE QUEEN'S BIRTH.

Curiously enough, neither the birth, baptism, nor confirmation of Queen Victoria is a matter of official public record. One might suppose that, filed away in its appointed place among the State archives, there could be found a document formally setting forth the birth of the child who, though not heir-presumptive to the throne at the time of the birth, was removed from it by only three degrees. But such is not the case. With regard to her birth, all that was deemed necessary was its announcement by the State officials whose duty it was to be personally cognisant of the fact.

In the huge public records building in Chancery Lane, wherein are jealously guarded the muniments of ancient landed titles and the records of Royal treaties, one may see the marvellously well-preserved Doomsday Book, which is the beginning of all things to the English convenancer; the solemn compacts of cardinals, envoys, ambassadors, and ministers; the priceless records of Royal prerogatives side by side with the grants wrung from unwilling monarchs to the growing power of the people. There, also, are preserved, and with equal care, a multitude of writings which have no other interest, despite their antiquity, than that which comes from the fact that they have to do with the trivial details of the most common incidents in the lives of the kings and queens of England. But among them all there can be found no official or other record of the coming into existence of a certain child, one Alexandrina Victoria, who was destined to become greater than all those whose merest doings are so faithfully recorded.

" *Daily Mail," July 7th, 1897.*

# Predictions.

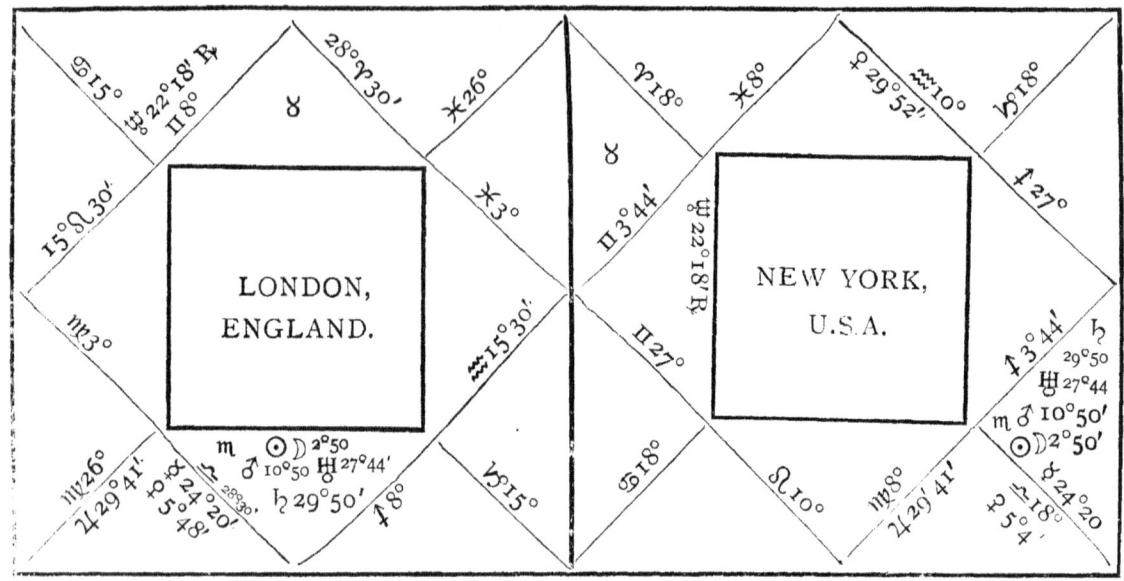

E have already given some of the predictions for this month of November in our last issue, under the heading of Predictions. For England the map is by no means an unimportant one, no less than five planets falling in the fourth angle, in the fixed and malignant sign of the scorpion.

From the above twin maps we may add to our previous remarks, obtaining our judgment from the houses in which the planets are placed. Considered in conjunction with the map for the year, March 20th, the majority of the planets fall in the unfortunate sixth house ; the ruling sign of the fourth in that map being upon the cusp of the first in the above figure. As we have before remarked, everything depends upon the judgment in reading the mundane figures. The new moon for the month of November is very decidedly an unfortunate one, and in it we can forsee grave disasters, and every indication of this month being serious for the nation. The death-rate will be unusually heavy, and before the lunar month is ended there will be many very shocking and sudden deaths. Strange and mysterious murders will again remind us of those unfortunate and horrible crimes which occurred in the East-end a few years back, and women of the unfortunate class will again be the victims of atrocious crimes, many of which will remain undiscovered. We shall be shocked by terrible tales of rape and seduction. There will be much sexual disease, causing the medical profession great activity.

Spiritualism will find many fresh adherents, and advance their cause. We shall hear of important discoveries in chemistry, and an extension of electrical appliances, the Rontgen rays making way for a still more important discovery, to the profound astonishment of the scientific world, the discoveries being concerned with the ether, etheric waves or vibrations. The women's movement will be active and there will be progress made toward their liberation and freedom. A theatre is threatened by fire.

The weather will be particularly rough, and severe during the lunar month, and towards its close we shall have heavy gales, and snow storms, and the news of heavy losses at sea will be frequent.

From shipwrecks and murders, also violent deaths of many kinds this month will be noted by its heavy mortality.

The map for New York indicates much sickness, and great danger of a serious epidemic in the United States. There will be an unusual tendency of the people toward phenomenal magic, and a spiritualistic prophet will arise, who will create an extraordinary sensation in the States. Some important discoveries with regard to air machine inventions may be expected, and for America generally the month will be full of important psychological magical phenomena.

Although the outlook for November appears so gloomy, there is a bright ray of hope shining out from the benefic Jupiter, who throws his beneficent rays to the sextile of Saturn and Uranus.

This will mitigate, and ward off a considerable amount of the evil, and, to a great extent, tone down the dark influence of the Scorpio conjunctions.

Just as a single ray of sunshine may light up the darkened places, and break of day scatter the darkness of the night, so may this Jupiterian brightness overcome the shadows that loom around us this winter.

If the powers for good can stay the overcrowding world's fate, then we may feel that the spiritual tide has turned upon the upward arc.

# Birthday Happenings.

**A**LL persons born in November are distinct from those born in any other month; each month marking off a division out of the twelve signs of the zodiac, through which the Sun appears to pass in the course of the year of 360 degrees, or 365 days. The division ruling this month is that called by name, Scorpio.

The negative, or night house of Mars, this is the eighth sign, ruling all matters of occultism, and change out of the physical, or concrete, into the plane next above it, called the Astral plane. The Novembrians, to coin a new word for them, are in many ways very remarkable people, they have tenacious wills, an undercurrent or deep reserve, and a great deal of secretion in their nature. When Venus and Mercury also fall in this sign at birth, they can be very proud, extremely jealous, and self-willed. More or less the Scorpio tendencies are toward the mystical, and occult, they know the value of silence, and do not waste many words in speech, and in all their attachment they work along the plane of action.

In giving the following indications for the month of November, it should be understood that the information can only be general. The birth time is always essential where accuracy of detail is required. Persons who know their nativities will understand how much reliance may be placed upon the information.

1st.—This is not a favourable birthday, persons in the employ of others will be in danger of losing it, they should avoid all pride, and obstinacy, and try to be submissive until they come under better influences. There will be trouble through correspondence, and children. New acquaintances will be made, and a friend added to the family circle.

2nd.—Some trouble may be expected during the year, arising from disputes, or accidents, keep the blood pure, be careful in love affairs, and study diet.

3rd.—Sudden events will happen, and the year will tend to be very unfortunate. Avoid speculation, theatres, and elderly persons. Do more by correspondence than personal interview.

4th.—There will be some pleasure during the year, courtships for the young, and offspring to the married. Travel will bring pleasure.

5th a.m.—You will travel, and have many strange experiences during the year, take pleasures quietly. P.M., take care of your health, avoid all rashness, and take no journeys.

6th.—Inflammatory complaints threaten you, avoid all feverish excitement, and live quietly during the year.

7th.—You will have disappointments in love affair, which will produce sickness through grief. You will profit by the year's experience however.

8th.—The year will be unimportant, be careful who you lend money to.

9th.—Domestic strife and law suits will bother you, your finance may prove a source of worry, it will be a very unfortunate year, and unless you are exceptionally careful one that will be full of losses and trouble.

10th.—Much unhappiness is indicated, losses through death, but gain thereby financially.

11th.—Deaths will occur, causing you much worry and mental anxiety, trouble will come through your relatives, or neighbours.

12th.—Watch your dreams, you will obtain some very valuable information while your soul is away from your body during sleep.

13th.—You will have many obstacles to contend with during the year, travel is indicated, probably through domestic affairs.

14th.—You will have changes, which in the end will turn out beneficial, accept things as they come, it will be best.

15th.—New light will dawn upon your mind this year, and some very beneficial changes will place you in a much better position, expect advancement, and progress.

16th.—Sudden and unexpected mental experience will break up some of your convential tendencies, in advanced and higher thought you will find a new field of activity.

17th.—Your heart will suffer, be prepared for shocks, the year will be a very trying one, be very careful of your honour and good name.

18th.—You will gain by the loss of an aged person, beware of dishonesty, and fraud, you will lose an old friend and gain a young one.

19th.—There are some good influences at work, with care all will go well.

20th.—This is the most fortunate day in November, and will prove to be a most successful and lucky birthday anniversary. Great benefits will come to all born on this very fortunate day, whatever happens will bring eventual good, and out of the most sudden events harmony will spring, all energy wisely expended will bring a tenfold interest.

21st.—Sudden crashes, and much sorrow is threatened, avoid marriage and all new ventures and enterprises.

22nd.—You will gain through the sudden and unexpected death of some relative.

23rd.—Some sorrows are looming, do nothing rashly or hastily.

24th.—A complete change in your surroundings is indicated, and your actions should be the result of very careful premeditation, or you will find yourself involved, through public bodies, and persons in authority.

25th.—This is a very unfortunate birthday, and you will bring many troubles upon yourself by your own actions. Avoid horses, and all sports of every kind.

26th.—Financial losses are threatened, look well to your business and your honour.

27th.—There are good and evil influences at work, and on the whole the year may be made very prosperous.

28th.—The year will be successful, and you will gain, both mentally and physically, many benefits through industry are promised.

29th.—For correspondence and literary matters the year will be successful, but in love affairs, and social matters expect disappointment.

30th.—This is not a fortunate birthday, yet amid the gloom there will be many streaks of bright sunshine. Pain is the teacher, and through pain we realize.

---

## GENERAL ADVICE.

The whole of the above remarks have reference to the personality, or the physical, and limited concrete part of our nature. We are free by knowledge, and it is not until we know, that we are able to act with discretion, and forethought, therefore all experience should be welcome, as it enables us to free ourselves from the bondage of convention, and limitation. The self side of life clings to the objective, and material, and all breaking away from it brings Pain, *the teacher.*

# Editorial Comment.

E have expended over one thousand pounds upon this magazine, and we are now making further arrangements to expend a large sum of money, and also a considerable amount of time upon its future developement. If we can carry through our ideas, we hope to issue with the next number the finest Christmas number ever before attempted by an astrological monthly. This new venture will raise MODERN ASTROLOGY to a very high position in modern journalism, the nature of the contents for next month, being in its tone, literary ability, and illustration as perfect, as superior art and skill can make it. We propose publishing an occult and magical story of the very finest description, in which a strange occult power is abused by an Astrologer who turns his abilities into the black art, and thereby becomes a terrible Black Magician. We want all our readers to tell everyone of their friends about the Chistmas number of MODERN ASTROLOGY this being a splendid opportunity for making our science known to all classes of readers. Regular readers and subscribers have now an opportunity to induce the news agents in their various towns to stock the Christmas number amongst their other various periodicals. We can assure our readers, that it will reflect to their credit, any efforts they may put forth. If possible the price will remain unchanged, unless the size is considerably increased, the whole idea being to increase the circulation, and thus popularize the grand truths of Astrology. May we rely upon your support, and help to make Astrology wider known? If you have appreciated our work, here is a grand opportunity to show your gratitude, and help us to at once double the sale and usefulness of MODERN ASTROLOGY.

MAY WE ASK YOU TO SPEAK TO EVERYONE YOU KNOW ABOUT THE GRAND DOUBLE CHRISTMAS NUMBER OF *MODERN ASTROLOGY* AND ITS REMARKABLE AND WEIRD OCCULT STORY. READY NOVEMBER TWENTIETH.

# The Students' Corner.

Puzzle Horoscope, No. 1.—The remarkable event that occurred to the native, was, the loss of his foot, on the date mentioned.

The competition for the various prizes stated in the August issue, will close at the end of this year, so that the successful contributions may be published in the present volume; which closes with the January number.

*　　*　　*　　*　　*　　*　　*

The following data has been received from various members of the Astrological Society :—

Female child, born at Manchester, at 1.55 a.m., July 28th, 1897. Died of convulsions at 3 a.m., August 19th, 1897.

Male, 7 months child, born, 10.30 a.m., May 22nd, 1887. Lived just 10 hours.

Male, born 11 a.m., November 17th, 1888, Brooklyn, U.S.A. Died, 2.35 a.m., December 26th, 1896.

Female born, at Ramsgate, 4 p.m., June 20th, 1871. Died at 1.40 a.m., September 4th, 1891, at Margate.

*　　*　　*　　*　　*　　*　　*

The passage of Saturn, and Uranus, is probably responsible for the following cutting ;—

"Readers of the newspapers cannot have failed to notice the remarkable epidemic of murder through which London and the neighbourhood is passing. Every day of late has seemingly brought one or more ghastly crimes to swell the list, and it may well puzzle the shrewdest physiologist or most experienced magistrate to account for this September death-roll. Statistics used to show that France surpassed us in crimes against the person, while English criminal records showed the way for crimes against property. At the present rate, however, London will soon be able to compete with the slums of Naples, and some of Professor Lombroso's theories will have to be remodelled."

*　　*　　*　　*　　*　　*　　*

Female, born at Barkworth, 3.30 a.m., March 6th, 1866. Has been deaf and dumb from a child.

Female, born 6 a.m., March 10th, 1880, Leeds. Is now supposed to be in a consumption, her mother died of this, and a complication of diseases on April 7th, 1894.

The City of Liverpool is undoubtedly ruled by Scorpio, as the following cutting willshow :—

"LIVERPOOL KNIFE OUTRAGES.—" Mr. Justice Bruce, who after his indisposition resumed his seat on the bench at the Liverpool Assizes on Saturday, passed various sentences of penal servitude for wounding with knives: John Kelly, labourer, six years; James Kennedy, aged twenty-two, five years; William Sunderland, aged twenty-nine, six years; James Baker, aged eighteen, barber, five years; Joseph Donovan, nineteen, labourer, five years; John Jordan, four years, and a number of others to twelve and eighteen months' imprisonment.

"His lordship, before pronouncing the sentences, said from the character of some of the cases one would almost think that Liverpool was a barbarous country instead of a Christian community, men and women appearing to use the knife with very little provocation. It was necessary for those who administered the law to inflict severe punishment in such cases."

T. P. states that Mrs. Maybrick was born at Alabama, U.S.A., at 6 a.m., September 3rd, 1866.

A member of the Beginners' Class sends the following :—

Male, Born June 14th, 1891, 8 hrs. 15 mins. a.m., Portsmouth.

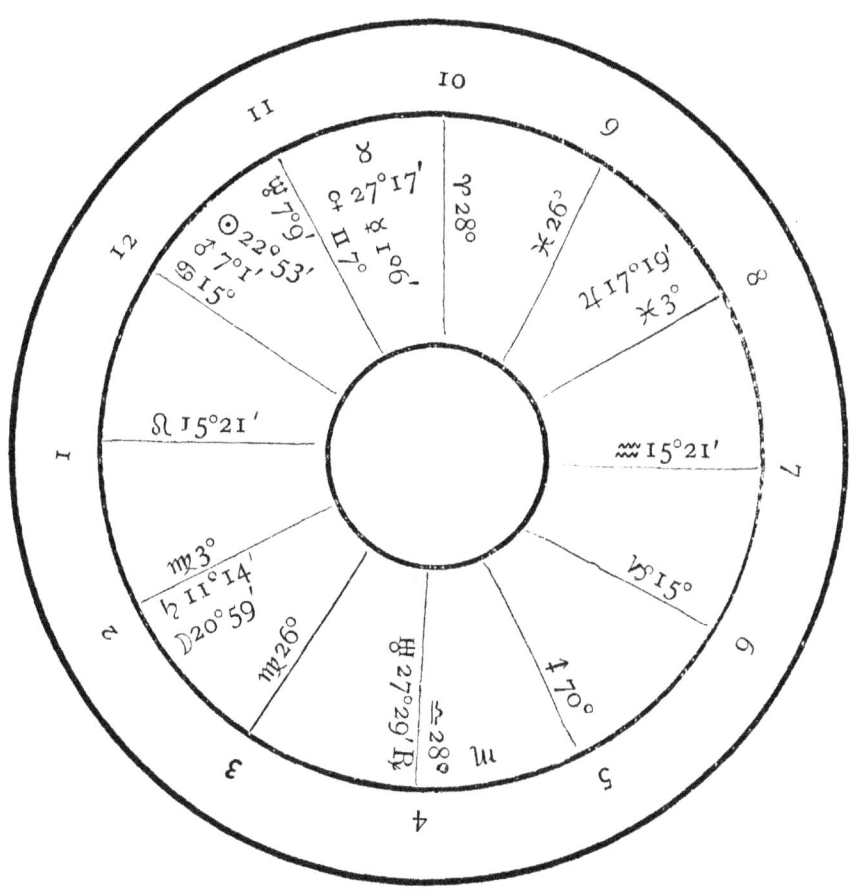

Declinations.

| ♅ | 10° 5' | ♃ | 6° 8' | ☉ | 23° 16' | ☿ | 17° 56' |
| ♄ | 9° 13' | ♂ | 24° 14' | ♀ | 18° 16' | ☽ | 8° 14' |

Boy born at 8.15 a.m., June 14th, 1891, although apparently strong at birth, has been ill almost ever since, but now appears stronger. He has had bronchitis several times, congestion of the lungs twice, pneumonia (for which he had an operation) and croup.

The boy's mother (who was born January 1st, 1867, at sunrise, in India, and who is of a very nervous, hysterical, and passionate temperament), was at death's door for many weeks after his birth, with puerperal fever, but ultimately recovered. He is the only child.

The mother married September, 1890, and the marriage has not proved a very happy one ; in fact, separation has more than once been contemplated.

* * * * *

Another writes as follows :—

With regard to the recent conjunction of ♅ and ♄ in ♏, do you not think that the outbreak of Typhoid at Maidstone may be attributed to it ?

I see by paper that the first 2 cases were reported on the 11th September, so probably the first outbreak of the epidemic was on the 10th of that month.

Now on the 9th September ♅ ☌ ♄ occurred at 9.54 a.m. on the same day the ☽ was □ to both ♅ and ♄, and applying to ☍ ☉, the complete aspect being at 2.12 a.m. on the 11th, and on that day being also ☍ ♃ and □ ☿. This certainly is remarkable, and surely would point out to some unusual occurrences.

The great fire in the Blackfriars Road shortly after midnight of 1st October seems to have occurred with ☽ ☍ ♅.

The positions being :—

☽ 22° 50″ ♐.

♅ 22° 33″ ♊.

"The Astrologer of 19th Century" states according to *Coming Events*, that 24° to 28° of common signs are calamatous degrees, and the transits of planets in them are productive of great destruction of life and property, both these planets being very near, but not quite in these degrees.

However, we find ♃ in 14° ♍ 36′ and ☿ almost then being 23 ♍ 37, so that they would be □ to both ☽ and ♅. This is a coincidence, and evidently points to an astral cause, and not mere chance.

\*    \*    \*    \*    \*

R. H., born 5 a.m., June 14th, 1890.  Lat. 50° 54′ N.  Long. 5 m. 35″ W.

The boy **was** adopted when 5 weeks old by a doctor and his wife, who are anxious that he should never know that they were not his real parents. Will he ever discover it? The doctor guarantees the time of birth, being present at the occasion.

The *Cymric*, a new steamship for the White Star Line, was launched at Messrs. Harland and Wolff's yard, at Belfast, on Tuesday. Her gross tonnage is 12,300 tons and displacement 23,000 tons, and she is by far the largest cargo steamer in the world. The exact time for this event was 10 hours, 29 minutes, 30 seconds a.m., October 12th, 1897.

\*    \*    \*    \*    \*

The launch of the *Canopus* took place at Portsmouth at 0.35 p.m., October 13th, 1897. The planet Mars had just culminated in Scorpio.

\*    \*    \*    \*    \*

A PROPHESYING COMPETITION.—The Khan of Baluchistan has lately lost his Court Astrologer, who was fortunate enough to die by a natural death. It is said to be an honourable and a lucrative post, and when the Lord High Commissioners of the Baluchistan Board of Examination notified the general public that the office of official star-gazer was vacant, no less than twenty-one candidates gave in their names for the forthcoming examination. An examination of astrologers personally supervised by the ruler of the land is surely something picturesque for a prosaic era, but ex oriente miracula. The questions and their answers would be interesting, for the adviser is adviser also in politics, and only consulted on great occasions. After two days Mir Mahmud Khan dismissed fifteen candidates; probably their paper work, as an Oxford don would say, was not satisfactory. Six he kept for the viva voce. These six are now on their trial for a certain number of weeks. They have each to prophesy freely during that period, and their forecasts are written in a book. These prophecies may only deal with events that can be verified in the six weeks' probation, and the man who comes nearest to the truth he is the new Court Astrologer.—" Pall Mall Gazette."

# Letters to the Editor.

Sir,—"J. W." puts me a question about the Paris fire. This occurred on May 4th last. The figure for the Spring Quarter shows the beginning of Aquarius culminating, and the early part of Gemini rising. The Sun, lord of the fourth, was at 0° ♈ in square to Mars in the second at 29° ♊ 15′. Apart from its bearing upon money, this would naturally indicate danger to houses from fire; for the Sun is lord of the fourth house, and Mars is just entering the fourth sign. On the day of the fire the Sun had reached 14° ♉ 15′ (at noon), and therefore was in exact semisquare to the place of Mars in the quarterly figure.

The New Moon preceding the event occurred on May 1st. Mars, lord of the ascendant and the fifth, was at 20° ♋ 45′ in the eighth house in square to the cusp of the fifth—signifying death at places of public entertainment. The lord of the fourth, Jupiter (in the fifth at the quarter) was in square to Saturn, rising. Mars had also reached the square of the quarterly Moon at 20° ♎ 14′, so that two very bad "directions" measured to the time.

But I imagine the real question to be—"could any Astrologer have foretold that this would take place in France and not in England?" I think it impossible with our present knowledge of the subject. As "J. W." remarks, the figures were practically the same for both countries. Very often the mundane figures for London will, for all practical purposes, serve also for the whole of the Western end of Europe; and I am not aware that any Astrologer pretends to be able to say in which of the various included countries the worst effects will fall. This difficulty is constantly arising. It cropped up over the assassination of President Carnot (see *A. M.*, Vol. v., page 4). Sepharial, in referring to the subject at the time, wrote that, while danger to rulers was indicated, "it would have been difficult to have centred the prediction upon France."

It is not uncommon for mundane predictions in the almanacks to fail in England but eventuate in France.

I am obliged to "J. W." for his reference to my predictions. My only reason for discontinuing them was lack of the necessary time. Will not "J. W." carry them on? I have no doubt the Editor will be pleased to afford him space.

Yours truly,

H. S. GREEN.

DEAR SIR,—I am sorry to see Mr. Pearce on the war-path. I was stupid enough to think he had had enough of wrangling, but it seems not. As for your system of astrology being 250 years behind the times, what of that? It does not matter whether it is 250 years or 2,500 so long as it is the most accurate, and I maintain that it is.

But I must be careful what I say, for Mr. Pearce is not in the roll of common men. He was actually born *twice* according to his own showing, the second birth occurring just 35 minutes after the first! In other words he has two remarkable horoscopes of himself. The explanation of this wonderful feat of natal juggling I leave to him to explain.

His latest effusion appears to be that of an anonymous letter which he publishes, and in which the writer sighs for the early death and burial of MODERN ASTROLOGY, oblivious of the fact that it has lived longer than all the magazines of Mr. A. J. P. put together, and is likely to live longer still. The same writer makes an attack on me. He says I give the longitude of ☿ on January 1st, 1862, as 28° ♓ 24′, which is false, as any of your readers may see by referring to the reprint.

Before looking too closely into my figures he should see that Mr. A. J. P. is blameless. If he wants some of this gentleman's errors here they are:— January, 1898, latitude of ♀ given as N should be S. Longitude of ♂ September 13th, 1896, 15° ♊ 43′ should be 15° 33′. The rising of the ☽ from May 26th to June 10th, 1896, is something like an hour wrong, more or less, each day. These are errors I have come across in a casual manner and without any seeking.

I do not blame Mr. A. J. Pearce in any way, but simply mention these errors to show your readers that he is no more accurate than I am. Mistakes will occur, although I use every precaution to prevent them.

RAPHAEL.

---

## Questions answered by the "Astrologer."

*(See August Number for Particulars).*

*Enclose Twelve Stamps for Post Answers.*

---

*No. 58.—Mr. N. Swaminadhaiyar.* Yes, you will take a long voyage which may be to England, the change is not for the better financially, but in other respects yes, very much.

*No. 59.—Jyekishan.* One of your sons will be very successful in connection with theatres, but his moral character will be ruined.

*No. 60.—Frankenstein.* Yes, five years hence.

*No. 61.—Nix.* You would have a strange marriage three years hence, but it would be wiser for you to remain single.

*No. 62.—November.*  Yes, you may marry the person born at the time you state.

*No. 63.—Carnation.*  Yes, you will marry.

*No. 64.—Pshaw.*  A very sudden change of mental attitude, and an uncommon event in connection with travelling, which in some way will affect your honour, and finance.

*No. 65.—T.H.*  The weak points will express themselves in an unhealthy love of pleasure, he must be early taught to respect the purity, and chastity of women.  His conduct in the pursuit of pleasure will produce serious, and incurable diseases, his mind and senses are curiously interwoven.  Teach him how to control his passions.  (Boy born 5.56 a.m., April 30th, 1890.)

*No. 66.—Clara Ghys.*  Yes, there is some likelihood of a happy marriage, but not just yet.

*No. 67.—G.A. 44.*  Long voyages are indicated about the 35th year, you will soon take some shorter journies.  Always travel in a south-easterly direction, travel will bring pleasure.

*No. 68.—D.M.O.*  Your request is far too serious, and demands more time than we can give gratis, but we will publish your letter in the Student's Corner if you desire, please let us know per return.

Theodore Wright is requested to send his address at once, a letter awaits him at this office from abroad.

––––––

In future the following COUPON must be sent with all questions to which a reply is required under the above heading.

Special replies are sent by the editor, through the post to those who remit **2/6** Stamps, or Postal Order with their question :—

---

*November, 1897.*

[COUPON].

TO THE ASTROLOGER.

––––

Kindly answer through the pages of "MODERN ASTROLOGY," the question attached to this Coupon.

––––

*Nom de plume*......................................

---

LONDON :

Printed by the Law & General Printing Co., 1 & 2, Bouverie St., & 66, Borough Road ; Published Monthly by the Proprietor, Alan Leo, at 9, Pleydell St., Fleet St., EC.

# Modern Astrology

### Edited by
### ALAN LEO, P.A.S.

## The Official Organ of the Astrological Society.

Vol. 3, No. 5.    ✳    DECEMBER, 1897.    ✳    Price 1s.

## To Our Readers.

THIS year we are, for the first time in our history, trying the experiment of a Christmas Number; whether we have been successful or not in pleasing all our usual readers, we wait to learn. To those who prefer our ordinary monthly, with its deep and metaphysical handling of the Science of Astrology, we hope they will not this month be too much shocked and surprised at its altered appearance. To those who are in full sympathy with our work, we would ask them to take this opportunity of recommending this number to all who are likely to be drawn, for the first time, to our special study. Personally, to us, Christmas time is no different to any other time, although the Sun lays for three days and three nights at the same declination, but it will rise again and ascend into heaven. But it is a general holiday-making, festive period, and we have broken out of our usual style to scatter a few crumbs, for those who prefer some lighter reading, into which, we hope, the undercurrent of truth may attract to its more serious side. To those who are reading this magazine for the first time, a few remarks upon what the Science of Astrology teaches may not be out of place. Astrology is an *exact* science, but it is a science connected with causes first, and effect afterwards. Every soul in this

world is clothed with a physical body, the fate of which is governed by law—that law acting through the planetary spirits as governors, and rulers under the Great Power at the head of our Solar system, upon the ether and finer portion of substance, affect the various inner bodies in which the Soul is *en rapport*. Our actions, through the direction of the mind, disturb the etheric vibrations, and sets up between ourselves and the law, a vibration which affects our future thoughts and actions. Hence we are only free within a limit, and that limit marks our fate. It is therefore necessary for us first to know the law, or by correspondence *know ourselves*, and with this knowledge guide our future. If custom or habit binds us, then are we bound to its limitation and not free. The astrologer sees the limitations and the will, also the character and mental qualifications, and knows what the nature of the past must have been to produce the present reaping of past sowing, and to a certain extent he sees the future of that soul and its struggles to unbind its own bindings. In the very essence of things each soul is free, being of the same spiritual essence as the absolute, but it is bound by its vehicles and its desires. Freedom comes when we work for the evolution and benefit of humanity, and not against it. It is a freedom of choice to serve under the great law for good and harmony. From the lowest to the highest all are under the one law, and it is the work of Astrology to unravel the mysteries, and this MODERN ASTROLOGY seeks to do month by month.

With regard to the astrologer's idea of Christmas. The birth of the Saviour of the World of the virgin is interpreted as nothing more or less than the descent of spirit into matter, or the Virgin soil of the very highest and refined substance, down into the lowest and most concrete physical matter, from which the spirit is to ascend again, and rise triumphant, having obtained the Christ's or individualized soul, into the heaven of bliss, where it may attain the at-one-ment with its parent source the Father or God of the universe. The only crucifixion that Astrology can believe in, is this spirit upon the cross of matter, and the only sacrifice that unspeakable act, whereby our Divine Ruler circumscribes himself to sustain the life of His universe.

# THE MYSTERY OF EUNICE;
## — OR —
# THE HAND OF FATE.

" Our birth is but a sleep and a forgetting ;
    The Soul that rises with us, our life's star,
Has had elsewhere its setting,
    And cometh from afar."

*Written for Modern Astrology by* B. LEO

N the year 1797, railway, telegraph, and telephone were not in existence, and the rush and turmoil, consequent on these increased powers of communication, had not yet disturbed the placid tenor of individual life. Conventionalism and orthodoxy were general, and those larger minds, that dared to think for themselves, were pointed out as objects for scorn and derision.

Superstition and ignorance, being rampant among the many, the advanced few kept their views and opinions more or less secret.

Mesmerism or magnetism, was being tested by the medical schools of the day, the lesser mysteries in connection with the Delphic oracle were now under the title of physiognomy, receiving attention by a few scholars, chief amongst whom was the celebrated Lavarter, who in 1783 had written a remarkable manual upon this subject.

Astrology was practised, having almanacs and mystic publications, and although this art was studied secretly, it was fast making many converts, who still preferred, as in the present day, to keep their knowledge from ridicule and abuse. In the masonry of the times some of the ancient truth had been preserved, and its teachings lay at the root of all mystical societies, and occult orders.

It was upon the occult arts, and mystical subjects in general, two persons were discoursing, as they strolled along side by side, all engrossed with each other, unheeding and unheeded by, the few chance pedestrians, who happened to be within their vicinity.

It was the spring time of life with both, though the man was the older of the two; that they were wealthy their appearance would denote;

that they were cultured, both voice and manner betrayed; that they were in love could be seen at a glance.

"Julian," said the girl, raising her blue eyes to the face of her companion, and speaking earnestly, "we have had so much time for study and thought, and so little of life's cares to worry us, is it any wonder we think more seriously than the ordinary man and woman of to-day? It is, however, somewhat curious, that both our minds run in an occult groove; we are both seekers of hidden causes, rather than the effects produced. It is a vast problem to solve, Julian, the inequalities of the human race are so very obvious. Why have we so many advantages that others lack? However, it gives me joy to realise that we shall help to raise the world's standard of thought, Julian," she said, and her eyes grew misty with emotion, "I feel loving God is serving our brothers and sisters, and so many blessings seem to have fallen in my way. The love of my parents, a childhood of bliss; and now, you have come into my life to fill my cup to the brim. My heart is full of gratitude; I would that all were as happy as ourselves."

She put her little hand within his arm, and he clasped the small fingers, feeling all too deeply at the moment for words, realizing as he did, that the girl beside him had become his world, his life, and his hope. Yet it was not the subtle spell of beauty that held him captive, though Eunice was fair to look upon; no, it was her character, her soul, and the purity of the maiden, for he had met nothing like it in the world he knew so well.

"Eunice," he said at last, looking at her sweet face, radiant with love of the loftiest kind, "can it be but two years since first I saw you? To me it seems a life time. The poets write of an immortal love, a love that lives on when the bodily form has long been dust. Did we meet in some other world in the far-off ages, I wonder? I cannot believe the feeling we have for each other is the outcome of only two years' growth." His eyes assumed that far-away look that Eunice had learnt to know so well.

Julian Stanton was not only a scholar and metaphysician, but an earnest soul. To all queries as to his religious views, he would simply answer, "I am a truth seeker, but only a religion that will satisfy head and heart will content me. I realize the heart in the Christ, but my head cries out for knowledge." A strange man, said friends and acquaintances; not yet thirty, and holding such strange and peculiar views; what a pity he is not more orthodox!

The sun was just setting, and here and there clouds of gold melted into faint crimson, while others stood out like snow-capped mountains in the distance, and seemed even whiter than the rest, by contrast. They looked at the sinking monarch of the day, these two so shortly to become one, and a silence fell upon them; they felt that mysterious magnetic power of sunset, the hush that seems to fall upon all nature made itself felt.

The sympathy between them was so perfect, that each understood the other's feelings, without any words. Only six weeks to-day, and Eunice Graham and Julian Stanton were to become man and wife, linked together, one in soul, heart and mind; that perfect union wherein the tastes and sympathies all agree.

Eunice Graham was an only child, and the very idol of her parents' heart, for she, (the youngest of their four), alone had lived.

She had been educated by a refined gentlewoman of mature years, who grew to love her charge, well nigh as tenderly as the girl's own parents. This lady's death had been the only grief Eunice had ever known. Occurring when her sixteenth birthday had only just passed, it caused Eunice to lose the thoughtlessness and playfulness of early girlhood, and seek to realize life's purpose, and its problems. The presence of that grim adversary, who, notwithstanding all that medical skill and Eunice's care could do, swept away from touch and sight a loved presence, gave the girl her first realization of sorrow, parting, and pain; but it stirred her slumbering soul to action, and although Eunice, at the time our story opens, had seen scarcely twenty-one summers, she was grave and thoughtful, beyond her years; what the sunshine of joy could not affect, the rain of tears brought about, and some of life's deepest problems found a place in the mind of Eunice Graham.

" Our Eunice has never been the same since Emma died," her mother would remark, "she is not like other girls of her age, she is too serious."

"Bless her sweet face!" said her father, "she is better so: the little lass will forget bye-and-bye, Joan, when a new love comes into her life." But years passed, and Eunice did not forget, but studied, read and thought deeply, and the mystery of life and death was the thing she most desired to know.

The inequalities of the human race, why some were found in such abject poverty, and others wealthy, troubled Eunice greatly. Father, mother, minister, all told her it was the will of God, but this did not satisfy either her sense of justice or her reason.

Some two years previous to the date, upon which this story opens there had been a series of lectures, given upon physiognomy and character. Eunice had been a regular attendant, at these very interesting lectures, and upon one occassion had persuaded her father, who was a man of scholarly habits and tastes, to accompany her, and he had consented. Julian Stanton, who happened to be there, on that evening, had noticed them come in, and the great beauty and intelligence of the girl's face had rivetted his attention.

The room was unusually hot, and Mr. Graham, unaccustomed to public gatherings, was taken ill. Julian saw what had happened, and noticed the distress upon the girl's face. He leant over (he was sitting just behind them) and said, "Don't be alarmed young lady, it is only the heat that is thus affecting the gentleman." He pushed down a window near, and taking Eunice's fan proceeded to wave it rapidly in front of Mr. Graham, who slowly revived. Julian then assisted him outside.

To call their carriage was the work of a moment, and as Julian knew of a friend near, a medical man of note and reputation, driving there occupied little time. The doctor assured them, after examining Mr. Graham, it was only the overheated atmosphere, that had caused her father's attack, and that there was not the slightest cause for alarm or anxiety.

"How can I ever thank you, sir?" said Eunice, at parting, her lovely face lit up with gratitude, the tender mouth quivering with emotion, the sunny curls falling in disarray about her shoulders. A vision of youth, purity and loveliness calculated to fascinate and charm a man of more mature years than Julian Stanton.

"You must come and see us," said Mr. Graham, and then cards were exchanged, when greatly to his surprise Mr. Graham discovered Julian's father and himself were old schoolmates, and close friends in boyhood.

Colonel Stanton, Julian's father, was dead, but the old regard for the father was extended to the son. So it happened, that with the full consent of both parents, Eunice was now Julian's promised bride. Julian's only brother was in India—the land in which their mother died—and Julian, who had been a great traveller, had at last settled in London, and was living alone in true batchelor fashion.

So the Grahams' old fashioned house near Hampstead, became in time a perfect home for the young man, while as the months rolled on, a fair face watched for his coming, and grew crimson at his step, while the frank blue eyes smiled their welcome.

With Julian, love's passion flower first unfolded, but he realized the extreme purity, and ideal tendencies of Eunice's nature, and for at least a year they were but friends, reading and discussing the poets, or in the twilight Eunice would play soft melodies on the spinet, or anon they would all discuss graver themes. Eunice's mother was orthodox, but her father, with his keen intellect and larger mind, saw religion did not explain life's purpose, or its mysteries. "Joan," he would say tenderly enough, if he felt he had shocked his wife's sensibilities, "thou art a good woman truly, but a philosopher, never."

So time passed on ; with each day that Julian spent beside Eunice, he realized more and more her lofty, moral nature, her tender heart and intelligent mind ; unlike most men he loved character, not the form only, but the mind and soul behind, and one day he told Eunice he loved her and desired her for his wife. "I am not so pure as you, my Eunice, and yet methinks my ideal is purity, and with you to help me, I may yet live it. To have one woman only, one mate to whom I can devote my life, that is what I have often desired. Out from the world you stand for me ; for you alone have touched my heart ; for other's my lower nature has been stirred to action, but my heart, never ; and now I ask you, dear Eunice, will you take me just as I am ? a man of the world in a way ; some call me hard, positive, and proud, yet you know something, dear, of that higher side of my nature, my better self ; for your sweet sake I can become anything, and yet I would not be selfish, if you do not care for me in this way, Eunice ; say so, we can still be friends, but I feel the devotion of my heart must have entered your own."

Eunice rose, and came over to him. " Julian, I am yours ; let us help each other to live a noble life. Dear Julian, I have never loved any but you, for you alone have responded to that inner something I feel, but cannot describe. Do you remember our talks of Plato, soon after we met, and you said you believed there was a love not born of the senses, but of the soul ; that a perfect union between two might be had, even as between Christ and the Church. It would be perfect, because no self could enter into it, or the animal nature ; and you quietly remarked, 'If I could get a woman to live with me in friendship, and share my name as wife, my ideal would be realised.' Julian, that was my ideal too, only I heard it voiced for the first time by you ; I loved you then, and I love you now. To me marriage ever meant congenial tastes, mind, and desires. What your past has been I do not seek to know, but if there be any page in it not fair to look upon, it is past, and you have grown wiser by the experience. Besides, I, too, have many faults and shortcomings, Julian, but together we shall find mutual help and comfort."

" You must not take Eunice out of England, when she is your wife," said Mr Graham, " that is our only proviso. The travelling days of the wife and I are over, Julian, but I can trust your father's son, my old friend's son, to be a tender husband to our darling. She has never known harsh words or anger, but the little maid is not spoilt."

" We could not spoil her," said Mrs. Graham, "dear Eunice has never given us one sorrowful day. Only I think she is too earnest and sober for her age. She has such deep, devotional feelings, and spiritual emotions, but like her father, she is, as you know, unorthodox in her views, and inclined to think for herself, and I fear she will grow more so, as you and Julian encourage all her mystic tendencies and peculiar thoughts. You will be good to her " the mother cried, " a strange feeling of trouble is about me, a presentiment of danger to the child.   Only last night I dreamt that she had left us for ever," and Mrs. Graham stopped, overcome by emotion.

" Joan what ails you ?" said her husband "you are not becoming a dreamer, wife, or a visionary, surely ? "

" Dear Mrs. Graham, Eunice will be my constant charge, I know she is not strong, but I will shield her as far as  man can do from outward pain and sorrow; beside, bethink you, Eunice would be left alone, when in the course of nature you two are called away.   I am but just thirty, and  hope to cherish Eunice for many a long year to come."

" Yes, yes, it is all for the best," said Mrs. Graham, "and I feel a great trust in you, Julian, it is not altogether that, but some instinct that seems to warn me of approaching danger and disaster."

" Who is talking of disaster pray," said Eunice tripping up to her father, and fondly kissing him. " Why mother you look distressed, is it on my account ? remember dear, you only gain a son, you can never lose your daughter," and she came and sat upon a footstool, and laid her fair head upon her mother's lap.  " Mammey (her childhood's pet name for her mother), dear mammey, you are dearer than ever now to your daughter's heart."

" Julian, who is Jubal Tankard ?" said Eunice, as they entered the house together about a fortnight later on.  " As I was playing the spinet last night I heard you talking to father of someone, and the name, Jubal Tankard caught my fancy, is he a friend of yours ? "

" No, darling," said Julian, " not a friend of mine at all.   It was Dr. Richardson who mentioned him to me.   He says he is a mesmerist and magician, has queer gifts of occult power, and also practises what some

people are foolish enough to term the 'black art,' I mean Astrology.
Dr. Richardson says he knows the cause of disease, and can prevent a
person feeling any pain by a few passes of his hand; that he can live for
several days without food, and that he told him he could (by putting his
body to sleep) visit other countries and patients, in a finer one, and
diagnose their diseases."

"Oh! Julian, is it possible?"

"I know not, Eunice, but he has some strange secrets and magical
powers, because my friend say's he believes it to be quite true that
Jubal Tankard can see the interior structures of persons and diagnose
their diseases and so often cure them.   He has got a most tremendous
will, I hear, and can work miracles with it."

"Have you seen him, Julian?"

"No, Eunice; but I fully mean to do so later on, for in spite of all
his skill and power, I hear he is poor.   He has written some most
valuable books on herbs and magic, but for want of funds is quite unable
to publish them ; this he is most desirous of doing, my friend tells me,
as he wants to become famous and is most remarkably ambitious for
power, money and fame.   You see, Eunice, I might be able to help him
financially, and that is the reason why I intend to see him for myself
some day."

"Is he a good man, Julian," said Eunice.   As she spoke a strong
shudder shook her, and anxiously, Julian turned up the lamp.

"Are you cold my darling?" and he took her hand in his.   "Yes,
you are; and you lock pale too, love.   Are you sure you feel
quite well?"

"Oh, yes, Julian, it was only a nervous feeling ; it seemed to me as
if this man was going to be our evil genius.   Don't think me superstitious,
but indeed, Julian, I feel he is not a good man.   If he is a magician, he
may gain some strange power over you, don't have anything to do with
him."

"Of whom are you speaking my child?" said Mr. Graham, entering
the study at that moment.

"Eunice and I" said Julian, "were discussing Jubal Tankard."

"Yes," said Mr. Graham "he practises magic, does he not, or something of that kind? I remember you telling me something to that effect; Eunice, you look pale, my child, I hope you do not feel ill."

"I have only a slight headache, father," said Eunice, rising as she spoke, to take off her outdoor wraps.

"Eunice sometimes has a curious fragile look," said Mr. Graham, as she left the room, "and yet she has never been ill in her life. Ah, yes, that reminds me, Julian, typhoid fever and diphtheria are prevalent at present, so Dr. Richardson tells me. He stopped me as he was riding by, to caution me not to let Eunice go her Samaritan rounds at present, nor enter any of the cottages in the valley—diphtheria is terrible there.'

"Sanitation is not carried on properly" said Julian, and then the two became engrossed in practical plans for helping and relieving the distress.

"Good night, Julian," said Eunice a few hours later, as she stood in the porch to watch his departure. In the silvery moonlight her face looked almost transparent; "God be with you, my beloved," she said in her sweet voice— "Good night."

He mounted his cob, and doffed his cap as he rode away. Some curious feeling of dread was upon him to-night, again and again he tried to shake it off, still that curious indescribable sensation held him, he tried to overcome it as he cantered on, but it was of no avail. "Good night, Julian," and again some echo softly breathed "Good Bye, Julian."

"Tush" he cried, "am I, too, growing superstitious and fanciful? I, Julan Stanton, the philosopher (his friends nickname for him). A good night's rest will put me right, I shall laugh at this to-morrow."

## CHAPTER II.

It was close on midnight, and bitterly cold; almost all day a gale had been blowing, while the air had that peculiar rawness, that only an east wind posesses.

In the top room of a rather dreary house, in one of the suburbs in the North of London, sat a most peculiar looking man. The room was plain enough, the chief articles of furniture being a camp bedstead a bookcase that had seen better days, two or three peculiar looking chemical appliances, a much worn globe, several musty looking manuscripts and volumes of books were piled upon the chairs, table and floor in careless disarray. Hanging against the wall were cabalistic symbols and figures, mounted on parchment. There was a strange smell of incense pervading the atmosphere of this somewhat weird looking apartment.

The occupant of the room was crouching over a somewhat scanty fire, slowly rubbing his hands, one over the other, in what appeared to be a brown study, the mind being apparently absent. His age was uncertain, for his coal black hair was as yet untinged with grey. His complexion appeared a curious ivory white, while his eyes, from out their sunken sockets, wore a peculiar sinister expression; dark, cold and piercing eyes, in which lurked a weird glitter; if you looked long into their depths you became conscious of a strange power overcoming you, as though will, life and vitality were all being drawn away.

He moved at last, sat upright and glanced at his watch. "To-night" he muttered, "I stand between the forces of good and evil. Which will win? For so many years I have said evil be thou my good, that the inevitable action must now take place, and power of choice may be no longer mine. What if I 'gain the whole world, and lose my soul,' said one who knew! Oh, how I hate humanity! I only long for power! I only thirst for fame! Is any price too dear to pay for power? To kill by a wish; to injure by a word; to slay by a thought! Fame and power; I would give my Soul itself for that! All my attempt at transmutation of base metal into gold have proved a failure, for my heart is evil, and my hands unclean; failure, ever failure, and yet gold I must have or my books will not be known, my years of labour wasted. I do not want posthumous fame, I want it to-day, now. Hark! what was that?" He sat upright, and raked together the cinders of the decaying fire.

Some vehicle being driven at a furious pace could now be heard rattling up the street. It stopped at the magician's door, and out of it sprang a young and slender man, who proceeded to pull the bell furiously.

" Old Judkins has not gone to bed yet " the figure upstairs muttered ; as he looked out of the window to ascertain who so late a visitor might be " if she is not too drunk, she will show him up. Ah! Here he is."

In another moment, breathless with agitation, a young man rushed into the room, hatless, with coat unbuttoned.

" Are you Jubal Tankard ? " queried a voice husky, and thick with emotion.

" That is my name sir," said the magician standing up, and now it could be seen what a very tall man he was, as he stood erect, coldly regarding the figure before him. " Why have you sought me at such an hour, pray ? You want something of me I suppose, they all do that come here."

" I am in dire distress, in agony of mind," replied the young man, " for the one who is dearest to me in all this world, lies to-night at the point of death." Jubal Tankard rapidly glanced at his watch. " She is my promised bride ; we were to have been married to-day, but she has sickened of fever, and to-night both doctors say they can do nothing more for her ; can you save her ? Have you any herb or simple you can give me, by your powers of magnetism or magic can you heal her ? I am wealthy, and you can name your own price, even to the half of my fortune. What is money to me who would give my life for her's ! Speak."

Unheeding much of this agitated pleading, Jubal Tankard had been making a strange circle, with a pencil on a piece of parchment ; a curious circle like a star, and within it were strange figures. He stood up at last and drew in his breath with a hissing sound. In the gloom of the room his eyes shone with their strange glitter. " She dies at three this morning " he softly muttered, " the stars never lie ! I can do nothing here ; again fate has played me a scurvy trick."

"Why are you wasting time?" said Julian Stanton, for this young man was he; "why do you hesitate? Directly you restore her the money you want shall be yours, within the hour if you like, so come back with me once, at once, I say, minutes are precious in this case; return with me, you have saved others, you must save her."

In another moment the two were driving furiously away.

Meanwhile sweet Eunice lay on her little white bed, like a faded flower, all unheeding, and unknowing the agony that racked her lover's heart. She had contracted the fever in its worst form several weeks earlier, and to-night Dr. Elliotson and Julian's friend Frank Richardson feared the worst.

Beside the bed sat her mother broken-hearted. The father white and grave, tried to keep up for the mother's sake, though now and again a dry sob would shake his frame. "My little lass" he muttered, "why can't your poor old father die instead?" All that the best medical skill of the day could accomplish had been done, a skilled nurse was there attending her. Her mother's tender care by night and day availed not, the fiat had gone forth, and the soul of sweet Eunice Graham was near its departure.

Julian as a last resource had bethought him of the magician and his wonderful power, and this last straw was eagerly snatched at, for either of the three would gladly have surrendered their own life, to save that of the beloved one.

Eunice was perfectly unconscious, her face had grown pale and emaciated, but still it looked like the face of a sleeping angel, so pure and calm. The clock ticked on in the silence—tick, tick, tick— as if it were slowly beating out the last heart-throbs of Eunice Graham. Now and again, a slow tear would drop in the mother's lap as she inwardly prayed to the great "All Father" to save her child. In the library below sat the doctors in consultation. "Nothing more can be done," said Richardson at last. "It is an awful case;" in all my medical practice I never met a sadder" . . . . Poor Julian, God help him," she was his idol, and glancing at the clock, "they were to

"BY MY COMPELLING WILL ENTER HER."

have been married this morning. I think this grief will break up the old couple, for they well nigh worshipped Eunice."

"She is practically dead now," said the other quietly. "Her pulse was scarcely perceptible a few moments ago."

"Jubal Tankard may suggest something, he is the oddest man I ever knew," said Dr. Richardson, "he magnetised a girl for me the other week, and I took her leg off; she felt no pain, in fact knew nothing about it at the time, she is now recovering; of course I paid him well, he will do nothing without that. He is selfish to the back bone. Well, even he cannot bring the dead to life again, at any rate," said the other, with a glance at the clock, "its just one, if they delay much longer they will only find a corpse."

"There they are" said both men simultaneously, Julian entered first. "How is she now?" his white lips questioned. His agonised eyes scanned the faces of the doctors. "In exactly the same condition, I am sorry to say Julian," replied his friend. Jubal Tankard unfastened his long cloak, and shook hands with Doctor Richardson. "You will excuse us gentlemen," said Julian, "Mr. Tankard desires to see Eunice at once, and alone."

As they entered the chamber Julian's eyes sought that quiet figure on the bed, in a whisper he told the parents he had brought Jubal Tankard, and then sank on his knees beside the bed, indifferent to all save its occupant. "Eunice," he called softly, "my beloved! oh, live for me; do not leave me! the sun of my existence fades with you, and all is dark."

"Hush!" said Jubal Tankard sternly, "Hush! not a sound; I must have perfect quiet here, or I can do nothing." He saw what the others could not see! He sensed what the others could not feel, and strong man though he was, beads of cold sweat rolled off his brow. "What shall it profit a man, if he gain the whole world, and lose his own soul." He brushed the thought away as though it had been some noxious insect: and in that moment his better self turned, and fled. He raised his hand and pointed in the direction of Eunice. "By my compelling will enter her," he cried. Somewhere in the air a mocking laugh faintly sounded.

The forces of the black that night had won.

The magician poured out a glass of brandy, and drank it rapidly, and then said "you can call up the doctors now, if you like. Your patient will recover!"

Jubal Tankard stood like a marble statue, while mother, father, lover, each in turn blessed him, shook his hand, and poured forth their gratitude, then turning to Mr. Stanton he said, " Remember our compact." I will attend to it at once "replied Julian," come down-stairs with me." Already the colour had returned to the face and lips of Eunice, the breathing and pulse had become strong and natural once more.

Truly a worker of miracles, said both doctors, after carefully examining the still unconscious patient. The crisis is over, and she will live.

" It may be a few days before she recovers consciousness," said Jubal Tankard on leaving, " you must be patient, the system has had a great strain, but she will be quite conscious soon." To himself he smiled, *too soon*, he said softly, and hurried away.


## CHAPTER III.

After three days, Eunice Graham rapidly recovered, but seemed to have become altogether a different woman. She who once loved beautiful sunsets, fair dawns, and Nature generally—she who had desired for knowledge and spiritual yearnings, now sat most of the day over a yellow-backed novel. The Eunice who had been a most abstemious eater, almost a vegetarian, often dining from fruit and bread, had now become a very epicurian, and eat meat several times a day; she who used to be a total abstainer now drank champagne, ale, and other drinks with avidity. The Eunice who loved simple dresses and soft colours, now, apparently, found her greatest delight in decking herself out in gorgeous apparel of brilliant hue. The Eunice who had been a most devoted daughter, now cared little for her parents, while for Julian she had, at times, mad outbursts of curious passion that quite astounded, nay horrified, the young man. The doctors said, be patient, her mind has become slightly unhinged she will become her normal self later on, and when Julian marries her and takes her away for change of air and scene, she will certainly return to you quite herself.

Julian sought Jubal Tankard, but in vain. His rooms were shut up; he had vanished, and no one knew where. Mrs. Judkins shook her head lugubriously, she was in a sober fit at the time—"I be glad he be gone, sir, that I am, sure, for he wor the devil hisself, I know. I heard voices a-talking where only he was there, and sometimes orful wailings, come through the closed door."

That was all Julian could gather. Jubal Tankard had vanished, and none knew whither. He might have vanished into thin air, so total and complete was his disappearance.

Eunice expressed her desire to live in the West end of London, "I want big rooms," she cried, "where I can have all my friends to visit me."

"I did not know you had so many, Eunice," said Julian in astonishment.

"Never you mind what you know or don't know! I want to enjoy myself."

That was the burden of the cry—enjoy. But, curiously enough, the enjoyment meant pleasures of the senses now, once they were pleasures of the soul!

A curious thing happened one day; Julian had begged Eunice to play for him again on the spinet, when, to his amazement he discovered she could only thump the keys, emitting most horrible sounds as she did so. Since her illness she had forgotten all her music—melody had left her.

\*　　\*　　\*　　\*　　\*

It was the eve of Julian Stanton's wedding-day, and as he sat in his study one might have noticed how haggard and anxious his face had grown; his hair in places had become quite white. This had been an awful day for Julian, for at the wedding breakfast Eunice had fallen from her chair, not in a faint (though such had been the

**P**

explanation), but drunk—dead drunk, and in this condition had been driven to her new home, and now lay on the bed upstairs in a drunken sleep.

" Oh God," groaned Julian in an agony of spirit, " what does it all mean ?  She must be mad !  Her parents are dying by inches through her conduct, faugh, it makes me sick.  I am married to a sensual animal—a mad woman—yet I will not complain.  Maybe, by tenderest love and care I can yet restore her.  Did her mind  partly leave her, or quite, on that night she nearly died, I wonder?  Oh, Eunice, better hadst thou died, thy virtues and thy sweetness would then have been mine for ever ; as it is, I see the same beautiful form as of yore, yet from out those once dear eyes something now appears so awful, that at times it makes me shudder.  I could fancy it was the gaze of some mocking, jibing fiend."

The hour was late, the house was still, and in the silence the man's heart was racked with agony—his mind torn with conflict.

" She will be my disgrace," he cried ; " and our lives were to have been pure, noble and useful.  All now is changed ; what if, after all, there be no ruler of the universe ?  If atheism is true, and the mind is everything, then there is no soul ; and so, neither God or hereafter."

His forehead was wrinkled in deep thought ; his hands were clenched in pain.  At last, worn out with mental conflict and physical fatigue, Julian Stanton fell asleep in his chair, and in his sleep he saw Eunice as she used to be, only grown fairer, in the same soft, clinging garments she used to wear ; her blue eyes had the same love shining in them, her sweet face was smiling, all around her was a luminous cloud, while her figure was radiant with light.  Woman, yet angel, she seemed ; the air was perfumed with violets—the scent radiated from her as she breathed.

She gazed at Julian with tender compassion, and, extending her white arms, she cried, " Oh, Julian, my beloved—thou hast the casket, but the soul of Eunice is here ; many times I have been near thee, and tried to impress thy mind, but, in your waking consciousness, it was of

"THOU HAST THE CASKET. THE SOUL OF EUNICE IS HERE."

no avail—I could not reach you. Dear Julian, there is a land of beauty and light; the heaven-world, is a world of bliss and joy unspeakable, there every noble aspiration becomes realized—there, those who love each other purely live together in pure joy. It is called the shining land, for all is light there. Do not grieve for me, there is no death, but change. I am the same Eunice, only clothed in a finer, lighter body. Pray for me to pass on swiftly; prayers do much for those we love. No one should leave their dead to go on their lonely way unattended by loving hosts of guardian angels, for thoughts, Julian, are real things here; loving thoughts are angel forms, helping us forward to peace and rest. In that shining land, where all is bliss, I shall wait your coming, and when you are in deep sleep, dear Julian, if you live purely, we may sometimes meet. Do not think of this as only a dream when you awake, for you have been most grossly deceived.

The animal soul of a sensualist and drunkard is at present using my body, drawn in by magical power, it will in a short time run its race, when you must speedily burn the form. This poor dark soul was drawn by Jubal Tankard's magic into my body attracted by the drink imbibed by the nurse who attended me, for oh! Julian, ladies little know when they drink their champagne, or wine, the evil things that are near them trying to push themselves into their bodies to snatch their desires through the medium of those still on earth, for their animal desires live on when their physical bodies decay. As we are on earth, so we are here, and each goes to his own place.

Give my dear parents this message, 'Eunice waits their coming to the land of bliss.' We shall know each other there. They have not lost their daughter. Tell my mother to grieve no more, for Eunice is not dead, but living! and the hour of their release from the burden of earth draws nigh. Julian, when your consciousness returns to your brain, remember this is no dream. You have been permitted to see behind the veil. You have seen the living truth! If your mind be sceptical, here is a proof, you will find the room perfumed with violets, you know it was the scent I always used. Fear nothing my beloved. God is indeed Love! Pure love brought the universe into being, pure love maintains it, pure love draws it upward to perfection, and to bliss. For

P I

you, Julian, much work on earth remains to be done, but you will find a teacher later on, and your mind will be illuminated. Go out into the world, and serve, for service to man is love for God. Farewell!"

With a start Julian Stanton awoke, to find he had slept but half-an-hour. The atmosphere of the room was heavy with violets. He realised that he had seen the real Eunice, and that the other was a fraud, a masquerade. A deep peace settled on him, what after all was a few short years of preparation, when an eternity of bliss awaited him. Yes, he would live purely, truly, and nobly, for her dear sake, and then and there he pledged himself to the "service of mankind" in any way possible, physically, mentally, morally, and spiritually—henceforth the world's sorrows should be his sorrow.

"My saint in heaven! sweet Eunice, thou hast given me back faith, hope, and love. Pass on, dear soul, in prayers will Julian ever help thee; if thou art happy, then surely I must be."

He sat up all night, and wrote several long letters, one to Mr. and Mrs. Graham, giving them an account of the vision, and Eunice's message, one to Frank Richardson, enclosing him some money, and asking him to look after the supposed Eunice. "I can never live with her again," he wrote, "but we can keep the affair secret, she will drink herself to death, and never be any better. I leave England in the morning, a sadder, yet a wiser man. My old life of travel will be commenced again. I will forward addresses, because I want you to do all you can for the old couple, they will not want to see Mrs. Stanton again, I think; meanwhile, supply her with money. I will send you more later on.

You may think me as mad as Eunice, but the fact is Jubal Tankard has betrayed us, and the mystery of that night only he and I know; it is a different soul, and a wicked one in the body that once belonged to Eunice. For Eunice died that night. I don't expect you will believe me, nor can I tell you by what means I became possessed of the knowledge of the villany that has been perpetrated. You must think exactly as you please, only carry out my wishes."

## CHAPTER IV.

Nearly three years have passed away since the events narrated in the former chapters of this story took place.

Julian Stanton had travelled far and wide seeking to benefit humanity, while now and again news from home would reach him. Mr. and Mrs. Graham, he learned, only survived their daughter one short year. They died within a few days of each other, and left their property in trust to Julian Stanton, for the founding of a home for young and friendless girls, in memory of their beloved daughter Eunice. On two occasions only had Julian received information from Mr. Graham, who, (notwithstanding Julian's advice,) had called on Mrs. Stanton, with the result that he was refused admittance. " The shock of the whole affair," wrote Mr. Graham, " has quite broken the mother's heart. Each night she dreams of Eunice, and I know Joan will be glad when her earthly days are done; for myself, I care not how soon release comes."

Dr. Richardson wrote—" I have at length been obliged to get a keeper for Mrs. Stanton, as she has shocking fits of mania, induced by drink. Certainly madness is the only thing, Julian, that explains the mystery, the other idea you put forth is really preposterous, such a thing could not be."

A year later Julian learnt his wife was dead, and the body burnt in accordance with his earlier instructions.

On the 24th December, 1800, Julian was travelling by stage coach in the North of England, when he was addressed by a fellow-passenger, who had been regarding him earnestly for a considerable period.— " Pardon me, sir, but are you related to a Mr. Maurice Stanton ? "

" He happens, sir," replied Julian, " to be my brother, resident in India ; may I ask whether *you* are acquainted with him, for it is several years since I had news of him ? "

" I am but now returning from that part of the world," replied the other, "where I happened to make his acquaintance. Permit me, therefore, to introduce myself—my name is Adrian de

Fermier. It may, however, be a greater passport to your confidence if I show you this letter, which you may, doubtless, recognize as being in your brother's handwriting."

" To Julian's surprise his companion then produced a letter in the well-known handwriting of his brother Maurice, addressed to Adrian de Fermier.

" You apparently know my brother intimately then."

" That is so," replied the other ; " and many a serious conversation has passed between us."

" You are French I presume, sir," said Julian, " judging by your name ? "

" My father was a Frenchman," replied his companion, " but I am a cosmopolitan ; I have no country nor land—I go where there is anything to be done."

Both men found they were bound for the same destination ; and when, towards the close of the day, it was discovered that owing to the increasing depth of snow, which had been falling thickly, the coach could not proceed, it was rather pleasant than otherwise for each to find that he had a congenial companion in the other.

During the following day, which was Christmas, the conversation turned upon religious and spiritual topics.

" Maurice, my brother, is more or less an atheist," said Julian.

" Was, you mean," quietly replied his companion. " Stay," he said, seeing the look of surprise on Julian's face, " I will bring you his letter, and you shall read his altered views for yourself. You will learn also the nature of the subjects upon which we have exchanged thoughts."

" Maurice become religious !—Is the world coming to an end ? " soliloquised Julian. He opened his brother's letter.

" My beloved teacher," it read, " since first the great truths of human life and purpose reached me through you, the world has worn, a different aspect. The knowledge that we live many lives upon this earth, for the purpose of gradual growth towards spiritual power—an acquaintance with the working of that profound Law of Karma, as the Hindoos call it—or the inevitable sequence of cause and effect in all departments of life; has helped me to realize the deep import of existence. I struggle hard for that thought control, so necessary for progress, now I know thoughts are living things, instinct with life; that we create them, and are therefore responsible for them; that we are ever sending angels and devils into the world of men; that we can heal people, or cause them disease by the potency of our wills. I look at the sun now, and remember that it is the outward form of the great God of this world, and that 'in Him we move, live, and have our being.' As I realize that perfect justice rules the world, that men suffer from themselves, and that it becomes possible to make an end of suffering, everything is changed. My gratitude is for ever yours. Atheist, unbeliever, I was fast becoming, for so-called religion was nothing but husks. I asked for bread, they gave me a stone. But in the ancient wisdom, I found satisfaction for head and heart; I felt an inner conviction of its truth from the first; it explained as nothing else had done, the problems of life, it solved the mystery of death, and the inequalities of the human race.

" The growth of many earth-lives is the perfect flower—love, will, and wisdom. God, or love, you said created us, and the only destiny is fate for good. We must become perfect. 'Even as our Father in heaven is perfect.' The struggle with the lower nature is severe, yet separated though we are, I feel you help me by thought, and I often wake out of sleep feeling I have met you somewhere during the night. Those books and pamphlets you lent me have been deeply studied. I struggle with the animal side of my nature, and I struggle with my mind; ever hoping the forces you have at your command to day may, in some future life, be mine, used by me for the helping, and service of mankind.

Farewell, your ever grateful, and devoted pupil,

MAURICE."

The letter was a long one, but each word was eagerly scanned by Julian; and as both men were bound for London, Julian begged his companion to allow him to accompany him, as a student of this wisdom.

"I have been seeking truth all my life," said Julian, and "Oh sir, I have suffered much, and I am sure I have done nothing in this life to merit such agony of soul and mind." If, as you say, we have lived before, it may be in my past life, I was a wicked man, but I don't remember any past life at all," said Julian, turning to his companion. "Why do I not? Do you?"

Mr. De Fermier sat regarding Julian earnestly for a moment, and then said quietly, "You have a new brain and body each earth life, my friend, and neither brain or body have been here before. But the soul can never die, it is immortal in all. I have now some writing I must get through," said Mr. De Fermier, rising; "but as you seem so desirous of a better acquaintance with this Divine Wisdom, I will leave you some books on the subject to study. Come to my private room to night at eight, and then we will go deeply into these problems that your brother has written about. Shall it be so?" He rose and shook hands with Julian, warmly; as he did so he turned his large brown eyes on Julian's face, and smiled.

Why did the image of the Christ suddenly flash through Julian's brain.

"Thank you very much," he said, earnestly, and they parted for a time.

It was some hours later, and in a private room of the hotel sat Julian and Adrian de Fermier in deep conversation. The older man, for he must have been quite fifty, listened most attentively, while the young man recounted the events we have depicted in the former chapters. He never moved, except to occasionally mend the fire.

"Well," said Julian, at last, "can you tell me what sin I did, say in a past life if you will, to have suffered such terrible pain and sorrow. Eunice did not tell me why she was taken, and I left. Can you?" Julian leant forward, and looked earnestly into the face of his companion.

"What good could this knowledge do you," said his friend, "even if you had it?"

"Just this" replied Julian, earnestly, "I should realize for myself the justice of the law, and be yet a more willing servant of humanity. I seem to have suffered so unjustly. Even Eunice herself, did not explain the mystery of our tragic love."

"Realize, then," Adrian said, placing his hand on Julian's shoulder.

A curious peace stole over Julian, he seemed to shake his body off as if it were a heavy garment, to be outside it, as it were, and everything seemed changed, for all had become transparent ; he could see through things, and the objects in the room, before so solid, now seemed like glass ; then they disappeared, and only the grand and glorious figure of his companion shone before him, and in reverence Julian would have knelt, for he thought it was an angel.

"Kneel only to the Divine, my son," said a voice of tender softness, "and now open thine eyes and see. Every act and deed of mortals s chronicled in nature's book which can never be cheated."

As Julian looked, a picture seemed unrolled before him. At first it vibrated so rapidly he could not see, but it presently grew steady, and he saw clearly.

"Your past," said a voice, "REALIZE."

In the picture stood a fair young girl, somewhat like Eunice, and a man who, though taller and darker, Julian knew was himself. The girl seemed pleading for something, her face was sad and her mien sorrowful. "Do not leave me," she entreated, "to the world's scorn." In the picture he saw his thoughts, and they were black, for he wished this girl out of his way in order to marry a rich woman, that through her he might be able to pay his gambling debts ; and this maiden was very poor, though fair and young. He saw the girl's agony of mind, he saw as in a cloud about her, what her future would be ; that she would be spurned by the world, having lost her all. He saw his own struggle to do right, then the girl lay sobbing on the ground, and he turned and fled. He saw himself wealthy, and married to an old woman, yet wretched in the midst of wealth. He gave money generously—it was the one thing he could do. He sent money to the girl but she had fled—friendless, poor, disgraced—into the cold, hard world alone ; for she was an orphan and friendless, and he realized that he had wrecked her life.

"Be not deceived," a voice said gravely ; "vengeance is mine, I will repay, saith the Lord. As a man soweth, so he must reap. This girl, left, betrayed, deserted by you, was this very Eunice Graham.

Torn from *you* this life as you tore yourself from her your victim, in the past. The law of perfect justice spareth none—it is unalterable; you then sowed, this life you reap. But in that girl's past misery her soul grew apace; she loved you ever, her destroyer, prayed for you with her last breath, and, in the fire of suffering, the virtue of purity was burnt into her soul. For a few years of blessedness she came on earth, this life to add knowledge to her love, and you, in your later years, last life, sought philosophy and higher thought, and gave great sums away, and so you were born wealthy, for the law awards you just what you earn. Give and it shall be given unto you It is finished, your time of full realization is at hand. You deceived and betrayed—you, yourself, were deceived and betrayed. But that old debt is now wiped off, and a long course of usefulness lies before you. In many lives past you were of great use to me; in this life I shall pay the debt."

A curious shock and pressure, and Julian opened his eyes to see his companion still sitting in the chair opposite, exactly as before, and only eight minutes had passed,

"Why, dear me," said Julian, "this is marvellous. What spell have you put upon me?"

"The power of love alone, my brother, which, touching you, made you pass from life's illusions to its realities. You can no longer doubt, for now you have seen and realized at first hand, and know 'that perfect justice rules the world.'"

\*       \*       \*       \*       \*

Julian Stanton never married, but rumour said he had joined a Brotherhood in the far East.

In the year 1801, the following curious story was published in a journal :—

"A man was found stabbed in the environs of Paris. He is entirely unknown to the authorities, but a letter discovered upon him, which we print below, may possibly lead to his recognition. It is addressed merely to Julian Stanton, and reads as follows:

'You will remember me—I did you harm enough to deserve your recollection. That you discovered, by sources unknown to most, the secret of the substitution I know, never mind how. The trick I played you has cost me dear; my wealth, (your wealth perhaps), I should say, melted like snow, and I am ruined now, with every hope of fame and power crushed hopelessly. Soon, say the stars, I must die. They never yet lied to me, devil though I be. You may, perchance, learn of my death, at least you should know what the end of J. T. is. There seems no good at last, for evil done, in this cursed life of man. Farewell!'"

" Mad of course," said the editor, "quite insane; but it is a curious coincidence that he should meet his death as he had foretold. But we all know Astrology to be an exploded fallacy, only practised by charlatans, and fortune-telling swindlers, and quite on a level with card-laying, and other superstitious foolery."

Is it so, dear reader? or is there a great plan of the universe with God as architect, and the stars as His ministers.

---

### BORDERLAND.

It is with much regret that we just learn of the temporary suspension of that very admirable quarterly *Borderland*. From a psychic standpoint, no words can express our admiration for the courage and fearless efforts of its able editor—Mr. W. T. Stead—to bring the physical world to the borderland of the psychic, and we await with hope and pleasure the re-opening of its pages with the first-hand knowledge that Mr. Stead has gone to seek, and we feel assured that when this is accomplished, Mr. Stead's supporters will be more than doubled.

In the last issue of *Borderland* there is a concluding note under the heading of Astrology, which we reproduce below. Coming from an independent source it may fairly be considered free from bias, but it substantiates our own opinion :—

"As a rule Astrologers will answer a question for two shillings and sixpence; but the price to be paid for the delineation of character and the drawing of a horoscope depends entirely upon the length of the time that is required. You can get some kind of a horoscope for five shillings, whereas, if you wish to go into the whole thing very elaborately, astrologers will undertake to put in as much time as you will pay for.

" At present there are few who imitate Oriental potentates, who maintain an astrologer permanently for advice, but a very elaborate horoscope could hardly be drawn under fifty pounds, but this, of course, is a luxury which very few persons will indulge in."

## Character from the Face; or Physiogonomy in a Nutshell.

THIS is a novel as well as an instructive form of, amusement suitable for Xmas, and when the usual frivolity has made way for a little change the elder portion of the party may in this manner be entertained and amused. By followin the few hints I am about to give you, you wil be able to pose as a character reader.

Bring a spice of wit to this feast of intelligence and a little of the salt of wisdom, carefully avoiding vinegar, mustard or pepper, though a modicum of oil may prove a valuable auxillary.

First regard the nose. A small straight nose (the Grecian)—love of beauty, and art. The Roman nose (this has an excresence in the centre)—love of power, ability to organize and direct. A nose tip tilted like a flower "—a thirst for finding out secrets, inquisitive. A nose flattened at the tip and broad—a great desire for economy, good bargainers. Long, thin and pointed nasal organ— suspicious, despondent, yet persevering. A very short nose—impulse and lack of caution. A very long nose—careful, cautious and plodding.

Next comes the mouth, that most bewitching feature of the face. First notice the shape of the lips, if full and red—a strong and active love nature. Very thin lips—an undemonstrative character.

Lips that turn up at the corners, very merry and happy disposition; lips that turn down are just the reverse. When the under lip is the most full, the desire is to be *loved*. When the top lip is slightly projective, a desire *to love* is present. The top lip is active, and the bottom passive. A fulness either side of the lower lip—the green-eyed monster lurketh near. Lips firmly pressed together—a firm character is shown. Mouth generally slightly open—a weak will and great impressionability is discovered.

The eyes. Ah! those windows of the soul! how shall I best describe their witchery? A large eye, soft and tender in expression, indicates a large soul with great capacity for feeling. Narrow, small eyes give intellectual ability, but not so much emotion or feeling as large orbs. Blue-eyed people have a gentle nature. Black — powerful and passionate. Green—clever and original. Brown eyes give a faithful nature, and so on.

A word for the chin. There are broad, narrow, pointed and square chins. The broad chin—this gives a faithful nature, stable and enduring. Narrow chins are more changeable in their affections, and somewhat difficult to please. The chin with a deep dimple in the centre—a desire to be loved. A pointed chin is called the ideal chin, because those possessing it will only marry their ideals. It is the chin of the old maid and the old bachelor, and maybe, that is why so many live to-day in single blessedness; they have not yet found their ideals. The face that is long, and pointed, and narrow, seeks solitude. A face that is round bears the insignia of a warm genial nature with plenty of energy and force on hand.

With these hints we hope, if you follow them, you will instruct and amuse all your friends at Xmas.

VIOLA.

---

Books and magazines are but white paper unless men spend in action the wisdom they get from thought.—BULWER LYTTON.

\*    \*    \*    \*    \*

Who is powerful? He who can control his passions. Who is rich? He who is contented with that he has.—TALMUD.

# The Utility of Astrology.

A T 3.20 p.m., October 14th, a lady came rushing into the Editorial Office of MODERN ASTROLOGY with an excited request that we might instantly take a figure, and, amidst suppressed tears of agonized emotion, we were informed that it was a most urgent case, and necessary to relieve the sad distress of several persons.

When the lady had sufficiently calmed herself, we were able to ascertain the facts, which were these.—A child had been lost for two days, and although it had been reported to all the police stations, no trace of the boy could be found, and the worst was feared. Every suggestion had been raised—was he drowned ?—had he been stolen by gipsies ?—and, finally, did we think that he would ever be recovered dead or alive ?

After calmly noting the time, and endeavouring to keep our mind fairly under control amid this mixture of emotion and excitement, we proceeded to erect the following map of the heavens at the time given above.

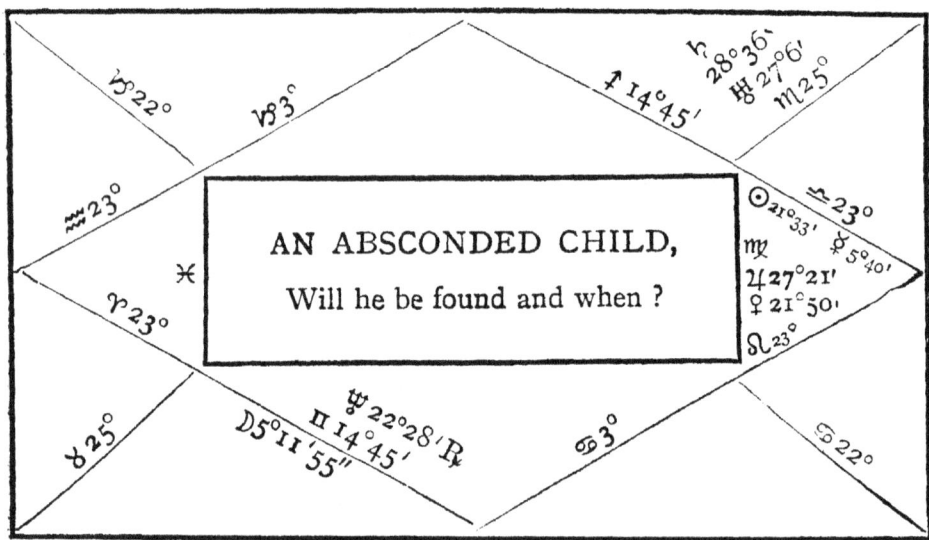

The above map represents what is called a Horary figure. It is possible to answer any material question under the sun by the use of Horary Astrology, providing that the mind of the questioner is perfectly clear, and his thoughts properly defined at the time of asking the question. The mind of the person asking the above question, concerning a child lost, was really anxious and concerned. Apart from the apparent earnestness of the questioner, the figure is what is called radical, that is, a definite portion of a sign rises, showing a definite thought behind all the excitement. Had the person been well balanced, the thought would have been expressed calmly, and probably with feeling, without emotion. It was a question expressed with a strong desire to help the parents and relieve them of their distress. This is indicated by the eleventh sign, the sign of pure desires, hopes and wishes being on the ascendant, or first house; the person's excitement and emotion being clearly marked by the conjunction of the ruler in the emotional sign Scorpio, the motive being good from the sextile of the ruler to Jupiter and Venus.

Now, in all questions of children, Mercury is the ruler, and in the figure the moon was applying to the trine aspect of Mercury. Mercury and the 5th house being the indicator of the child, the ascendant indicating the father, and the Moon the mother.

Our judgment was instantly given the moment that the figure was complete, that the child would be found, either the same evening, or the first thing in the morning by the parents, and that the child had gone in a northerly direction from his home.

He was found on the evening of the same day, at Islington, very little the worse for his experience.

The parents are upholsterers living at Fortune Green, and their relief was great when they were assured that the child was perfectly safe, though with strangers, and no harm whatever had befallen him.

These are the cases of horary astrology we believe in, for in this way it is of practical help to humanity. But when frivolous questions are asked of the astrologer, then we think that the time is wasted. That horary astrology is true is undoubted, as the above facts, which can be verified, go to prove. But the mind must be anxious, and the motives pure to obtain reliable results.

The rules of horary astrology are very simple, and there are several good books upon the subject, which will enable any person of ordinary intellect to become proficient. But the one essential thing required is *judgment*.

# Calendar for  December.

The Sun passes through Sagittarius, the ninth sign, entering Capricorn on the 21st.

### THE LUNAR TABLE FOR DECEMBER.

| D M | D W | Moon at Noon. ° ′ | LUNAR ASPECTS at GREENWICH. Before Noon. | After Noon. |
|---|---|---|---|---|
| 1 | W | 13♓58 | □⊙ | Venus a Morning Star |
| 2 | Th | 26 ,, 40 | □♆, ☿, △♀ | △♅ |
| 3 | F | 9♈ 6 | △♄, ☍♃, △♂ | △⊙ |
| 4 | S | 21 ,, 20 | ✶♆ Noon. | Jupiter a Morning Star |
| 5 | S | 3♉24 | △☿ | |
| 6 | M | 15 ,, 21 | ⊙ sets 3.50 p.m. | |
| 7 | Tu | 27 ,, 15 | ☽ souths 10.50 p.m. | ☍♅, ♀ |
| 8 | W | 9♊ 6 | ☍♄, ♀ ☌ ♅ | ☍♂ △♃ |
| 9 | Th | 20 ,, 56 | ☍⊙ ♀ Par. ♄ | ☌♆ |
| 10 | F | 2♋48 | ☽ sets 9.15 a.m. | □♃, ☍☿ |
| 11 | S | 14 ,, 42 | ☿ □♃ | ☽ rises 5.45 p.m. |
| 12 | S | 26 ,, 42 | ⊙ rises 8 a.m. | △♅ |
| 13 | M | 8♌49 | △♄, ♀, ✶♃ | |
| 14 | T | 21 ,, 8 | ✶♆, △♂ | △⊙ |
| 15 | W | 3♍42 | □♅ | □♄, ♀ |
| 16 | Th | 16 ,, 34 | □♂, △☿ | □♆ |
| 17 | F | 29 ,, 49 | □⊙ | ✶♅, ✶♄ |
| 18 | S | 13♎28 | ☌♃ | ✶♀, ♂, □☿ |
| 19 | S | 27 ,, 35 | △♆ | ✶⊙ |
| 20 | M | 12♏ 6 | ☿ Par. ♂ | ✶☿ |
| 21 | Tu | 27 ,, 0 | ⊙ enters ♑ | ☌♅ |
| 22 | W | 12♐ 7 | ☌♄, ✶♃ | ☌♀ |
| 23 | Th | 29 ,, 19 | New Moon 7.55 p.m. | ☌♂, ⊙. ☍♆ |
| 24 | F | 12♑26 | □♃ | |
| 25 | S | 27 ,, 20 | ☌☿ | ✶♅ |
| 26 | S | 11♒51 | ✶♄ △♃ | |
| 27 | M | 25 ,, 56 | △♆, ✶♀, ♂ | □♅ |
| 28 | Tu | 9♓34 | ✶⊙, □♄ | |
| 29 | W | 22 ,, 45 | □♆ | □♀, ♂ |
| 30 | Th | 5♈33 | □⊙, △♅ | ☍♃, △♄ |
| 31 | F | 18 ,, | ☿ Par. ♅ | ✶♆ |

THE new moon, which occurred on the 24th of last month (November), would indeed be a serious one, far exceeding in calamities our anticipations of last month's predictions, were it not for the benefic sextile of Jupiter from the sign of the balance. As it is, the conjunction of Sun, Moon, Mars, and Saturn, will not separate from their orbs without making the close of 1897 remarkable for its disasters and misfortunes. We are, at the time of writing, on the eve of a national calamity, and one which we doubt if the sextile of Jupiter will do much to avert. All we need remark is *Tempus Omnia Revelat.*

# Fortune Telling by Cards.

## By an Astrologer.

STROLOGERS at the festive season may be excused if they find themselves lost amid the pleasure seekers, whose only thoughts in connection with their subject, are concerned with the star-shaped tinselled plates that decorate the Christmas trees.

It happened one Christmas, many years ago, that I was one of those unfortunate individuals whose resources were severely taxed by the hostess persisting in the request that I should suggest something new and novel to entertain the guests.

What could I do? My mind was more occupied in star gazing than parlour entertainments. At last a bright idea fell upon me. I would play the part of gipsy fortune teller, and with a pack of cards see what my inventive genius could conjure up to tell the fortune hunters.

It must have been a favourable moment considering the rate my ideas got into shape. It occurred to me that the twelve houses as used in astrology might come in as a key to the reading of the cards.

Throwing a Paisley shawl across my shoulders, and quickly improvising a tent out of the screen over which I had thrown a travelling rug, I summoned the crowd to the gipsey's tent. Then the real fun of the evening began, and for the benefit of those who may be similarly placed I give the following simple rules as a guide to assist their future ingenuity.

The following diagram represents the position that the cards are to hold when properly laid out.

Q

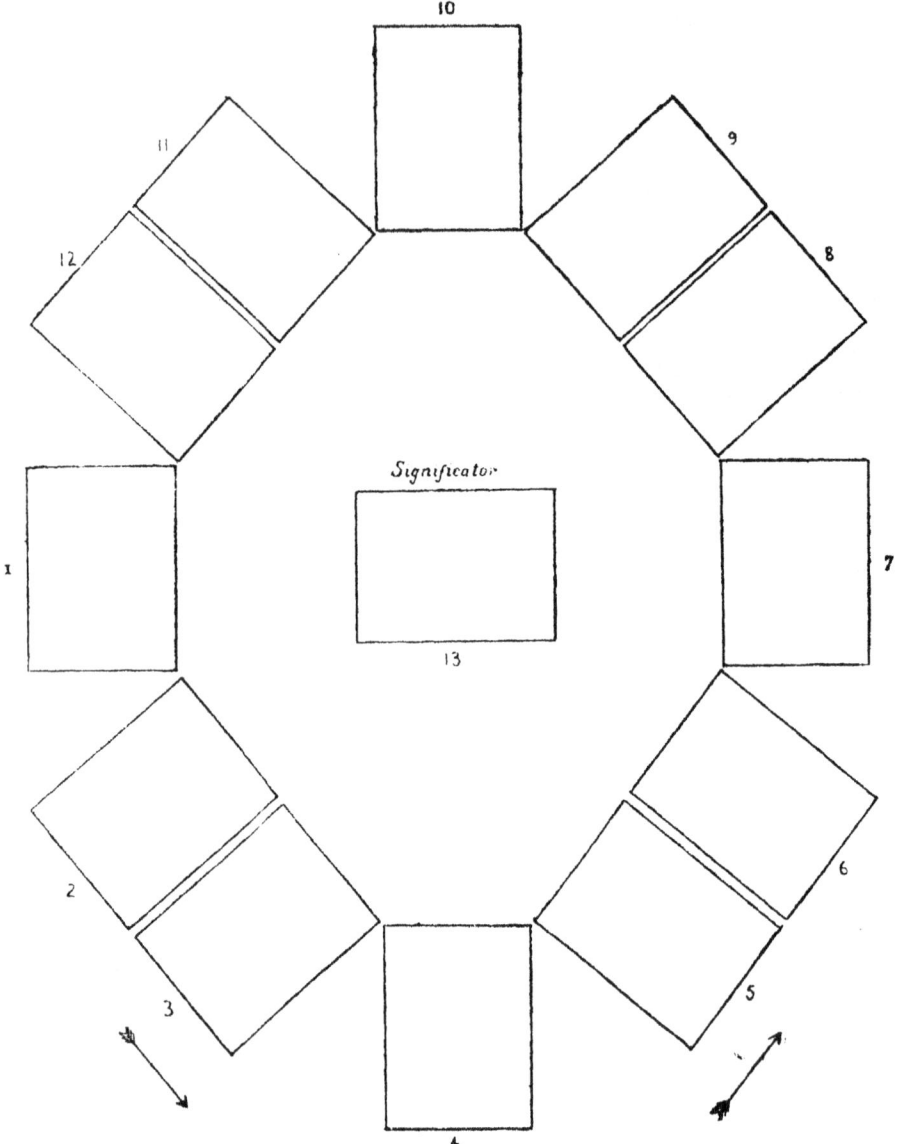

Hand the lady or gentleman the pack of cards to well shuffle and cut, then deal out 13 cards, starting from 1 going round by way of the arrows, finally placing the 13th card in the centre as the significator. The position marked 1 is to be taken as the ascendant, or the first house, for reading, generally speaking it will describe the condition of the person, their disposition, and character. The next division marked 2, will describe the financial condition such as the wealth, or monetary expectations.

No. 3 will govern all that is connected with the mind, showing its state, whether bright or dull, foolish or wise ; it also is concerned with travel, and journies, and general correspondence.

No. 4.—The house you are in, removals, and the end of affairs.

No. 5.—Pleasure, such as concerts, theatres, speculation, and the young ones, children, &c. Also courtships.

No. 6.—The food, health, servants, and **mystery**.

No. 7.—Marriage, law, and partners.

No. 8.—Legacies, and the partner's money.

No. 9.—Philosophy, foreign travel, and correspondence.

No. 10.—The honour, and moral character, also fame, and profession.

No. 11. — The hopes, wishes, and desires. Friends, and acquaintances.

No. 12. — Disappointments, and misfortunes, mystery, and **romance**.

Now, whatever the centre card happens to be, this card is the index for the whole reading. If the ace of hearts, or any of the heart cards is the centre card, then in whatever house you find a heart card read the fortune.

For the guidance of those who find it difficult to form the best opinion as to the descriptions, the following centre card cypher key will help to distinguish the significator or its meaning. Generally speaking kings representing adult males, and the queens adult females, and the knaves young persons ; but if a queen, is significator for a negative or feminine character, or *vice versa.*

# CENTRE CARD.
### Brief Cypher Key.

| Males. | Personalties. |
|---|---|
| King of Hearts ... | Romantic lover, good hearted man, or traveller. |
| „ „ Spades ... | Elderly person, very just, but cold. |
| „ „ Diamonds... | Wealthy person of authority. Generous. |
| „ „ Clubs ... | A doctor, or military person, very courageous. |

*Females.*

Queen of Hearts  ...  A fair lady, gentle and tender, **loving.**

„  „ Spades  ...  **A very dark person, diplomatic, proud.**

„  „ Diamonds  Very fair, noble, true and sincere.

„  „ Clubs  ...  Neither dark or fair, talkative, **active and alert.**

*Young Persons.*

Jack of Hearts  ...  A changeable but affectionate person, a flirt.

„  „ Spades  ...  Not well disposed, artful, and very subtle.

„  „ Diamonds ...  Rather bashful and timid.

„  „ Clubs  ...  Argumentative person, hasty and impulsive.

The 10, 7 and 4 of any suit range next to the king, and are modifications of the reading, and the 9, 5, and 3 range under the queen, while the 8, 6 and 2 are modifications of the knave. Space will not allow us to give fuller details.

Now if there are any cards of the same suit as the significator which is the centre card, out amongst the twelve in the circle, note the houses they occupy, and judge these as the indications of the fortune.

The following illustration will simplify the method. Suppose the centre card is the jack of hearts, and the person young, read out the description as follows:—

" You are quite a flirt I see, and you want to know something about your sweetheart."

If an elderly person then read you are somewhat frivolous, and evidently on pleasure bent, and so on.

Now, supposing that hearts is the centre card, and the 7, 8, or any other number, of hearts, occupies the seventh division, then judge marriage, &c., &c.

It may perhaps be as well to give a short sketch of a reading. A card of the same suit as the significator (No. 13) in the first division (No. 1) a well disposed person, honourable and sincere, but ambitious with thoughts upon themselves. In the 2nd, thoughts on money, desire for wealth ; in the 3rd, a strong and useful mind. In the 4th, thoughts on removal, or it may be sympathy with the house. In the 5th, thoughts on courtship and pleasure. The 6th, some slight indisposition. In the 7th, desire for marriage. 8th, money coming by legacy. 9th, prospects of a long journey. 10th, very honourable, and the probability of advancement in profession. 11th, very strong hopes and wishes, they will obtain their desires. In the 12th some misfortune is threatened.

In a general way the reading of the houses may be obtained from a blending of the cards in the various houses.

The ace of hearts represents all that is joyous, hopeful, friendly, pleasurable, and in a general way love and happiness.

The ace of spades is the reverse, signifying sorrow, bereavement losses, disappointment, ill-feeling, trouble and worry.

The ace of diamonds stands for finance, gain, success, and prosperity.

The ace of clubs represents everything connected with correspondence, writings, papers, letters, journeys, travel, business, commerce.

When reversed they are not good and indicate delay, hindrances, &c.

With very little study quite a new method of card reading may be introduced, and based as it is upon an astrological foundation some reliable results may be obtained if care is taken to watch a few details. Diamonds falling in the 8th house may be interpreted gain by a legacy. Spades in the fifth, some disappointment in courtship, or hearts in seventh, a speedy marriage, while spades in the seventh danger of litigation. Clubs in the third, correspondence, &c. Time may be judged as follows :—

Clubs, days ; diamonds, weeks ; hearts, months, and spades, years. A card should be chosen from the pack to decide the time when events will happen. This may be best left to the ready wit of the experimentor. Also any other details in addition to the broad outlines as sketched above.

The plan is decidedly novel, and much amusement may be obtained by a clever cartomantist, which is perhaps the best term that could be applied to the operator.

# The Principles of Graphology Astrologically Considered.

By RICHARD DIMSDALE STOCKER.

*Author of " The Human Face as Expressive of Disposition," "A Concordance of Graphology and Physiognomy," &c.*

HE handwriting of an individual, the "style" that is to say, which comes easiest to him or her, and is in every way natural and unstudied, is a sure guide to the temperament and disposition possessed by the native, revealing, as it does (and that in a minute degree), the spirit, soul, and bodily constitution—as well as the whole physical and mental condition. Laying aside the reasons why this is the case—for much upon this branch of our subject has been already, and will be, written—we will for a few moments pause to consider the astrological aspects of the subject.

It is, however, the *theoretical* phases of the matter which we are about to consider and with which we will deal; for the scientific side of it can be studied at leisure without going deeply into details.

By those who have studied astrology, the handwriting adopted is referred to the influence of those planets which govern the native, and each of the seven principal planets impart his or her own peculiar 'styles," which will be developed in a given direction—taking the autography in the abstract—according to the graphological equivalents of the mental faculties, which, in their turn, give life and character to the whole organization.

Now it will be admitted that there is no manifestation of *mind* without *brain* matter; hence certain organs thereof (42 being the sum total at present generally recognised) have been attributed to special planets.

Briefly:—*Mercury* rules the *intellectual* (perceptive, literary, comparative, and reflective); the *Moon*, the *perfective;* *Jupiter*, the *moral;* *Saturn*, the *egoistic;* *Mars*, the *selfish;* the *Sun*, the *aspiring;* and *Venus*, the *domestic faculties.* Of course this only gives a rough idea of the nature of the actual organs and their functions, to say nothing of the combinations produced by the various aspects and positions of the planets themselves.

But having now given the basis of the matter, let us for a moment consider what the nature of *handwriting* is. It is nothing, more or less, as a matter of fact, than a series of more or less regular *straight* and *curved* strokes. Just so; and the *keynote* to its interpretation rests in the *astrological symbolism*—as previously discussed in MODERN ASTROLOGY in such an able manner.

In order to elucidate my meaning I will give the characteristic features of the types of handwriting assigned to those influenced by the planetary bodies, after the following manner :—

| PLANET. | | WRITING. | Symbol. |
|---|---|---|---|
| ☉ | *Sun* ... | *Curved* ... | *Circle*—enclosing dot—of course undemonstrable. |
| ♂ | *Mars* ... | *Angular, linear* | *Cross* in the ascendancy. |
| ♀ | *Venus* ... | Curved ... | *Circle* surmounting cross. |
| ☽ | The Moon | Full and *rounded* | Double *semi-circles.* |
| ♄ | Saturn ... | Neat, linear ... | *Cross* over semi-circle |
| ♃ | Jupiter ... | Curved ... | *Half-circle* uppermost. |
| ☿ | Mercury ... | Indefinate, indeterminate | Complex—half-circle in circle over cross. |

If we take these elements—for such, in truth they are, not only of astrology, but also of every other science—we obtain the complete secret of graphology ; in fact, we get the whole matter in a nutshell.

The lines by which the handwriting is founded—which constitutes it—offer a satisfactory clue to the natures of the planets, and consequently to those pertaining to them, and this is so because they follow out, in the main, the formation of the symbols, as has been shown.

Thus, as we have seen, the *circular* element—which indicates love, peace, concord, harmony, feeling, faith, and so forth—is peculiar to those of the Sun, Venus, the Moon and Jupiter ; while the *linear* is characteristic of those of Mars and Saturn more especially, it being significant of energy, force, self, positivism, materialism, reason and so on. Without entering into the minutiæa of the subject—without attempting to indicate the individual graphic signs—which, after all, are built upon the foregoing foundation, and are only one, referable thereunto—we have in these elements the whole outline of the universe, of which man is but a complex reflex, being, as he is, either dominated by the laws of precision, method, and " wordly wisdom," or else governed by such qualities as mercy, pity, and intuition.

I have already stated that the characteristic features of the handwriting of those of the planet Mercury are not so easily exemplified ; still the *circle* will be found to dominate the *line*.

If the line and angle are *substituted* for the curve or spherical form or *vice versa,* so will the characteristics symbolised be of a like pronounced description.

---

The mind is the man. If that be kept pure, a man signifies somewhat If not what difference is there between a man and a beast, save that the man has the greater power for the larger mischief ?

\*　　\*　　\*　　\*　　\*

The first symptom of a really free man is not that he resists the laws of the universe, but that he obeys them.—CARLYLE.

\*　　\*　　\*　　\*　　\*

The Siamese method of computing time was, before April 1st, 1889 based on a lunar reckoning, each day being referred to as such a day of the waxing, or such a day of the waning moon, and each year being one of a cycle of twelve years (derived from the Chinese), each of which bore the name of one of the constellations of the zodiac. According to this system it was most difficult and tedious to calculate the corresponding European date. Assistant-Consul Beckett says, the Siamese year, as now reckoned, contains twelve months, like the European year, with corresponding leap years and number of days in each month, the only difference being that the Siamese year commences on April 1st. Each month is now called after one of the constellations in the Copernican system.

\*　　\*　　\*　　\*　　\*

Never treat money affairs with levity ; Money is character.—LYTTON.

# Christmas Hints on Palmistry.

AT this festive season of the year, when the mind is naturally on pleasure bent, and merry-making is the order of the day, it may not be inappropriate to give one or two hints, or short cuts to knowledge, in so far as hand-reading is concerned.

To the amateurs who wish to surprise and startle their friends by blossoming out into a full-blown palmist, we give the following wrinkles. To convey the ideas quickly, we will condense the tips into the following details :—

First, choose the prettiest young lady of the party, if you be of the male sex, and note if she holds out her hand with a smile, if so, she is agreeable by nature. Then, holding her hand in yours with the palm spread outwards, note the kind of hand.—Short fingers and long palms—impulsive. No perceptible joints, smooth fingers—intuitive, not calculating. A full mount of Venus (which is that plump part at the root of the thumb, called the ball of the the thumb)—a very loving and affectionate nature. A full mount, or cushion, at the root of the first finger—a love of society, friends, also social gatherings. A full mount under the little finger gives quickness, agility, and the "gift of the gab." If the thumb bends back well—pliability and adaptability ; if quite stiff, the opposite. Long thumb, from the first joint to the tip,—a strong will. A broad thumb—strength of character. Pointed tips to fingers,—not fond of work (suggest a rich husband). A large mount opposite to the mount of the thumb,—a large imagination. If the little finger be a long one, great tact is shown. If short, the reverse is the case. If there should be a cross, thus ×, on the mount of Jupiter, which is the mount under the first finger, predict a good marriage ; if two crosses, two marriages. If over the whole palm many lines are seen, and they are fine, and form a network, the person worries very much, often over small things. Lastly, note the line running round the ball of the thumb in each hand. If clearly marked and unbroken in each hand a long and healthy life may be expected.

You can quickly note the temperament or character by the back of the hand. Turning the little palm over in your own, ascertain if the finger tips are broad, spatulate, or pointed. If broad, and the nails very pink, the vital or ease-loving nature is abundant. If spatulate, the motive, the character of the worker is found. If pointed tips and oval nails, the mental, ideal, and refined character is indicated.

If the hand as a whole turns outward, instead of inclining inwards, a very generous nature is described. N.B.—We extend the hand in the giving, and we close it in retaining. Thus comes the expression, *close-fisted*. Note the colour of the skin; if very yellow, a tendency to biliousness and liver complaint. If hard, and tense and firm to the touch, a healthy organization. If very red, a tendency to feverish complaints, and so on.

These few remarks are likely to cause the young lady to think that you have the wisdom of Solomon. That being the case, remember the motto "a still tongue makes a wise head," and wisely retire on your laurels. Many may be afforded some rare fun, in which truth has been nicely wrapped up, and the saying " shall I tell your fortune, my pretty maid " will be met with entire approval, and your invitation to the next Christmas party assured.

VIOLA (PALMIST).

When alone we have our thoughts to watch; in the family our temper, in society our tongue.—HANNAH MORE.

\*      \*      \*      \*      \*

The years write their record on human hearts as they do on trees, in hidden inner circles or growth which no eye can see.—SAXE HOLIN.

\*      \*      \*      \*      \*      \*      \*

Paradise is always where pure love dwells.—JEAN PAUL RICHTER.

\*      \*      \*      \*      \*

Every bond of your life is a debt. The right lies in the payment of that debt; it can lie nowhere else.—(GEORGE ELIOT.)

# The Nativity of Jesus.

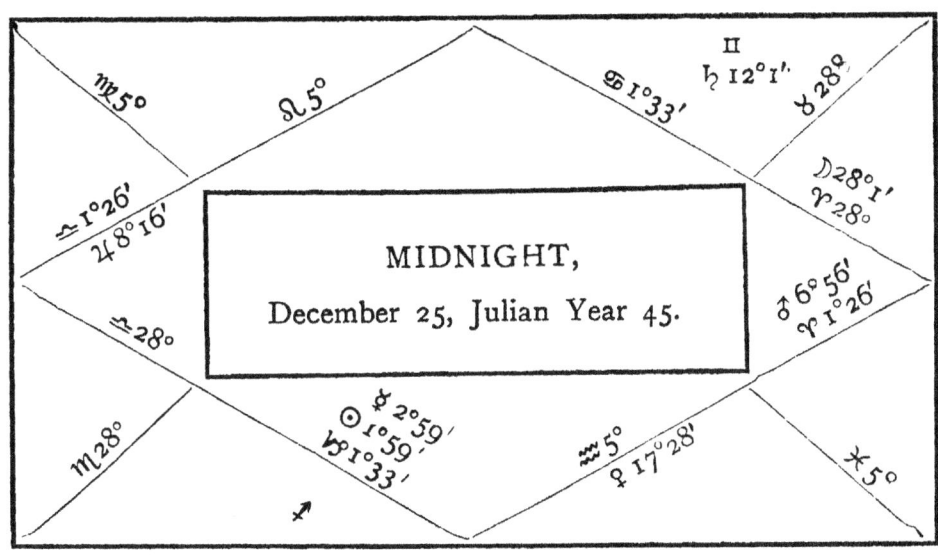

MIDNIGHT,
December 25, Julian Year 45.

*In the first number of the first Volume of the Astrologer's Magazine, we published the above Nativity of Jesus, formerly published by the Rev. Dr. John Butler, Rector of Litchborough in the year 1668. The Rev. Doctor took up the study of Astrology with the set purpose of disproving its truths, but as in the case of all others who have undertaken the same task he became a convert, and one of its most able exponents, but the true meaning of the Christ or Christos he does not appear to have understood as his remarkable reading of this nativity goes to prove.*

---

## CHRISTIANITY AND ASTROLOGY.

THIS subject is so vast and important, requiring so much tact, and consideration in its expression, that one shrinks from the responsibility of wounding in any way the extreme sensitiveness of those who cherish the beauties of the ideal contained in their early teaching with regard to Christianity. Yet the real truth must some day be faced, and at this time of the year when so much misconception is prevalent, it may not do so much harm if the light of Astrology be turned upon some of the actual facts as they really are represented. It may be taken for granted that Jesus lived and taught within the present cycle of two thousand years ; but that He was born of a virgin mother, a feat unknown in nature, must always remain a question until the real facts are known.   But we may suggest as a part of our studies a possible explanation of what appears to be a literal translation of the early initiations into the mysteries.   No matter from what point we study the subject we shall be met with the same internal meaning, from the birth of the Christ, until the crucifixion and the ascent into Heaven.   Taken from the consideration of the Zodiac we have the birth of Spirit, or the Sun (Son), out of the sign Leo, through the Virgin soil, or sign Virgo.   (It is said in the New Testament that the Lord overshadowed the Virgin).

Taken from another standpoint, Astrologically, the Sun is representative of the Father, and the Moon the Mother.   The Sun overshadows the Moon monthly.   The Moon is the preserver and nourisher, while the Sun vitalizes, and all things are generated by heat from water and moisture.   Now the Moon rules over all liquids which are clear and pure, hence the Moon is always called a pure and perpetual Virgin.   When the Sun and Moon (circle and half-circle), are linked to the Cross, the planetary symbol of Mercury is formed and all through the circle of the Zodiac it is this messenger of the Gods whose house is the Virgin sign Virgo, He is the Virgin youth, the outcome of the Solar, Lunar union.   The whole meaning of the birth and crucifixion is concealed in Astrology, let him who would disprove it, study and learn the true meaning of all its wonderful symbology.

The concentrated essence of all the past history of the world and the true meaning of the world's evolution is contained in the planetary symbols and the twelve signs of the Zodiac.   The Cross symbolizes matter or substance, and upon *this* cross the Spirit is crucified.

From Aries to Pisces we may take the beautiful symbology of the Cross over the circle ($\mars$) Mars, in his journey through the twelve signs to finally end as love in Pisces, the exaltation of Venus, circle over the Cross ($\venus$).   If we follow the Moon from her own sign, we find her reaching her exaltation in Taurus ($\taurus$) finally to end in the twelfth sign from her house, Gemini $\left(\text{II}\right)$, here she becomes again linked to matter $\left( \text{☿} \right)$, or the Cross. It is in Aries that the Sun of Man is crucified, for in this sign spirit begins its cycle through the twelve signs of the Zodiac.

And this is why Aries $\left( ♈ \right)$ has always been known to astrologers as the sign of sacrifice; though few realise the real signification of the word sacrifice. Its root is derived from *sacer*—sacred, or holy; *facio*— to make, to make holy. "And Leah said a troop cometh, and she called his name Gad," the biblical name for the sign Aries, and one in which the pioneer is so aptly expressed. The sacrifice takes place at Easter, the time of the Passover, when the pascal lamb is slain (Aries, the ram). Even if we note the symbol of the sign Aries, made from the horns of the ram, we see in it the meeting of the intellect and intuition, or the head and heart. And in this the sacrifice becomes complete. In the horns of the ram are outpouring rays of love and wisdom, both rising out of the will at the root or base. And then, tracing the Sun's progress, we have in Whitsun or white sunday, the arrival at Cancer, the house of the Moon, when the white garments are put on for initiation, the period of the older *Pentecost*. Here is the mystery of the Trinity, in which the past, present, and future are concealed; or father, mother, son. It is from the Virgin Mother (Virgo) that the Christ comes forth. At this point the Libran scales are equally balanced. Aries has evolved its opposite, and from Mars, the warrior, is evolved the Venus, whose mission is love; the Old Testament closes, to be taken up by the New. Light dawns upon the world, and Jesus takes up his cross.

Reaching Capricorn, the foot of the Cardinal Cross is reached, and for three days he lays buried, to rise again and pass into the sign of the perfected man; then finally we see the ☉ has surmounted the Cross, and the Exhaltation into the double half-circles (♓) Pisces is complete, then if we can see in this sign the closing up of the Cross into the one straight line and the half circles joined we can see the perfected individuality as it were, within its own circle, to which the consciousness of all other circles is added. Such an one was Jesus, upon Him descended the true Christ or Christos, and He became one with the Father in heaven. His disciples were fishermen, and He left with them the legacy that they might become fishers of men, for Pisces ends the cycle of the serving trinity. In My Father's house are many mansions He said. Eternal and Divine bliss awaits the perfected ones but the truth alone can set us free.

# Dreams.

AVICEN makes the cause of dreams to be an ultimate intelligence moving the Moon in the midst of that light with which the fancies of men are illuminated while they sleep. Aristotle refers the cause of them to common sense, but placed in the fancy. Averroes places it in the imagination. Democritus ascribes it to little images, or representations; Plato, among the specific and concrete notions of the soul. Albertus, to the superior influences which continually flow from the sky through many specific mediums.

Some physicians attribute the cause of them to vapours and humours, and the affections and cares of persons predominant when awake, for, say they, by reason of the abundance of vapours, which are inhaled in consequence of immoderate feeding, the brain is so stuffed by it that monsters and strange chimera are formed, of which the most immoderate eaters and drinkers furnish us with sufficient instances.

Some dreams, they assert, are governed partly by the temperature of the body and partly by the humour which mostly abounds in it, to which may be added the apprehensions which have preceded the day before, which are often remarked in dogs and other animals which bark and make a noise in their sleep.

In dreams, they observe, proceeding from the humours and temperature of the body, we see the choleric dream of fire, combats, yellow colours, etc.; the phlegmatic, of water, baths, of sailing on the sea, etc.; the melancholic, of thick fumes, deserts, fantasies, hideous faces, etc.; the sanguine, of merry feasts, dances, etc.

They that have the hinder part of the brain clogged with vicious humours, called by physicians ephialtes incubus, or, as it is termed, nightmare, imagine, in dreaming, that they are suffocated; and those who have the orifice of their stomach loaded with malignant humours are affrighted with strange visions, by reason of those venomous vapours that mount to the brain and distemper it.

Cicero tells a story of two Arcadians, who, travelling together, came to Megara, a city of Greece between Athens and Corinth, where one of them lodged in a friend's house and the other at an inn. After supper the person who lodged at the private house went to bed, and, falling asleep, dreamed that his friend at the inn appeared to him and begged his assistance, because the innkeeper was going to kill him. The man immediately got out of bed, much frightened at the dream, but, recovering himself, and falling asleep again, his friend appeared to him a second time and desired that, as he would not assist him in time, he would take care, at least, not to let his death go unpunished; that the innkeeper, having murdered him, had thrown his body into a cart and covered it with dung. He therefore begged that he would be at the city gate in the morning, before the cart was out. Struck with this new dream, he went early to the gate, saw the cart, and asked the driver what was in it. The driver immediately fled, the dead body was taken out of the cart, and the innkeeper apprehended and executed.—THE ASTROLOGER.

# Editorial Comment.

WING to the special nature of this Christmas Number, our ordinary and usual articles have been suspended. In issuing this number we have endeavoured to make an appeal to the minds of those who are not accustomed to our metaphysical style, and symbolical interpretations of planetary influence, with a hope that they may find food for reflection in this lighter reading.

Every reader of this number may obtain a knowledge of our fascinating science, and be enabled to understand the laws of Fate and Fortune, if a continuance of subscription be made to the following issues. Month by month we explain the laws which govern human destiny, and illustrate those peculiarities of human inequalities that so often puzzle those who are limited to the conventional methods of investigation and research.

The web of destiny is unravelled in a clear and simple manner, and the science of Astrology is taught by a system that is adopted by no other work upon the subject. It seeks to explain the laws of Fate, and the theory of re-embodiment of the Soul.

Every person whose intellect is seeking an explanation of the problems of life, should support this magazine in its endeavour to spread a knowledge of Astro-philosophy.

Our object in running this magazine is to assist in expanding the minds of all those whose lines of thought run upon similar ideas, and we are willing and anxious to share our experience by throwing out hints and suggestions in symbolical language ; so that readers may become fellow students of that particular branch of occultism known as Astrology.

Each month we place at the disposal of our readers a special page, for the purpose of answering any questions that may be put to the astrologer who has charge of this department ; all that we require is that the coupon, which appears month by month, may be sent with the question, so that we may be satisfied with the bona-fides of the enquirer.

Month by month, a portion of our energies are devoted to a study of the phenomena of planetary influence, and by tabulation, and the help of older students, combined efforts are made to elucidate the law of our life upon this planet, and the influence of other planets upon it.

All readers who have found in themselves sympathy with our plan, are earnesty entreated to help us in this work of spreading knowledge. Our motives are quite impersonal, and above the taint of self-interest, the sole desire being to unravel the mysteries, and learn the Will of God.

Those who have been our valued supporters up to the present, are now asked to extend their help and support, by introducing this number to every one they may meet or know. From a very small beginning over seven years ago, we have rapidly grown in influence and public favour, and this mainly by the help of our friends and helpers.

With hearty good wishes to the whole world, we only need express one desire, and that is for a few to realize the full astrological meaning of the birth of the Saviour of Mankind. To every one the Christ will some day come; all that is required of us is that we make the Temple a fitting sanctuary, wherein the Christos may dwell.

Take up thy Cardinal Cross, upon it the Sun of Man is crucified, and upon it all limitation must be overcome.

---

Christians, awake, and hail the rising Sun,
  Within thy heart there dwells the link divine.
T'was he who overcame, whose Soul proclaimed the song,
  Thy will be done ; peace on earth, until the end of time.

# Questions answered by the "Astrologer."

N.B.—*If you are in doubt as to the future, seeking advice upon the problems of life, or desirous of testing the truth of Astrology, then consult the Astrologer into whose hands the management of this part of the Magazine has been entrusted. All communications should be addressed to the Editorial offices of* MODERN ASTROLOGY, *9, Lyncroft Gardens, West Hampstead, N.W., and the envelopes marked Q. The correspondence must be written upon one side of the paper only, and no more than one question asked at the time of sending. We shall require the following particulars with the question :—* TIME, DATE, *and* PLACE OF BIRTH, *full name and address, or instead, a suitable non de plume, which alone will be used when sent. All questions are answered free of charge. Answers will be sent by post to subscribers if desired, or on receipt of twelve stamps to non-subscribers. Questions are answered in rotation as received. The numbers to each question have reference to the map which has been erected for future requirements. The particulars of question run through in the following order :—No—, nom de plume, birth data, place, question. The birth data will be suppressed if required.*

In future the following COUPON must be sent with all questions to which a reply is required under the above heading.

Special replies are sent by the editor, through the post to those who remit **2/6** Stamps, or Postal Order with their question :—

---

[COUPON.]                                        *December, 1897.*

## TO THE ASTROLOGER.

---

Kindly answer through the pages of " MODERN ASTROLOGY," the question attached to this Coupon.

---

*Nom de Plume*..................................................

Edited by
ALAN LEO, P.A.S.

The Official Organ of the Astrological Society.

Vol. 3, No. 6.   *   JANUARY, 1898.   *   Price 1s.

## Announcements.

With this number we are closing the present volume owing to the increase in bulk of the numbers issued. The price of the volume, bound in cloth, will be seven shillings.

We propose in the next volume to continue improving the quality of the magazine as far as lies in our power, assuming that the support required from subscribers is maintained.

In future the volumes will close with the half year, and subscriptions may be sent half-yearly, or annually, as desired. The annual subscription is twelve shillings, or half-yearly, six shillings and sixpence, post free to any part of the world.

During the next three months we offer a free horoscope, or one year's directions to all subscribers who introduce a fresh subscriber. And to those who introduce three new subscribers we will present a copy of Vol. 3 Modern Astrology bound in cloth. Any student introducing five fresh subscribers, will be presented with a bound volume of Ephermerides for any ten years selected.

Students may send us the names of likely subscribers, to whom we will send a specimen copy, and should they become subscribers eventually, we will credit them the same as though they had introduced the subscriber. We want one thousand direct subscribers, and we are prepared to pay a premium to obtain them; and as we are determined to accomplish this object, we shall be glad of your support, help and assistance. The new features of the next volume will be found mentioned elsewhere.

R

# A Simple Method of Instruction in the Science of Practical Astrology.

## HEALTH—(*Continued.*)

WE have stated that the several parts of the body are governed by certain signs, but these signs have also a wider meaning than the mere control of the physical parts. The division of the signs into groups of fire, air, earth, and water, more important than is generally supposed.

Taking the earthy signs into consideration, first, we find that they control the centres of physical action. The three earthy signs are Taurus, Virgo and Capricorn, governing respectively the throat, neck and bowels, and solar plexus and the knees. Hence we have speech, sensation and motion, governed by Venus, Mercury and Saturn, and having control over the purely physical form or side of the body.

The watery signs are connected with the body through the emotional or sensational centres. The three watery signs are Cancer, Scorpio and Pisces, governing the stomach, secret parts and feet.

Under the control of the Moon, Mars and Jupiter, are the centres of the psychological part of our composition, the vapoury bodies called the etheric, astral and auric.

The airy signs preside over the mental body and the centres connected with the mind. The airy signs are Gemini, Libra and Aquarius.

Mercury, Venus and Uranus, are the planets having control.

Where the Nativity indicates that Uranus is latent as a ruler, then Saturn governs Aquarius. The three airy signs govern the lungs and chest, reins and kidneys, ankles and blood.

The last three are the fiery signs, having direct connection with the soul, or the highest manifestation in the majority of humanity.

The fiery signs are Aries, Leo and Sagittarius.   These signs are ruled by Mars, Sun and Jupiter, and they govern the head and face, heart, back and the thighs.

It will be noticed, that the central signs of each group are the vital and most important, as they govern the most active centres.

We have now a tabulation as follows :—

| Symbol. | Sign. | Part of Body. | Ruler. | Symbol. | Nature. |
|---|---|---|---|---|---|
| ♈ | Aries | Head and Face | Mars | ♂ | Fire |
| ♉ | Taurus | Neck and Throat | Venus | ♀ | Earth |
| ♊ | Gemini | Chest and Shoulders | Mercury | ☿ | Air |
| ♋ | Cancer | Breasts and Stomach | Moon | ☾ | Water |
| ♌ | Leo | Heart and Back | Sun | ☉ | Fire |
| ♍ | Virgo | Bowels and Solar Plexus | Mercury | ☿ | Earth |
| ♎ | Libra | Reins and Kidneys | Venus | ♀ | Air |
| ♏ | Scorpio | Secret Parts and Muscles | Mars | ♂ | Water |
| ♐ | Sagittarius | Thighs and Sacrum | Jupiter | ♃ | Fire |
| ♑ | Capricorn | Knees and Bones | Saturn | ♄ | Earth |
| ♒ | Aquarius | Ankles and Blood | Uranus | ♅ | Air |
| ♓ | Pisces | Feet | Jupiter | ♃ | Water |

To locate diseases, and all physical derangements, we must note the positions of Saturn and Mars, and the points from which afflictions come. If they occur in the cardinal signs, then the disease will be functional but if in the fixed signs vital, while the common signs will indicate the nervous system.

The sign upon the cusp of the ascendant will indicate the nature of the disease, or the parts most susceptible and easily affected, while planets in the ascendant will indicate also the nature of complaints. Saturn giving cold complaints and Mars fevers.

In the same way the signs govern the various parts of the body, so may it be said of the houses.  The first house governs the head and face, the second the throat, and so on through the twelve houses.

It has been found that Uranus governs incurable diseases, or as we should say, diseases at present not understood, and their causes lying beyond the knowledge of the ordinary physician.

Apart from physical heredity, it is within the range of everyone, whose mind is not affected, to secure good bodily health, and Nature provides the means, as will be seen from what we shall have to say as we proceed.

Persons who have the majority of the planets in the earthy signs, should pay especial attenti n to the purity of their food, and everyone who can in any way manage it should avoid eating the flesh of animals, this not being at all necessary to sustain life. The impurities taken into the system by way of animal foods are at present very little thought of; apart from the pyschological impurities drawn around the system, the various functions of the body are clogged up and over-loaded. All foods should be properly cooked, and every care should be taken to insure their cleanliness and purity, and if possible all bad magnetism should be eliminated from their preparation.

The earthy or physical types of humanity to be healthy require good, plain wholesome food and plenty of exercise.

Those coming under the watery signs, or having the majority of planets in watery signs, should be exceedingly particular with regard to cleanliness; proper and regular daily bathing, and the frequent change of under-wear are essential. All damp and chills should be avoided, and cleanliness should be made a feature of the life. They should associate only with very clean persons, and avoid contagious places, looking wel to the drains of the housesthey reside in, or are visiting; being very receptive, they need care in the choice of surroundings; they should be as far removed as possible from slaughter-houses, butcher's shops and public-houses, and above all things they should avoid intoxicants.

Those coming under the airy signs, either by the rising sign or by having the majority of planets in airy signs, require abundance of fresh air and artistic surroundings; as they are essentially refined in nature and purity of mind is for them the best condition. The higher the tone of their mental conditions, the better will the health be. With them the mind will so re-act upon the body, that the mind should have the first care. Living in the plane of the mind as they do, they should study the culture of the mind; they should associate themselves with cheer-fulness, brightness and hope, and should read the best authors, and poets, changing the mental vibration when weary or depressed. With this class the artistic and beautiful will always act as a tonic, and before taking drugs and physic they should get the mind in to order. Living as they do in their mental or mind body, they should make refinement and harmonious surroundings their first care.

Those coming under the last group, the fiery, require an ideal and subjective world to live in. In all cases of ill-health the spiritual element must be aroused, and that which appeals to the soul or ideal life needs attention. They can have no ideal too high ; and all that is gross and common will act like poison to the soul and re-act on the body. To be in touch with their true self they must look to the spiritual and live in the highest part of their nature ; if not they will in time sicken, pine and die. Music will do much to dispel the clouds that gather upon the horizon of the fiery types of humanity.

All students of Astrology look upon the physical body as the temple or medium through which the ego can manifest upon the physical plane, or the world of gross matter. But they have not yet fully realized that the mind is also a medium though which the ego functions therefore, after running through the physical requirements with regard to health, later on we shall take up the necessary mental purifications essential to perfect health.

## CAUSE AND EFFECTS.

Nature is a vast circular chain of causes and effects. Causes joining produce effects, and these effects unite, becoming causes for other effects. This chain of causation is universal and constant. The elements of the vital principle are common to all; they pervade the universe, and extend their influence over all animated nature. The atmosphere is universal as regards terrestial beings, and a common support to them all. Then, as fire consumes the tangible parts of bodies, and converts their natural structure into another form, so does the vital principle consume the atmosphere and become united with its vital elements converting food to the nourishment of the body, and preserving itself from decay by its affinity to the elements of life diffused throughout the universe.

# An Essay on the Astral Forces and the Relation of the Planetary Rays to Art and Science.

## No. I.—MUSIC AND COLOUR—(*Continued.*)
### By AGAR ZARIEL.

ERE we find the first or key-note C, represented by the Sun and orange ray, is linked by contrast with the sixth or saturnine note A, the blue ray, which in musical parlance is called the "relative minor key." It represents an opposition of tonality in quality and in colours; orange and blue are known as complmentaries or contrasts.

This first or solar tone forms the foundation of the key—the top and bottom of the scale-octave, from which the other tones evolve. It is bright, warm and genial in character, like the sunshine of spring time, tonic and reviving like its colour ray, orange, while its contrasting note A is melancholy, and cold as its colour, blue.

The second or supertonic D is linked in a similar manner with the fourth or sub-dominant F, and these are contrasted tones in musical art, while their respective colours, yellow and purple, are also known as contrasts or complementary. It is the Venus tone, of highly romantic and beautiful quality, and is strangely attracted towards the fifth or red martial note, so much so that some authors call it the pre-dominant, because, when used as the bass of a fundamental chord, it seems drawn to the Mars tone, and in this form is much used in constructing the concluding harmonies of a musical phrase :—

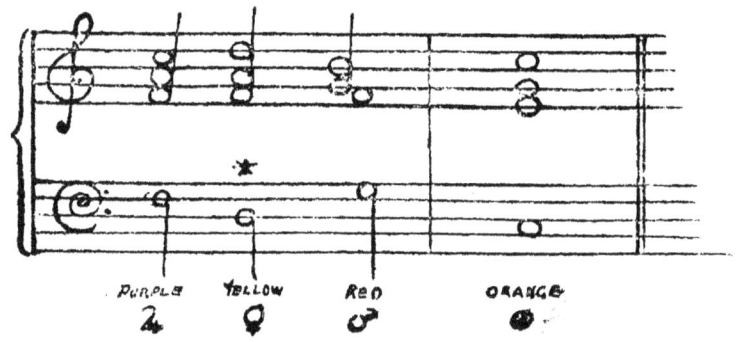

Venus being the natural symbol of love, repose and the feminine nature, and Mars the symbol of force and the masculine nature, so in musical art, which acts upon the sentiments by the symbolic nature of sounds, the Venus impulse leads to repose and perfection through the martial dominant to the solar tonic, bringing a state of perfect rest.

The third of the scale or mediant E is the lunar or green tone, and forms a powerful contrast with the fifth or Mars note G, and these give complementary tones and colours, green and red. This green, mediating note E, has a sympathetic affinity with A, the blue saturnine note. The name of mediant by which this tone is called is very significant, for not only is its colour green a powerful mediant in Nature, but the satellite under whose influence it falls bears also the same character in the great planetary scale. It lies exactly midway between the orange key-note or tonic, and the red dominant, supplying in this position the two primary elements of colour which are absent from the red, viz., blue and yellow mixed.

The fourth of the scale, sub-dominant, the Jupiter tone and purple or indigo ray, is the most majestic and royal note of the series. A simple chord formed upon this tone is used to give an expression of awe and grandeur, as in the Amen of the old Church music. Its effect is unmistakable and at once suggests something great, good, just and impressive.

This purple symbol contrasts in influence with the Venus or yellow tone, being complementary in sound and colour.

The fifth of the scale, dominant or red martial tone, is the most forcible and flaring sound in the scale, from which fact it derives its name. It forms the chief trumpet-note in military music, and in every

sense bears out its true domineering martial character.   It has a strong
affinity to the orange or key-note and a powerful contrasting or complementary effect with the Lunar mediant or green tone.

When it is desired to proclaim a new key, or to establish a firm
tonal effect, this note is used for the purpose ; therefore, when modulating
from one key to another, the dominant or martial tone of the new key
is employed to announce it and herald it into prominence.

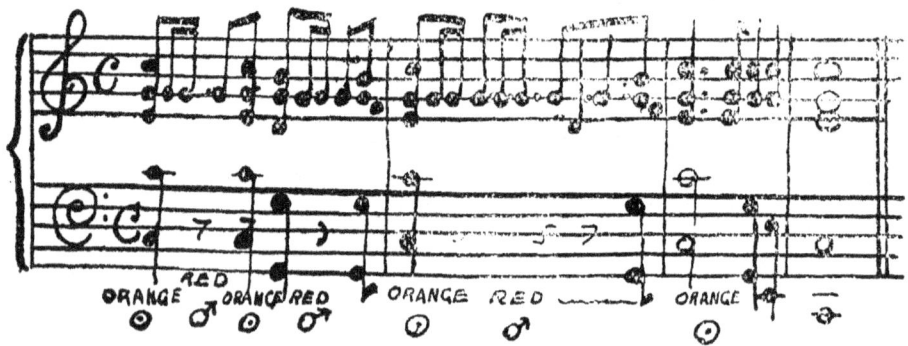

The sixth of the scale, the sub-mediant, or saturnine blue ray, is sad
and  melancholy in character, exciting  meditation and memory of the
past.   It has a strong affinity with the Lunar green tone, and a powerful contrasting effect with the tonic, orange tone, as chords founded
upon these notes will show :—

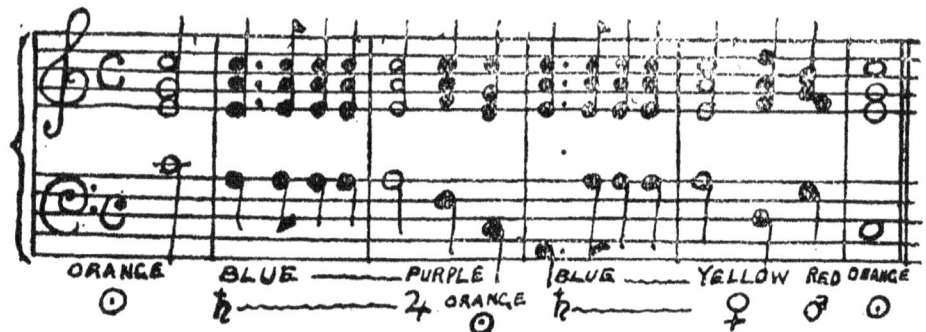

The seventh of the scale, leading note, or sensitive note, the mercurial
or violet tone forms the highest of the series.   It has no special affinity
or contrast with the others excepting the tonic or solar tone, into which
as the " Messenger  of the Gods, " it leads the others,  hence its
name of " leading note."  When allied with the purple or indigo
note it sets up a peculiar mental impression of keen anticipation which

demands that the violet should become absorbed into the orange and the purple into the green :—

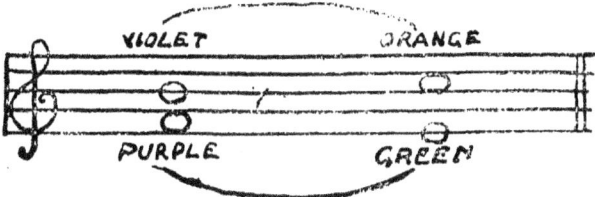

This has a very significant application in relation to astro-philosophy, for Jupiter and Mercury (purple and violet) when well-connected symbolize the highest grade of justice and intellect, worthy of being received by the two monarchs of heaven—the Sun who rules by day, the material King of Glory, holding the supreme position, and the Moon who rules by night, the material Queen of heaven holding sway as the mediator with the great Lord of Day.

As before observed, there are other arrangements of the colour and tone scales bearing on different lines or planes of action, physical and mental, where the planetary colours become modified and more or less altered by the retardation or acceleration of the vibratory action in different spheres.

In the old magical ceremonies the colours or planetary vibrating rays are at considerable variance with what has been noted regarding these influences on modern music and medical art.

In the occult sphere of the ancient ceremonies connected with magical rites, the colours are :—⊙, deep yellow or orange (gold) ☽, white (silver); ☿, light purple (violet) (quicksilver); ♀, green (copper); ♂, red (iron); ♃, blue (tin); ♄, black (lead).

In this scale of application the change of zodiacal influx has no doubt much influence. For instance, Venus would give the green when associated with the earthly sign Taurus, which is the exaltation of the Moon, whereas the yellow Venus colour is connected with her Libra nature in the action upon the human excretory system, and the artistic qualities of the sign Libra.

Saturn's black ray is associated with his earthly night-house Capricorn, and his cool and sedative blue ray with the airy waterman Aquarius.

In like manner, Jupiter's blue ray would be connected with the watery sign Pisces, and the purple ray from Sagittarius, yet this blue would partake more of the indigo ray than Saturn's aquarius blue.

The Moon's white ray is her own silvery sheen, but when treated in connection with a complete planetary scale, the Sun becomes the great master and transmitter of the combined planetary rays, which, as a sum total, are white until separated by partial absorption, reflection, or refraction.

Since the olden days of Astrological research the planets, Uranus and Neptune have been discovered, or perhaps re-discovered, and observation and experience are associating them with certain mixed tints. The following table gives the various colour-rays connected with the planetary action on different planes of manifestation :—

### TABLE OF PLANETARY COLOURS.

⊙  Orange, gold, and yellow brown.

☽  Green, white, pearly tints, and bright sparkling hues.

☿  Violet, light purple, grey and mixed colours which partake of the three primaries, red, blue and yellow.

♀  Yellow, pale green, and pale delicate hues.

♂  Dark red, scarlet, and fiery colours.

♃  Dark purple and indigo blue.

♄  Sky-blue, black, and dark brown.

♅  Streaky and mixed colours, plaids, and uncommon eccentric loud combinations.

☿  Whitish, luminous blue, and yellowish green, novel ethereal tints, sometimes reverses to darkness.

As indicated in the musical scale and medicinal influences, we find the relation of colour with the planetary influx proving itself by natural association of character and condition.

But this is not all, for herein the great voice of Nature speaks again. If we associate these colour and planetary rays with the sounds as naturally produced in the scale of harmonics, there is presented to us for contemplation a wonderful symbolism of human progress through the long vista of time and evolution, from the lowest grade of savage life to the highest conception of wisdom and intellectual attainment :—

First, we have the very lowest elementary manifestion of animal force and life in the martial ray. This becomes accentuated by another and more active vibration of the red ray, giving increase of the martial and lower instincts, before the first dawn of love, as also greed, self-preservation and combative propensities in their earliest stages—a mere gratification of the physical appetites.

After this comes the first Venus ray, ushering in the dawn of the earliest development of the love instinct. This brings the joint influence of the two nearest planets, Mars and Venus, into combined action on their lowest planes of manifestation. The crude savage is only dominated by these two approximate planets—the male and female propensities—red and yellow.

Then comes another flash of the red martial ray on a somewhat higher and more active plane, though still of a low and undeveloped type, without the knowledge of good and evil being developed beyond a mere sense of personal like and dislike.

After this is suggested the first dawn of knowledge and mental expansion from the earliest emanation of the Mercurial ray, bringing the mind into progressive action with expression of thought, memory, and a sense of good and evil. This is naturally followed by a higher grade of the instinct of love, with increased purity of intention, as shown by the succession of the Venus tone on a more exalted plane immediately after the first Mercurial ray.

Then follows, as a consequence, the first Jupiter tone, signifying the acquirement of a sense of veneration and justice—the inevitable out-come of the elements of knowledge and expansion of intellect, combined with increase of purity and discretion in the love sentiments.

After this follows the highest unfolding of the red, martial tone, bringing nobility and adjustment of better conditions in warfare, com-bined with skill in weapons, knowledge, justice, and the extension of manufacturing and trading faculties.

This is succeeded by the blue saturnine note, which, as a consequence of all the foregoing leads to a development of the meditative and higher reflective and religious propensities, with regret for past misdeeds and with contemplation of the infinite, thus completing the first round of the mental faculties.

This is followed by the highest grade of human knowledge in the last projection of the mercurial or violet ray in its most exalted sphere, bringing to light the greatest perfections in human mentality on the physical plane, noble and scientific inventions, altogether beyond all former attempts, marvellous mechanisms and increased inter-communi-cation between nations, bringing the whole race of mankind face to face with interchange of knowledge between nation and nation.

Then comes the great solar tonic or orange tone, showing the spread of spirituality and perfection of the mental attributes extending from the physical towards the development of the soul and the psychic plane. This final is succeeded by the most exalted vibrations of the Venus ray, the perfection of all that had gone before, the acme of wisdom, spirituality and true divinity of love.  This meets the last emanation of the human, physical, mental, evolutionary stage in the Lunar green ray, typical of the great mediating link, which lies between mortality and immortality, the perfection of the human soul, the fruitful green of peace, good-will and plenty, the Mediator between the known and the vast unknown—the Buddha of the East, the Christ of the West—the perfect Man.

AGAR ZARIAL.

Sydney, Australia.

# The Winter Quarter.

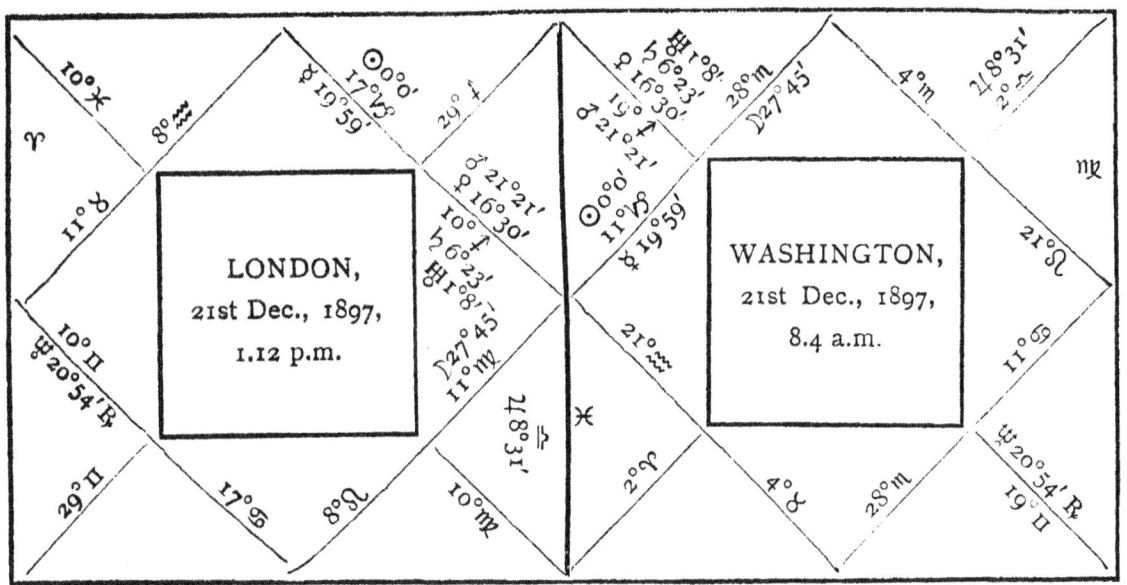

THE same sign rises in each of these maps as in the corresponding figures for the last autumn quarter. Foreign affairs are likely to be very unsettled throughout the greater part of Europe, but especially among the western nations. Disputes about colonies and settlements over seas will cause much trouble to more than one country. Financial affairs and business will not be fortunate; a high expenditure will rule in all money relations, London is sure to suffer in business, through heavy failures and is under a cloud generally. With the affliction of Neptune in Gemini and the elevation of Mercury, it looks very much as if there will be an attempt to carry out the announced changes in the government of London; but if so it will be under very unfavourable auspices.

The Government is unpopular and its power wanes, but it has a firm hold on Parliament. Some statesman may die, and an aged dignitary of Church or State. Divorces, outrages, and crimes against women will abound. There will be disputes rising out of religion and education in the land and especially in London. The death-rate will be high and there will be much sickness.   Thefts of money, swindling and forgery will be frequent and heavy.   The influences are not favourable for the health of the Queen.   There will be storms and loss of life round our coasts, especially when Mars passes over the Sun's place early in January.   One great strike will come to a peaceable end, but others will spring up during the quarter.

In the United States, crime will increase, outrages, murders, and robbery.   Affairs will go far from smoothly in the legislative chambers. The Government and the President lose in popularity.   The health of the country will not be good; some eminent man will die, and the death-rate will be high.

The passage of Mars and Venus over the Sun in both maps and over the angles close by, should be carefully noted during January.

The eclipse of January 8th will be very unfavourable for governments, rulers, and monarchs in countries where it is visible; there will be loss of power and prestige among such, and the death of great and aged people; suffering and discontent among the common people.

H. S. GREEN

If a man conquer in battle a thousand times a thousand men, and if another conquer himself, he is the greater of conquerors.—DHAMMAPADA.

\*          \*          \*          \*          \*

All planets of the Earth make a man illustrious and generally known far and near, and being all swift in motion, renders them dexterous and nimble in the despatch of affairs.

\*          \*          \*          \*          \*

The qualities bestowed upon humanity coming under the influence of Saturn are mysticism, secrecy, contemplation, patience, steadiness, and a love of justice.

\*          \*          \*          \*          \*

If the mind can be considered as having dual attributes, such as subjective and objective, then the planet would govern the objective half, and Jupiter the subjective.   Saturn ruling all the concrete, limited and bound conditions, is the planet of what we may, therefore, call the lower mind.   When the ice-bound conditions of Saturn are melted by the solar rays the Uranian influence in Aquarius begins.

# Studies in Leaves.

O the student of Nature, whose delight is to commune with bird and beast, with flower and stone, the visible universe is a chalice in which he may see the Invisible. It is true that often the images are blurred and indistinct, yet even then a glimpse is caught of the realities beyond. As the sight grows clearer and the senses keener, more and more one realizes the truth of the ancient Hermetic axiom " As above, so below."

Think, for a moment, of some forest giant. Note its massive gnarled stem, its labyrinth of branches, and its graceful foliage. This is the form sheathing a living entity, whose astral shape clear-seeing eyes can view in all its beauty.

Now compare this tree to one's greater life, the life of one's immortal ego, and the leaves to the lesser lives, the lives of our successive personalities, by which the ego, manifests itself. In early spring the tree bursts into leaf. After the leaf, the flower, and finally the fruit. As the parts of the flower and fruit are but modified leaves, we may speak of the foliage-leaves, the flower-leaves and the fruit-leaves.

The studies of botanists during the last two decades have shown the paramount importance of the leaves to the plant. The tree elaborates the materials growth, within the cells of the leaf. It is here one sees the chief living processes by which raw materials form external sources are disintegrated and then built up into the food substances of the plant. Thus the tree, by means of its leaves, comes into touch with the external world, and laying hold upon the forces therein, moulds them into itself. When the leaves fall and the winter rest is at hand, these elaborated substances are indrawn into the stem and root. Similarly the human ego puts forth its foliage of earth lives or leaves, and builds by means of these its spiritual body. It seeks experience in these lives, destroying, constructing, adding little by little to the vestures of the spirit. Sometimes a leaf is blighted and useless, yet a new one will arise in the coming spring, for progression, Nature's own law, triumphs over retrogression. Very beautiful, too, are some of these foliage-leaves, exquisite in shape and glowing with the tints of a future condition.

When the lesser life fades away, and the ego enters into its rest, the assimilated experiences are stored for the coming spring ; when again it will clothe itself in a garment of flesh.

The growth of foliage, however beautiful it may be, is not the ultimate of the tree's existence. There *are* trees which will not go further, like the fig-tree which Jesus saw and found nothing thereon but leaves. The tree must bear flowers and from these will arise the fruit. In the flower the leaves have taken on a new character, and new work. It is the period of blossom when the soul expands and grows into a beautiful flower.

The reserve of strength and will gathered in countless lives is now to be used in producing the lotus blossoms of the soul. To the ego comes the opportunity for accelerated progress, and then (as referred to before in this magazine) it is born into the solar month of Taurus, when earth puts forth her flowers as a token of the heritage of her children.

Yet here again these flower-leaves must die. These exquisite petals rich in perfume, painted and pencilled as only the Divine Hand can devise, must fade that the innermost leaves of the flower may grow into the perfect fruit.

Watch the opening of a lotus lily bud and note the method of unfolding. First, the outer protecting whorl, the calyx, separates its green sepals. until we see within the tender, tinted petals. Then the petals increas in size, unfold, expand, until the sepals are fogotten in the beauty of the corolla. Next the stamens, and finally in the centre is seen the pistil from which will arise the fruit. From the outside to the centre along our spiral of progression, unfolding and growing silently, we pass until fruition begins. Then are we born in the Solar months of the Lion and the Virgin, that the opportunity may be given for the formation of fruit. We must grow until the harvest, when the husbandman will gather in the results of his toil. It was of this final stage that the Hebrew Psalmist sang, "And he shall be like a tree planted by the streams of water, that bringeth forth its fruit in its season, whose leaf also doth not wither." Then, and then only, will the vision of prophet and seer be realized.

EBN EL DELOU.

# Calendar for  January.

## THE LUNAR ASPECTS FOR THE MONTH.

| D M | D W | Moon at Noon. | Before Noon. | After Noon. | Influence. |
|---|---|---|---|---|---|
| | | ° ′ | | | |
| 1 | S | 0 ♉ 12 | △ ♂ | △ ♀ | Finance and pleasure |
| 2 | S | 12 „ 13 | △ ☉ | △ ☿ | Devotion and meditation |
| 3 | M | 24 „ 6 | (☿ Par. ♄) | | Fast day |
| 4 | Tu | 5 ♊ 56 | ☍ ♅ | ☍ ♄ △ ♃ | Avoid travel |
| 5 | W | 17 „ 46 | (☉ centre of ♑) | ☌ ♆ | A day for uncommon events |
| 6 | Th | 29 „ 38 | (☉ ☌ ☿, ☿ ∠ ♅) | ☍ ♂ | Control the energies |
| 7 | F | 11 ♋ 35 | □ ♃ ☍ ♀ | ☍ ☿ | An unfortunate day |
| 8 | S | 23 „ 39 | ☍ ☉ | (☿ 36° ♄) | Fast day |
| 9 | S | 5 ♌ 50 | △ ♅ | △ ♄ ✱ ♃ | Very fortunate |
| 10 | M | 18 „ 12 | ✱ ♆ | (☿ ☌ ♀) | Artistic influences [events |
| 11 | T | 0 ♍ 45 | (☉ Par. ♆) | □ ♅ | Uncommon and unexpected |
| 12 | W | 13 „ 31 | □ ♄ △ ♂ △ ☿ | △ ♀ | A steady influence |
| 13 | Th | 26 „ 32 | △ ☉ □ ♆ | ✱ ♅ | Business active |
| 14 | F | 9 ♎ 50 | ✱ ♄ ♆ □ ♂, ☿ | ☌ ♃ | Disputes end peacefully |
| 15 | S | 23 „ 26 | △ ♆ □ ♀ | □ ☉ | Socially, unfavourable |
| 16 | S | 7 ♏ 21 | (☿ Par. ♄) | ✱ ♂ ✱ ☿ | Meditation & deep thought |
| 17 | M | 21 „ 35 | ✱ ☉ ✱ ♀ | (♀ 150° ♆) | Good influences |
| 18 | Tu | 6 ♐ 5 | ☌ ♅ | ☌ ♄ ✱ ♃ | Mixed |
| 19 | W | 20 „ 47 | ☍ ♆ | (☉ Par ♄, ☿ Par ♅) | Fast day |
| 20 | Th | 5 ♑ 37 | (♀ ∠ ♄) | □ ♃ ☌ ☿ | Unfavourable |
| 21 | F | 20 „ 27 | ☌ ♂ | ☌ ♀ | Purify the passions |
| 22 | S | 5 ♒ 9 | ☌ ☉ ✱ ♅ | ✱ ♆ △ ♃ | Fast day [thought |
| 23 | S | 19 „ 37 | (22nd ☉ ✱ ♅) | △ ♆ | Favourable for higher |
| 24 | M | 3 ♓ 44 | □ ♅ | □ ♄ ✱ ☿ | Strange influences |
| 25 | Tu | 17 „ 28 | (♂ ∠ ♅) | □ ♆ ✱ ♂ | Irritable |
| 26 | W | 0 ♈ 47 | (♀ Par. ♅) | ✱ ☉ △ ♅ ✱ ♀ | Favourable |
| 27 | Th | 18 „ 41 | △ ♄ ☍ ♃ □ ☿ | □ ♂ | Accidents and disputes |
| 28 | F | 26 „ 14 | ✱ ♆ | (♁ 150° ♆ ♀ Par ♄) | |
| 29 | S | 8 ♉ 29 | □ ☉ □ ♀ | (☿ Par. ♆) | Unfavourable |
| 30 | S | 20 „ 31 | △ ☿ | △ ♂ | Intuitional |
| 31 | M | 2 ♊ 24 | 30th ☉ ✱ ♄, △ ♃ | ☍ ♅ | Changeable |

THE month of January is governed by the planet Saturn, who is lord or ruler of the zodiacal sign, Capricorn. The earth passes through the sign from December 22 to January 20, when we enter Aquarius. Saturn means the sower. Chronus, in the mythologies, was the God of time; he was the youngest son of Uranus and Terra. The myth informs us that he devoured his own children as soon as they were born, but Jupiter, or Zeus, escaped this fate and eventually ruled, while Chronus became an exile and wandering into another country taught the people agriculture.

# A Microcephalic Idiot.

Born 5h. 30m. a.m., Sat. 7th Sept., 1895.  Poles 11th, &c.=40°30'
Long. 4h. 58m. 58.4s. E.  Poles 12th, &c.=9°30'21"
Lat. 13°20'30" N.   Worked from ⊙'s Arc and Semi-Arc.
M.C.

| | Lat. | | Declin. | | Rt. Ascen | | | Mid.Dis | | | S. Arc | | | A.D. under Pole of Horos. | |
|---|---|---|---|---|---|---|---|---|---|---|---|---|---|---|---|
| | ° | ' | ° | ' | ° | ' | " | ° | ' | " | ° | ' | " | ° | ' |
| ⊙ | ✕✕✕ | | 6 N | 15 | 165 | 22 | 34 | 82 | 57 | 53 | 88 | 30 | 42 | 1 | 29 18 |
| ☽ | 2 N | 46 | 8 N | 11 | 12 | 9 | 50 | 56 | 10 | 37 | 91 | 57 | 16 | 1 | 57 16 |
| ☿ | 0 N | 13 | 0 N | 3 | 180 | 58 | 4 | 67 | 22 | 23 | 89 | 57 | 39 | 0 | 2 22 |
| ♀ | 7 S | 59 | 8 S | 18 | 179 | 1 | 15 | 69 | 19 | 12 | 91 | 58 | 58 | 1 | 58 58 |
| ♂ | 0 N | 50 | 2 N | 38 | 176 | 4 | 13 | 72 | 16 | 14 | 89 | 30 | 0 | 0 | 30 0 |
| ♃ | 0 N | 16 | 20 N | 20 | 122 | 41 | 28 | 54 | 21 | 1 | 95 | 30 | 54 | 5 | 2 30 |
| ♄ | 2 N | 15 | 10 S | 29 | 212 | 16 | 40 | 36 | 3 | 47 | 92 | 30 | 54 | 2 | 30 54 |
| ♅ | 0 N | 18 | 16 S | 33 | 224 | 18 | 12 | 24 | 2 | 15 | 94 | 2 | 29 | 4 | 2 29 |
| ♇ | 1 S | 27 | 21 N | 28 | 77 | 6 | 9 | 8 | 45 | 42 | 95 | 21 | 10 | 5 | 21 10 |
| ebaran | 5 S | 28 | 16 N | 18 | 67 | 29 | 8 | 0 | 51 | 19 | 93 | 58 | 39 | 3 | 58 39 |
| Regel | 31 S | 8 | 8 S | 19 | 77 | 22 | 56 | 9 | 2 | 29 | 88 | 0 | 48 | 1 | 59 12 |
| Sirius | 39 S | 35 | 16 S | 24 | 100 | 8 | 11 | 31 | 47 | 44 | 85 | 57 | 16 | 4 | 2 44 |
| Castor | 10 N | 5 | 32 N | 7 | 111 | 59 | 5 | 43 | 38 | 38 | 98 | 33 | 40 | 8 | 33 40 |
| Regulus | 0 N | 28 | 12 N | 29 | 150 | 42 | 3 | 82 | 21 | 36 | 93 | 0 | 32 | 3 | 0 32 |
| Spica | 2 S | 3 | 10 S | 37 | 199 | 55 | 14 | 48 | 25 | 13 | 92 | 32 | 52 | 2 | 32 52 |
| Antares | 5 S | 45 | 26 S | 12 | 245 | 45 | 9 | 2 | 35 | 18 | 96 | 42 | 10 | 6 | 42 10 |

O.E.$= 23°27' 10.41''$

| | H. | M. | S. |
|---|---|---|---|
| Sidereal Time, noon, 6th September ... | 11 | 1 | 18.42 |
| Correction for Longitude, E. ... ... ... | 0 | 0 | 49.11 |
| Sidereal Time at Udipi ... ... ... | 11 | 0 | 29.31 |
| Birth Time ... ... ... ... ... | 17 | 30 | 0.00 |
| Difference S. and M. Time ... ... ... | 0 | 2 | 52.49 |
| | 28 | 33 | 21.80 |
| | 24 | 0 | 0.00 |
| R.A. of M.C. ... ... ... ... ... | 4 | 33 | 21.80 |

M. Arc ... 68° 20' 27''.

THE above Map has been sent to us by a member of the Astrological Society for publication, so that those who are not members may have the benefit of some of the society's work of tabulation.

At first glance the ordinary student might be forgiven if he passed this case over as one that he could not solve, and although it has been dealt with by the Society at one of its social meetings we have thought it advisable to give some of the leading professors of the science an opportunity to offer their opinion as to the case from an astrological standpoint.

We therefore make bold to invite the judgement of the gifted astro- logers, " Sepharial," A. J. Pearce, Esq, " Raphael " and " Herschel." Also any of the known astrologers whom we have not mentioned.

We hope that prejudice will not prevent these gentlemen, each of whom claims to possess astrological ability, from giving an opinion since we have no other object than to get at truth.

The gentleman who has supplied the data can be relied upon, and for the information of those who may have any doubts we will state that he is a superintendent of police, and a student whose mathematical ability is beyond question. We may state that he was unable to solve the problem.

The question to be solved is :— " What is the Astrological cause of this case ; also how long will the child live ?" Replies should be sent in as early as possible, and we should prefer that none but astrologers who have in some way come before the public, should send in answers.

The value of the Wisdom Religion does not appear to have been fully recognised by students of astrology, and this is probably owing to the mistaken attitude of a few who prefer to maintain a sect, or cult, excluding all investigations from others, even those who know that this science is the oldest in the world. Unity is needed among all students ; sooner or later this great fact will have to be recognised, and to this end we would earnestly advise all astrologers to tone down their Uranian nature, for since they are undoubtedly strong, they should be tolerant as well as merciful.

The following interesting reply to a question in the Vâhan under the well-known initials "A.B." may throw some light upon our subject, so for the benefit of astrological students we reproduce it.

### QUESTION CCCLXXXI.

*L.D.—What kind of evil-doing in past lives is the karmic cause of insanity ?*

A. B.—Insanity appears to be the karmic result of grave crimes committed against knowledge and bringing serious ills to others. That which may be termed ordinary wrong-doing, committed from ignorance, heedlessness, or under the blind impulses of passion, works itself out in the ordinary sufferings of life, and by these the ego learns the existence of law and the folly of setting himself against the evolutionary process. But there are crimes committed against light and against knowledge, especially those which drag back a soul progressing in the higher life, and these may bring about insanity as a karmic consequence. Let us suppose that an ego has definitely entered on the pathway which leads to discipleship, and is within measurable distance of that condition ; another ego—prompted by envy, by lust, or by any other evil feeling, or by some deeper motive into which the mental element largely enters— allures or tempts the rapidly advancing soul, shakes it from its balance, and thus causes it to fall from the point it had attained, and perchance entails on it many a weary incarnation ere the lost ground is recovered ; such a criminal reaps as harvest the appropriate fruit of insanity, during which his own ego, tethered to a body physically incapable of serving it as its vehicle or expression, suffers on the astral plane all the tortures of impotent longing to progress, a sentence, as it were, of penal servitude, cut off from human association and from the joy of activity. Thus fettered, the ego learns that it is an evil thing and bitter to hinder the growth of another soul, and experiences in his own person the delay he has induced for another. It seems not unlikely that Jesus had this penalty in mind in his impressive warning to any who should cause to offend "one of these little ones," whose "angels do always behold the face of my Father which is in heaven." Quoth the Teacher: " It were better for him that a millstone were hanged about his neck, and that he were drowned in the depth of the sea (See Matt. xviii. 6, 16.) The loss of a physical body is a light thing compared to the being bound to a physical body which is dead to every higher impulse.

# The Flat Earth Theory.

ROM time to time we receive many strange letters and pamphlets with regard to the earth and the sun ; and it is still an open question for Astrologers to consider, whether or not, when speaking of the Sun's position in the horoscope, the earth should not be substituted. To one or two of our persistent friends we should like to quote the following from the *Astronomical Alderman:* "Sir," he exclaimed, between his bumpers, "Copernicus and Tycho Brahe, and all those chaps, have had their day; they've written monstrous lies, sir, thumpers! Move round the Sun— its talking treason, the earth stands still ; it stands to reason. Round as a globe ?—stuff—humbug—fable! It's a flat sphere, sir, like a table; and the sun o'erhangs this sphere, and lights it like a chandelier." "But," quoth his neighbour, "when the sun from East to West his course has run, how comes it then he shows his face next morning in his former place ?" "Oho! a pretty question truly," replied the knight, with an unruly burst of laughter and delight—so much his triumph seemed to please him; "why, blockhead, he goes back at night, and that's the reason no one sees him!"

The system of Astrology in use by all Astrologers has always considered the sun as the centre. The Zodiac used is the lunar Zodiac, or that around the earth which is considered as a miniature copy of the Greater or Solar Zodiac. Of this we know very little, if anything, the knowledge being in the hands of the adepts and great Masters. Students will be wise in first mastering the Geocentric positions of the planets before speculating upon the Heliocentric.

Famous are those persons in whose nativities the Moon receives the light of many planets, or is joined to some powerful Royal Fixed Star.

\* \* \* \* \* \*

There is no greater curse to posterity than that of bequeathing them an increasing population of imbeciles and idlers and criminals. To aid the bad in multiplying is, in effect, the same as maliciously providing for our descendants a larger host of enemies.—HERBERT SPENCER, "The Study of Sociology."

# Astrological Stories.

## CHAPTER V.

N a crisp, bright morning in February, some four years later, Squire Lennox, his wife and daughter are seated at breakfast. With the exception that the Squire's hair and beard are now white, and a few extra wrinkles may be traced on the brow of Mrs. Lennox, the march of time has apparently passed unheeded.

It is only when we regard Bessie Lennox herself that we realize that four years have indeed glided away since the events narrated in our last chapter occurred.

The little maiden with sunny curls and short frocks has become almost a woman. At that epoch " When childhood and womanhood meet," as the poet puts it, stands Bessie Lennox. Her hair no longer flows about her shoulders, but is gathered up and fastened back on her head revealing the broad white brow ; the face has gained in expression while losing none of its candour and innocence ; she is tall for sixteen summers, and womanly in appearance.

" The postman must be late to-day, I do wish he would make his appearance," remarked the squire, putting down his empty coffee cup and turning towards his wife, " I am getting anxious about those railway shares ; the Company was unable to pay the half-yearly dividend and the report was anything but satisfactory."

" I think, dear, it would be far wiser to give up these speculative investments," said Mrs. Lennox, " they only cause you anxiety and worry. I wish you had listened to my intuitions respecting those mining shares you took in Bessie's name. What was the name of the mine ?"

" The 'East Wheel Nursel' is all right, wife, don't you concern your-self with business. The stars are more in your line," said the squire, with a sly twinkle in his blue eyes.

" There is the postman, Dad, coming up the drive," said Bessie ; " I will run and get the letters." She opened the window and ran lightly down the gravel path, and, holding out her hand, said : " Please give me the letters, Rogers, father is in a hurry to get them this morning ; " back she came, breathless, holding out to her father one long blue envelope marked " urgent," and then sat down to finish her breakfast.

" Old Rogers grows more feeble every day, mother, it is really time he was superannuated." Mrs. Lennox smiled at her child's determined tone, and was just about to reply, when a groan from Mr. Lennox arrested their attention. The squire had fallen back in his chair, his face was crimson, and the veins on his forehead stood out like whip-cord. His breath came in gasps, and before either Bessie or his wife could reach his side he had fallen to the floor in a fit. Mrs. Lennox loosened his collar, and took his head on her knee, while Bessie, out of whose face every tinge of color had vanished, rang the bell loudly. " Jane," she said, " Let James saddle the mare and fetch Dr. Scott immediately. Father is taken suddenly ill ; " and then—for her mother, usually so capable and clear-headed, now seemed unable to think or give any orders.—Bessie had a fire lighted in the squire's study, just opposite, a bed got ready, and assisted the cook and gardener to carry the unconscious form of the squire there and lay him on the bed.

His wife sat by his side, stunned by the shock, and it was on Bessie the household relied in that hour.

As she passed through the dining-room she found, lying on the floor, the letter that had caused this trouble, and read the announcement of the ruin that had befallen them vainly she strove to understand its purport fully, but only here and there a word stood out. " The company was a swindle ; " " The mine flooded ; " " No hope of recovery," etc. etc. As Bessie Lennox endeavoured to steady her nerves and gather some self-control in that hour of mental agony ,the bud burst into a blossom, the child became the woman with the burden of womanhood upon her : to support, to succour, and sustain.

She locked the letter carefully away, and then returned to her father's bedside.

The laboured breathing, short and heavy, was the only token that life was still in the body, while Mrs. Lennox was so absorbed in watching him, that she was almost unconscious of aught beside.

" Mother, darling," said Bessie, " Dr. Scott will be here soon ; you have always said he was such a clever man, he will know what to do and bring father round.   There he is ! "

At that moment Dr. Scott entered the room and with his keen professioual instincts tpok in the bearings of the case at a glance.

He stooped gently over the unconscious figure on the bed and slowly lifted one of the eyelids, then felt the pulse and examined the heart.

" How long has the squire been ill ?" addressing Mrs. Lennox, who vainly endeavoured to give some coherent reply.

" Father received bad news in a letter this morning at breakfast, then fell from his chair, and has been in this condition since."

Dr. Scott was a middle-aged man, with wife and daughter of his own, and tenderly he spoke to the stricken woman.   " Mrs. Lennox, you must try and bear up ; I will send your husband a dose that I hope will relieve him, but we shall have you on our hands next if you do not rouse yourself ; for Bessie's sake, be brave ! "   He put a white powder in a glass of water and made Mrs. Lennox drink it ; then he took Bessie's hand and led her from the room and softly closed the door.   " Sit down," he said.   He had known the girl from early childhood and she was dear to him.   " Bessie," he said, " my dear child, I am going to tell you the truth, for I know it will be the truest kindness in the end.   Your father has had a seizure of apoplexy ; that is not the main difficulty, however, because we could pull him through that, but his heart is affected, and, in short, there is nothing to be done, your father's hours are numbered." Bessie spoke no word ; the piteous feeling of misery and desolation paralysed her.   Her world had smashed up in two hours ; her eye saw the disarranged breakfast-table, with its empty cups and saucers.   In the shock, hurry and agitation of the morning, the usual work of the day

**had been neglected.** The milk jug had been overturned and milk lay in a pool on the polished boards, with cat and kitten lapping it unconcernedly.

"It must be a dream!" No ; she hears the doctor's voice still speaking. "Your mother has only you, Bessie, to comfort her, remember, and she is not strong." By an almost superhuman effort of will Bessie put self on one side, she must think for her mother.

Though Dr. Scott was used to scenes of sorrow, he felt a curious thrill in the region of the heart, as Bessie Lennox clasped her small hands together in the extremity of her pain, and without a tear, calmly said : "I will do all I can, Dr. Scott, but you know I have had so little to do with sickness."

"I shall send you in a nurse as soon as possible, Bessie, of course, but is there any help I can give you? You spoke of a letter causing your father this seizure."

"Oh, yes, Dr. Scott! and I think mother has quite forgotten all about it." Bessie took it out of the writing bureau and handed it to Dr. Scott. "God bless me!" he ejaculated. "Poor Lennox! No wonder. This is a bad job! Bessie, dear, I will bring back a nurse with me, and as soon as possible (I have two serious cases I must see) will return and stay with you. Don't mention business to your mother, nor let her know your father's condition for a few hours."

"She could not stand more now; she has not your constitution! Cheer up, Bessie, you must be brave for the mother's sake. I won't be long, child."

"Jane," he said, turning to the housemaid, who opened the door for him, "see to Miss Lennox ; coax her to eat."

"How is master, sir ?" said the weeping girl.

Dr. Scott shook his head as he hurried away.

Bessie stood for a moment with her hand pressed to her heart, this was what uncle Sapal meant, "In the hour of any sorrow, don't be afraid to call out for help, invisible helpers are ever near." Then Bessie Lennox prayed for help, for courage, for strength ; and some curious peace fell upon her and a voice whispered, "Not alone, little heart, never alone, for 'God is Love.'"

A week later Squire Lennox died without recovering consciousness. Mrs. Lennox and Bessie, after everything was settled, found themselves with only practically fifty pounds a year to live on, besides a few hundreds in ready-money. All had been swept away by rotten securities.

Dr. Scott and Bessie held counsel together of ways and means, for Mrs. Lennox was utterly prostrate, and on her daughter's young shoulders, the whole burden fell. She it was who paid and dismissed the servants—Jane alone utterly refused to be separated from them in their time of trouble.

" We have not the means to pay you, Jane, we shall have to live in rooms and do for ourselves," said Bessie to the weeping girl, but she spoke in vain.

" Miss Bessie, I only want food and shelter. I love the mistress and you, let me go with you—for a time at least—until something turns up," and Bessie had not the heart to deny her pleading, besides, she, Bessie, must earn something to eke out their scanty means, and Mrs. Lennox really needed someone with her, so utterly broken down in health had she become.

" I always felt I should like to be a nurse, Dr. Scott," said Bessie, " But I suppose that idea is utterly useless now, there would be a premium and——

" No, no, Bessie, I have a brother in Scotland—in Edinborough in fact, who is connected with the training home for nurses and women doctors, and the fine Scotch air would pull your mother round again. If your desires run that way, my child, I do not really see anything better could be done. You have a fine constitution and will be a credit to the Institute."

A month later saw Mrs. Lennox, Bessie and Jane settled in Scotland, and Bessie began her new life, so different to the other. The past life —the life of luxury, and the present one, the life of service, Miss Lennox the squire's daughter, was now Nurse Lennox, in gown and cap. Yet Bessie loved her work, and in the shade of life's pathway, the grit and energy of the girl's character stood the test. She comforted her widowed mother, who sometimes fretted at her own inability to provide means for her child's comfort.

"Mother, darling, whatever is, must be best," said Bessie, "and you believe in God's law, darling, and the stars as his agents. You taught me that in years gone by. We have enough for our needs mother dear, and believe me, I would not exchange my work of ministering to the needs of suffering humanity, for any enjoyment. I am quite content, mother, and quite well; so cheer up, we have got each other, we are not apart—our evenings together are sweeter for the separation by day."

She pressed her rosy cheek close to the white one of her mothers, and Mrs. Lennox recognised, with the rapture mothers know, the noble nature and sweet content of her child's character.

\*    \*    \*    \*    \*

Several years passed and almost the last month of Bessie's time in the Institute was drawing to a close. She had won golden opinions from all. The matron and the doctors considered Nurse Lennox one of their best and most capable nurses. She would have many engagements in the near future, and could command a high fee. Bessie Lennox cared little for fame or name, save as it enabled her to support her mother and be able to supply all the little delicacies and comforts Mrs. Lennox's health and age required. This was, indeed, a joy to Bessie. Being a Leo by birth-right, child of the Sun—her greatest joy was in the "giving" and she was indeed the Sun of the little household, her bright and sunny spirit dispelling all gloom. As she passed up the stairs of the Instiute on this fair autumn morning, the Sun, turning to gold the lustrous coil of hair under the nurse's bonnet, few fairer pictures could be found. Bessie was a pretty child, but she has grown a beautiful woman. Her face has that earnest, spiritual look together with the peace of supreme content, that most faces so sadly lack; the beautifully cut mouth and firm chin indicates the strong characer, while the frankly earnest eyes, with their intelligent expression, shadow forth the soul's nobility. As she enters the door she is greeted by the Matron—

"Oh, I am glad you are early this morning, Nurse Lennox, read this;" and she handed the girl a note, which read:—"Send one of your most capable nurses at once; severe accident. "Gillwinnie House,' Gillwinnie.'"

"I hope it is not Lady Gwendoline Earlmont," remarked the Matron, I did not like the look of the mare she was riding yesterday when she called here."

Bessie lost little time in packing a small handbag and set forth.

At "Gillwinnie House" all was confusion, no less a person than the mistress of the mansion had sustained serious injuries. She had been thrown from her horse and sustained a fracture of the skull and was perfectly unconscious; beside the bed was the doctor, a tall, grave man, who turned round as Bessie entered.

"Are you the nurse from the Institute," he said.

Bessie quietly said she was.

"I am Dr. Arter," he said, " of London. I am here as a guest (really taking a holiday). What is your name?"

" Nurse Lennox."

"Well, Nurse," he said, "you must keep Lady Gwendoline perfectly quiet; admit no one for the present, not even her husband to this room." Dr. Edward Scott and myself have the sole charge of the case. By the way, he mentioned you as the best nurse we could get, or I should have telegraphed at once for one of my specials from London." He took out his watch as he spoke, and gravely counted his patient's pulse. Bessie stood by his side, earnestly regarding him; somehow his face seemed familiar, like a face seen in a dream. Then her eyes travelled to a watch, quaint and oldfashioned and swiftly an intuition flashed through her soul. It was Willie Arter. As he put his watch back in his waist-coat pocket, she saw an inscription at the back; yes, it was the same watch that years ago she and her father chose for her little friend, Willie Arter. She, with her woman's wit, remembered him at once, but he had forgotten her, and Bessie feels, with a throb at her heart, how greatly their positions have changed. He was once the poor farm labourer's son, and she the squire's daughter. Now he is Dr. William Arter, the guest of Lady Gwendoline Earlmont, and she, the trained nurse.

He gave her all directions; and then retired to consult with Dr. Scott, Lady Gwendoline's own adviser.

After an earnest counsel, Dr. Arter said, "I like the nurse; she seems a very capable refined woman. She is not Scotch, by her accent."

"No; she is English and a gentlewomam. I have my brother in England to thank for Nurse Lennox (and not in the least knowing the antecedents of the famous nerve and brain specialist Dr. Arter.)

Dr. Scott spoke of Squire Lennox losing all his property suddenly, and his (Dr. Scott's brother) sending Bessie Lennox and her mother over to Scotland, and he wound up by saying, " George was certainly right, for Miss Lennox is a born nurse, and a credit to our Institute."

Dr. Arter said no word to Dr. Scott, but he determined he would seek out Mrs. Lennox and pay back in part if possible some of the debt contracted to the Squire in the past. Bessie had altered so greatly ; no, he should not have remembered her and doubtless she had quite forgotten him.

On the following Sunday as Bessie (off duty) tripped upstairs to her mother's room, a gentleman stood up to greet her.

" Bessie my child," said her mother " this is your old friend and playfellow, Willie Arter."

"Why, you are not even surprised, Miss Lennox," said Dr. Arter, shaking hands warmly with the smiling girl.

" Why should I be ?" " I knew you at once, Dr. Arter" said Bessie, "partly through the watch you held to count your patient's pulse on our first meeting."

Dr. Arter took out the watch with the insscription and said earnestly and with deep gratitude, "I have never used any other. I was grieved to find your father had passed away. He was always very good to me, I have never forgotten those past days, never ! "

$$* \quad * \quad * \quad * \quad * \quad *$$

Two years later Bessie Lennox became Dr. Arter's wife and passed indeed from storm to peace, the union being that rare bond of mutual friendship and love.

They often compared their horoscopes and remembered Sapals prediction, for Dr. Arter and his wife, together with Mrs. Lennox, believe in the Stellar ruling. They have had the practical proof in their own natus, and are daily noting the same occurring with their friend's nativities, " for the history of the world is written in the Zodiac," and " as above, so below," "man being an epitome of the Cosmos."

**THE END.**

# Mr. Bishop Culpeper and Raphael.

(To the Editor MODERN ASTROLOGY.)

DEAR SIR,—Mr. Culpeper, in his remarks as chairman at the special meeting of astrologers, reported in this month's magazine, takes me to task for the remarks in my almanac for 1898.

He says the Society has accomplished *much*, but he mentions nothing in particular, except that it has become known to astrologers the world over ; a feat, by-the-bye, very easy of attainment and by no means expensive in this case.

What I wish to know is this :—What has the Society actually accomplished for the benefit of Astrology and astrologers between its inception and the end of last June, when I wrote that paragraph ?

Although I have Saturn rising, I am not subject to " fits of depression " but I had in my mind the ideal that it would not be right for me to praise the Society and invite my readers to join or subscribe to it, when, to all appearances, it existed in name only.  Respecting Mr. Culpeper's invitation to me to be present at the council meetings, the President knew full well when he invited me to become vice-president that I should not be able to attend meetings, and since then, I *think* I have, for this very reason, asked him to elect some one in my stead.  Anyhow, I will now tender my resignation as Vice-President, as it is not right that I should keep a much more capable person from filling the office and attending the meetings.  Mr. Culpeper appeals strongly for *funds*.  With my own money I do as I like, but in dealing with other people's, I am very very, particular.  I would, therefore suggest that a balance sheet of the society be published, showing its receipts and items of expenditure.  Let it be distinctly understood that this suggestion does not imply the least doubt or suspicion in my mind.  I simply make it because I think the subscribers are entitled to it.

In my letter in last month's magazine there is a misprint, ☿ (Mercury) is printed for ♆ (Neptune).

RAPHAEL.

A reply to this letter and a full report of the Society's work with the balance sheet will be found in our next issue.— [ED.]

# Degrees of the Zodiac Symbolised.
## By CHARUBEL.

### CANCER.

1° Symbol:—A large clock, with weights in sight, suspended from a high place, on which I see a large dial-plate, with hours and hands complete.

This denotes a splendid timist in music, and one who will delight in the study of dynamics; a shrewd observer in what pertains to cause and effect.

2° Symbol:—A man in a green-house with a watering-can, watering some flowering shrubs.

This denotes one whose delight will be in the study of the beautiful in Nature, and who will devote time and energy to the development of the beautiful, more especially in the floral kingdom.

3° Symbol:—A deep shaft descending into the earth, and, right overhead, a balloon.

This denotes an all-round person, one conversant with the different strata in the formation of the crust of our globe. In the meantime the native will make himself familiar with those graduated densities in the atmosphere, that are witnessed at different altitudes. He will be a scientist of some note.

4° Symbol:—I see that side of the Moon, which is never seen by the inhabitants of this planet. As this is a thing I dare not look at, inspection being dangerous, I will simply give character it typifies.

A strange character, one whom no one will ever understand. A person possessed of powers unknown to the present race, and, unless the mind has been much distorted, he will pursue studies with which the age is not conversant. He will not be tied down to any religious tenets, as he can *never* be brought to submit himself to any. He will be a magician, but not of any known type. Such one may be called insane, whilst the brain, and intellect generally are quite healthy. But the powers are what I will call *Moon-set!* That is, such a man is out of the ordinary groove of every-day life, but is not insane. All that the average person may be taken up with is uncongenial to him. There is ever a gulf between such a character and ordinary humanity.

5° Symbol :—A person holding up a scale in his hand with even beam.

A just person, one whose mind will spontaneously detect a falsehood, or an injustice, or any wrong.

6° Symbol :—I see a large tract of land mapped out, and enclosed with posts and rails, divided into what are intended for a farm and homestead in the near future.

This denotes one possessed of boundless resources; an adventurer; a person who generally accomplishes what he purposes. His speculations are successful.

7° Symbol :—I see one large, ripe, nicely-tinted apple suspended from a bough. There is but this one on the tree.

This denotes one who will advance himself from comparative obscurity to a position where there will be no compeer to rival his excellences.

8° Symbol :—A man pulling at a rope attached to a bell, which is suspended near the top of a high tree.

A person who will take a delight in publishing what he knows about everybody. As the conducter of a newspaper he may be in his sphere; but it will be with difficulty that he will preserve himself from the crime of defamation of character.

9° Symbol :—I see a spider in the corner of a room, intently watching the giddy dance of silly flies, as they needlessly approach the confines of its dominions.

This denotes a student of law and order; a shrewd lawyer; he would make a good detective.

10° Symbol :—A bulbous plant, just pushing its way upward from beneath the sod, and beginning to unfold itself in order to show forth its beauties.

This denotes one possessed of a great amount of soul-force in whom the principle of life is very strong. He may make a powerful magnetist, as he will have a strong will.

11° Symbol:—A young girl playing on a lyre.

A gay person, fond of youth and youthful amusements artistic and musical.

12° Symbol:—A cypress tree.

A person of melancholy and fretful disposition, mournful and gloomy. Will suffer much through bereavement.

13° Symbol;—A man delving.

An industrious person; most particular in all small matters ever partial to manaul labour.

14° Symbol:—A man standing before an audience, with all the paraphernalia of a juggler.

This denotes one having all-round accomplishments. He is never at a loss through lack of resources. He is capable of turning his hand or his wits to anything.

15° Symbol:—A pool of water.

An easy-going person, content with only a little. Poo abilities; rather unstable; fond of home.

16° Symbol:—This is a blank degree. What this implies I cannot say, as the books are mysteriously silent about this degree. There is some mystery about the number four and its square.

17° Symbol:—An artificial globe.

This denotes one who will travel, a student, and one who may make many discoveries.

18° Symbol:—A bull tossing a man with his horns.

This denotes a wilful person, one who will be always on the defensive, and too often on the aggressive. Personal property will have but little sacredness with him, his motto being, " What I can get is my own."

19° Symbol:—A man with a very old-looking book before him. I has the appearance of some ancient record.

This denotes a studious person, a profound thinker, one capable of grappling with abstruse studies. He loves his

books, and his studies are more for self-amusement than
with the object of appearing in print.    He is free from that
craze.

20° Symbol :—A large building, with walls of granite, having a
dull or sombre appearance.

This denotes something lasting.    This person will do some
great deed in life which will be handed down to posterity.    His
chief characteristic is firmness, not ghoulish.    He will live
to a ripe old age.

21° Symbol :—A King, an Emperor, or Commander on horseback.

This is the degree of power, and should raise the native to
some post of honour, where he will be in a position to command more than obey.

22° Symbol :—A quantity of toys, or common ornaments of glass
and tinsel.

This denotes a proud person, fond of the artificial, and is
highly superficial; one of a fretful and peevish disposition,
creating misery wherever he or she may reside.

23o Symbol :—A burly man, with an apron before him.

This degree governs work connected with catering for the
public.    It will answer for the manager of a restaurant, an
inn-keeper, or a butcher.

24° Symbol :—A small church, but highly ornate, having all the
sacerdotal display usually met with in larger places of that
class.

This denotes one who will be very religlious, a strict
observer of feasts, fasts and festivals, but a very narrow-
minded person and a most intolerant bigot.

25° Symbol :—A very lofty pine-tree.

This denotes a noble person, one whose mind is fired with
grand aspirations, whose good influence will be felt beyond
the limits of his own neighbourhood.    His deeds will speak
louder than words.

26° Symbol:— A gentleman with a number of ladies in a carriage.

This denotes a good, and kind disposition; a person very liberal with his presents, in whose nature benevolence bubbles sides, lacking in of circumspection; a veritable " Timon of Athens."

27° Symbol :—A pear-tree loaded with large ripe fruit.

This person abounds in [goodness; his nature is charged (so to speak) with good influences which flow from him spontaneously. He is a living *talisman* for the healing of discord and strife; a peacemaker.

28° Symbol:—Heaps of gold and silver coin.

This person will grow rich, however poor or low his birth may have been; he will get money, and he will know how to look after it. He loves money for its own sake, hence becomes a miser.

29° Symbol :—A man driving a bull or an ox.

A person who will be fond of dealing in cattle; a cattle dealer. He will prosper by such means.

30° Symbol:—An acute triangle, with a cross on the top.

A person of peculiarly strong will; very lofty in his deportment, and commanding in appearance; he would succeed in some official capacity under Government.

———

Pythagoras held that the Celestial bodies were immortal and Divine; that the Sun, Moon, and stars were so many gods, who possessed a superabundance of heat, which is the principle of life; that the rays of the sun, penetrating the air and the water down to the profoundest depths of the ocean, spread the genius of life everywhere.

Pythagoras therefore placed the substance of the Deity in this ethereal fire, of which the Sun is one of the sources; this fire circulating throughout matter, constitutes the universal soul of the world, or the Deity, of whom each soul or each principle of individual motion and life is an emanation.

Pythagoras brought from the East the idea of re-incarnation; it was there held that the soul, enchained in the circle of necessity, assumes successively the shapes of different animals. Pythagoras made Mercury the depository and and the leader of these souls. From him it passed into the mysteries, where men were persuaded to escape from the circle of these successive changes by virtuous conduct.

# Editorial Comment.

THIS month we bring another volume to a close, and for the first time in our history conclude with the half-year.

The new plan, we hope, will greatly add to our subscription-list and will also give our readers—subscribers who wish to gain for us new friends—the opportunity of making a New Year's gift of the half-year's bound volume. The extraordinary sale of the Christmas Number has left us but few copies for binding and there are only a limited number at our disposal. We have had the volume nicely bound and as a present we are sure it will prove acceptable to all persons interested in the occult sciences.

Commencing with the next volume, we shall introduce a valuable addition to the Magazine which will greatly increase its value. Also some new ideas and instructive articles will be published, and we hope to still further improve its pages.

The prizes offered at the beginning of the volume have not been so eagerly sought after as we had hoped; if the subject be considered of sufficient interest we shall take it up during the next volume.

Students will be pleased to hear that Mr. H. S. Green will resume his reading of the mundane maps each month and we feel sure that this branch of the science has no better exponent. Some very interesting articles from this most able astrologer's pen will be published in the next volume, in which a series of papers will be commenced dealing with the signs of the zodiac.

We wish to draw the attention of all students to the Bureau advertised on cover. All who desire good work should subscribe, and assist the Bureau in forming what we believe will become a very useful institution. Also with regard to the classes forming for Astrological instruction, those who are able to join them, will find this a splendid opportunity to obtain some practical and useful instruction. Full particulars will be found in the advertisement.

This Number will reach all our subscribers before the New Year, excepting those who are beyond a nine days' mail; therefore, to one and all we wish a "Very happy and prosperous New Year," behind which, we have the internal desire that their knowledge may be turned into wisdom, and their hearts filled with purity and peace.

# Students' Corner

I am deeply interested in ".Practical Astrology," by Alan Leo, but there are many things therein I do not understand ; for instance page 11. Do you consider planets abused when afflicted by evil aspects or ill-dignified, and the middle column to mean their innate meaning, and the first column their nature when well aspected or dignified ?

On page 147 you clasify the signs for character and mind building, but, as far as I am able to discern, give no example of how to use the tables or signs as arranged.

Page 156 you judge the map to be more positive than negative by planets in the electrical portion of map, but fail to give the meaning of the decision, viz., being positive.

On page 158 you point to the sign containing ♐ as giving the energy or trend to the expression of Nature upon the physical plane through ♉, the throat. Can this rule always be relied upon, and applied to all signs which ♐ may be in ? What is meant by " over-coming these two elements and progress is sure " on page 194, second paragraph, and again by " rising above the limitations of ♄," how can this be done ?

It seems to me that, if astrology is true, a prediction can be made to-day that will eventuate ten years hence, and as its rules are founded upon immutable laws that were the same yesterday, to-day, and for ever, that whatever man does he cannot change these laws nor alter their working. Certainly he cannot control his birth nor alter his invironment, nor *always* make conditions for himself. Events will occur in his life, good or bad, over which he *cannot possibly have any control*. If, by information received through astrology, he *thinks* he is avoiding certain unfortunate periods, or making the most of the good, he is only deceived, for then he is only following out a part of fate, for he certainly was fated to receive the information, whether an astrologer is clever enough to discover it in his natal chart or not. This illustration will apply equally well to health, accidents, marriage, financial affairs, etc., etc.

If man is able to modify events in life, why not avoid them? It looks to me that man is powerless to alter one particle of his fate, for if he did how could any reliance be put upon *any prediction* by an astrologer? How, then, is man to rise above the mundane houses and come under the signs of the zodiac, or rule his planets? If he *does* rise above the influence of the mundane houses and come under the signs, how is one to tell, when writing a horoscope, which he will be the most influenced by?

I have written this for your students' page, believing the question will be of interest to all students, and hope to see an early reply.

I remain,

Sincerely yours,

"PLAINANT."

Watertown, N.Z., Oct. 20th, 1897.

The answer will be given next month. Students may reply to any queries appearing in this page.—[ED.]

\*        \*        \*        \*        \*

Twins: male, born 3 p.m.; female, born 3.30 p.m., August 17th, 1870, Lincs. Female died December 26th, 1887, typhoid fever. The male had an attack, three or four months earlier, but recovered, and is now living.—(Sent by T. Cook.)

F.A.H., female, born 2.45 a.m., October 21st, 1866, Hants. Three days after childbirth she lost her reason and died in an asylum.—(Miss B.)

Male, born 7.30 p.m., September 24th, 1863, Dorset. He is subject to fits; the first occurred at 8.15 a.m., March 30th, 1879.—(P.)

G.S., male, born 3.15 a.m., January 4th, 1849, Dumfries, sends the following data:—" Father, who was head gardener to Sir James Graham, died December 27th, 1879; mother died December 21st, 1889; married first wife May 20th, 1869; she died May 2nd, 1873; married second wife August, 1876; she died 1887. He was apprenticed to gardening May, 1864, and as a carpenter April, 1866."

# Our New Volume.

Next month we enter upon a new departure from our usual method of conducting this magazine. Hitherto we have been heavily handicapped with regard to the work attached to writing, publishing and editing MODERN ASTROLOGY; in the latter department we have been fortunate enough to obtain the assistance of those whose only motive in aiding us is a universal interest, the self element being entirely eliminated; hence, we can promise our readers an almost perfectly edited journal in the future. We are also making arrangements with regard to the publishing, so that this department may be in the hands of publishers whose interests it will be to make the magazine more generally known by advertising and other means. The publisher's name will appear on the cover next month.

These arrangements have left us free to devote more time to the writing of articles, the collection of useful information for students and readers, and research work.

Beginning with the new volume we commence a gigantic task, the full particulars of which, at present, we do not think it advisable to disclose. But as the months pass on, each number will increase in value, until there will be nothing of equal value published in the astrological world. So confident are we of its success that we make the prediction that twelve months hence No. 1 of Vol. 4, MODERN ASTROLOGY, will be honestly worth half-a-crown instead of one shilling.

If Mercury be chief ruler, he signifieth such events as are of the nature of the planet with which he is in conjunction and in configuration.

\*   \*   \*   \*   \*   \*   \*

When eclipses occur in Taurus, Virgo or Capricorn, they signify a scarcity of the fruits of the earth, and corn; in Gemini, Libra, or Aquarius, famine and disease, pestilence and mortality; in Cancer, Scorpio, or Pisces, the death and slaughter of obscure, common, plebian people; continual quarrels and seditions, and great damage to navigators; in Aries, Leo, or Saggittarius, sudden and frequent motions of armies, assaults and batteries tumults, controversies, great heat and drought, corruption of fruit trees, death of prominent women, death of some eminent prince, anxiety to rulers, rapines, profanation of holy places, diseases among horses, destruction of woods by fire.

# Letters to the Editor.

Dear Sir,—" Star Lore " is not right in my case in stating your system of Astrology to be two hundred and fifty years behind the times; it is up-to-date with me. I can prove this over and over again, from the advice I have had year by year from you for the last seven years. Now you informed me in Subscribers' Directions, 1897 and 1898, on September 6th, 1897, " that the passage of Saturn over the radical place of your Sun is likely to cause you some trouble and anxiety at the close of October and through November this year." True, it did, by my father losing a very dear old friend and holding public meetings in native towns, which caused strong opposition to him. As I am in business this does me a lot of harm by what people think of us, and trade suffers.

I hope, from the bottom of my heart, that the death and burial of Modern Astrology will not take place for many years to come, as I look forward with much pleasure, from month to month, to receiving same and enclose my card, so that if anyone wishes to know me, you can give them my address.

Yours faithfully,

SOMEWHAT BLACK

———

Dear Sir,—So the Princess of Wales, that kind, good-natured, amiable person is born under the harsh, cruel, blood-thirsty, vivisecting sign, Scorpio ? Thus saith Mr. Pearce, who, born under a double-bodied sign, has allocated to himself a double nativity!

You, Mr. Editor, and myself, when we remonstrated with him for his stupidity and conceit, were said to be guilty of using Billingsgate language! He very considerately warns students against any false teachings on directions. I now repeat what I have said before, viz :—" That all the systems of directing

Placidian especially) are fallacious and unreliable, but that the one taught in my ' key ' comes nearer the truth than any other, although even that is sadly deficient."

Can anyone, with any common sense, believe that the planets form aspects or directions within a few hours or days after birth, which do not operate for fifty or more years ? And can any Astrologer believe that the Princess of Wales is born under Scorpio ?

The map for the birth of the Princess published by " Sepharial " with Libra rising, and Mars and Venus in the ascendant, is very nearly, if not quite, correct.

RAPHAEL.

DEAR SIR,—In " Raphael's Almanac " for 1898, where he refers to the Astrological Society, he states—" the Society has now been in existence nearly two years, and, so far as I can learn, has accomplished nothing." This is a choice remark from the vice-president of the Society !  A pertinent question is ' what has *he* done in his official capacities as (1) vice-President and (2) Editor and Proprietor of " Raphael's Almanac.' " I have attended many of the Society's meetings, and as far as I can make out Raphael ha*s never* attended. Had he put in an appearance he would have found out that something had been done. One of the objects of the Society was and is to " Purify Astrology," and he would find had he attended that this object formed a most important portion of the deliberations of the members. We want an Astrological Almanac one on the lines of R. C. Smith's ("Raphael I "), and Commander Morrison's " Zadkiel I ") a combination of the two, and the sooner a genuine one comes out, the better for Astrology.

Yours truly,

Sept. 20th, 1897.     A MEMBER OF THE ASTROLOGICAL SOCIETY

SIR,—Some months back I, as a humble student, asked for information respecting oblique ascension and the equal division of the *Zodiacal Circle à la Zariel*. In April Mr. H. S. Green wrote that I was a little hard upon him and *Zariel*, but he gave no answer as to which of the modes he thought best, and advised me to study both, and form my own opinion. This, Sir, I think very hard, as I have so little time, and wish to employ it to the best advantage. I sought bread (advice) and Mr. Green gave me a stone. A parallel case would be if a student, with limited time and means, asked his tutor which language he should learn to be of the most use, and got for answer—" Study them all and form your own opinion ! " Will you, Sir, or some of your learned contributors kindly show me and very many other students, by comparative work, which of these methods is the better. Life is too short to waste in travelling over old and new roads when the best road is known ; old or new it matters not, we want the best. I know opinions differ, but if these two warriors would kindly work out the issue on the same battle-field, not each picking a suitable natus for his particular scheme, the whole of the Astrological Science would benefit, no matter which won.

Yours etc.,

JOHN NICHOLAS,

August 12th, 1897.                                    AUSTRALIA.

## AN EXPOSURE.

DEAR SIR,—Having recently made, with exactness, a new Ephemeris for 1898, I have examined all the planets' longitudes given in each " angelic " one for that year, and the result is the following summary of errors as compared with our strict computations.

Not counting the very numerous instances where it varies only 1', the Zadkiel one is wrong in fifty-three instances by 2' or 3', and four times is 4' wrong. This comparatively small number of errors proves, to one familiar with such work, that it was done by the right mathematical method, though very carelessly.

The Raphael one is ten times as bad. In 530 cases it is 2' or 3' in error! Nine times it is 4' wrong, and for November 9 to 17 Mars is 5' and 6' wrong! This shows up their cheap and easy *judging* process—the " ready reckoner " they have boasted of. It is fair to presume that for many previous years it has been as unreliable.

The usual amenitites of discussion are out of place in treating such an atrocity, yet I shall not apply the extreme language that this fraud deserves but by accurate and honest work expect to do much to check the condemnable imposition, in this country at least. Both the works in question are also manifestly deficient and ill-arranged.

J. G. D., BOSTON, U.S.A.

## Astrological Periodicals.

 E believe there are now half a dozen Astrological periodicals published in England and America. Occasionally one or two of these reach this office ; some day the history of Astrological journalism will make interesting copy. It is now ten years since *The Astrologer* was started by Mr. Powley, and it was owing to its failure that the *Astrologers' Magazine* was published ; since that time, there have been many attempts to run a successful publication, but none have yet existed more than two years.

As far as we can ascertain, the following are now in circulation besides MODERN ASTROLOGY.—*Coming Events*, owned by Messrs. W. Foulsham and Co., and edited by " Sephariel," also *Star Lore*, by " Zadkiel." In America, *The 20th Century Astrologer, Planets and People*, and the latest arrival *The Radix*, the latter is edited by Mrs. A. E. Lloyde, not Professor Henry, as we stated in a former notice. There is plenty of variety in these periodicals, each one differing entirely in its tone and style, and each having an apparently different aim as a motive for its publication, but none having an avowed object before them as far as we can gather. *Planets and People* appear to advocate a Heliocentric system of Astrology, but, so far, we have been unable to make either head or tail of its teaching or methods ; its pages seem to be more occupied with the people than the planets, probably it does not come under the heading of an Astrological journal. There are some very useful paragraphs in *The Radix*. The only copy of *The 20th Century Astrologer* we have seen was the first number, which contained some reprints from MODERN ASTROLOGY. *Star Lore* is a pamphlet of Zadkeilism, but *Coming Events* bids fair to improve, judging by the current issue.

# Questions answered by the "Astrologer."

N.B.—*If you are in doubt as to the future, seeking advice upon the problems of life,
then consult the Astrologer to whose hands the management of this part
of the Magazine has been entrusted. The correspondence must be written
upon one side of the paper only, and no more than one question asked at
the time of sending. We shall require the following particulars with the
question :*—TIME, DATE, *and* PLACE OF BIRTH, *full name and address,
or instead, a suitable nom de plume, which alone will be used when sent
All questions are answered free of charge, and in rotation as received.
All communications should be addressed to the Editorial offices of* MODERN
ASTROLOGY, *9, Lyncroft Gardens, West Hampstead, N.W.*

———

In future the above COUPON must be sent with all questions to
which a reply is required under this heading.

Special replies are sent by the editor through the post, to those
who remit 2 6 in Stamps or Postal Order with their question.

———

*Actress.* Sprained ancle or injury to the lower limbs; should you by
care escape this a severe cold will work out the physical effects of the aspects.

*Nuchum.* Delay marriage for three years; marriage prospects not good.

*Clara Ghys.* Yes, but a prospect of widowhood as well.

*T. Hy. Stoddart.* By using common sense and a strong will in eighteen
months you will be free.

*December.* Within five years from now.

*Scorpio.* During 1898.

*Violet.* He will have a very bad temper and be inclined to habits of
intemperance.

*Ruby.* Light employment, shop assistant, lady help, or companion.

*Aries.* In three years' time.

*Libra Justice.* Yes, one event in particular, which was a shock.

*A.B.R.* Toward the close of 1898 they will be better, but avoid speculation.

*David W.* Farming, during 1898.

*Herschelite.* You will understand astrology in three years' time, but it will not be successful financially.

*Parson.* Not until your 30th year is past.

*F. L. Chandler.* Death will release you from the bond earlier than you expect. Within two years a great change will take place.

*B.P.* Land pursuits, such as gardener, florist, or horticulturist.

*Nix.* There will be changes in the spring which will lead to the breaking up of your home.

*T.W.* A great change at 33, good; again at 47, bad.

*Cordella.* A very serious illness after a year's sojourn in a foreign land from which he will recover.

*Niobe.* ♎ 27° (Libra).

*E.B.* Your coupon has been disqualified. Try again.

*Gavior.* Four years hence the tide will turn.

*Ella.* Yes, we think you will.

J. H. L. Your coupon only arrived in time for this issue. The calculations required will take up some time, send in again.

*E. S. Penny.* Yes.

*Mundane.* The indications are ☉ ⚹ ♅ and ☽ in ♉. The issue will be as you desire; all you require is to continually energize the WILL.

*Venus.* See reply to J. H. L.

*Gavior.* If you postpone the idea for seven years it will be favourable, there are no good aspects for this affair until then. To attempt it before would be disastrous.

*Domestics, Yorkshire.* For employers January 22, 29, or 31, February 2, 8, 28; March 5, 24. Employees January 11, 12 and 13, 20, 21, 22, 24, and 25. February 8, 9, 16, 17, 18, 21 and 22; March 7, 8, 16, 17, and 21.

---

Each month we exchange with *Intelligence, Mind, The Esoteric, Notes and Queries, The Vegetarian, Light, The World's Advice, Thought, The Exodus, Light of the East,* and the *Theosophical Review.* In the latter Mr. Glass concludes his very interesting articles on " The Geometry of Nature." Mr. Leadbeater relates the story of an astral murder, and Mr. M. U. Moore deals with some Astronomical note under the title " The Age of the Vedas." *Intelligence* is remarkably interesting, especially in the opening article upon the origin of symbolism with its numerous illustrations; a new volume begins with the oriental holiday number.

CPSIA information can be obtained
at www.ICGtesting.com
Printed in the USA
BVOW09*2117150217

476316BV00006B/174/P

9 781161 366556